INDIGENOUS PEOPLES AND THE COLLABORATIVE STEWARDSHIP OF NATURE

INDIGENOUS PEOPLES AND THE COLLABORATIVE STEWARDSHIP OF NATURE

Knowledge Binds and Institutional Conflicts

Anne Ross, Kathleen Pickering Sherman,

Jeffrey G. Snodgrass, Henry D. Delcore,

Richard Sherman

Routledge
Taylor & Francis Group

LONDON AND NEW YORK

First published 2011 by Left Coast Press, Inc.

Published 2016 by Routledge
2 Park Square, Milton Park, Abingdon, Oxon OX14 4RN
711 Third Avenue, New York, NY 10017, USA

Routledge is an imprint of the Taylor & Francis Group, an informa business

Library of Congress Cataloging-in-Publication Data
Indigenous peoples and the collaborative stewardship of nature : knowledge binds and institutional conflicts / Anne Ross ... [et al.].
p. cm.
Includes bibliographical references and index.
ISBN 978-1-59874-577-1 (hardback : alk. paper)—ISBN 978-1-59874-578-8 (pbk. : alk. paper)
1. Indigenous peoples—Ecology. 2. Traditional ecological knowledge. 3. Philosophy of nature. 4. Conservation of natural resources. I. Ross, Anne, Ph. D.
GF50.I5198 2010
304.2—dc22
2010037437

Cover design by Allison Smith
Cover illustration: Sign at the entrance to Pine Ridge Indian Reservation, South Dakota, USA. This image symbolises the journey from the Western world to the Indigenous world and demonstrates that Indigenous people should have responsibility for making rules and administering stewardship responsibilities over resources. Photograph by Richard Sherman.

ISBN 978-1-59874-577-1 hardcover
ISBN 978-1-59874-578-8 paperback

CONTENTS

ACKNOWLEDGMENTS

This book would never have eventuated if it had not been for our Indigenous research collaborators. Each of us has spent many years working in our case study areas with our Indigenous colleagues and friends, who have shared with us knowledge about natural resource stewardship – and many other things. We feel very privileged by the trust shown to us in the provision of this knowledge and in allowing us to use stewardship information in this book as one way of giving Indigenous people a voice in the wider natural resources management discourse.

Although there are far too many field collaborators to thank individually, we would like to specifically mention the following key partners (and friends) in our research: Annie Ross thanks the Coghill family, especially Shane, Brian, Leonie, Denise, and Brendon, Uncle Dennis Moreton, Auntie Joni Moreton, Auntie Shirley Moreton, Uncle Keith Borey, Cliff Campbell, Dale Ruska, and Greg (Chegg) Eggert. Jeff Snodgrass would like to thank the many members of the Bhil, Girasia, Kathodia, and Sahariya communities, on whose knowledge and generosity his research rests. He also expresses gratitude to the employees of the Rajasthan Forest Department and the government of India who supported his research, as well as the administration, faculty, and students of Bhupal Nobles' P. G. College (Udaipur), Mohanlal Sukhadia University (Udaipur), the Indian Institute of Forest Management (I.I.F.M., Bhopal), and the American Institute of Indian Studies (A.I.I.S., New Delhi), who assisted with field arrangements and provided other field support. Special thanks go to Satish Kumar Sharma, friend and research collaborator, who contributed deeply to Jeff's understanding of Adivasi relationships with the environment. Further, he thanks in particular the collaborative assistance of Mohan Advani, N. K. Bhargava, Debashis Debnath, Yuvraj Singh Jhala, Michael G. Lacy, Sirisha Naidu, Kristina Tiedje, and Chakrapani Upadhyay. Hank Delcore would like to acknowledge the following field collaborators: in Silalaeng and Ban Toey, Pho Serm Takaew, Somsak, Thawin, Thanom, and Thira; at Doi Phukha National Park, Sakonsak Patchianuwat and Sathit Wongsawat; and for support in Nan Province generally, Phra Khru Phithak Nanthakhun, Sathaporn Somsak, Lamphaen Jommuang, and Ruangdej Jommuang. Kathy Pickering Sherman and Richard Sherman would like to acknowledge all the Lakota people of Pine Ridge Indian Reservation for their assistance and friendship during fieldwork and on other occasions.

7

For each of us, our research has necessitated long periods in the field, and we thank all those organizations who have sponsored this fieldwork. In particular we thank our home institutions: The University of Queensland, Colorado State University, and California State University, Fresno. We also thank the following funding bodies: for Ross's Australian research, the Australian Institute of Aboriginal and Torres Strait Islander Studies; the Fraser Island World Heritage Area Scientific Advisory Committee; and The University of Queensland; Pickering Sherman's Pine Ridge research is based on work supported by a National Science Foundation Career Award; a USDA-Cooperative State Research, Education, and Extension Service NRICGP Rural Development Grant; an award from the Oglala Oyate Woitancan Empowerment Zone; and the Monfort Family Foundation's Colorado State University Monfort Professorship; Sherman's work on Pine Ridge has been supported by the Northwest Area Foundation; Winona La Duke and Honor the Earth and the Tides Foundation; Christina Voormann of The Lakota Village Project; Terry McCabe, University of Colorado, Boulder; Rebecca Adamson and First Nations Development Institute; and many others. Delcore's Thailand research was supported by California State University, Fresno; the Wenner Gren Foundation; and the U.S. Department of Education's Fulbright-Hays Program. Snodgrass gratefully acknowledges funding support from both Colorado State University and the National Geographic Foundation.

Annie Ross's involvement in the project would not have been possible without the support of The University of Queensland, which gave financial assistance and approval for her to undertake two long periods of study leave, and several shorter stays, at Colorado State University.

As we indicate later on, the idea for this volume arose out of a session at the American Anthropological Association annual meeting in Chicago in November 2003. We thank the original presenters in that session and all those who provided comments to us during that session, as well as other academic colleagues who discussed ideas with us subsequently, as the project evolved. Dr. J. Peter White (University of Sydney) and two anonymous referees provided feedback on the final draft of the manuscript. We thank them for their insightful comments, which improved the structure and readability of the volume.

Jennifer Collier at Left Coast Press has provided editorial advice and assistance over the past six months. Elana Stokes drew the figures. Stacey Sawyer was the copy editor. Her attention to detail and knowledge of grammar is unrivalled! The book is a far "cleaner" production for her patience and care.

Finally, we thank our families who have, in many ways, undertaken this writing journey with us as they supported us throughout the project. We particularly thank Greg Siepen, Emma Siepen, and Darcy Siepen.

INTRODUCTION

THE WAY FORWARD

I suggest [that] the terms for genuine participation have hardly been glimpsed, let alone put in place. (Campbell 2004: 164, speaking of Indigenous participation in natural resource co-management in Nepal)

In this book we build and argue a case for the utility of collaborative natural resource management partnerships between Indigenous communities and government agencies, particularly in protected natural areas. We examine the reasons why Indigenous peoples and their knowledge about natural systems are so often denied a place at the natural resource management table. We critically evaluate a range of methods and procedures that have been enacted over recent years in which Indigenous peoples and their knowledge have been ostensibly integrated into mainstream natural resource management. We particularly focus on so-called co-management agreements, which have gained such popularity in recent years. Despite the promise of the various forms that co-management has taken, our research demonstrates that these supposed 'modern', 'scientific', and 'progressive' methods and approaches generally perpetuate epistemological and institutional barriers to the recognition and incorporation of Indigenous knowledge and practices related to natural resource stewardship. We argue that Indigenous people remain excluded from decision making and are sometimes even denied access to their own resources. We not only point to problems but also suggest numerous ways to avoid such exclusions. We end by outlining an innovative, alternative example of co-management, the *Indigenous Stewardship Model*, developed in a North American Native context, which has the potential to transcend some of the usual barriers to equal partnerships in natural resource management.

There are now a host of excellent books, both monographs and edited volumes, about Indigenous knowledge – for example, Basso 1996; Berkes 2008; Berkes and Folke 1998; Berkes, Colding, and Folke 2003; Bicker, Sillitoe, and Pottier 2004; Bomford and Caughley 1996; Bradley et al. 2006; Milton 1996; Odora Hoppers 2002; Sillitoe, Bicker, and Pottier 2002; Williams and Baines 1993. These volumes have demonstrated that Indigenous knowledge exists, having survived various colonial and other state-based land and resource management activities that have attempted – and sometimes succeeded in – the disempowering of local traditional resource owners. These volumes argue cogently that Indigenous knowledge should be recognized as having a role in mainstream natural resource management. Although strongly influenced by these writings and analytical perspectives, we neither repeat these claims nor do we systematically restate definitions of 'Indigenous knowledge', 'community', 'resources', or other similar terms already well-defined in this existing literature. Pragmatically, we define terms when we feel it necessary – for example, we present shortly our understanding of 'Indigenous peoples' – but we focus most of our energies on advancing our case regarding what we consider to be a genuine form of natural resource co-management between modern settler states and Indigenous communities. This is a book about how Indigenous knowledge can actually be harnessed to natural resource stewardship – a project much rarer within the anthropological and natural resource management literatures – rather than a systematic analysis of Indigenous knowledge structures per se.

We also avoid the format of the edited volume. Our study mainly compares Indigenous communities in four nations – Australia, the United States, India, and Thailand – and their experiences living in or near government-protected natural areas. Rather than presenting a compendium of case studies drafted in isolation, linked only by theme, we have collaborated to design an integrated analysis that develops a unified analytical framework for assessing the potential of genuine state-Indigenous co-management of natural areas. For the sake of analytical clarity, and based on our own training and experiences, we develop a scheme that separates 'epistemological' from 'institutional' barriers to such co-management. Looking even deeper, we identify subforms (see Chapter 3) of these two categories of barriers, which we then systematically apply to each of our four case studies. Unlike an edited volume wherein analyses remain largely independent, our chapters typically interweave analyses across these four examples. Such an approach, we believe, allows readers to more clearly identify common themes and processes that might otherwise go undetected. Likewise, such an approach allows us to speak to and learn from one another in a manner that would be impossible in other formats.

We believe that we have identified a potential management path that could overcome some of the obstacles we outline and that, if properly implemented, could lead to opportunities for compromise and genuine partnerships in natural resource stewardship. We point to – and indeed passionately argue for – the depth and richness of Indigenous knowledge, even promoting its 'scientific' merit. However, we do not call for the elimination of a role for scientists from other traditions, such as the West, through this valorizing of Indigenous knowledge. On the contrary, we appeal for an integration of the knowledge of managers trained in Western education systems with a science paradigm and those who have grown up in Indigenous knowledge systems.

CASE STUDIES

Most of the data on which we base our arguments and analyses derive from four culture areas, which we briefly introduce here: the lands and waters of the Dandrubin Gorenpul people of Moreton Bay in Queensland, Australia; the Pine Ridge Indian Reservation in South Dakota, central United States of America; the lands occupied by the Adivasi of southern Rajasthan in India; and Nan Province in northern Thailand (Figure I.1). We use the empirical data from these case studies to ground our review of the barriers to building collaborative partnerships between Indigenous peoples and their knowledge of natural resource management, on the one hand, and 'mainstream' land and sea managers and their Western scientific paradigms of knowledge, on the other. We also use the data from the case studies as a springboard into an analysis of various co-management strategies that have operated or are currently operating in various national parks.

Dandrubin Gorenpul Land and Seascape, Moreton Bay, Southeastern Queensland, Australia (Annie Ross)

There are more than 360 islands in Moreton Bay, southeastern Queensland, providing a rich and varied resource base for people practicing a subsistence economy. Most of the waters of the bay have been classified as a marine park, managed by the Queensland Parks and Wildlife Service (QPWS). There are four land-based national parks within the Moreton Bay region, also managed by QPWS. Three Aboriginal clans occupy the lands and waters of the bay: the Dandrubin Gorenpul, Ngugi, and Noonucal. The clan that Ross has worked with most closely is the Dandrubin Gorenpul. Collectively these clans refer to themselves as the people of Quandamooka (Barker and Ross 2003; Ross and Quandamooka 1996a). According to their knowledge,

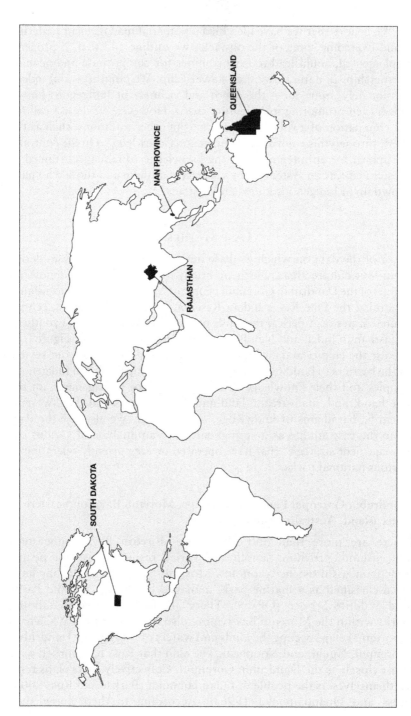

Figure I.1 Map showing location of case study regions.

people have been living in Moreton Bay since the beginning of time and have always relied on the resources of the sea (Figure I.2). Based on archaeological evidence, they have occupied the bay for at least 20,000 years, during which time the Aboriginal subsistence economy has been based principally on marine resource harvesting (Ross and Moreton in press).

Many Quandamooka Aboriginal people were removed to missions on North Stradbroke Island in 1892, but the isolation of the missions there meant that inhabitants were able to continue to practice many of their cultural traditions. Today the people of Quandamooka are becoming increasingly vocal about the decline in natural resources in Moreton Bay. There are few legal and policy mechanisms to allow Indigenous people to be involved in decision making about the management of national or marine parks, but Dandrubin Gorenpul people are permitted to provide an input into development planning when development may adversely affect native title rights and interests. This input, however, is not a veto, and all final decisions rest with various government agencies.

Figure I.2 The sea is a dominating influence in Quandamooka country – Cape Moreton stone quarry (foreground) and workshop and trade site (background) on the northeastern tip of Moreton Island, southeastern Queensland. As well as stone tool manufacturing, these locations also contain evidence of marine exploitation and are associated with stories of marine resource creation and stewardship laws (Ross, Anderson, and Campbell 2003) (photograph by A. Ross).

Methods

Annie Ross has worked with the Dandrubin Gorenpul Aboriginal people of Moreton Bay since 1993. Data collection began as a cultural heritage mapping exercise, wherein Indigenous knowledge relating to cultural and natural resources of the bay was recorded in terms of physical location and oral histories about archaeological sites and resource places (Prangnell, Ross, and Coghill 2010; Ross, Prangnell, and Coghill 2010), with these data supported by ethnohistorical research and archaeological excavations (Ross and Tomkins in press).

Respondents were selected for interview based on the snowballing technique, very much favored by Aboriginal communities in this part of Australia. In this technique, knowledgeable elders are first invited to provide responses to open-ended questions posed by the researcher. As gatekeepers in the community, their approval for the research and for the questions being asked is an essential requirement before any project can proceed. Once senior members of the community had provided their responses to the open-ended questions, they then nominated others whom they regarded as having both the necessary knowledge of and the essential right to speak about the issues of concern. These research collaborators then nominated others for interview, and so on.

In Aboriginal Australia not all members of a community have equal levels of knowledge about all aspects of the environment. Since the research for this project was largely based on marine resources and their exploitation (including by-products of resource harvesting, such as shell midden deposits), the research collaborators interviewed were mostly those people with specific knowledge of marine resources. These research collaborators were both men and women, and mostly people in their 30s or older.

Additional information on natural resource stewardship knowledge comes from other Queensland coastal Aboriginal communities, especially those on Fraser Island. Once again, most information has come from senior research collaborators who have both the knowledge of and the right to speak about particular resources. Other comparative information comes from literature analyses.

Pine Ridge Indian Reservation, Southwestern South Dakota, United States (Kathy Pickering Sherman and Richard Sherman)

Badlands National Park in South Dakota consists of two units: an area that was once called Badlands National Monument, now known as the North Unit, and an area comprising the northern portion of the Pine Ridge Indian Reservation, known as the South Unit (Figure I.3). Because the land in the South Unit still belongs to the tribe, tribal members continue to engage in activities in the South Unit that would never be allowed in other national parks. Badlands is the only national park in the United States that allows local people to herd cattle and grow hay. Tribal members hunt and gather wild plant food in the South Unit, although the park superintendent has the power to regulate these activities. Furthermore, tourists are restricted from visiting certain parts of the South Unit, which are sacred ceremonial sites of the Lakota/Oglala. This situation makes Badlands an interesting case study, because the traditional park ideal frequently comes into conflict with the people whose land it has enclosed. The South Unit is a classic example of a contested landscape. It is contested in the very literal sense that several different groups claim rights to it. It is also contested in the ideological sense that these various groups define it in different ways: as a sacred place, as a wilderness to be preserved, as a resource to be developed, and as a fun place to go off-road, just to name a few. All these claims and perspectives make management of the South Unit very difficult indeed.

Figure I.3 Landscape of Badlands National Park (photograph by K. Pickering Sherman).

Methods

The data presented here are based on Richard Sherman's lifetime connection to the Pine Ridge Indian Reservation as a Lakota hunter-gatherer and landowner as well as a career dedicated to implementing culturally appropriate and scientifically sound natural resource and wildlife management on the Reservation, and on Kathy Pickering Sherman's work with Lakota people for more than 20 years, first as an attorney and then as an anthropologist. The study has included both qualitative and quantitative data. The qualitative data were collected during an eight-year longitudinal study of 300 Lakota households on the Reservation from 2001 through 2008. The participants were chosen at random from aerial photographs of the housing units on Pine Ridge, located with GIS coordinates, so the statistical results could be generalized across the Reservation population. Residents were asked a range of questions relating to their perceptions of natural resources and their approaches to natural resources use and management. Some examples of questions asked are summarized in Table I.1 (see Pickering and Jewell 2008 for more details). From the responses to the survey questions, it is apparent that many traditional beliefs are still operative at the grassroots level.

Many of the quantitative questions generated qualitative responses, which have been amalgamated with longer-term earlier qualitative studies, and the case study analyses presented in this volume include many examples of Lakota voice provided as a result of the comments received as part of the mainstream studies. Among the qualitative responses provided by the participants, three dominant themes were expressed in relation to Lakota conceptions of humans and nature. First and foremost, humans, animals, and plants are interdependent on one another to survive and thrive. Second, to keep that interdependence successful, humans must show respect for, not dominance over, the natural world. Finally, greed, waste, and selfishness in relation to the ecosystem are the human behaviors that endanger the health of not only plant and animal populations but ultimately of humans as well.

Phulwari ki Nal Wildlife Sanctuary, Rajasthan, India (Jeff Snodgrass)

Phulwari ki Nal (the 'Abode of Flowers') is a dry tropical deciduous forest reserve of 511 square kilometers, located in the southern portion of the Aravalli mountain range in Udaipur District near the Rajasthani town of Kotra (Figure I.4). Before Indian Independence in 1947, this area was a hunting reserve of the rulers of the Princely Kingdoms of Bhumat and Mewar. In 1983 the area was declared a state wildlife sanctuary under the Wildlife Protection Act of 1972 and the Rajasthan Forest Conservation

TABLE I.1   Examples of survey questions relating to natural resource perceptions and use, and summary of responses (Pickering and Jewell 2008).

Question	Response
Do you feel your spiritual beliefs are connected to the way you feel about nature?	Almost 88% answered in the affirmative.
Plants and animals have as much right to exist as humans.	Virtually 100% of respondents agreed with this statement.
When was the last time you ate wild game?	Almost 45% within the last month.
When was the last time you ate wild plant food?	50% within the last month.
When was the last time you ate traditional Lakota food?	63% within the last month.
Nature is strong enough to cope with whatever humans do.	Only 40% agreed with this statement.
It is important to have lots of wild animals on the reservation for people to use.	64% of respondents agreed with this statement.
Plants that were introduced to the reservation (for example, agricultural crops) are more important than plants that are native to this area (for instance, *tinpsila* [wild turnip]).	Fewer than 35% of respondents agreed with this statement.

Act of 1980. At this point, all hunting, and most local rights of access to wood and non-timber forest products (NTFPs) were ended. The area's primary aim was declared to be the preservation and restoration of wildlife.

Indigenous persons in India – termed *Adivasis* (literally, 'first inhabitants,' or 'natives'), *Janjatis* (often translated as 'tribals'), and 'Scheduled Tribes' (an official state designation) – make up 8% of India's population. These Adivasis continue to inhabit many of India's protected and reserved forests, parks and wildlife sanctuaries. The Phulwari ki Nal sanctuary contains 134 villages, in many of which reside members of the Bhil tribe, the dominant local population (about 75% of the area's population) and indeed the third-largest tribal group in India. Other Adivasi associated with Phulwari ki Nal include the Girasias and Kathodias, although they are in fewer numbers than the Bhils.

In the recent colonial and postcolonial past, the forests of Phulwari were valued primarily for their economic benefits to the Indian state, rather than for their economic value to local communities, or for their natural or environmental value to locals or India as a whole. Today

Figure I.4 Phulwari ki Nal's distinctive rock outcroppings (photograph by J. Snodgrass).

tribals depend on the forest for their economic survival, although in law no one is allowed to take, as Snodgrass was told, 'even a single blade of grass' from within the sanctuary's boundaries. The Adivasi communities living in and adjacent to the park are impoverished and growing in numbers. They place an increasing pressure on natural areas such as Phulwari ki Nal, and these pressures bring conflict over resource use in this protected area. As a result conflicts between the needs of humans and wildlife, and how and even whether both can be accommodated, are thrown into particularly sharp relief in this Indian setting.

Methods

The data analysis and practical recommendations derive from ongoing research in which Snodgrass initially hypothesized a potential causal link between animist nature reverence (Bird-David 1991) and consciously pursued conservation (Smith and Wishnie 2000). To examine this relationship, he employed both ethnographic and formal survey methods.

The ethnographic phase involved fieldwork in 20 tribal villages in or near the proposed ecological core of Phulwari ki Nal each summer from

2003 through 2008, and over a four-month period in the fall of 2005. Unstructured and semistructured interviews with tribals and Rajasthan Forest Department (RFD) employees in villages and forests, participant observation, and oral histories were used to clarify the changing nature of Indigenous relationships with the forest and the RFD. A structured survey was then employed to more formally elicit the environmental thought and reported practice of religious specialists (shamans) in comparison with demographically matched non-specialist tribal members. The sample comprised 234 individuals – 117 religious specialists (almost all of the locally known and recognized specialists in the area), and 117 non specialist research collaborators (who were chosen to match on age, gender, tribe, education, village of residence, and economic status). By comparing persons with especially intense religious commitment to 'matched' persons otherwise similar but of lesser religious commitment, the question of whether more intense animist *religious* commitment might lead research collaborators to more vigorously protect, conserve, and sustainably manage their lands was illuminated (Snodgrass, Lacy, et al. 2008; Snodgrass, Sharma, et al. 2007, 2008; Snodgrass and Tiedje 2008; Tiedje and Snodgrass 2008).

Doi Phukha National Park, Nan Province, Northern Thailand (Hank Delcore)

Pua District is a multi-ethnic district in Nan Province, northern Thailand. Pua, like much of Nan Province, is predominantly an upland topography, and most of its land is classified as forest. In the 1960s, the area and its people entered into an accelerated process of social and economic change spurred by the Thai state's resource intensive drive for development. The changes that accelerated then have since combined with a myriad of local, national, and international trends to produce a massive expansion of state protected areas. One such park is Doi Phukha National Park (DPNP). Thai national parks prohibit any kind of productive activity; they are 'landscapes of consumption', meant largely for the enjoyment of domestic and foreign tourists. The people who live in and around DPNP, the lowland Thai-Lue and the upland Lua, face a serious challenge to their existing ways of interacting with their environment. This case study focuses on the resource management controversies surrounding Doi Phukha National Park and the difference in the relations between park managers and the Thai-Lue and Lua communities (Figure I.5).

Methods

Hank Delcore first visited the DPNP area in 1997 while conducting a study of development and environmental activism by Non-Governmental

Figure I.5 Lua swidden field inside Doi Phukha National Park (photograph by H. Delcore).

Organizations (NGOs) and local people (see Delcore 2000, 2003, 2004). At that time, he interviewed Thai-Lue farmers, who lived at the park's edge, about their environmental activism and relations with local NGOs.

He later returned in 2003 and 2006 for short field visits that included interviews and periods of observation with all three major ethnic communities in and around the park: Thai-Lue, Lua, and Hmong. He also interviewed two park directors and other national park and forestry officials assigned to the area. Delcore has focused interview questions on the following topics: relations between ethnic communities and park officials; relations among the ethnic communities; traditions of resource use and management practices; and evolving local political and cultural responses to environmental change and increased state regulation of resources (see Delcore 2007).

The Notion of 'Indigenous' Peoples

In the most straightforward formulation of the term, 'Indigenous' peoples are 'native' to a particular place, original to their lands rather than having migrated from elsewhere (Clifford 2007). In recognition of these communities' purported ancient connections to their territories, North American Indians such as the Lakota Sioux are also referred to as 'Native' and 'First Nations' peoples, whereas in Australia they are termed 'Aboriginal peoples' and 'Torres Strait Islanders'. In India, Indigenous communities are called 'Adivasis', which translates as 'First Inhabitants'. In Thailand, there is no one term that captures the idea of 'Indigenous people' in the same way as 'First Nations' or 'Aboriginal'. However, the Lua, a focus of the Thailand case study, are sometimes referred to as *khon phuun muang*, or the 'native people', referring to a common belief among Thais that their occupancy predates the settlement of the area by Tai-speaking peoples. (However, the more common Thai term for non-Tai speakers is *chaaw khaw*, commonly translated in English as 'hilltribes', a term with negative connotations and imprecise application to a very diverse group of mostly upland peoples – see Chapter 4).

Many Indigenous communities claim in their histories and myths to have either literally sprung from their lands, and thus to have been created by or from the land, or to have themselves created their territories. In both cases, such myths express the important symbiotic relationship that Indigenous groups feel for their lands and its resources. Examples can be found in Native American 'earth diver' creation myths, wherein a supreme being sends an ancestral animal into primal waters to find material with which to build habitable land (Dundes 1962). In this respect Indigenous societies can be contrasted with European settler societies, whose founding legends often feature transplantation through violent conquest of a seat of high civilization (Waswo 1997).

Still, it is not always easy to establish Indigenous peoples' prior occupancy in the lands they currently inhabit. The descendants of India's pre-Independence 'Princely Kingdoms' – such as the Rajput states of Rajasthan that relied on intensive irrigated agriculture – claim in many instances as deep a connection to local territories (Beteille 1998). In Thailand, Indigenous communities are highly mobile, having complex histories featuring migrations and interminglings with outsiders. There, groups such as the Hmong, who are now found throughout Southeast Asia, are in fact believed to have originated in southern China or even Tibet (see McKinnon and Wanat 1983; Tapp 1989; Tapp et al. 2004).

If the histories can be murky, Indigenous peoples do often display distinctive forms of social, political, and economic organization. In comparison to members of settler societies, Indigenous peoples typically live in 'segmentary' systems, organized around kin-based groups claiming descent from common ancestors, who themselves are either opposed to or affiliated with other descent groups (Evans-Pritchard 1969). Lacking centralized forms of authority characteristic of states, Indigenous peoples' segmentary lineage systems create forms of political authority that are largely egalitarian and diffused through multiple individuals and groups and that are thus spread over large territories. Indigenous groups also often inhabit isolated hills and forests are foragers and/or swidden agriculturalists, and are thus largely independent of settled society (Xaxa 2003). Living in such close proximity to forests and other natural areas, Indigenous communities typically display a deep connection to the natural world. Indeed, their survival typically depends on their depth of connection to nature (Gadgil and Guha 1992, 1995; Merlan 2009).

Likewise, Indigenous peoples have usually been incorporated, often by force, into states dominated by others and within which they have been marginalized or dominated (Clifford 2007; Merlan 2009; Trigger and Dalley 2010). Native communities in the United States and Australia were incorporated into states controlled by persons of European descent. In addition to the prejudice that members of these Indigenous communities continue to experience, Indigenous peoples also are among the poorest citizens of these nations (see Pickering 2004; Reynolds 1987a, 1987b, 2001; Rowse 2000). In western India, Indigenous power was eroded in the precolonial period first by emerging Rajput kingdoms and then by the Marathas of Maharashtra. The British pushed Adivasis further into isolated forests, which were subsequently largely appropriated by the British in their empire's hunger for lumber for ships and railways. British commodity-extraction policies continued in post-Independence India as the newly formed Indian state sold clear-cutting and mining contracts to outside groups and pursued national 'development' projects such as dams that alienated Indigenous peoples from their increasingly degraded forest homes (Arnold and Guha 1995; Baviskar 1995; Guha 1999). Currently, most of India's Adivasi groups – 67,758,000 persons by the Census of 1991, or 8% of India's population (Xaxa 2003) – are officially categorized as 461 distinct 'Scheduled Tribes'. That is, they are 'scheduled' – along with India's marginalized and formerly untouchable caste communities (Snodgrass 2006) – for government aid programs aiming to alleviate their poverty and social 'backwardness'.

The category 'Indigenous peoples' is a legal and bureaucratic term in three of the nation-states where our research unfolds. In Australia, concepts of 'Indigenous' have necessarily been linked to legal definitions and requirements of the Native Title Act of 1993. Under this Act, to be successful in having one's traditional connections to land and sea (termed 'country' in Aboriginal English [Rose 1996b]) recognized, Aboriginal and Torres Strait Islander Australians must demonstrate their indigeneity through an ongoing performance of tradition (Weiner 2002). In the United States, Indians must demonstrate affiliation to known Native 'tribes' as well as have certain percentages of Indian blood in order to qualify as 'Native' or 'First Nations'. And in India the government maintains lists of recognized Indigenous groups under the category 'Scheduled Tribes', who have special legal rights and privileges. In Thailand, although upland minorities have been subject to intense state interest ranging from counter-insurgency to development, there is no single bureaucratic category for 'Indigenous peoples' that carries particular rights and privileges; if anything, non-Tai minorities are often subject to insecure citizenship and other prejudicial policies and practices (see Chapter 2).

Acknowledging the complexity of this terminological issue, we use the phrase 'Indigenous peoples' somewhat loosely in ways that reference the ideas sketched above. Each of the groups featured in this book claims to have ancient ties to the land, claims that are enacted in both oral histories and contemporary rituals. They tend to possess egalitarian and decentralized forms of social organization. They typically inhabit lands somewhat removed from mainstream society, for example, semi-isolated hills and forests and sparsely populated plains, to whose natural processes they are closely attuned. Their claims of prior habitation and thus distinctive identity are bolstered by these communities' awareness of both their difference from and subordination to persons more closely affiliated with the dominant states into which Indigenous peoples have been subsumed. Further, each of these groups' claims to be 'Indigenous' are legal according to the laws and mandates of the states they inhabit.

Our use of the term 'Indigenous' thus aligns closely with that prepared by José R. Martinez Cobo for the United Nations:

Indigenous communities, peoples and nations are those which, having a historical continuity with pre-invasion and pre-colonial societies that developed on their territories, consider themselves distinct from other sectors of the societies now prevailing on those territories, or parts of them. They form at present non-dominant sectors of society and are determined to preserve, develop and transmit to future generations their ancestral territories, and their ethnic identity, as the basis of their continued existence as peoples, in accordance with their own cultural patterns, social institutions and legal system. (United Nations 2004)

That is, following a number of contemporary anthropologists, we do not insist that groups demonstrate actual prior occupation to qualify as 'Indigenous' (Bodley 2008; Maybury-Lewis 2002; Merlan 2009; Trigger and Dalley 2010). Rather, we apply the term to groups who self-identify with precolonial societies, even if those societies have found their deep historical links to particular lands to be disrupted or compromised. Nor do 'Indigenous' groups, in our usage, necessarily demonstrate particular forms of sociopolitical organization. The social relations of the communities featured in this book are generally egalitarian and decentralized; the people typically hunt, gather, and practice horticulture. However, we recognize the possibility of Indigenous *states* tied to other forms of subsistence, such as full-scale irrigated agriculture, even though we do not find such historical formations among the communities with whom we work most closely. For us, 'Indigenous' is a category of identity, itself recognized by modern bureaucratic states, that emerges as much from current feelings of oppression and marginalization as from actual history. Of note, throughout the book, we capitalize the term 'Indigenous' in order to bestow on members of these communities the same dignity as is given to the other citizens of such modern states as Australia, the United States, India, and Thailand.

It is thus difficult for us to draw clear and absolute boundaries between Indigenous and non-Indigenous persons. Using 'Indigenous peoples' in this broad and somewhat imprecise manner might seem unsatisfying to certain readers. Still, such usage does potentially permit us to generalize broadly from our case studies. These case studies were chosen in order to demonstrate a range of Indigenous experiences, two emerging from historical processes of groups subordinated to Euro-American societies (Australia, the United States) and two others from communities dominated by local 'Indigenous' states or even by both local and European powers (Thailand, India). In fact, we believe that many of the processes described in this book can be extended to the 'practical environmentalism of the poor' (Guha and Martinez-Alier 1997; Snodgrass, Sharma, et al. 2008), which is characteristic of many pre- and non-industrial subaltern societies that fail to be classified as 'Indigenous', but that nevertheless demonstrate deep and abiding connections to their lands.

THE BOOK

These case studies provide the examples and comparative materials used throughout the book, but we begin with a more general and theoretical overview of the issues that provide the framework for our discussion of the case studies.

We begin our analysis in earnest, in Chapter 1, by exploring how best to frame the concept of 'Indigenous knowledge'. Relying largely on a cognitive anthropological vocabulary of knowledge 'frames' and 'models' (D'Andrade 1995), we present the idea that Indigenous knowledge is not some form of 'primitive ecological wisdom' (Suzuki and Knudtson 1992; cf. Milton 1996). The dangers of reifying Indigenous knowledge, itself a culture-specific collection of socially transmitted 'frames' and 'models' of reality, as an answer to all the world's environmental problems have been well analyzed by others – for example, Agrawal 1995; Brosius 2000; Krech 1999; Milton 1996; Redford 1990; Sillitoe 1998. These authors provide many examples of Indigenous peoples having an environmental impact that is contrary to (modern) conservation ideals (see also Diamond 2005; Sillitoe 2002; Smith and Wishnie 2000). There is no essential non-industrial cultural response to the environment.

Nevertheless, there are Indigenous societies and other local groups that are not clearly or straightforwardly 'Indigenous' (Antweiler 2004), who do have laws, rituals, beliefs, and other social norms that relate to the management of their local environment. Where such cultures *do* have knowledge that promotes human intervention to sustain the environment, we argue that there is an opportunity for modern societies to take note, particularly where current environmental management practices are clearly unsatisfactory.

In many Indigenous cultures people have lived in and managed (and often modified) their surrounding ecosystems for hundreds if not thousands of years. Over time their knowledge evolves to deal with newly emerging problems presented by the environment. David (2006) argues that Indigenous societies have undergone numerous changes over time, and as a consequence there can be no single, 'traditional' response to the physical and spiritual world that surrounds a particular group. Knowledge is therefore not a belief system that is somehow fossilized or unchanged – locked in some romantic time warp of a recreated past. It comprises 'a pastiche of transmitted knowledge and recent invention' (Antweiler 2004: 5). Consequently, if we do need to adopt a definition of Indigenous knowledge, we prefer definitions that recognize the evolving nature of Indigenous knowledge, that understand that it encompasses more than just natural systems, and that emphasize the social context for knowledge (for example, Berkes 2008: 8; Bradley et al. 2006; Posey 1998: 96–97).

In this volume we do not aim to perpetuate the myth of the non-industrial world living in harmony with the environment, ideas we challenge in Chapter 1 and elsewhere. On the contrary, we acknowledge that environmental knowledge includes knowledge about how to manipulate and even change the environment, and we include examples of such manipulation among our case studies. The point we are making is that, where Indigenous knowledge includes knowledge that relates to environmental stewardship, and where that knowledge leads to conservation, whether or not such conservation is 'by design' (Smith and Wishnie 2000), such knowledge should not be ignored by environmental managers today.

In Chapter 2 we look at the history of the way in which the epistemological conflicts between Indigenous knowledge and scientific knowledge have evolved. We further develop our cognitive and constructivist approach, arguing that the world around us and the way we understand our place in the world are historical constructs, based on the ontology we acquire as a result of our social and cultural upbringing. This constructivist methodology sees culture as the determinant of a person's understanding of the environment, by defining the nature and boundaries of that environment and by giving meaning to what that person sees in that environment. An open field may be seen as either a wasted area or a landscape abundant with wild resources, depending on whether it is being seen by a cattle rancher or a hunter-gatherer.

Milton argues that constructivism is not helpful in environmental debates. She claims that: 'If the environment were nothing more than a cognitive construct, we could change it by constructing different truths, different meanings' (1996: 54). Furthermore, she argues, '[Constructivism] implies that the real, unconstructed world is unknowable or at least has no inherent meaning' (1996: 60).

Milton develops an alternative paradigm for understanding how people see the world:

> [N]ot everything that exists in people's minds is 'constructed'. At least some of what we know, think and feel about the world comes to us directly through our experience, in the form of discovered meanings . . . . these meanings, these 'perceptions' are part of culture. (1996: 62)

However, our view is that this is exactly what constructivism is. Our perceptions of the world come from our experiences with the world, and our experiences are shaped by culture. There is no single way of understanding the world. To claim that the world is knowable is to privilege one set of facts about the world over all others.

We use this perspective to outline a history of exchanges and conflicts between states, or settled peoples inhabiting so-called civilizations, on the one hand, and Indigenous peoples, on the other. These interactions present themselves to us as a history of marginalization of Indigenous knowledge and dispossession of Indigenous peoples from their lands. Understanding such processes throws into relief many of the social processes still at work in our case-study sites today.

An appreciation of the significance of constructing reality is vital to understanding Indigenous dissatisfaction with current co-management arrangements, which continue to privilege Western goals for conservation over Indigenous goals for harvesting (Stevenson 2006). In Chapter 3 we outline specific barriers to the development of integrated systems of management that aim to value Western and Indigenous perspectives equally. These barriers relate to how people think and to the ways they organize activities. Cultures construct various contrasting understandings of the environment and the human role in the environment. Consequently, different management goals result, contesting co-management objectives. In Chapter 4 we develop our specific case studies as examples of these barriers to equal collaborative partnerships, with individual though interwoven sections devoted to Australia, the United States, India, and Thailand. We explicitly compare and contrast the range of different management styles and situations in these four parts of the globe.

Each of the authors of this volume has undertaken research over many years with the various communities that make up the case studies in this book. Although we aim for a large degree of analytical unity across these case studies, each of us has worked independently in our research, and we have all been trained in a range of methods and theoretical perspectives. As a result we have each applied different methods in acquiring data, depending on the nature of the communities, the requirements of the research collaborators, and the specific goals of our original research. In this way, each case study is discrete and stands alone, and indeed can be read that way.

In Chapters 5 and 6 we review some of the mechanisms that have been introduced to reduce or eliminate the barriers to genuine collaborative partnerships. In Chapter 5 we show that co-management goes part of the way to addressing the problem of imposing Western viewpoints onto Indigenous lands. Nevertheless, we find that the privileging of scientific approaches to management and Western cultural perspectives still dominates, even in co-managed areas. Because Australia has been at the forefront of international developments in co-management of protected natural areas, we concentrate here on Australian examples. Case studies from elsewhere in the world, and notably from our own experiences in India and Thailand, provide comparative analyses. In Chapter 6 we present an alternative model that provides a central role for Indigenous constructs of stewardship of the land, developing a common language that allows for balanced contributions from Western land managers and Indigenous communities. This chapter draws exclusively on Pickering Sherman's and Sherman's experiences with Native communities in the United States, in a setting where Indigenous management of natural areas is particularly well developed. In the book's conclusion, after summarizing the principal threads of our arguments, we each present our vision for the way forward in state-Indigenous partnerships in natural resource stewardship.

THE STORY OF THE BOOK

The idea for this book germinated in 2003 when Annie Ross, Kathy Pickering Sherman, and Jim Igoe (formerly of the University of Colorado) organized a panel for the 102nd Annual Meeting of the American Anthropological Association (November 19–23, 2003 in Chicago). The aim of the session was to present a global comparison of obstacles to collaborative conservation between Indigenous communities and 'mainstream' resource managers. Papers were to present encounters with conservation, exploring both positive and negative examples of conservation alliances.

Papers by Ross (Australia), Pickering Sherman (United States of America), and Igoe (Africa) were joined by presentations from Delcore (Thailand) and John Wagner of University of British Columbia (New Guinea) and later by Snodgrass (India). The synergies between ideas, and the commonalities in the widely varied case studies, generated the desire to bring these case studies together in a single volume.

At first all the authors agreed to be part of the development of the volume, but pressures of other work led Igoe and Wagner to leave the project during 2004–2005. In 2007 Richard Sherman (Oglala Lakota tribal member) joined the writing team, contributing the chapter on the Indigenous Stewardship Model (Chapter 6), originally developed for Lakota people but now expanded to be applicable anywhere in the Indigenous world.

The analytical schemes and models presented in this book evolved over the course of several years and many discussions between the members of our writing team. For example, the distinction between epistemological and institutional barriers to collaborative conservation (see Chapter 3) was generated by what we might call both deductive and inductive forces. *Deductively*, our different anthropological trainings led some of us to pay particular attention to knowledge structures, others to political and economic relationships of inequality. With his training in cognitive anthropology, with its emphasis on unraveling processes associated with the social transmission and sharing of cultural knowledge and values, Snodgrass is an example of the former. A focus on the way in which local Indigenous social economies in North America intersect with global market forces and settler nation-states makes Pickering Sherman a particularly good example of the latter. *Inductively* we generated innumerable examples of problems arising in the implementation of collaborative conservation in our four field-sites. As we grouped these examples into larger categories, we began to see, slowly, how analytically useful it was to distinguish between *epistemological* problems associated with the recognition of Indigenous knowledge and *institutional* issues typically connected to the economically and politically marginal status of Indigenous communities. With its many subheadings (used throughout Chapters 3 and 4), this analytical scheme may seem unwieldy, and even arbitrary, in places. Nevertheless, we find it a particularly useful set of categories that do justice both to our own individual anthropological traditions as well as to the thought and practice of the Indigenous peoples we know so well.

THE WAY FORWARD

Overall, this book addresses what each of us identifies as being among the most pressing problems of our time. In the name of conservation and the protection of biological diversity, Indigenous peoples are being systematically excluded from lands and resources they occupied, utilized, and indeed protected for generations. Labeled poachers and trespassers in newly created parks, wildlife sanctuaries, and other protected and often fenced areas, part of the problem rather than a solution, Indigenous peoples find it increasingly hard if not impossible to participate meaningfully in the sustainable management of their own ancestral territories. We believe such exclusions are deeply dangerous, both for the future of our planet and its myriad species as well as for the future of the Indigenous peoples with whom we have spent so many years of our lives. Such exclusions set up confrontations that transform Indigenous peoples into enemies of biological diversity rather than potentially its staunchest defenders. We also think that many of the problems we sketch, which are related to conflict between Western resource managers and NGOs (who are committed to conservation and sustainability) and Indigenous peoples (who are similarly committed to sustainable resources stewardship), are largely avoidable. For this reason we lay out a framework that both identifies problem areas and also points to potential resolutions. In doing so we hope to help to assure the futures of the lands and the animals cherished so much by us and by the Indigenous peoples with whom we work and count as friends, colleagues, and fellow scientists in these conservation and management challenges.

In a recent review article Pretty and associates (2009) laid out a compelling case for policies that pursue the joint and combined conservation of biological and also cultural diversity, given the way natural and social systems are intertwined and also threatened by the same historical drivers. This book does not assess barriers associated with the conservation of sociocultural diversity. Rather, it focuses on epistemological and institutional problems that Indigenous peoples encounter when they attempt to manage nature collaboratively with parties external to their own societies. Indigenous peoples, somewhat 'bound' to their traditions and systems of knowledge, find themselves in contemporary 'binds' as they try to translate their knowledge and practice into the frameworks of contemporary language. However, we applaud and in fact align our work closely with Pretty and associates' (2009) proposal. We place tremendous value on the Indigenous societies featured in this book. We hope this is evident on every page. And we also hope that more fruitful collaborative land stewardship partnerships between Indigenous peoples and others, which our book ideally might facilitate, will help to preserve both nature and the Indigenous peoples whose lives and histories are intertwined with that nature.

Chapter 1

INDIGENOUS AND SCIENTIFIC KNOWLEDGE

The whole of science is nothing more than a refinement of everyday thinking. (Einstein, quoted in Ellen 2004: 425)

In his book *A Forest of Time*, Nabokov (2002) describes a meeting between an archaeologist and an elderly Navajo man. The archaeologist was keen to know what the Navajo man thought of archaeological descriptions of the past. The elder began to explain that, for Navajo, one could not understand the origin of people on the land without first knowing about insects and corn kernels and their place in the creation of people and the landscape. The archaeologist, mystified by these stories, tried asking his questions in different ways. He laid out maps of migration routes across the Bering Strait and held up pictures of Folsom points and Clovis arrowheads. The Navajo elder, however, indicated that horny toads had made these stone tools. At this point, the archaeologist appears to have given up his quest for Navajo corroboration of scientific knowledge (Nabokov 2002: 29–31).

Nabokov uses this vignette to demonstrate the nature of Indigenous modes of narrating history and imparting knowledge about the past. For the Navajo and other Indigenous communities, according to Nabokov, objects and archaeological sites are not just neutral and 'objective' records of past human events (cf. Appadurai 1986; Bradley 2008; Byrne 2005). They are locales that document interactions between those human and nonhuman persons who have come before the present generation and, as importantly, who continue to interact in contemporary times. History for these communities is thus a living entity that documents but also *maintains* past and present relationships of dependency between humans and nonhuman persons such as insects, corn kernels, and horny toads. In Indigenous worldviews, as Nabokov explains, these relationships have structured the naming of places and the creation of such material artifacts as arrowheads; but they continue to structure the contemporary production of places and artifacts (Nabokov 2002: 126–149; see also Bradley 2008). For Indigenous communities, as Nabokov elaborates, the narration of history is a multimedia production involving the communal creation of stories, songs, dances, music, and visual art. For Indigenous groups to separate the past from these contemporary performative and social contexts, like separating the past from human relations with corn kernels and horny toads, would entail killing history by robbing it of most of its power to evoke commitment and passion in living human beings (Nabokov 2002: 29–57).

For Nabokov, the uniqueness of Indigenous epistemologies points to the fundamentally different understandings of time and space, landscape, and the past held by Indigenous peoples on the one hand and scientists on the other. In framing the past by evoking and paying homage to the 'subjectivities' of human and nonhuman persons, Indigenous peoples personify history in a way that cannot be easily heard or fathomed by archaeologists pursuing purely 'objective' forms of analysis (cf. Bradley 2008; Godwin 2005; Nabokov 2002: 150–171; Ross 2008; Rowlands 1994). It is not surprising, then, that the interaction between the archaeologist and Navajo elder described above, informed as it is by these individuals' contrasting assumptions and priorities regarding the past that literally 'crackle off the page', is characterized by 'halting exchanges' that never quite take off (Nabokov 2002: 31).

Solomon Islands nationals, Gegeo and Watson-Gegeo, discuss this and other related issues in the context of their comparative analysis of Indigenous and Western (scientific) epistemologies. They define Indigenous epistemology as 'a cultural *group's* way of thinking and of creating, reformulating, and theorizing about knowledge via traditional discourses' (2001: 58, emphasis added). Scientific epistemologies, in contrast, are rarely recognized as having this social and communal context, despite anthropological discourse to the contrary (Nabokov 2002; Nadasdy 1999; Sillitoe 2002; Stevenson 2006). To most Western-trained academics, science is based on an objective 'knowledge without a knower' that is usually foreign to Indigenous peoples for whom knowledge is very much personalized and social (Gegeo and Watson-Gegeo 2001: 62). Although Indigenous knowledge is owned and shared asymmetrically (Ellen and Harris 2000: 4–5) – often only certain individuals have the right to speak about certain aspects of local knowledge (Rose 1996a) – such knowledge is put back together as a whole when the community gathers together on practical and ritual occasions (Gegeo and Watson-Gegeo 2001: 62).

At this general level, then, Western scientific and Indigenous ways of knowing would seem to constitute distinctive modes of thought. In this chapter we analyze the nature of both difference and similarity between these two knowledge systems, dealing not so much with *what* is known but rather with *how* different ways of knowing are valorized and institutionalized in modern scientific and Indigenous contexts. In grappling with these epistemological issues we realize that we are in illustrious and daunting company. Anthropological luminaries from Frazer to Tylor, from Malinowski to Evans-Pritchard and Tambiah have all wrestled with the separation or lack of separation between science and magic, which we see as a proxy discussion for the relationship between scientific and Indigenous knowledge more generally. Further, an immense literature spanning most of the social sciences as well as philosophy and history has attempted to define the nature of science and thus, by extension, the nature of nonscientific forms of knowing. Indeed, this literature has been polarized into what has been termed the 'science wars' (Anderson 2000; Ellen 2004). In this discursive 'war', one side argues for the distinctive and superior nature of scientific forms of understanding: scientists discover 'truths' about the way the world really works. The other side, in a position with roots in extreme 'postmodernist' forms of cultural relativism, denies any special status for scientific forms of understanding: 'science' is merely a label used to privilege certain forms of knowledge and thus to denigrate and marginalize other nonscientific modes of thought (see the discussion on constructivism in the Introduction).

We are not under the illusion that we will resolve all the contentious issues related to how scientists and nonscientists understand the world. However, in this chapter we sketch a position that lies between the two poles of this debate, a position that frames the arguments of this book. We do believe that there are good reasons to separate scientific from Indigenous modes of thought. We argue, however, that such differences lie primarily on the level of cultural ideals and methodological prescriptions: scientists privilege impersonal and decontextualized knowledge, for example, in a way that Indigenous peoples generally do not; they strive to follow a method that seeks to eliminate observer bias and the peculiarity of context in a way, again, that Indigenous peoples usually do not. Nevertheless, we still see important continuities between scientific and Indigenous ways of knowing, especially on the level of actual epistemological practice: for example, we accept that scientific knowledge, like Indigenous ways of knowing, 'draws its form from its social and cultural roots' (Nader 1996b: xi; see also Ede and Cormack 2004; Peloquin and Berkes 2009). To decontextualize science from its social roots is to grant science a privileged status and an unfounded superiority over other ways of knowing (Agrawal 1995; Nadasdy 1999; Nader 1996a; Sillitoe 2002). Alternatively, to argue that only Indigenous knowledge has a social context tends to produce views of Indigenous peoples as 'ecological savages' (Krech 1999; Milton 1996; Redford 1990) with no 'objective' knowledge of value in a modern political world (Kuper 2003). These are positions we cannot support.

Overall, we hope this chapter introduces some important differences between scientific and Indigenous ways of knowing without essentializing these differences or implying that they are absolute. To argue for an insurmountable 'cognitive divide' between scientists and nonscientists would in fact defeat one of the primary aims of this book, which is to show how barriers become *constructed* between government-based resource managers and Indigenous peoples and thus also how such barriers, as social *constructs*, might be bridged.

INDIGENOUS KNOWLEDGE VERSUS SCIENTIFIC KNOWLEDGE

From our field experiences, we have learned that Indigenous know-how is a form of '*local* knowledge', intricately bound to particular communities and places as well as to whole ways of life. Such knowledge is often learned through informal trial and error processes and thus comes from direct personal experiences. Despite the highly personal and even individualized character of this knowledge, however, the acquisition and preservation of Indigenous understandings are usually mediated by social others in informal apprentice relationships. Such apprenticeships, in turn, are structured by highly repetitive and often unspoken demonstrations by, and silent imitations of, local experts. In similar terms, Indigenous knowledge is often pragmatic rather than abstractly theoretical – a *knowledge how* rather than an abstract *knowledge of* or *knowledge about*. Likewise, Indigenous knowledge, as suggested above, is orally preserved not only in the living memories of individuals but also within the textures of local songs, stories, and other performance traditions. Further, Indigenous knowledge is almost invariably informed by references to elusive spiritual beings such as gods, ghosts, and ancestors. Such knowledge, again as indicated above, interconnects local human communities with nonhuman societies of animals and plants (Feit 1987; Gadgil, Berkes, and Folke 1993; Nadasdy 1999; Posey 1992, 2000; Scott 1996; Sillitoe 2002; Snodgrass, Sharma, et al. 2007, 2008; Snodgrass, Lacy, et al. 2008) and with past-human realms of spirit and creator beings and ancestors (Bradley 2001, 2008; Merlan 1998; Nabokov 2002; Povinelli 1993; Rose 1996b; Snodgrass and Tiedje 2008; Tiedje and Snodgrass 2008). Overall, such knowledge is explicitly acknowledged as partaking in local 'traditions' that build on the know-how of multiple preceding generations. And such 'traditional' knowledge, it is argued, has helped its practitioners to manage their lands relatively sustainably across large expanses of time (but see Chapter 2).

By contrast, scientists are said to pursue knowledge that is replicable across contexts that are strictly controlled, making such knowledge more abstract and universalizing, rigorously empirical and experimental rather than simply experiential (Ede and Cormack 2004; Kalland 2000; Lindberg 1990; Nader 1996a; Schafersman 1997). Scientific knowledge is also preserved in impersonal institutional networks such as written and digital texts rather than only in the minds and bodies of living persons and in the fluid and unpredictable language of story (Ede and Cormack 2004: 147; Goody 1977, 1986, 1987; Nadasdy 1999; Wallerstein 2003: 459). Further, scientists are certainly interested in gaining technological *knowledge how* to control and manipulate the world. Nevertheless, such practical know-how is often subordinated to abstract *knowledge of* in the form of coherent systems of explanation, even logical syllogisms and proofs, statistical tables and rigorous taxonomies, and mathematical equations. Modern scientists, more than Indigenous peoples, seem to be interested in consciously coding their knowledge in formalized representations that can be manipulated according to the rules of logical inference to retrieve such knowledge. Such a coding, it is sometimes argued, also makes knowledge easier to critique and thus facilitates the critical distance that prevents irrational and blind commitment to traditional authority. Mathematics and formal logic, then, not narrative, performance, and social authority, are the watchwords of modern scientific practice. In this same vein, scientists are committed to the generation of testable hypotheses that are systematic, logically coherent, and empirically grounded (Schafersman 1997), not to mercurial spiritual beings. And scientific knowledge, owing to the institutional and technological forms it has engendered and in seeming direct contrast to Indigenous forms of knowing, has led to an unprecedented control over, and even exploitation and degradation of, the planet. Indeed, many social scientists preserve the distinction between these two forms of knowledge on precisely these grounds (Gegeo and Watson-Gegeo 2001, 2002; Hunn 2003; Hunn et al. 2003; Kalland 2000; Nadasdy 1999; Scott 1996; Silberbauer 1994; Sillitoe 1998, 2002).

Indigenous knowledge, we would thus argue, is eminently social as well as *integrated.* Here we wish to be careful, however, not to occlude the personalized, and even individualized, nature of such knowledge. Institutional structures such as totems, kinship relationships, proprietary stories/myths, political status, and so on influence the construction and indeed *ownership* of Indigenous knowledge and therefore the exclusive right to speak about and regulate certain resources. This individual ownership, it should be pointed out, makes Indigenous knowledge potentially unstable: important traditions can be lost with the death of a single expert; likewise, such knowledge can be acquired, or re-acquired, with the help of a single Native genius. Indigenous knowledge, then, can be said to be fragmented in a certain sense. Nevertheless, one typically finds Indigenous mechanisms that ensure that knowledge, even when shared asymmetrically, is available to many. This sharing of knowledge can occur through the bringing together of specialists at appropriate times to address important resource problems, to direct the extraction of resources, and/or to grant rights of access over these resources. In addition, much Indigenous ownership of knowledge is not limited to specific individuals; instead, it is spread over entire clans or communities, or it is distributed over categories of persons based on their age or their gender. This form of knowledge management adds to the understanding that Indigenous knowledge is social, and indeed redundant, rather than merely individualized (see Basso 1996; Bradley 2001; Feit 1987, 1994; Kearney 2008; Mearns 1994; Merculieff 1994; Pickering and Jewell 2008; Povinelli 1993; Rose 1996b; Silberbauer 1994; Williams and Mununggurr 1989).

To elaborate on the social nature of Indigenous knowledge, Feit (1994) and Nadasdy (1999) argue that the ritual and political nature of Indigenous knowledge is central to the successful sharing of knowledge within a Native community as well as between Indigenous peoples, on the one hand, and scientists and resource managers, on the other. For Feit, local relations of power are particularly important in the praxis of hunting. Passing on the hunting culture from one generation to the next not only regenerates the hunt, it also 'reproduces the social system of relations, including social differentiations that both hierarchically separate and link generations' (Feit 1994: 436). For Nadasdy (1999), power lies in the choices made about the kinds of information brought to the management table. Local experience is the key to understanding management problems and to developing solutions, and social networks inform experience. Indigenous resource managers combine their knowledge and experience in a social context that ensures that all relevant elements of knowledge can come together regularly. Because Indigenous peoples form communities, their social structures ensure that they interrelate on a regular (often daily) basis, coming together for a range of social activities – including but not limited to the stewardship of natural resources and the resolution of ecological crises – as part of normal community activities.

In contrast to Indigenous peoples' 'holistic' distribution of knowledge, scientists' knowledge tends to be specialized, with research concentrated on narrow fields of knowledge. This highly specialized way of knowing, which is the dominant tendency of science, is often experienced by outsiders to the scientific enterprise – or to certain narrowly demarcated dimensions of the scientific enterprise – as the extremely esoteric nature of certain kinds of scientific knowledge and expertise. In 2003 one of us (AR) attended a workshop presenting scientific research undertaken in national parks in Queensland (Australia) as a collaborative venture of university and other scientists and national parks staff. Dr. Don Sands, from the Australian Commonwealth Scientific Industrial and Research Organisation (CSIRO) Division of Entomology discussed his work in communicating scientific research into *Lepidoptera* (butterflies) to the general public. His was the only paper relating to invertebrates. Most of the other speakers discussed research into ecosystems supporting rare and threatened plant and animal species, with large vertebrate mammals dominating the day's proceedings. In speaking about butterflies and moths, Sands distinguished himself from his colleagues by referring to the other speakers at the gathering as 'you vertebrate people'. He then outlined why his talk was only about *Lepidoptera*, explaining that he was interested only in collecting and researching butterflies and moths: 'although I will do ants if someone needs me to'.

Suzuki documents a similar experience while on a visit to the Amazon rainforest: 'Three scientists, frog experts, were there at the time, and their knowledge of their subject was impressive. One of them took us on a night hike and in pitch dark, could find frogs that were barely half an inch long. But when I asked about a bird we scared up and a strange plant on a tree, he shrugged his shoulders. "Don't ask me, I'm a herpetologist", he said' (1992: xxxvi).

Kalland (2000) argues that this sometimes myopic knowledge bind of scientists is due to a one-dimensional focus on causation that is at the heart of the separation of scientific disciplines. As a result, scientists like Nabokov's archaeologist often cannot understand the complex interconnections between different animal species that characterize Indigenous explanations of problems (Feit 1987; Nadasdy 1999; Scott 1996; Silberbauer 1994; Sillitoe 2002; Stevenson 2006). This problem is not so marked in those scientific fields that adopt a holistic approach to the environment, such as ecology, but even here there are some ecologists who take a narrow perspective on the discipline and therefore fail to realize the level of holism that is characteristic of so many nonscientific communities (Taylor 2001).

Such myopia is often evident in resource management. In most management agencies, especially those dealing with the protection of important – often endangered – species, individual species management plans are the most common instrument of fauna and flora conservation. Although holistic management of the entire protected area is desired and even required by legislation, holistic management is achieved by the separation of each element of the protected area and the development of individual management plans on a species-by-species basis. A review of any plan of management for a national park, for example, demonstrates this point. The plan is divided into separate management components, with a separate, individual, isolated set of policies and procedures for each compartment. Management of the whole is simply the sum of the individual, isolated parts (Golschewski 2004; Nadasdy 1999).

The segregation of knowledge and understanding, as we have argued, is not entirely foreign to most Indigenous communities. Indigenous experts, too, maintain technical and esoteric knowledge that is unequally distributed within a community. However, we would suggest that Indigenous experts must continually translate their knowledge into terms that are meaningful and practical to the community as a whole. Western scientists also participate in communal gatherings – academic conferences, for example. And interdisciplinary gatherings are increasingly common. We would suggest, however, that these more holistically defined occasions have been precipitated by a perceived failure of or crisis within normative science which is, by its nature, fragmenting and compartmentalized.

DISENTANGLING SIMPLISTIC DISTINCTIONS I: INDIGENOUS PEOPLES THINKING LIKE SCIENTISTS

Despite these examples, ample anthropological research breaks down simplistic distinctions between Indigenous and scientific knowledge. Bourdieu (1960, 1972), for example, has demonstrated that knowledge that is usually presented as characteristic of Indigenous societies – knowledge that is context-bound, practical, largely unspoken and unsystematic, often beyond challenge, and deeply embodied rather than abstractly theorized – is also characteristic of communities as diverse as Algerian peasants and the French bourgeoisie.

Simplistic distinctions between Indigenous and scientific knowledge tend to occlude important features of Indigenous thought that we have all encountered in our various field-sites. For example, an emphasis on Indigenous knowledge as 'traditional' knowledge handed down from generation to generation, tends to suggest that Indigenous peoples inhabit 'closed' epistemological systems, thus denying them their creativity and ability to learn and respond flexibly to new situations (Berkes 2008; Hunn 1993; Merlan 1998; Nadasdy 1999). Belying such assumptions, we have all witnessed Indigenous incorporations of scientific knowledge into local Indigenous systems of land management (cf. Stevenson 2006). Similarly, the emphasis on Indigenous knowledge as experiential and sacred rather than experimental and purely empirical – the fact that Indigenous peoples are willing to be guided by unseen forces and entities – can obscure the reality that Indigenous peoples may produce accounts of their environments that are just as objective, detailed, rigorously grounded, and coherent as those of ecologists. And the suggestion that Indigenous knowledge is largely informal, pragmatic rather than abstract, again denies the fact that Indigenous peoples often speculate in the most nuanced and conscious of manners not only about their environments but also about what they know about their environments, even if such speculations are often encoded in folktales and myths rather than abstract propositions.

Berkes (2008; Berkes and Kislalioglu Berkes 2009; Peloquin and Berkes 2009) has documented careful empirical quantitative thought among his Cree hunter research collaborators. Although hunters' and Indigenous land managers' knowledge is experiential, shared, and communal (Peloquin and Berkes 2009), the complexity of variables involved in decision making about hunting requires highly complex ecological knowledge and 'direct immersion in and constant observation of countless elements' (Peloquin and Berkes 2009: 538). Berkes likens Cree and Inuit resources management to the adaptive management regimes and 'fuzzy logic' of Western science, arguing that 'some indigenous groups have resource-use practices that suggest a sophisticated understanding of ecological relationships and dynamics' (Berkes and Kislalioglu Berkes 2009: 6; see also Peloquin and Berkes 2009).

Other researchers have drawn similar analogies between Indigenous knowledge and scientific methods. Nadasdy (1999) describes Kluane First Nation Canadians working with scientists to count Dall sheep using rigorous monitoring and counting techniques. According to Nadasdy, the difference between the scientists and the Kluane was not in the methods used to achieve the quantitative data but in the readiness to rely on small sample sizes as well as the eventual use made of these observations. Nadasdy demonstrates that knowledge that Kluane believed was significant in the management of the sheep was ignored by the scientists, because the total count, by scientific standards, was too low for meaningful statistical analysis. Kluane felt the data were important, because they demonstrated a serious decline in total sheep population numbers, observations that were born out in other contexts, such as Indigenous oral history (Nadasdy 1999: 9).

None of us would deny that our Indigenous research collaborators, like us, can and do think inductively and deductively. Native peoples certainly think abstractly and build hypotheses. For example, the Dandrubin Gorenpul Aboriginal people of Moreton Bay in southeastern Queensland, observing numbers of rainbow lorikeets (a small, brightly colored bird) will know that large numbers (as one variable) portend a large haul of sea mullet (as a second variable), which will lead the Aboriginal community to invite kin and trading partners from neighboring areas for the forthcoming feast. Alternatively, low numbers of lorikeets will lead to hypotheses of a lean fishing season and a consequent cancellation of plans for festivities. Western scientists have not, as yet, accounted for the causal chain that explains this connection between variables, although the correlation is evident.

Likewise, although Indigenous knowledge is often characterized as holistic and thus in contrast to the compartmentalization of science, it still supports the existence of specialists among Indigenous resource managers. In Rajasthan, for example, where another of us works (JS), we sometimes find compartmentalization of knowledge occurring among, say, herbalists specializing in curing a particular stomach affliction in cattle and who are consulted and paid for their services. These specialists typically know little to nothing about, for example, how to treat children's flu or even such human stomach ailments as common indigestion.

Disentangling Simplistic Distinctions II: Scientists Thinking Like Indigenous Peoples

Some philosophers do continue to argue for the special character of scientific knowledge and continue to conceptualize the scientific enterprise as a search for universal and objective 'Truth'. Here we are especially thinking of certain neo-Popperian philosophers of science who seek to identify and define the formal method and logic that separates scientific thought from everyday or Indigenous thought. Still, formal definitions of science – for example, in terms of an idealized hypothetico-deductive method – are increasingly difficult to defend and have been largely abandoned (Ellen 2004: 420). And a new consensus among philosophers of science has emerged that suggests that we should look more closely at the social and cultural roots of science and thus at the way science is actually performed rather than at scientific knowledge as simply 'true', 'objective', or 'accurate' knowledge of the world (Ellen 2004: 420–421; see also Bruner 1996; Dunbar 1995).

Indeed, anthropologists have for some time now been studying scientific 'tribes': biologists in the Pasteur Institute in Paris; high-energy physicists; and employees of the CETUS Corporation busily piecing together the human genome (respectively, Latour 1988; Traweek 1988; Rabinow 1996). If these 'science studies' are to be believed, scientists are also story-tellers: laboratory folklore serves to transmit knowledge within the scientific community as well as to cement social networks; stories also work to render scientific knowledge compelling as well as understandable both to insiders and outsiders to scientific endeavors. More generally, ethnographic and historical studies of laboratories and real scientific practice suggest that science is as much an irrational Weberian 'calling' as an objective enterprise. Scientists, it seems, are driven as much by hunches, inspirations, quirks of personality, and irrational passions as by the numbers. Furthermore, the answers to scientific questions may be as much structured by local oral traditions, culturally peculiar definitions of 'nature', hidden assumptions about what are valuable and testable, networks of patronage and tutelage, the next paycheck, ritualized relationships of jesting and familiarity, and worries over reputations as by cool reason.

One example of the social dimension of science comes from our sister subdiscipline of archaeology. For many years, archaeologists in most parts of the world have asserted the primary place of 'science' and scientific methods to their discipline (Cole 1993; Hiscock 1996, 2008; Loy and Wood 1989). As early as 1973, David Clarke argued:

> In the new era of critical self-consciousness the discipline [of archaeology] recognizes that its domain is as much defined by the characteristic forms of its reasoning, the intrinsic nature of its knowledge and information, and its competing theories of concepts and their relationships [i.e., its scientific methods] – as by the elementary specification of raw material, scale of study, and methodology. (Clarke 1973: 7)

Yet it is clear that archaeology does not, and cannot, operate outside a sociopolitical framework, especially when the past of Indigenous others is the focus of research (see arguments in Fforde, Hubert, and Turnbull 2002; Swidler et al. 1997). At the first World Archaeological Congress in Southampton in 1986, Indigenous owners of heritage vocally challenged the findings of 'scientific archaeology' conducted outside an Indigenous construction of the past (Rowlands 1994). In response to concerns raised by Indigenous peoples, and by archaeologists working closely with traditional owners, we have since seen numerous nations develop Codes of Ethics that recognize that archaeology has a social place and that Indigenous ways of understanding the past have a legitimate role in the interpretation of archaeological remains. In response to the re-emergence of archaeology as a 'soft' as well as a 'hard' science, genuinely collaborative projects between archaeologists and Indigenous heritage managers have grown. Termed 'community archaeology', such research recognizes Indigenous explanations of the past even when such interpretations may not always concur with the analytical models and specialist language of standard scientific investigations (Clarke 2002; Cole et al. 2002; Field et al. 2000; Greer, Harrison, and McIntyre-Tamwoy 2002; Harrison 2002; Marshall 2002; Ross 2008; Ross and Coghill 2000; Smith and Burke 2003, 2004).

Increasingly, archaeologists are redefining their discipline as an enterprise that cannot put aside passions, politically driven purposes, and collective imaginations of the past (Rowlands 1994: 133; see also Nabokov 2002; Perkins 2001). Neither can this discipline ignore the fact that some methodological choices are unscientifically arbitrary, linked as they are to certain historically specific developments. As one critic puts it:

> The social construction of archaeological pasts is more than personal values getting involved in the academic enterprise. In the differing contexts of nationalism, development and the postmodern, we encounter the silences and gaps in archaeological explanations that determine which sites are excavated, what kinds of artefacts are privileged in the legitimizing of expert archaeological knowledges. (Rowlands 1994: 141; see also Byrne 2005)

Archaeologists and other 'scientists', to put it bluntly and to summarize, also inhabit communities and possess cultures (Nader 1996a; Rowlands 1994). Or, in Kuhn's terms (1962), scientists possess 'paradigms' to which they are largely blind but that nevertheless guide inquiry, structuring the kinds of questions scientists ask, the way they interpret their data, and indeed the very way they inhabit the world (Hytten and Burns 2007). Ellen (2004) refers to these Kuhnian paradigms as 'framework theories', which he believes contrasts with Popperian-like methodologies for testing more context-dependent and narrowly defined hypotheses. One can certainly define science in terms of its formal methods of hypothesis-testing rather than in terms of its paradigms, framework theories, and social practices. Likewise, one can remove from one's definitions the messy, unplanned, and contingent side of science and instead focus on an idealized methodology and program by which hypotheses are generated and tested against objective 'data' – although, as Ellen (2004) and other observers of science point out, the elimination of the social and cultural dimensions of science may remove features of science that are absolutely integral to our understanding of the way science actually works and thus critical to our understanding of the way scientific knowledge is generated and validated.

We noted in the previous section that Indigenous people sometimes make generalizations based on small samples. Yet, scientists, too, sometimes draw conclusions based on small samples and slim data. Brower (1991), for example, describes the case of a fine but narrow ecological study of slope processes in Sagarmatha National Park in Nepal. A Western-trained researcher studied one slope for one season, observed vegetation decline and erosion, and blamed Sherpa grazing and juniper harvesting as the cause of degradation without any further assessment. As a consequence of these observations the researcher advised adoption of 'strict land-use policies' (Brower 1991: 177). However, Brower notes that a more in-depth and longer-term study would have demonstrated that the local micro-environment of the slope was drier than nearby areas. Long-term sampling of the area by Brower indicated the ecological resilience of the Khumbu region, including diversity of grasses and juniper regeneration, despite this dry micro-climate. She argued that the relatively sparse distribution of juniper on the slope compared to elsewhere may be because, unlike adjacent areas, Sherpas live near the slope year round and thus harvest the slope's juniper for fuel more regularly than elsewhere (Brower 1991: 178). She argued that the scientific study's conclusions, although highly compartmentalized and based on a narrow base of data, were accepted because they fitted the dominant view of Himalayan ecosystems as fragile and under serious threat from human occupation (1991: 5–7).

A Case Study of Scientific Thought: Tanzania and the Tragedy of the Commons

Another example of scientific practice being influenced by the 'discourse of science' and the consequent rhetoric of knowledge can be seen in Igoe's (2004: 554–558) critique of an application of the famous work of Hardin (1968). We provide a detailed review of Igoe's study here, because Igoe's analysis shows not only that Indigenous people can indeed 'think like scientists' but also that, even when such rational approaches to resources management are taken by Indigenous people, they are not always recognized by scientists who may, at times, be blinded by the perceptions of their discourse.

In his influential 1968 article in *Science*, Garrett Hardin powerfully articulated the idea known as the 'tragedy of the commons'. Drawing on the 19th-century work of William Forster Lloyd, Hardin describes tragedy unfolding on a common pasture. Given population growth and scarcity, herders who graze cattle on the common pasture are faced with a dilemma. Each herder knows he can increase the number of cattle he grazes on the pasture, but if everyone does this the pasture will be degraded. But each herder also knows that if he steadies or decreases the number of cattle he grazes, he has no assurance that others will do the same, and so the pasture will be degraded anyway. The first option is thus preferable to the second. 'Freedom in a commons brings ruin to all' (Hardin 1968: 1244).

Hardin's tragic pasture occupies hardly a page in his entire article and serves as but one part of his larger argument about the need for population control. But the fate of Hardin's 'tragedy of the commons' in scholarly and popular consciousness illustrates the workings of the discourse of science. Igoe (2004) argues that Hardin's model of the 'tragedy of the commons' has gained the status of authoritative 'scientific fact' among some conservation experts. As 'scientific fact' it demands acceptance and obviates the need to collect empirical data to test its validity. In this sense, some claims about the 'tragedy of the commons' in conservation circles are examples of the discourse of science at work, rather than sound scientific practice.

Igoe critiques Hardin's 'tragedy of the commons' at a number of levels. First, the pasture Hardin describes is hypothetical, and Hardin assumes that the herders are rational maximizers; they consciously weigh costs and benefits and act in ways that maximize their utility. Furthermore, Hardin describes a specific kind of common – an open-access or unmanaged common – although the injudicious reader could take him to be talking about all kinds of commons. This is a crucial point to which we return later.

Second, Igoe notes that a form of 'tragedy of the commons' thinking has bled into popular consciousness. Hardin's model appears scientific and so carries the prestige and authority of science. Westerners are drawn to the idea of the 'tragedy of the commons' because it puts the stamp of scientific authority on deeply held cultural beliefs about human nature.

In later work, Hardin (1991, 1993) clarified his position on the commons: 'Clearly, the background of the resources discussed [in the 1968 *Science* article] was one of *non*-management of the commons under conditions of scarcity' (1991: 178, emphasis in original). He admits that the title of the 1968 article should have been 'The Tragedy of the *Unmanaged* Commons' (1991: 178, emphasis in original). He also notes that the article examined the 'logical properties' of the unmanaged commons model and that '[w]hether any particular case is a materialization of that model is a historical question' (1993: 179).

But a popularized version of Hardin's original 'tragedy of the commons' model lives on in some conservation initiatives. The popularized version, which perhaps we can summarize as 'selfish individuals will naturally degrade any common', is different from Hardin's more careful formulation. The popular version takes Hardin's model as 'fact', and as fact about not just unmanaged commons but all commons everywhere.

Igoe uses an example from east Africa to illustrate how a popularized version of the 'tragedy of the commons' is often wielded in conservation circles in ways that contravene best scientific practices. East African Maasai herders have employed social and cultural means to manage common pasture land effectively, yet in ways that differ markedly from Hardin's hypothetical pasture. Igoe presents evidence that Maasai pastoralism modulates herd size and distribution in a way that prevents degradation of pasture land and incorporates safeguards against disaster in dry years. This management regime promotes biodiversity of plant and wild animal species, including large mammals. Maasai resource use, therefore, is an example 'in which people have effectively managed a commons for the benefit of the group, instead of destroying it in the interest of the individual' (Igoe 2004: 56).

Despite this sustainable management system, Maasai pastoralism is under pressure from several directions. For example, under colonialism, British settlers took control of the best farm lands in the mountains, displacing local farmers who in turn encroached on Maasai pasture land. More recently, farmers have been forced into the lowlands by the enclosure of national parks in the mountains. Some Maasai groups have been forced to graze their herds on more ecologically marginal pastures. At the same time, parks and wildlife sanctuaries staff in the savannah have enclosed some Maasai pasture land in the name of wildlife conservation focused on big mammals, such as elephants. In this climate of competition for resources and increasing enclosure, the Maasai have struggled to maintain their herds. They have also been the target of various government and NGO development and conservation initiatives, sometimes driven by science as discourse.

Igoe recounts the Kenyan experience with group ranches as a specific example. In the1960s the Kenyan government encouraged Maasai herders to enclose common pastures and form smaller group ranches. The group ranches were intended to help the Maasai 'preserve' their pasture land by controlling access and by keeping smaller herds of larger cows. The policy makers assumed that in the existing Maasai system, access was uncontrolled and herders kept large herds of small cows, because they were maximizing their returns against their neighbors' profits. Actually, Maasai kept large herds of small cows as a hedge against dry years when pasture was scarce and scattered in small patches. Igoe notes that three 120 kg cows can be sent to three different pastures, whereas one 400 kg cow must graze in one place. A grazing scheme based on small, enclosed ranches and large cattle lacked the flexibility needed to account for the variable climate and landscape of the region, and the group ranches were a failure. In this case, policy makers worked within a discourse of science rather than applying sound scientific practices. They uncritically accepted the 'tragedy of the commons' rhetoric as 'scientific fact' rather than a hypothesis and applied its lessons to a case about which they lacked empirical data. Scientific practice could have involved, for example, first gathering empirical data on Maasai pastoralism and the way it structures individual behavior, then asking whether the Maasai situation conforms to the predictions made by Hardin's 'tragedy of the commons' model.

Igoe is not 'antiscience': 'Scientific method is an excellent way of understanding the world, although it is certainly not the only way. Having a hypothesis, testing that hypothesis, and being willing to reconsider that hypothesis in the face of contradictory evidence is what is meant by scientific practice' (2004: 54). Rather, he is noting the tendency for people working within a discourse of science to make 'scientific' claims without reference to rigorous empirical data or hypothesis testing.

In the conclusion to his discussion of the discourse of science, Igoe argues that some Western conservationists and NGOs, Western tourists and African elites all stand to benefit in different ways from the removal of Maasai herders from their pastures. It is useful, therefore, that enclosure of pasture land by parks and farms and a range of other initiatives finds 'scientific' basis in the idea of the 'tragedy of the commons'. The vesting of certain ideas with the status of 'scientific fact' is a powerful rhetorical strategy, given 'the [popular] Western faith that science can explain any mystery and solve any problem' (Igoe 2004: 54).

In this sense, then, scientific knowledge systems, termed the 'discourse of science' by Igoe, can suffer from the application of poorly researched models that are not based on the rigorous application of scientific methods – a common criticism of Indigenous ways of understanding. Clearly, quantitative and experimental knowledge is not purely a scientific monopoly. As we have demonstrated in the examples of Cree and Inuit hunters, Kluane land managers and Maasai pastoralists, Indigenous peoples may think not only quantitatively, in ways similar to those used by scientists, but also *experimentally*. As Ellen points out, '[e]vidence for the repeated and systematic evaluation of experimental situations has by now been well-documented in the local agroecological knowledge literature, with respect to plant-breeding and pest control' (2004: 428; for example, Cleveland and Soleri 2002; Richards 1985). Indigenous peoples, it seems, use an experimental methodology for manipulating certain variables and then evaluating the data against several alternative explanations. And this is especially the case in areas of vital concern to local peoples, such as agriculture, where Indigenous farmers 'year-on-year conduct experiments regarding the utility of different landrace seeds' (Ellen 2004: 439).

GENERIC HUMAN FACULTIES, CULTURAL IDEALS, AND INSTITUTIONAL PRACTICES

Agrawal (1995) points out that there may be as many or even more differences between the numerous and diverse Indigenous knowledges as there are between an amorphous and generalized 'Indigenous knowledge' and 'scientific knowledge'. To make gross generalizations about what either Indigenous peoples (as a whole) or scientists (as a whole) know is to essentialize groups that are, by their very nature, diversely defined (Agrawal 1995: 421; see also Berkes 2008; Ellen 2004; Ellen and Harris 2000; Hunn 1993; Nadasdy 1999; Posey 1998, 2000; Sillitoe 1998).

Scientific knowledge, we would suggest, shares certain features with Indigenous knowledge, and likewise Indigenous knowledge in some ways aligns with scientific reason. Following Agrawal and others (Agrawal 1995; Ellen 2004; Kalland 2000; Murray Li 2000), we would thus 'dismantle' any absolute divide between these two forms of knowledge. Indeed, we are in safe company here given that, as Agrawal points out, most anthropological attempts to locate 'savage' or 'primitive' minds that are radically different from Western mentalities – like most other 'us-them' dualisms such as traditional-modern, savage-civilized, oral-literate, religious-secular, irrational-rational, and capitalist-noncapitalist – have been abandoned as rife with contradiction and half-truths. Philosophers of science, from the logical positivists to the Popperians, cannot agree on how to demarcate a proper scientific methodology from a nonscientific one. Likewise, most contemporary social scientists cannot agree on what clusters of features – even 'polythetic' clusters of features of the 'non-necessary-and-sufficient' type (Needham 1975) – might be grouped to constitute a traditional, primitive, tribal, primal, or 'Indigenous' mentality. Given these difficulties and this genealogy of failure, who are we, no philosophers of science ourselves yet becoming increasingly aware of the epistemological differences in our various field-sites, to quixotically pursue the grail of identifying once and for all the differences between scientific and Indigenous knowledge?

Our Indigenous interview participants, then, are certainly capable of thinking in the same manner as the most careful and highly trained of scientists. In fact, certain anthropologists point to potentially pan-cultural cognitive universals related to, for example, the classification of colors and animals and thus to a 'natural history intelligence' and evolutionarily acquired 'algorithm for the recognition of animacy' (Atran 1990, 1998; Berlin 1991, 1992; Boster 1996; Ellen 2003, 2004: 425–426; Gelman 1990; Keil 1994; Mithen 1996). These arguments are controversial and contested. Nevertheless, we would suggest that science is best conceptualized as an elaboration and a formalization of generic human faculties and aptitudes related not only to 'natural history intelligence' but also to more basic processes, such as empiricism, quantification and the perception of number, induction and deduction, causal inference, abstraction, hypothesis-building, experimentation, the separation of human subjects from an environment of objects, and the compartmentalization of various experiences of the world.

Science, then, has built on a litany of generic human abilities, which it has elaborated and interconnected in a manner never before seen historically. Likewise, science has connected such modes of knowledge, or faculties, to institutional artifacts, structures, and powers that are certainly not found in our field-sites, such as test tubes, DNA extraction via PCR machines, NSF grants, centrifuges, and academic conferences. All human beings can think experimentally, but scientists conduct their experiments with extraordinary control and precision. Similarly, all people manipulate technology, although modern scientists have created instrumentation and prostheses that extend human senses and capabilities in never-before imagined ways (Ellen 2004: 440). Further, anyone *can* think inductively, though scientists seem to do so with more discipline than others, as most people find induction 'intrinsically difficult because the default form of folk explanation involves deduction: testing a pre-existing model of the world or current hypothesis against new data' (Ellen 2004: 441, citing Oatley 1996: 136). In these terms, we would follow Dunbar (1995: 58; cf. Ellen 2004: 425) and suggest that 'Western science is a product of a highly formalized version of something very basic to life'.

Put another way: scientists have enshrined a network of generic human faculties into a highly valued *cultural ideal*. Scientists, as compared to Indigenous peoples, are typically guided in their inquiries by different understandings of what counts as good or best knowledge of inquiry and thus about how they *should be* going about investigating the world. Such idealized understandings of inquiry, however, fail to capture the complex manner in which real scientists or Indigenous peoples actually do understand the world. Nevertheless, these cultural ideals are real and motivating. They are also enshrined in institutional norms and thus not entirely disconnected from actual practice.

Here we would be careful to point out the differences between cultural ideals and values, on the one hand, and actual practices, on the other. Although scientists may *strive* for knowledge that is context-free and universally relevant, expressive of linear causal relationships, grounded in empirical observations, unbiased by human intuitions and inspirations, replicable, systematic, and consciously framed in an abstract propositional form, they may not always arrive at such an end in actual practice. Likewise, scientists might be primarily interested in knowledge that follows the laws of logical induction and deduction, knowledge that is *induced* from observations in the world and that subsequently can be put into an abstract theoretical form capable of producing *deducible* novel propositions whose veracity can be empirically confirmed through rigorously controlled experiment. Still, as those previously mentioned anthropologists and sociologists of science so eagerly point out, scientists, despite their commitments, sometimes actually produce knowledge that is framed by unspoken 'irrational' paradigms, that is not purely or logically inducible or deducible, and that is at times pragmatic, inconsistent, nonverifiable, context-bound, driven by passion, and structured by social relations of power. In similar terms, scientists may be prone to question the foundations of their knowledge itself, demonstrating a distanced and objective scrutiny of their own assumptions and elevating doubt and uncertainty to a matter of principle (on this point, see the discussion in Ellen 2004: 441). Nevertheless, Kuhn (1962) reminds us that such critical distance and self-conscious reflexivity is more characteristic of scientific 'revolutions' and of unique moments in the history of science and not of ordinary, day-to-day, 'normal' science.

We would make similar points in regard to Indigenous knowledge. Despite sharing many features in common with actual scientific practice, Indigenous inquiry does not seem to be guided by the same scientific ideal of what counts as legitimate, valuable, and authoritative knowledge. We do think it is more difficult to identify the ideal that is common to such societies, given both the diversity of epistemologies we find at our field-sites and the fact that many Indigenous peoples do not as clearly, and often not as consciously and consistently, articulate their views on these matters. Nevertheless, we feel comfortable pointing to a variety of features in an ideal model of inquiry that cross-cut many of our field-sites. For example, we have found that Indigenous peoples tend to value knowledge that works within specific practical constraints over knowledge that is true in the abstract or that is logically consistent with other pieces of knowledge. That is, our Indigenous colleagues believe that knowing *how* to do something is more valuable than knowing *that* the world is a certain way. And knowledge that allows for action in situations of incomplete understanding is typically judged to be more valuable than knowledge rigorously proven to be true, as is knowledge that takes account of complex real-world contexts as compared to that which rigorously though artificially combines a few abstract variables.

Likewise, Indigenous peoples often value understandings that are linked to personal (or even spiritual), and thus idiosyncratic, experiences and feelings. For this reason, dreams and nonreplicable communications from the ancestors are judged to be intensely meaningful; deep connections to *specific* landscapes and people are judged to be more important than relationships or understandings of the land *in general*. Indeed, many Indigenous peoples see people and emotions as valuable gateways to knowledge rather than mere impediments to true understanding. Knowledge that helps to maintain harmonious social relations is more important than that which rigorously controls for, and seeks to eliminate, the human element. Furthermore, Indigenous peoples would suggest that sound knowledge, and thus sound natural resource stewardship, demands all the things that scientists wish to suppress, such as personal emotions and idiosyncratic experiences, the uniting of the head and the heart, relations of trust and intimacy between people both human and nonhuman, living and spiritual (see Nadasdy).

Indigenous knowledge, then, often works by informal 'rules of thumb' that are heavily context-dependent (Smith and Wintherhalder 1992). For example, in the case of Cree hunting, one such rule might be phrased as: 'Proceed along the creek bed until you intercept a track; then, if the track is fresh, search the upland patch to which it leads' (Ingold 1996: 37). Such rules of thumb cannot always be worked into a more abstract system of scientific laws given that they often come into conflict with other informal algorithms and given that they can be deeply personal and idiosyncratic, having been passed on from elders in highly charged emotion-laden learning contexts (Sillitoe 2002). This does not mean, however, that Indigenous peoples cannot, or do not, build theories that are abstract and logically consistent. They can and they do. But, in Indigenous systems of knowledge, abstract theorizing, like the systematic and seamless interrelating of different domains of knowledge, often takes a back seat to the need to get things done. Impersonal knowledge is often judged to be less important than the social relations that made such knowledge available in the first place. Similarly, rigorous empiricism is often subordinated to the need to act even in situations of incomplete empirical knowledge.

We hope, then, to have drawn the reader's attention to the fact that many scientists do more or less closely embody their ideals of objectivity, rigorously and systematically overcoming their human biases. But many do not. Likewise, many Indigenous peoples would not enshrine empirical knowledge in the same manner as scientists. But, again, others certainly do. All of us have met a hard-nosed Indigenous empiricist or two.

It may seem in this discussion as if we are simply re-instating the dichotomy between scientific and Indigenous knowledge that we wish to dismantle. In a sense, we are. We think scientists and Indigenous peoples do tend to set up very different ideals of inquiry, and thus we would preserve the divide on this level of analysis. We also think that the scientific and Indigenous enshrinement of different cultural ideals can result in very different institutional formations. Nevertheless, we do not think that these points detract from our earlier discussions related to the manner in which scientists can and do think like Indigenous peoples and that, vice versa, Indigenous peoples can and do think like scientists. Scientists, after all, do not always adhere to their values or institutional decrees and instead rely on informal, imperfect, and context-bound heuristic devices. Likewise, Indigenous peoples sometimes dismiss the social and emotional in favor of the empirical. Nevertheless, the fact that neither scientists nor Indigenous peoples invariably embody their cultural ideals does not dismantle these different cultural ideals or deny their motivating force.

It is clear, then, that Western science is dominated by a positivist, reductionist, theoretically constructed, reliable, independently verified, narrowly applied, and heavily compartmentalized way of understanding how the world works. It is also clear that many scientists, if not most science practitioners, believe that this way of knowing is the only true and 'correct' way of thinking. As Schafersman has so clearly put it:

> most people possess a lot of unreliable knowledge and, what's worse, they act on that knowledge! Other ways of knowing, and there are many in addition to science, are not reliable because their discovered knowledge is not justified. Science is a method that allows a person to possess, with the highest degree of certainty possible, reliable knowledge (justified true belief) about nature. (1997: 1)

By contrast, we emphasize in this book that science is neither the only *true* nor the only *tested* belief system in the world. Still, we are interested in the manner that idealized and simplified models of science are wielded by scientists and natural resource managers to valorize and denigrate various alternative forms of inquiry. When models are wielded in this way, we refer to them as a scientific 'ideology', or what Igoe called a 'discourse of science'. Scientific ideology, we will argue at various places in the book, is important not because it captures the diversity of actual investigative practice – it does not. Rather, it is important in the manner it is used to marginalize Indigenous peoples and their knowledge base. The issue of importance to this book, then, is less knowledge or cultural ideals per se than the issue of power-knowledge relationships, or how certain cultural ideals become linked to political concerns and agenda.

We would argue that it is difficult to find any feature in science that is not also found in some form in Indigenous practice. We do not think that scientific and Indigenous systems of knowledge are radically different in form or content, which is a common relativistic position. We see too many commonalities between these different modes of thought to hold such a position. Still, the contrasting cultural ideals, which are themselves connected to actual practices and institutional structures, set up differences worth noting. Thus, we would take a pluralistic position, acknowledging both the differences and the affinities, the unique characteristics of each system that nevertheless allow for common understandings and thus for communication across difference (see Table 1.1).

In fact, as we shall see, it is often the differences that motivate the desire for collaboration in the first place. Each system hopes to find answers in the other. But it is the similarities that allow for successful communication. Without common understandings, how could

TABLE 1.1 Comparison of Western and Indigenous knowledge.

Ways of Knowing	Western/Scientific Knowledge	Indigenous/Local Knowledge
Knowledge framework	Compartmentalized and specialized; narrowly constituted in a single or limited range of paradigms.	Holistic and integrated; broadly constituted in a wide array of paradigms.
Knowledge holders	Individuals or small research teams develop and explore specialist research questions (often rather like a small-scale society); knowledge is objective – knowledge without a knower. Knowledge is 'true' because of the rigor of data-gathering and theoretical framework of the knowledge research.	Knowledge is subjective and belongs to an individual or group of specialists. Knowledge is shared asymmetrically (based on social relationships between individuals in a society) but is socially constructed, available to all members of society involved in applying knowledge to solve practical problems. Knowledge is 'true' because of the social status of the knowledge holder.
Knowledge format	Knowledge is impersonal, factual, data-rich, and deemed to be decontextualized from external and unrelated aspects of society and culture (although expectations and dominant paradigms can influence knowledge application).	Knowledge is culturally and spiritually embedded in a social framework.
Methodology	Rigorous, empirical, and objective methodology, based in quantitative data and requiring replicable experimentation within rules of logic. Knowledge is theoretically framed, abstract, and universalizing.	Experiential, empirical, and subjective, based in both qualitative and quantitative data and requiring ongoing experiential reinforcement. Knowledge is pragmatic, concrete, and local.
Methods	Quantitative, empirical, replicative, and experimental; all results must be empirically grounded.	Quantitative, qualitative, spiritual, experiential, replicative, and experimental. All results must be experientially grounded.

Continued

TABLE 1.1 *Continued*

Ways of Knowing	Western/Scientific Knowledge	Indigenous/Local Knowledge
Transmission	Publication and peer review, rigorous debate and academic investigation/ corroboration. Transmission is designed to inform other specialists, although interdisciplinary research is becoming increasingly common.	Oral (including song and dance) and reviewed by social peers, debated in social circles. Transmission is designed to inform other members of a social group.
Application	Problems are resolved by experimental research based on theories that are 'true'.	Problems are resolved by application of knowledge that works in accordance with social and normative rules.
Knowledge structures	Institutional.	Social and spiritual.

either scientists or Indigenous peoples understand the others' worlds? Nevertheless, most collaborations do not unfold in such an idealized manner. Resource managers such as ecologists, politicians, and the non-Indigenous public often mistake simplified models of scientific inquiry for actual scientific practice. They are unable to see the systematic biases in their own science – the social and cultural models, theories, and paradigms at work. Likewise, they mistake the Indigenous ideals of best inquiry for the more complex reality of Indigenous 'science'. They are unable to see the just-plain accuracy and empiricism of Indigenous knowledge, often because Indigenous peoples do not insist on or valorize such empiricism. As a result, Westerners often find it very difficult to identify any features in common between the two systems of knowledge. And, more important, they often find it easy to discriminate against Indigenous knowledge as being of lesser value and validity than Western scientific knowledge (Nadasdy 1999; Stevenson 2006).

This misunderstanding of the relationship of simplified models of inquiry for the complexity of inquiry itself, we would argue, creates important barriers to successful collaboration between science-trained resource managers and Indigenous resource managers (see Chapter 3). Such a misunderstanding makes it difficult for government resource managers to critique their own systems of knowledge (Hytten and Burns 2007); likewise, it makes it difficult for them to see the value in other systems of knowledge that are at once empirical and social, intuitive and spiritual. It is easier instead to evoke their own authority, connected as it is to the wonder and mystery of science, and marginalize Indigenous others' knowledge and authority, emerging as they do from local 'superstitions'. This book traces the history of this hierarchy of knowledge, and these exclusions. But, more important, it traces the manner in which such hierarchies still work in our various field-sites to prioritize and privilege certain ways of knowing and to denigrate others.

COGNITIVE ANTHROPOLOGY AND THE FRAMEWORK OF KNOWLEDGE TRANSMISSION

In this chapter, we have recognized and prioritized the value of cognitive anthropology in understanding the contexts within which knowledge is constructed. Indeed, cognitive anthropology forms the bedrock of much of the analysis to come. We pursue this path because we consider Indigenous and indeed any form of inquiry to be a simplification of reality, not capturing the full complexity of embodied and living practice. Cognitive anthropology helps us to frame ideas related to the constitution and organization of such knowledge. In the language of this subdiscipline of cultural anthropology, we might call these ideas about the world 'cultural models' or 'frames' – abstract and simplified mental representations of the world that are intersubjectively shared and socially learned and transmitted by members of a community (D'Andrade 1980, 1995; Strauss and Quinn 1997). However, we hope that referring to Indigenous knowledge as a collection of 'simplified models' of reality will not hide the fact that such ideals are themselves complex (Peloquin and Berkes 2009). Cultural frames, we would suggest, bring together an array of human faculties related to quantification, abstract thinking, mathematics, deductive logic, and so forth. As such, they unite these faculties into new networks of meaning that, although somewhat firm and 'structural', can be reworked with changing historical contexts.

Similarly, we find it useful to refer to these knowledge models of reality as 'schematic'. They are incomplete simplifications of the world that do not provide their users with all the answers. Rather, they provide simple heuristic devices that allow for the generation of novel inferences. We would not think of models of inquiry as fixed or static, in the case of either scientific or traditional Indigenous models, but as providing a structure through which new ideas can be generated and fresh observations can be given meaning. As a result, they allow for constrained creativity, or innovation within the structures provided by tradition.

We would also suggest that these frames exist on both conscious and unconscious levels of thought, and even as a complex movement between these two levels. They largely guide behavior implicitly, although a little effort and cleverness can bring at least parts of the model into conscious awareness, where it can be articulated into more coherent scientific or folk 'theories', be they 'framework' or 'context-dependent' theories (Berkes and Kislalioglu Berkes 2009; Ellen 2004). We have observed that scientists are more interested than are Indigenous land managers in bringing implicit cultural models into conscious awareness, where they can be put in propositional form, whose logic and consistency can be tested and systematized, and can in turn consciously guide action. Still, Indigenous peoples may also bring cultural models into consciousness, although their articulated theories are often stored in the form of narratives like folktales or myths, or alternatively in proverbs, songs, and sayings, and thus in a way that involves an alternative expression and logic (Nabokov 2002).

We would also point to the way that the models of concern to us here set up cultural ideals of action that are rewarded in their respective societies and thus can be highly motivating. However, we would emphasize that these frames are *variably* motivating. The models become 'internalized' and connected to inner emotions and life histories that vary from individual to individual. Thus these cultural ideals are neither automatically nor necessarily enacted.

In similar terms, we would consider these models to be mental representations of the world that are inside the head. Nevertheless, these mental frames are themselves in complex interaction with public artifacts and institutions: individuals create simplified mental models of the world based on their observations; in turn, mental models serve as frames for action that lead to the creation of new artifacts and practices that serve as the basis for future observations.

Finally, we would point out that multiple models of this kind are to be found in any given culture at any given moment in time, although some are dominant while others are subordinate. This is particularly the case in the areas in which we work, where the scientific model may be known by Indigenous peoples but is not found to be relevant or motivating for a number of reasons. One of the reasons may be that, although the models might be recognized by the Indigenous resources managers, they are often configured and interpreted in a manner different from that of the scientists. In many cases, these frames come into conflict, such as when Indigenous actors invoke frames that are more mystical or emotional than those proffered by science, which renders the Indigenous use of scientific frames less respected by wildlife managers (Stevenson 2006).

In pursuing these issues, we do not wish the reader to get lost in the concerns of cognitive anthropology. We have simply provided the preceding discussion to help the reader see the complex interrelationships between thought and practice and between simplified models of the world and the world itself. Indeed, even the Western idealized model of science is complicated, and philosophers of science do not agree on what it entails. Still, we feel comfortable pointing to a simplified version of science that circulates in our various field-sites and that many natural resource managers find highly motivating. Cognitive anthropology usefully frames these issues, and thus we rely on its vocabulary at various places in our book.

LOOKING AHEAD: THE POLITICAL ECONOMY OF KNOWLEDGE

In the next chapter we trace some of the reasons for the rise in the inability to see and understand knowledge that is constructed and contextualized in ways different from our own, whether we be Western-trained academics or Indigenous peoples. We review the rise of science and the privileging of 'truth' in a Western ontology, and we provide an overview of the dispossession of Indigenous peoples – of their lands and waters, their resources, and their knowledge – and the consequences of such dispossession for the retention and recognition of 'traditional' knowledge. In particular, we review the historical evidence for the rise of the compartmentalization of knowledge that seems to characterize modern scientific ways of knowing. We find 17th-century philosophers, such as Bacon, Boyle, and Newton, to be the fathers of this approach (Ede and Cormack 2004; Harrison 2007). Influenced by the rise of capitalism, which emphasized the need for orderliness in the arrangement of economic systems (Merchant 1995), Bacon in particular argued that truth could be accessed only by the investigation of the individual parts that provided far more information than did the whole. Such a conjunction of philosophical and economic forces led to a fragmentation of knowledge and society on many different levels.

In subsequent chapters we go on to argue that barriers to collaborative management of natural resources are partly epistemological – related as they are to different ideas, and ideals, about what constitutes best knowledge and inquiry. But we also argue that they are economic and political. And the most interesting and important barriers to collaborative management emerge at the intersection of epistemologies with these economic and political forces.

As an example, we could point to the way that the scientific ideals of free and open inquiry and shared knowledge come into conflict with the modern economic imperative of individually owned knowledge (Eamon 1990: 333). Scientists may wish to engage in collaborative research, but the need to protect and claim any potential wealth that emerges from scientific research leads to a system of patents, trade secrets, and contractual ownership that discourages such collaborative work (Ede and Cormack 2004: 145). This capitalist imperative, in turn, has implications for the manner in which Indigenous peoples themselves are encouraged to manage their resources. They are encouraged, for example, to establish *individual* ownership over their lands and their knowledge of their lands, even if no such ownership of nature and knowledge existed beforehand (Riley 2005). Such an establishment of Indigenous property rights works to bring capitalist and Native systems of thought and practice into alignment, which can facilitate the appropriation of Indigenous resources.

A similar situation exists in the relationship between science and the State. On the one hand, modern science flourishes in the philosophical climate of freedom and democracy, allowing full expression to individual creativity and exploration. At the same time, science has been used by the emerging political economy of state-sponsored capitalism to exploit the world's resources, making science a necessary ingredient for operating modern nation-states (Eamon 1990: 346; Ede and Cormack 2004: 182, 196; Needham 1954 [2000]: xii). Scientific expeditions feed not only the intellectual hunger of scholars but also on the commercial hunger of burgeoning industries looking for new raw materials for production (Ede and Cormack 2004: 201–203). The scientific appropriation and transplanting of these new materials, such as bread fruit, tea, and rubber, have become the normal business of establishing empire (2004: 203).

In this chapter, then, we have discussed the interconnection of epistemological ideals and institutional formations that manage and regulate the way in which these ideals are connected to real practice (on 'instituted models', see D'Andrade 2008; Shore 1996). In subsequent chapters, however, we emphasize the manner in which epistemological ideals are connected to economic and political institutions. We especially scrutinize the manner in which *modern* scientific ideals and practices inform and bolster a number of economic and political processes. We argue that the modern scientific ideal of objectivity, neutrality, and knowledge for knowledge's sake can in fact hide the way that scientific inquiry is often driven by economic and political forces. One need only think of Kloppenberg's (1988) discussion of the manner in which modern agricultural innovation has been driven by the profit motive and the corporate bottom line; although one could as easily look to the history of the tobacco, defense, biotechnology, and pharmaceutical industries to see many examples of the way that modern scientific inquiry and invention have been historically driven by political and economic forces.

The scientific ideal of 'knowledge without a knower' – along with other dimensions of the modern scientific ideal – may therefore do more than fail to capture the complexity of actual scientific practice, as we have argued in this chapter. It may serve as an ideology that validates scientific authority and that thus legitimates the working of a political and economic system that, as we shall see, has systematically appropriated and in many cases destroyed Indigenous know-how. Indigenous peoples readily acknowledge that knowledge is connected to economic and political forces – if not always to *individual* ownership and control of such knowledge. Science, however, often denies that any such connection exists. Science is science, some would argue, a quest for knowledge driven by a desire for truth and understanding. We would not deny that such motivations can and do exist, if only in certain contexts and on a certain level of analysis. However, we hope to draw attention to the fact that such an ideal is also a powerful political ideology that might justify the superiority of Western epistemology – and indeed of Western society – and thus that might also justify the epistemological and social hierarchies that we scrutinize in subsequent chapters of this book.

Chapter 2

Untangling the Historical Origins of Epistemological Conflict

Despite the commonalities between Indigenous knowledge and scientific knowledge identified in Chapter 1, the historical relationship between these two ways of knowing the world have been rife with misunderstanding, conflict, and contestation. In this chapter we examine the origins of these two approaches to knowledge and the processes that resulted in Indigenous knowledge being subordinated to science on a global scale. Understanding the history behind this epistemological conflict is essential both to interpreting the current status of Indigenous knowledge relative to science and natural resource management and to articulating a shift in the current knowledge hierarchy as it relates to natural resource stewardship that not only accommodates but also truly integrates both ways of knowing.

Before Science

The natural resources of the globe existed and thrived long before the development of science. Although most of the history of these resources has been told through the lens of science, human systems of natural resource stewardship were in place for centuries before the arrival of management regimes dictated by science. In premodern times, for example, Indigenous owners of the land and sea had the political, spiritual, and moral authority to engage with the environment, conveyed through social and kinship relationships, totemic systems, ritual practices, and religious beliefs and other sources of rights and responsibilities. Land and resource stewardship was an integral part of the entire social system, often linked to political, cultural, spiritual, and economic responsibility.

Both science and Indigenous knowledge support a considerable antiquity for the human involvement in creating natural resource abundance. Archaeological evidence, for example, confirms that Indigenous peoples have had a long connection with their lands and waters and with the natural resources that sustained them during tens of thousands of years of human history. During their long association with the world, even before the rise of agriculture, Indigenous peoples changed the land with fire (Bowman 1998, 2000; Sponsel 1998: 384–386); modified fauna distribution and abundance through hunting and management practices (Ross 1994; Sponsel 1998: 385); brought about alterations to plant communities through the use of fire and the development of plant cultivation techniques (Balme and Beck 1996; Engelhardt 1989: 134; Peacock and Turner 2000; Surin 1985: 215); and used water-control mechanisms to ensure regular supplies of water and irrigation (Bellwood 1985: 253; Engelhardt 1989: 134; Lourandos 1980, 1997) or to farm fish and other aquatic resources (Barker and Ross 2003; Ross and Pickering 2002), thus modifying water courses and even tidal areas. Archaeological evidence demonstrates that all these land and resource stewardship techniques have a considerable antiquity, dating long before contact with more advanced settlers of the recent past and extending back to 'hunter-gatherer' times.

Archaeological evidence from Australia, for example, documents that the Aboriginal people of Moreton Bay in southeastern Queensland have been involved in fisheries stewardship for more than 100 generations (Ross and Tomkins in press; Ulm, Petchey, and Ross 2009), including oyster farming, the construction of artificial reefs, and the management of sea mammals (Ross and Pickering 2002). From northwest coastal United States there is evidence for several management regimes used prior to European settlement, including construction of artificial reefs; closure of rivers and lakes to fishing to conserve fish runs when stocks were low; careful selection of village sites to ensure that waterways were not polluted; and confining fisheries areas to allow regulation of the catch and protection of the run (Boldt 1974: 359–385). Such techniques ensured the sustainability of the salmon resource for future generations (Cohen 1986: 30; Ross and Pickering 2002).

Growth and change to trade systems is an example of the variations that occurred in harvesting practices over time. Where once production was for local consumption only (Jones and White 1988; McBryde 1984), the development of new trade networks meant a change in collection, storage, and dispersal strategies (Cottrell 1985; Gould and Saggers 1985; Torrence 1986); or changes in rights of access to resources (McBryde 1984; Ross, Anderson, and Campbell 2003); or the development of more rigorous access control provisions (Jones and White 1988; Ross,

Anderson, and Campbell 2003). These trade systems, in particular, were vital cogs in the formation of alliance networks that not only supported social ties and kinship relationships but also provided support mechanisms in times of hardship (Cottrell 1985; McBryde 1984).

Consequently, the biosystems of the world have been influenced by human actions since the earliest inhabitations by modern humans. Throughout the period of modern human occupation of the earth, people have been conducting activities that have resulted in the ongoing management of the land and its resources. Indigenous land and resource stewardship practices in the past were supervised by the Indigenous peoples who had the political and moral authority to exercise control over land and resources without interference from outsiders and who had the right to speak about the land in accordance with local laws. Indigenous peoples had complex systems of laws and social obligations that ensured an acceptable social order and provided for stewardship of land, water, and resources (Berkes 2008; Head 2000). Although not without disputes and problems, these systems evolved to support the continuing livelihoods of communities within particular ecological regions.

Land and resource stewardship was an integral part of the entire social system, embedded in wider social, kinship, totemic, and religious and ceremonial systems, reinforced by the reciting of accounts from the past that warned of the consequences for those who failed to meet their obligations. Indigenous landowners exercised rights and responsibilities for 'negotiating' with the land and its resources (Bradley 2001) as given to them by spiritual beings or handed down through generations via ritual and other social practices. They were stewards of the lands and waters of the world through an evolving understanding of the relationship between plants and animals and their habitats, and between humans and the natural world. This stewardship approach was embodied in systems of Indigenous knowledge that placed natural resources in a totally conceived cosmic order. In this way, Indigenous knowledge, and particularly its manifestation as resource stewardship, was integral to the governance of the entire community. Knowledge could never be expressed or practiced outside its social and political context.

THE ORIGINS OF MODERN SCIENCE

The history of development of Indigenous knowledge contrasts with the processes that constructed science in Western Europe. So-called modern science is the product of a particular set of historic conjunctures that brought about a fundamentally new form of social organization in Western Europe, now known as capitalism. This new form of social organization transformed not only assumptions and ideals surrounding knowledge but also the entire social, economic, and political fabric of European life.

Modern science emerged from a specific set of historical and cultural conditions in Western Europe during the 16th and 17th centuries. These same historical and cultural conditions, simultaneously and dialectically, also produced the modern capitalist world economy (Eamon 1990; Ede and Cormack 2004; Taylor 1996; Zilsel 1939 [2000]). Other forms of inquiry and knowledge were prevalent in other parts of the world for centuries before Western Europe took the helm (Ede and Cormack 2004; Needham 1954 [2000]), yet, in the history of the science discipline, these non-European modes of inquiry were deemed to be constructed outside the truly 'scientific' paradigm and tended to be discounted as incomplete by those regarding science from a Western outlook (Needham 1954 [2000]). In contrast to these non-European forms of knowledge, European sources, particularly those from Greece and Rome, are embraced as the roots of modern science (Ede and Cormack 2004; Harvey 1999; Lindberg 1990).

Several schools of thought have developed as to why Western European science is now regarded as superior to all prior systems of knowledge. Some might contend that the reason is pure European chauvinism (Ede and Cormack 2004: 14). Others look to the historical development of a particular Western way of knowing. The separation of religion and science was at the heart of the rise of this modern scientific knowledge (Ede and Cormack 2004). The Greeks, whose knowledge construction was the precursor of that adopted in Western Europe, made a separation between the natural world, which is knowable, and the supernatural world, which is unknowable. This difference is often subliminally read to mean that the rational (knowable) world is superior to the irrational or superstitious or religious (unknowable) world. Ede and Cormack argue that this Cartesian divide established the roots for modern science, with the consequence that religion is absent within science (2004: 24).

The paradox that arises from this perspective is that, for more than 10 centuries after the Greeks separated science and religion, Western Europe was under the complete authority of the Christian Church, which had a monopoly on truth, knowledge, and ways of thinking and knowing (Ede and Cormack 2004: 57–102). In 1662 Robert South preached that in the beginning, God created Adam as all knowing: 'till his fall it [Adam's knowledge] was ignorant of nothing but Sin' (cited in Harrison 2007: 1). The consequent aim of 17th-century scholars was the re-establishment of Adam's knowledge through the search for truth and a right relationship with God. Philosophers such as Francis Bacon argued that if sin could be identified and neutralized, knowledge would return. Science, he argued, was the best prospect for achieving 'Truth' (the enemy of

'Sin') and consequently the restoration of Adam's knowledge, 'or at least repairing the losses to knowledge that had resulted from the Fall' (Harrison 2007: 4). As a consequence, the aim of 17th-century science philosophy was to re-establish man's *control* over reason and the natural order of things, using the technology of science:

> the restoration of Adamic knowledge would be accomplished through re-establishing control of the passions, thus enabling reason once again to discharge its proper function. If the Fall had dulled Adam's senses, this deficiency might be overcome through the use of artificial instruments capable of restoring to weakened human senses some of their original acuity. (Harrison 2007: 6)

In response to Bacon's call, scientists such as Galileo sought to reconcile religion with natural philosophy (Ede and Cormack 2004: 134). The 'Enlightenment' period saw scientists simply place God into their epistemological system, arguing that 'all physical processes are governed by rational natural laws established by God', a perspective that continues to be prevalent among some scientists today (Zilsel 1939 [2000]: 10). In theory, science and religion were not separated until the 16th century, and consequently it is unlikely that this Cartesian divide was the sole driver of the development of modern scientific ways of knowing. Certainly many other factors have also been raised as possible explanations for the origins of modern science in Europe. The developments of collaborative research, controlled experimentation, empirical induction, calendar-calculation, and mathematics have all been cited as examples of European advancement. But all these theoretical and methodological developments existed in China well before the Scientific Revolution in Europe's 17th century (Needham 1954 [2000]: xiii) and are therefore as unsatisfactory as the separation of religion and science as explanations for the rise of current Western knowledge ontologies.

Mathematics + Nature = Commerce

The key to the rise of modern science in Europe appears to be embedded in the development of a distinct form of economic system, ultimately known as capitalism. Mathematical writing in Europe between the 14th and 17th centuries was intimately connected to the needs of tradesmen, bankers, architects, craftsmen, and engineers (Zilsel 1939 [2000]: 3, 9). 'Science was born when, with the progress of technology, the experimental method eventually overcame the social prejudice against manual labor and was adopted by rationally trained scholars' (7). Science was valued for its utility in advancing production and capital accumulation, a link that continues into the present (Kleinman and Vallas 2001).

Capitalism also brought about a fusion of mathematics, experimentation, and natural science (Needham 1954 [2000]: xii). All human societies have struggled with the issue of how we know what is true. Modern science provided its answer to this question of 'truth' by being sure of the knowledge it had. The best way to be absolutely sure, the European founders of modern science argued, is to reduce complex natural situations into small enough units to make definite measurement (mathematics) and analysis (scientific method) possible. Anything sufficiently isolated, controlled, and measured to produce truth should be reducible to a mathematical equation. This quantification of nature is what allied mathematics to the evolution of positivist science. Mathematics became the language of natural science and consequently formed the foundation for the modern scientific understanding of the natural world.

In this sense modern science was really born of a 'new natural philosophy', developed and promoted by such scholars as Bacon, Boyle, and Newton. As we saw above, Bacon asserted that knowledge was flawed by man's fall from grace and by the idols men carried within themselves. The only way to disabuse oneself of idols was to look at 'small, discrete bits of nature' (cited in Ede and Cormack 2004: 144). The inductive method used to divide up the natural world in this controlled way isolated and compartmentalized the individual parts of the natural system to produce increments of information gathered by a community of individual investigators, put together in a tabular form and then explained by elite interpreters (Eamon 1990; Harrison 2007; Zilsel 1939 [2000]). Ultimately, elaborate classification systems had to be developed to provide structure for the endless minute details that erupted from the modern scientific method (Ede and Cormack 2004: 205), but in the meantime the fascination with minutia came to dominate the search for 'truth'.

While incomplete knowledge limited comprehension, science filled any temporary gaps in knowledge through the development of sophisticated mathematical models. Probability theory, for example, helped smooth the path when all the determining factors could not be known with certainty. As a result, modern science was satisfied to know that there was a 75% probability that a mine worker would contract lung disease, but it recognized no requirement for the development of explanations for why one individual worker became ill while another stayed healthy.

Experimentation was the favored method for isolating and then proving small pieces of truth, promoted by Bacon as the essential counter to speculative ideas of earlier investigations (such as occurred during the Inquisition and philosophical explorations of a variety of phenomena) (Lindberg 1990: 7). To be absolutely true, the same outcome should emerge from multiple experiments following the same process, creating the notion of 'replicability' as a hallmark of scientific knowledge and methodology. It is interesting to note that Bacon's duties as Lord Chancellor included overseeing torture to make men tell the truth, so it was only a minor increment in philosophy to subject nature to similar forms of experimentation that would force her to reveal her secrets (Ede and Cormack 2004: 158). Having gained these secrets, people obtain the power to control nature.

Through the development of specialist research, scientists and philosophers turned their gaze in the search for truth from 'big picture' investigations to the pursuit of understanding the particular. As Auguste Comte explained, through 'positive' science, the mind gives up the quest for 'absolute notions, the origin and destination of the universe, and the causes or phenomena, and applies itself to the study of their laws – that is, their invariable relations of succession and resemblance' (1856: 26, cited in Lindberg 1990: 11). Consequently, while the ancients looked for final causes and deep understandings, 'positive' science looked for individual and particular laws of nature. It is perhaps not surprising, then, that both Francis Bacon and René Descartes were lawyers.

Structurally, modern science emerged from a 16th-century system of patronage that privileged practical uses for science that would support spectacle, power, and wealth (Ede and Cormack 2004: 103, 121). Bacon expressed this union of science, nature, and political economy in his famous phrase: 'Knowledge is power' (Zilsel 1939 [2000]: 29). Scientific societies, such as the Royal Society of London in 1660, were created to set the standards of expertise and qualification for membership. Ultimately, these societies were instrumental in defining scientists as independent intellectuals. They also promoted the ideal of scientific communication as essential to guarantee the veracity and reliability of experimental results, creating journals and other scholarly publications to publicize the outcomes of research (Eamon 1990: 345; Ede and Cormack 2004: 169–172). They nevertheless relied on the patronage of wealthy interests to support ongoing research, creating a nexus between economic pursuits and the pure discovery of science.

A by-product of defining the outcome of science as sure knowledge was the belief that truth resides in one right answer (Schafersman 1997; see Chapter 1). Bacon was explicit that, if used properly, the scientific method would provide *the* truth, transcendent of opinion, point of view, or degree of intellect. 'Induction, if properly carried out, "leads to an inevitable conclusion"' (Bacon 1623: 20, cited in McMullin 1990: 47). Since then, philosophers of science and scientists themselves have come to recognize the ever-provisional nature of scientific knowledge. Indeed, one of the hallmarks of scientific knowledge is that it must be open to refutation. Nevertheless, the development of modern science reinforced

Western tendencies to see truth as unified and complete, and at least partially accessible given the proper procedures.

This view of a single, verifiable truth, accessed only through the scientific method, clearly required the rhetorical separation of science from religion, but the reality was twofold: a redefinition of God and the transference of belief from the supernatural to the scientific. Science was originally defined in opposition to syllogistic logic and theology and was therefore credited with taking the monopoly on truth away from the (largely Christian) Church. Before Bacon's admonition to seek truth in the elements of nature, natural science was viewed as the study of God's work. But by the 18th century, the fiery, vindictive, irrational God of the Old Testament had been completely replaced by the assumption that God's work was rational and therefore explicable (Ede and Cormak 2004: 141, 198). The laws of nature may have been issued by the Creator (Lindberg 1990: 4), but they were knowable through science.

Today, quantitative and particularistic results are argued to be the surest, most replicable and reliable form of truth, because it is 'surer knowledge than searching for final causes' (Ede and Cormack 2004: 147; see also Schafersman 1997; Wallerstein 2003: 459). The premise of modern science is that the world is comprehensible and utterly knowable. Technology provides the basis for this knowledge. Technologies capable of refined measurements take center stage as the instruments for revealing truth in many disciplines once reliant on less precise forms of gathering data. Navigational tools in particular helped spawn the Age of Exploration (Sobel 1995). Technologies from the world of science reinforce the conceptual view that nature is measurable, knowable, and therefore controllable.

This perspective captures the major belief structure of modern Western European society today: belief in the power of a scientific elite rather than a religious elite. In this sense, modern science is itself a belief system (Nader 1996a) and is not as separate from cultural construction as some scientists might like to assert.

Nader (1996a) provides a detailed analysis of the social and cultural context of science. As well as the social elements of scientific enquiry, demonstrated through ethnographic research in the scientific workplace (see Chapter 1), Nader analyses the way scientists create knowledge. She demonstrates that scientific knowledge is not free from political tensions and power struggles, nor is it free from social context. She provides numerous examples of popular beliefs informing scientific enquiry and subsequent knowledge production. The following recent case study from Australia can be added to Nader's examples.

As we discuss in Chapter 4, dingo management on Fraser Island, Queensland, Australia, has become a significant political issue since a young boy was killed by two 'rogue' dingoes in April 2001. To ensure that such human/dingo interactions never occur again, Queensland Parks and Wildlife Service (QPWS) scientists and managers have constructed dingoes as part of the natural environment (Hytten and Burns 2007). They perceive dingoes as apart from humans. Their very genus – *Canis lupus dingo* [that is, related to the wolf], recently changed from *Canis familiaris dingo* [that is, related to the domestic dog] – denotes the scientific view of this animal as wild, untamed, ferocious. As a consequence of this construct, or *belief* about dingoes, scientists and QPWS managers construct an ideal world in which dingoes and humans have no interaction whatsoever. The management strategy developed by scientists to implement this paradigm encourages the separation of dingoes and humans. Aboriginal beliefs about dingoes, however, are diametrically opposed to this scientific view (Phoenix-O'Brien 2002; Rose 1992). Aboriginal Australians believe dingoes are spiritually linked to humans (Rose 1992). According to Aboriginal cosmology throughout much of northern Australia, dingoes and humans were one in the Dreaming, and they retain powerful human kinship connections in the present (Bradley 2008; Phoenix-O'Brien 2002; Rose 1992). Controversy over management of the dingo on Fraser Island has resulted from this clash of different belief systems (see Chapter 4). Clashes between scientific and Indigenous belief systems are common and have their roots in colonial expansion.

Western Science and Indigenous Experiences of Global Expansion

Western European colonial expansion covered almost the entire globe over a 500-year period, imposing European perspectives and beliefs across most continents. The emergence of the resulting modern world-system was accompanied by a systematic lack of recognition by Europeans for the political, economic, and social autonomy of Indigenous peoples, which ultimately defined knowledge itself as an exclusive product of Western thought.

The ideologies of science helped to reinforce capitalism's geographic expanse, as most of the globe became the experimental ground of Western Europe. The natural resources of the world were destined to be studied, reduced to their elemental components, and then productively entered into the colonial commerce of Western Europe. The ideological creation of such concepts as commodities removed natural resources from the Indigenous social systems that had developed them and placed them into the price-fixing markets of capitalism. Natural laws joined Western juridical systems to construct concepts of land ownership and tenure, alienating generations of Indigenous control for failure to perfect title under the newly imposed rational regime of law. 'Superior rational intellect' then dictated that scientifically informed political systems of the West should govern the 'productive development' of the world's natural resources, conveying exclusive rights to their use and profitability to the colonizing powers of Europe.

The lands containing the natural resources to fuel Western capitalism were in most instances already inhabited by extensive populations with their own distinct historical trajectories and consequent forms of social organization. Once again Western science provided the justification and methods for establishing European control over these populations and their resources. The scientific method was extended into social studies and used to create social sciences. The methods and concepts of natural science were applied to human societies to produce an evolutionary trajectory for civilization, with Europe at the pinnacle of the social evolutionary process (Wallerstein 2001).

THE PLACE OF ANTHROPOLOGY

The object of social science was to discover laws that explained human behavior. For example, Adam Smith searched for natural laws regarding economic exchange and developed the principles of self-regulating markets that guide the discipline of economics to this day (Ede and Cormack 2004: 196). Social scientists endeavored 'to construct the most general laws possible about social behavior via quasi-experimental designs, using data that are presumably replicable and on the whole as quantitative as possible' (Wallerstein 2003: 455). Consequently, during the 19th century, disciplines were constructed to house discrete areas of social knowledge where fragments of knowledge could be further isolated for controlled study by more and more specialized experts (2003: 454). Stemming from the four traditional faculties of theology, philosophy, law, and medicine, six main disciplines emerged that defined social science for more than a century: political science, economics, history, philosophy, sociology, and anthropology. '[T]he centerpiece of social process was the careful delimitation of three spheres of activity: those related to the market, those related to the State, and those that were "personal"' (2003: 19).

In the development of social science disciplines, the field of anthropology has been intimately tied up with the expansion of the West. The unilineal evolutionists of the 19th century, such as E. B. Tylor, were concerned with outlining the standard set of stages of humankind, from 'primitive' to 'civilized', through which they believed all cultures passed. At this time this was the focus of anthropological endeavor (Wallerstein 2001).

To some Europeans and Americans, this fixed cultural evolutionary framework gave a supposedly scientific basis for the popular belief in the racial and cultural superiority of the West. For others, it helped justify colonialism and the 'benefits' it brought, via the perceived responsibility of the colonizers to lift the 'primitives' up and help them toward civilization. These views live on in many Western and elite non-Western circles. The widespread assumption that 'we' (Anglo Americans, educated and urban-based Thais, educated South Asians, and so on) are more civilized than 'them' (American Indians, Australian Aborigines, Indigenous minorities, tribals, and so forth) is inspired by latent unilineal evolutionist thinking.

In the late 19th and early 20th centuries the work of Franz Boas, Robert Lowie, and others helped to move anthropology away from cultural evolution and to make relativism – which posits the equality of all cultures and requires that cultural analysis must be scientific, neutral, and objective – a valid stance in the discipline. Nevertheless, the work of many 20th-century anthropologists remained tied in complex ways to colonialist projects. For example, the structural functionalist school in British anthropology has often been criticized for its synchronic approach, which, at least implicitly, left the impression that 'the natives' were locked in a timeless and (by implication) backward state (Fabian 1983).

Being on the front lines of cultural exchange, anthropology as a discipline soon recognized the problems of scientific claims for a single truth and therefore became one of the fields to encounter the postmodern sea change early on. Although a Western discipline, anthropology was in constant negotiation with other forms of knowledge and could therefore take a more constructivist view of the world than hard sciences could accommodate. Far from being insulated in the sterile laboratories of experimental science, anthropologists were in the field being confronted with accusations of ethnocentrism, appropriation, and subjective self-interest from the now unfrozen, constantly changing 'other'.

Although we do not wish to revisit the entire critique of anthropology and colonialism here, we point out that anthropology in its modern form can, at times, privilege the more material, objective aspects of culture over those that are more spiritual and subjective. A strong tradition of applying scientific and objective methods to the study of culture has evolved as the basis for recording the 'truth' about another culture (Salmon 2000). The labeling of anthropology as a social *science* has encouraged a view that anthropological endeavor should be scientifically rigorous. Luckily, emphases on the materiality of society and culture have declined in recent years, and anthropology as a discipline recognizes the role of many factors, including spirituality, religion, culture, and kinship, in defining all cultures (O'Reilly 2005). Our own research perspectives embrace this constructivist view of society and culture as a framework for understanding Indigenous knowledge and traditional mechanisms for understanding natural resources.

GLOBAL EXPANSION, INDIGENOUS DISPOSSESSION, AND NATURAL RESOURCES

Beginning in the late 1400s a new form of social organization took hold in Western Europe, one that would ultimately encompass the entire globe. Born of a simultaneous collapse in Europe of economic, political, and religious elites, and the demise of the external threat of the Mongol empire (Wallerstein 1992), Western European society reorganized itself into a new system in which capital accumulation was freed from the constraints of politics and religion, supported by a mutuality of interests with emerging modern nation-states, and fueled by a gradual geographic expansion of resources around the world (Taylor 1996: 10–11). In the path of the construction of this capitalist world-economy stood countless Indigenous societies with their own distinct forms of social organization. The encounter between Western Europeans and these Indigenous societies produced the foundation for suppressing Indigenous perspectives through an imposed and totalizing bureaucratic construct of colonization and capitalism.

The expansion of capitalism was accompanied by the creation and expansion of modern nation-states to facilitate the free flow of resources from peripheries of the globe to core centers of production and capital accumulation. Within a 500-year period, the lands of the entire world, and all the people living there, were neatly bounded into nation-states. The nation-state became the only legitimate expression of sovereignty, with all other potential forms of local authority subordinate to the ultimate control of the centralized state. While European nation-states evolved out of local social structures, most of the remaining global territory was shaped into nation-states out of externally imposed colonial processes or through a system of internal colonialism, directed by ethnic or class-based elites. Since the neat boundaries of states were often drawn by competing European powers negotiating for territory and spheres of influence, the presence of, or effects on, Indigenous peoples were rarely considered.

Warfare and resistance to Western invasion brought dramatic declines in Indigenous populations (Reynolds 1987a, 2001). But an even greater impact on Indigenous populations came in the form of disease. Often preceding direct European contact, epidemics brought from Europe and unleashed on Indigenous populations without immunities to these diseases had devastating implications for local Indigenous populations. In North America it is estimated that as much as 85% of the population was lost to epidemic disease, with some tribes being completely eliminated (Trigger 1969: 1–2). Russell Thornton (1987) has estimated that American Indian populations in Canada and the United States of America at first contact numbered 7 million, but that a combination of disease and warfare reduced that figure to a low of 390,000 (see also Bodley 2008: 44). In Australia, it is estimated that an original Aboriginal population of 3 million was reduced to a low of 60,500, victims of introduced diseases and physical violence (Bodley 2008: 44; Butlin 1983). The smallpox epidemic, which spread from Sydney in 1789 to reach the Murray River by 1830 and which affected only the Aboriginal population, resulted in the death of half the Indigenous population of the Sydney region alone (Butlin 1983: 19–24).

The combined effects of warfare and disease purposefully or serendipitously resulted in a significant silencing of the Indigenous voice. While Indigenous communities struggled to recover and regroup after the devastating loss of population, the ever-increasing numbers of European immigrants moved easily into the newly created 'empty spaces'. For example, the Puritans arrived in Plymouth in 1620 and thanked God for providing them with land that was not only vacant but already prepared for cultivation. They were unaware that New England tribes of sedentary agriculturalists had been wiped out by scarlet fever in 1616, and the handful of survivors had abandoned their homeland to join other communities from different tribes (Hurt 1987: 80; McNickle 1973: 4, 31). The consequent misinterpretation of the land as 'vacant' and of the landscape as 'wilderness' led Europeans to view Indigenous peoples and their subsistence systems as lacking any planning or forethought and to conclude that, without European 'help', the 'natives' would probably starve. 'Natives' were characterized as living from hand to mouth, with only the vicissitudes of nature to provide for them.

What slaughter and disease had failed to accomplish, explicit government policies of removal of people from their lands and resources achieved. Indigenous land was transformed into government and settler title. Indigenous land ownership and resource management systems, and the social structures that supported them, were utterly foreign to colonists familiar with European mechanisms for identifying land tenure and control of property – fences, gates, title deeds, tagged animals, and so forth. The more subtle ways of territory demarcation employed by most Indigenous communities were simply unable to be incorporated into the settlers' paradigms.

As colonialism progressed, Indigenous agents of stewardship were removed and new regimes imposed. Whereas the former were informed by centuries of experience with their particular ecological niche, the latter were based on the cultural perceptions of (mainly) Western European stakeholders. In this way Indigenous voices were largely lost from the management debate. There was no recognition that traditional owners had knowledge of the productivity of the land that would allow them to plan for their long-term survival. The totalizing expectations of the European settlers arising from colonization and state formation created the starting point for suppressing Indigenous knowledge systems. With no recognition of the pre-existing political, economic, spiritual, or social systems of Indigenous peoples, European ethnocentrism led to the misguided conclusion that there was no Indigenous knowledge. Anything that differed from European cultural constructs had to be the product of Indigenous ignorance, backwardness, and superstition, lacking the European logic of science and technology freed from the bonds of religious control. Writing was used as a litmus test of whether or not knowledge could be systematically transmitted from one generation to the next, and virtually all Indigenous societies were found to be lacking (Perkins 2001).

In tandem with European attitudes of political and economic superiority was what Niezen (2003: 211) calls 'philanthropic hubris' – that Europeans were 'liberating natives' from 'thralldom and superstition of their origins' and providing them with a superior model to follow: the model of European society. In moral terms, Indigenous peoples were consistently described as 'Godless', 'satanic', and 'immoral', desperate for the saving graces of Christian conversion. There was no recognition on the part of Europeans that Indigenous communities had their own spiritual systems and social organizations. Rather, whenever a European practice was absent, it was assumed that Indigenous peoples had nothing of value that took its place. Patriarchy was enforced globally, with no European conception of the possibility of matrilineal systems or egalitarian roles for men and women. Europeans assumed individualism to be a natural condition of humanity, and therefore interpreted any submission for the good of the group to be the tyrannical oppression of tradition. Social practices that strayed from monogamy and nuclear families were described as bestial, more of nature than of human existence.

Differences in economic production and land-management regimes were similarly viewed as backward, primitive behavior. Intensive domestication of plants and animals and rapid extraction of natural resources were prescribed by Europeans the world over, with limited concepts of sustainability, ecological capacity, or climate variability (Cronon 2003). In this atmosphere of asserting Western European cultural superiority, there was little room for appreciating or even recognizing Indigenous knowledge in relation to natural resource management. Indigenous experience was pushed aside in favor of so-called scientific and capitalist approaches to land use and resource management.

The capitalist construct of scarcity fostered the acquisition of all the resources possible, before they 'ran out' or were taken by someone else (Sahlins 1972). If the lands were not currently suited to intensive agriculture, cultivation would force the land to submit to the discipline of production. Any reluctance on the part of Indigenous peoples to participate in intensive agriculture or resource extraction was simply more justification for moving them off the land and bringing in European settlers who were ready to use the land productively. In the colonizing world of the 18th and 19th centuries, 'timeless' Indigenous peoples who wandered across an untracked and 'timeless' land were aligned with, and denigrated in the same way as, the ill-educated and gullible poor who believed in superstitions and called on the services of fortune tellers (Perkins 2001). Their failure to have made any 'improvements' to their lands marked them as lazy and lacking the ability to progress. The colonizers' view was that such peoples had forfeited their rights to the land.

Consistently, the pre-existing political systems of Indigenous communities were either not recognized or recognized only as subordinate to the superior authority of crown or state. International law in the 16th to 18th centuries recognized that 'colonization' was a legitimate way of acquiring sovereignty over lands that were *terra nullius* – that is, lands not perceived to be owned by the people who occupied those lands (Brennan 1992: 19–20). In some places, predominantly where armed conflict erupted between colonial forces and Indigenous peoples, treaties were negotiated primarily to solidify peace and legitimize territorial transfers and secondarily to provide limited recognition of the inherent sovereignty of the 'natives' involved. In places where there was no armed resistance, there were not even treaties to recognize Indigenous peoples' pre-incorporation autonomy. The European logic of centralization was used to discredit or manipulate Indigenous systems built on diffused power, consensus decision making, and ultimate local control.

Even where nominal land ownership rights were recognized through a treaty process, the beneficial use of Indigenous land was controlled by colonial and state policies that 'helped' Indigenous peoples make 'better use' of their natural resources. The concept of a trust relationship between the State and its Indigenous citizens provided the mechanism for diverting any potentially useful resource toward the forces of industrial production.

Without a recognized political authority or geographic territory, Indigenous communities were suddenly hard-pressed to assert their ownership of the land and resources on which they had subsisted for generations. The subversion of their pre-existing political systems was exacerbated by the failure of Europeans to recognize the existence, let alone the extent, of Indigenous land holdings and land use. European perspectives viewed intensive agriculture and intensive resource extraction as proof of 'productive' resource utilization and progress (Perkins 2001). Most Indigenous land-use practices left light footprints on the land in comparison with the impacts of the settlers. For example, Indigenous cattle herding involved transhumance, whereby livestock are moved from one landscape to the next in a broad seasonal cycle (Igoe 2004; see Chapter 1); Indigenous agriculture was based on swidden cultivation, whereby crops are planted with minimal disruption to the landscape and then rotated to other lands in 5- to 15-year cycles to maintain the richest soil quality (Kunstadter and Chapman 1978; Yos 2003). Europeans recognized only those land 'improvements' that resulted in a complete and irreversible change to the landscape and acknowledged only intensive exploitation of land as 'use'. Therefore, the centuries of gradual land transformation brought about by Indigenous land-management practices, including enhanced wildlife habitat, enriched wild plant harvests, and increased biodiversity, were viewed by Europeans as the products of 'nature' in an abundant but untouched 'wilderness' – as lands that were wild, untamed, untouched, and unmanaged by human hands (Taylor 1990: 11).

The lack of European understanding of Indigenous practices did not cause Europeans the same concern they had for Indigenous failures to understand European practices. Europeans began an immediate appropriation of the pieces of Indigenous culture that were useful to the expanding modern world-economy, without compensation to or recognition for Indigenous intellectual property. The tremendous capital wealth that Europe was able to accumulate, however, grew largely out of Indigenous management regimes and intellectual property. Such foods as tomatoes, corn, and squash; medicinal products such as quinine; tobacco; amazing stands of timber; fur and meat from apparently unlimited populations of wild animals – all these became commodities in the emerging world-economy for the enrichment of Europeans and to the detriment of the Indigenous communities responsible for their initial development (Mgbeoji 2007; Weatherford 1988).

Europeans exhibited minimal awareness of Indigenous voices in the wake of the new modern world-economy. Indigenous peoples were a transaction cost to be minimized in the European effort to access resources for rapid capital accumulation. Europeans believed that Indigenous communities had three 'choices' in the face of settler intrusion: they could blend in, physically relocate to unwanted or barren 'borderlands', or die off. But Indigenous communities often had other ideas. In the next stage, the 'native problem' began to impose costs on European expansion and capital accumulation as Indigenous peoples fought back. European capital accumulation could no longer be left to Indigenous 'choice'. The Indigenous obstacle had to be either removed from the modern landscape or forced to blend in with it (Reynolds 2001; Spence 1999).

Although many trends in the effects of global expansion and consequent dispossession of Indigenous lands are apparent, the historically specific time periods in which these trends were experienced locally are widely diverse. In some parts of the globe (for example, Africa and North America), initial contact was much earlier than in other parts (for instance, Australia and New Guinea). In some areas of the world, the creation of modern nation-states occurred earlier (United States) than in other parts where colonial status extended into the 20th century (Tanzania and India). In most places, the construction of colonization was carried out by Europeans themselves, but in some areas, such as Thailand and China, the political and economic incorporation of Indigenous peoples was mediated through local authorities who defined their own cultural norms and knowledge systems but who were eventually incorporated into this multistate global process. In some sense, the processes of Indigenous incorporation that took place in the United States 80 years ago were at work in Australia 40 years ago and are at work in Thailand today.

Therefore, any discussion of common trends will combine disparate historic periods under a thematic unity and will compress catalogues of difference below a surface of shared experience. Nonetheless, the emergence of the modern world-system was accompanied by a systematic lack of recognition by state authorities for the political, economic, and social autonomy of Indigenous peoples and by a denial that they possessed knowledge of the world on a par with scientific knowledge. The following example, from Thailand, demonstrates the impact of globalization on Indigenous peoples in that nation-state.

Globalization and Indigenous Peoples in Thailand

The Siamese are the dominant ethnic group in Thailand. They speak a dialect of the Tai language family and share many cultural features with other Tai-speakers, who together form a majority of the Thai population. The most numerous non-Tai peoples are the Tibeto-Burman, Hmong-Mien, and Mon-Khmer speaking groups concentrated in the largely upland areas of northern and western Thailand. Some, like the Karen and Lua, have occupied land in or around what is now Thailand for centuries. Nevertheless, they share subordinate political, economic, and racial positions within the modern Thai nation as the result of a process of internal colonialism that has created effects analogous to those that prevail in settler nations. It is by virtue of this subordinate position that Thailand's upland ethnic groups can be called 'Indigenous peoples'.

Before the formation of the modern Thai nation, legitimate inclusion in the realm of a Tai-speaking ruler, such as the King of Siam, was predicated on political loyalty and trade relations more than on ethnic identity or cultural affiliation. The political and economic roles played by different ethnic groups and communities varied. The Karen on the mountainous borderlands with the Burmese kingdoms to the west occupied a buffer zone and served as informal border guards (see Pinkaew 2002: 34–35). Many upland communities provided forest products and other goods (including opium) to lowland-based traders and as tribute to local Tai rulers (Tapp 1989). Through these roles, non-Tai peoples were integral to the political, economic, and social system in spite of the political dominance of lowland Tai rulers. (See Jonsson 2005; Richardson and Hanks 2001; Scott 2009 for a range of perspectives on upland-lowland relations in mainland Southeast Asia).

The rise of the modern nation-state altered the relations between the Tai-speaking majority and the upland minority peoples. Key groundwork for the emergence of the nation-state of Thailand was laid by the last few absolute monarchs of Siam and by the Western-educated civilian and military officials who overthrew the absolute monarchy in 1932. Since then, the institutions and ideological framework of the Thai nation-state and Thai nationalism have developed steadily. Nationalist ideology identifies 'Thainess' with the political and cultural features widely attributed to Tai-speakers. (See Winichakul 1994, 2000a, 2000b; Vella 1978; Wyatt 1984 on various dimensions of the formation of modern Thai nationalism). Hence, by the post-World War II era, non-Tai peoples came to occupy an uneasy place in the newly conceived nation. In the Cold War era, the upland minorities were increasingly seen as primitive and backward 'hilltribes' (or *chaw khaw*), a pejorative term that implied communist insurgency and opium cultivation (Pinkaew 2002). This exclusionary aspect of Thai modernity has forced upland minorities to struggle to balance commitment to local social and cultural forms with their location within the 'Thai' nation.

Starting in the 1960s the Thai State undertook a vigorous program to assimilate and integrate the upland minority peoples into the political and economic life of the nation by promoting adoption of Buddhism, discouraging opium production, and encouraging commercialized agriculture (Keyes 1989: 127–130). Yet, at the same time, full citizenship rights have often been denied to them on the basis of their perceived foreign status, even in cases of communities that have been present in Thai territory for a century or more. The result for many uplanders has been not political and economic integration but a marginalization from the mainstream of Thai society and exclusion from the benefits of increasingly open politics and economic growth (see McCaskill and Kempe 1997). The most recent bind for upland minorities has been increased state interest in restricting their access to natural resources. Since the 1980s, with the communist and opium production issues largely resolved, upland minorities have been framed as a threat to the Thai nation, because their swidden practices are supposedly harmful to the nation's environment (Lohmann 1999). This predicament is the result of some long-term changes in the Thai political economy and the discursive status of natural resources.

In 1988 flooding and landslides in southern Thailand wiped out several villages and killed about 350 people. The disaster, which many in Thailand attributed to over-logging in the area, brought deforestation to the fore of environmental politics in Thailand and forced the government to institute a nationwide logging ban in 1989. Since then, forest 'conservation' and 'environmental' concerns in general have been topics of extensive public debate and important components of state development policy.

The state has responded to upland environmental issues with a range of conservation policies. Abetted by the rise of scientific forestry in Thailand in the 20th century (Pinkaew 2002), Thai state agencies such as the Royal Forestry Department (RFD) have promoted the view that healthy forests require a lack of human habitation. So-called degraded forest (including fallow swidden land) is seen as a sign of the inherent destructiveness of upland agriculture. This view ignores the fact that upland communities have in fact successfully stewarded various kinds of forest zones around their settlements, including both agricultural areas and various kinds of 'reserved' forest areas, such as sacred groves. Nevertheless, the view that the upland minority peoples are forest destroyers par excellence enjoys great official and popular currency among the Thai majority and some sectors of the state bureaucracy. (Ironically, even the move of some upland communities toward opium replacement crops such as cabbage under the encouragement of Thai agricultural extension efforts has been excoriated by some NGOs and the RFD for their extensive land requirements). As a result, the RFD has pursued policies such as 'reforestation' and the increased establishment of protected areas. Farmers (both Thai and minority) who earlier pushed their fields into national forest reserve areas came under state scrutiny and criticism, and some had their lands expropriated for conversion to commercial tree plantations of eucalyptus and teak. The establishment of national parks and wildlife reserves was stepped up, removing huge swaths of land from smallholder agricultural activity, with particularly acute effects for upland peoples. Forested and upland areas have also been increasingly drawn into the Thai discourse of national security, with the health of forests (defined as free from human activity) framed as crucial for the ecological well-being of the nation. (Vandergeest and Peluso 1995 and Vandergeest 1996, 2003 detail the way resource management and state power have become intertwined in modern Thailand).

Thus, with the rise of the Thai nation, Thailand's Indigenous peoples have actually seen a loss of status and rights vis-à-vis central state authorities at the same time that those authorities have sought to assimilate and integrate them into the nation. Today, some of the most urgent resource-management and land-rights conflicts center on claims and counter-claims made by the State, upland peoples, lowland Tai-speakers, and other actors, such as Thai NGOs and the urban elite and middle class. The status of upland minorities, their claims to resource-use rights, and the nature of their knowledge about natural resources remain hotly contested issues in Thailand, played out in a context of political-economic subordination and assumptions of upland minority racial inferiority (see Delcore 2007).

INDIGENOUS RESILIENCE, SELF-DETERMINATION, AND THE WESTERN DOUBLE BIND

Indigenous Responses to the Colonial Process

Despite hundreds of years of conquest, colonization, and cultural subordination, Indigenous peoples have never ceased resisting their oppression or reasserting their own perspectives on how life should be understood. Resistance to colonization by Indigenous landowners came as a surprise to the European settlers. The early period of contact between colonizer and Indigenous landowner was often marked by hostile clashes over land and food. Early land appropriations were accomplished by simple declarations of right on behalf of the monarchs of Europe, with little concern for the original inhabitants 'discovered' on these new lands (McNickle 1973: 29; Reynolds 1987b: 7–11). When Indigenous groups observed European appropriation going beyond the accepted behavior of visitors, or when the European interest in maintaining decorum was strained by the unbridled lust for land and exportable resources, various forms of violence and brutality erupted on both sides. This was sometimes declared as war and fought by military personnel, but more often it was undeclared and uncontrolled either by the initial colonial administration or by the early national governments that followed. In Colonial America, for example, the English attacked the Pequots in 1637, destroying their principal village and confiscating their entire store of corn (Russell 1980: 187–188).

Over time European settler populations occupying colonial territories in North America, South America, South Africa, New Zealand, and Australia demanded self-rule and independence from Britain. They carved out new nations from lands that had been inhabited by Indigenous peoples when colonial expansion began, but they did not include Indigenous peoples when designing these new nations. Indigenous communities that withdrew from direct interaction with invading European forces toward interior 'regions of refuge' (Hall 1986, 1987) often found that their communities and territories now straddled the boundaries between two or more newly created nation-states. Later, when local independence movements arose in Africa and Asia to throw off the domination of European settler populations, the nationalism essential for centralized nation-states found no space for recognizing Indigenous difference or autonomy.

Assimilation had succeeded in robbing Indigenous peoples of many of their cultural ways, even if a strong sense of identity had survived. Consequently, Indigenous peoples who desired self-governance and access to original homelands often found it difficult, if not impossible, to prove their traditional ties to land to the satisfaction of Western legal systems. In some instances Indigenous peoples have been able to ignore legal channels to achieving their desires for self-determination. In remote parts of Australia, for example, Aboriginal people who wished to return to more traditional lifestyles simply moved off reserves and occupied vacant Crown lands. This movement was known as the 'Outstation Movement,', and there are groups who live on Outstations to the present day (Rowse 2000: 83–87). But such action was not, and is not, available to Indigenous peoples living in more settled areas.

Through state policies and institutions Indigenous peoples were denied access to their language, education, and cultural practices. They were encouraged to become members of mainstream society by adopting the economy, religion, and material culture of the mainstream society. Those who willingly renounced their 'primitive' ways were promised various forms of economic support and protection, while those who adhered to their cultural traditions were viewed as military and economic threats. Only those voices that spoke within an accepted Western structure, such as the 'educated native' or the artist who painted in a 'Western style', or the 'aboriginal pastor', were able to be heard by a bureaucratic system that did not recognize the 'heathen' ways of tribal peoples (Ellis 1994; Perkins 2001). Self-governance and self-determination were largely destroyed. The only Indigenous peoples who were able to operate successfully outside institutional controls were those who, at least outwardly, adopted a Western style of living (Ellis 1994; Reynolds 2001; Rowse 2000).

In Australia, Indigenous peoples who accepted (either willingly or by force) a Western education emerged in time as an 'Indigenous intelligencia' (Rowse 2000) who increasingly demanded a greater say in the management of their affairs. By the 1970s these Indigenous voices finally achieved a change in government policies from assimilation to self-determination and self-governance. But these policy changes have not necessarily led to any genuine opportunities for Indigenous peoples to return to the social structures of their ancestors. The only moral and social system recognized within government policy is that imposed by Western social systems and legal constructs (see Chapter 5).

Throughout the colonized world, government policies of protectionism and assimilation attempted to divest Indigenous peoples of their language, cultural property, and access to traditional resources. These policies have existed for so long that '[i]t is difficult for most environmental scientists and technocrats to accept the premise that so-called primitive or underdeveloped peoples possess knowledge of scientific worth' (Lewis1993: 8). Although such attitudes are beginning to change (Head 1990), the concept of Indigenous peoples having any knowledge about how to manage the land, the sea, and their resources remains foreign to many scientists, conservationists, and government land managers (King 1997).

Indigenous Self-Determination in Settler Nations: Structures and Substance

Despite concerted attempts by governments to ensure the erasure of Indigenous cultures, through programs such as the forcible removal of Indigenous peoples from their homelands and removal of children from their families in order to provide them with a 'white' education, many Indigenous peoples managed to retain a great deal of their cultural knowledge.

> [Missionaries and governments] were full of good will but didn't really understand the problems they were trying to handle. . . . [I]t is clear that, even in those places where Aborigines are living in close proximity to white people, the strength of their own traditions and ways of life is much stronger than most people are aware of and there is an unwillingness to accept the white man's way of life. (H. C. [Nugget] Coombs 1967, cited in Rowse 2000: 4)

Stories, traditions, and subsistence practices continued to be taught in secret long after people had escaped missions and other 'protectionists'. On North Stradbroke Island, (Moreton Bay, southeast Queensland), for example, Shane Coghill recounts how, as children, he and his brothers were taken on hunting trips during school holidays by their grandparents and great uncles while their parents were at work. They were taught the knowledge associated with tracking and hunting kangaroos and other local food animals. Their parents were not (officially) alerted to this activity, and, providing state authorities remained unaware of the practice, it could continue without adverse repercussions. It is clear from speaking to other Indigenous research collaborators that the continuation of youth training in this way was not uncommon. In remote communities it was even easier to continue to practice culture, language, and ceremonies, because government agents were rarely around to see (Reynolds 2001; Rowse 2000).

As a result, traditional ecological knowledge has survived as an integral part of Indigenous intellectual property in many parts of the world, despite attempts by governments to deny Indigenous peoples access to their cultural knowledge. The last three decades have seen a dramatic resurgence of Indigenous outcry about the dismal, scientifically constituted, management regimes that have resulted in declining plant and animal populations and diversity, soil erosion, and environmental degradation (Ross and Pickering 2002). Far from vanished, Indigenous peoples around the globe are mobilized to demand recognition, restitution, and respect for their distinct cultures, histories, and relationships to natural resources (Niezen 2003).

Land Rights Movements, the bane of government policy makers, mobilized both Indigenous and non-Indigenous peoples to voice opposition to policies that actively condoned cultural imperialism, and during the 1970s a movement for Indigenous self-determination and self-governance began to develop in many parts of the world (Castile 1998: 168–169; Rowse 2000). It was the Land Rights Movement that, in many ways, forced a gradual change in government policy away from assimilation and toward recognition of Indigenous aspirations for self-governance and self-determination. A new approach based on recognition of Indigenous rights and political self-determination became official government policy in many countries during the 1970s, although many governments were loath to see this policy change lead to genuine opportunities for Indigenous land ownership.

Today, contemporary Indigenous movements are operating within, and are often contextualized by, Western perspectives and institutional frameworks governing what Indigenousness is, is not, and ought to be. The intellectual backdrop that will allow Indigenous peoples a legitimate role in the management of the resources of their lands and waters is all based in Western intellectual and bureaucratic systems. Many Indigenous peoples living through governmental policies of assimilation were removed from their lands and forced to live like the neocolonial elites, occupying jobs and practicing all the outward signs of a homogenous national lifestyle (Wise 1985). The irony of self-determination is that generations of Indigenous peoples have now lived for so long under Western bureaucratic regimes that many, if not most, are unable to return to more tribal ways. For example, the young, articulate intelligentsia, who have largely led the movement for self-governance and land rights, are hardly the people who, under traditional law, would have been the leaders of an autonomous group (Rowse 2000; Stevenson 2006).

Furthermore, although government responses to calls for self-determination have varied across jurisdictions, all have one thing in common: any move to implement self-determination and self-governance for Indigenous peoples must be within the normal bounds of dominant law and government policy (see Chapters 4 and 5 for case studies). Indigenous law, even on Indian Reservations in the United States and on Outstations in Australia, has a very limited place in the modern neocolonial system, being firmly constrained by Western legal strictures (Hall 1986, 1987; Reynolds 2001; Rose 1986, 1996a; Rowse 2000). Even more enlightened administrations that championed Indigenous calls for self-governance have failed to recognize that self-governance and self-determination bounded within a dominant governance structure is no self-determination at all. Marcia Langton (1978) bluntly points out that although structures that allow Australian Aboriginal people to manage their own affairs have been put in place, these structures are white bureaucratic structures. Aboriginal bodies have been formally constituted, but at regional, state, and national scales, totally different from the small local communities that characterize more traditional Indigenous society structures (see also Rose 1986, 1996a; Rowse 2000: 131–148). In a policy move that Rose (1996a) terms 'deep colonising', governments have embedded allowable and recognized Indigenous self-governance organizations, such as Land Councils and Tribes, within Western institutions designed to control Indigenous activity. Indigenous communities have rarely been allowed 'to act in a wide range of issues of community concern so that they may adapt their customary law and traditions to the needs of their present situation' (Coombs 1972, cited in Rowse 2000: 107–108). A similar situation exists on Reservations in the United States (see Chapter 4).

Indigenous 'self-governing' groups are required by law to rely on mainstream government bureaucracies. For example, Marcia Langton points out that applications for funding, simply to run a government imposed 'self-governance' structure, must be submitted to white government agencies in accordance with dominant bureaucratic procedures. Only those projects that satisfy 'the values and prejudices of the white assessors' are funded (Langton 1978: 5). Conduct of projects must meet strict fiscal requirements, and expenditure must be acquitted in accordance with national taxation laws.

As a result of the failure of self-determination policies to deliver genuine opportunities for self-governance for many if not most Indigenous peoples, little opportunity exists for traditional land and resource stewards to present their case for involvement in land and resource management outside a Western management regime.

In this sense, one can argue that there is little difference in practice between assimilation and self-determination policies. Both policies require Indigenous peoples to operate within a modern world system and to act within a modern paradigm to achieve any form of control over their own affairs – but even then with the power controlled by the dominant bureaucratic system (Stevenson 2006). Local ways of dispute resolution are ignored. Customary roles for leaders are overlooked, and traditional power-brokers (often the elderly) are simply unable to make the long journeys to the cities and large towns where land-management offices are situated and where Indigenous land managers must go to attend meetings. Under this current regime of 'self-determination' and 'self-governance', most Indigenous peoples have none of the genuine political authority of the precolonial era. Lands have been appropriated and Indigenous political systems and laws dismantled. Indigenous peoples have few options other than to exist in a modern bureaucratic world – there is no other system in which their voice can be heard.

As a result, a double bind has developed whereby few paths are open for Indigenous peoples to promote and protect their ecological knowledge and property rights (but see Chapter 6). Indigenous communities who have mastered bureaucratic perspectives and the government institutions required for self-determination are slighted (often by both Europeans and their more radical neighbors) as culturally inauthentic and diminished, with no possible claim to any 'genuine' traditional ecological knowledge. At the same time, Indigenous communities who do not immerse themselves in such dominant institutions and modern modes of thought often cannot assert or protect their rights or knowledge, because they are usually unable to maneuver through the bureaucratic processes that control natural resource use and management. Indigenous communities who rely on others to articulate their rights often fall prey to the manipulations and appropriations of organizations deciding 'what is best for them'.

A new form of dispossession of Indigenous peoples from their natural resources takes place as a result. Limits are placed on hunting and fishing rights by freezing Indigenous cultures in time and arguing that the traditional resources of these peoples may be taken only with traditional technologies (Cordell 1991: 11; Lewis 1993: 9, 18; Whaley and Bresette

1994: 19–20, 36-37; see Ross 1994). Despite years of punishment for speaking traditional languages, carrying traditional weapons in public, and participating in traditional cultural activities, Indigenous peoples are now being asked to turn back the clock and re-acquire 'traditional' ways in order to be considered suitably 'traditional' to participate in customary land- and resource-management practices (for example, Hanson 1999).

Furthermore, there is the unfortunate prospect of many of those recognizing the potential benefits of Indigenous knowledge now engaging in a final wave of appropriation and exploitation. Indigenous communities are now being asked to reveal the knowledge they so diligently kept secret all the years during the onslaught of assimilation and land appropriation, not to increase their participation in land and resource management but to once again enrich the interests of the descendants of these colonizing forces (McNiven and Russell 2005; Roopnaraine 1998; Ross and Pickering 2002). Western legal systems and international trade organizations do not always recognize the concepts and social structures of Indigenous societies that would support their rights to own and apply their ecological knowledge to the vast resources they developed, once managed, and desire to control again (Riley 2005).

The Academic Debate: Tightening the Double Bind

Independent of Indigenous debates over efforts to reconcile their traditional heritage with the demands of the contemporary world, a vibrant debate is taking place *within* the knowledge system of science about the relationship between Indigenous peoples and natural resources. One school of thought romanticizes Indigenous peoples as being 'at one' with nature, employing 'primitive ecological wisdom' to ensure that they have no ecological impact on the land (see Milton 1996). Opposing scholars highlight the capacity of earlier Indigenous populations to cause species extinction, and they question the relevance and resilience of Indigenous concepts about nature in a severely changed world (Rowland 2004). As the Australian Aboriginal academic Marcia Langton observes:

> The popular definition of 'wilderness' excludes all human interaction within the allegedly pristine areas, even though they are and ever have been inhabited and used by indigenous people for thousands of years. Like the legal fiction of *terra nullius* which imagined us out of existence until the High Court decisions in the Mabo case, popular culture imagines us out of existence. The modern proponents of this wilderness cult dichotomise Aborigines into two extremes, the Noble Savage in harmony with the environment and the modern Aborigine who poses a threat of

extinction to rare and endangered species by virtue of wearing shoes, driving a Toyota and hunting with guns. (1996: 17)

Unfortunately, neither side of the debate allows for the concrete and constantly evolving contemporary practices of real Indigenous people in relation to resource management.

The Ecologically Noble Savage

Every part of this country is sacred to my people. Every hillside, every valley, every plain and grove has been hallowed by some fond memory or some sad experience of my tribe. . . . Even the rocks that seem to lie dumb as they swelter in the sun along the silent seashore in solemn grandeur thrill with memories of past events connected with the fate of my people, and the very dust under your feet responds more lovingly to our footsteps than to yours, because it is the ashes of our ancestors, and our bare feet are conscious of the sympathetic touch, for the soil is rich with the life of our kindred. (Chief Seattle 1854/1855 in Clark 1985)

This is an excerpt from arguably one of the most often-quoted speeches by an Indigenous person regarding his people's connection to their environment. Although Chief Seattle's speech is unlikely to have been the blatant fraud that was the 'Crying Indian' (Upshal 2000), there is now considerable doubt about the authenticity of the words spoken by Chief Seattle, and even about his name (Clark 1985; Kaiser 1985, cited in Suzuki and Knudtson 1992: xx–xxii). Yet there are many Indigenous and non-Indigenous peoples who view these words as those of the quint-essential Indian who meets romantic ideals of the ecological savage, living in harmony with the land.

These romantic ideals are often used by conservationists and others to promote a return to nature for industrial societies. These people claim to present *the* truth about what Indigenous peoples know (and knew) and how that knowledge should inform modern ecosystems management practice. Yet these texts are usually based on limited familiarity with the peoples they claim to represent and are often based on errors or misunderstanding of the nature of the Indigenous knowledge they convey. There are many possible examples of these statements, but two will suffice to illustrate our point. The first is from the work of J. Donald Hughes, who wrote that:

Everywhere they went, they [the Indians] had learned to live with nature; to survive and indeed prosper in each kind of environment the vast land offered in seemingly infinite variety. And they did this without destroying, without polluting, without using up the living resources of the natural world. Somehow they had learned a secret that Europe had already lost . . . the secret of how to live in harmony with Mother Earth, to use what she offers without hurting her; the secret of receiving gratefully the gifts of the Great Spirit. (1983: 1)

This exact statement is reprinted in the second edition of Hughes's book (Hughes 1996: 1), despite the fact that since the first edition new anthropological research had produced a 'more realistic picture' of Native American life. Hughes acknowledges that Indians had an impact ('All living things do; [even] buffalo make wallows and bees build hives' [1996: 4]) but claims that in the case of Indians this impact was negligible and did no harm to the earth or its resources.

Booth and Jacobs also recognize that natural communities changed as a result of Indian activities, but rarely adversely (1990: 31). This was because, unlike modern Europeans, who have forced the earth to change 'to meet their needs[,]. . . . Native American cultures had adapted their needs to the capacities of natural communities' (1990: 31). Consequently, Indigenous peoples (in this case Native Americans) are a model for 'a way humans can learn to live in harmony with the natural world' (1990: 41).

In both these ecological texts the writers do outline the social and cultural framework within which Native American knowledge about the environment is situated, but the complexity of these frameworks is poorly understood and is so oversimplified as to demonstrate only a shallow understanding of how knowledge applied (and still applies) in practice. This oversimplification has allowed these writers to overemphasize the 'sacred' and 'mystical' relationships between people and animals in American Indian cosmology and as a consequence to stress the romantic nature of Indian relationships with their ecosystems. This kind of misunderstanding and consequent romanticization of Indigenous knowledge is a common theme in much of this literature (see Milton 1996).

Brosius (2000) provides some excellent examples of how misunderstandings can occur and are perpetuated by those who desire to encourage an Indigenous narrative that appeals to preconceived and inaccurate notions of Indigeneity that today form much of the Euro-American gaze on Indigenous lifeways. Comparing his own detailed and long-term research into Penan environmental knowledge in Sarawak with that published by conservationists keen to save Sarawak forests from logging, Brosius records the misrepresentations of Penan knowledge that appear in the writings of these researchers who spend only short periods with their research collaborators. Brosius's main concerns are that the conservationists tend to reduce Penan knowledge to the sacred, to the exclusion of economic, social, and political concerns, imposing meanings on Penan knowledge that are largely constructed by Euro-Americans (2000: 309–311). Unfortunately some Indigenous peoples have internalized this rhetoric and adopted it as their own, at times genuinely believing the narrative ascribed to them but at other times adopting these narratives, because such beliefs are expected of them by outsiders (Brosious 2000: 306–311; see also Head 1990; Kuper 2003; Redford and Stearman 2003: 251; Stevenson 2006).

Despite the recent criticisms of works that romanticize Indigenous peoples' connections to land, and a growing body of anthropological literature that attempts to provide a more realistic and socially contextualized understanding of Indigenous ways of knowing, there are still some who insist on promoting the view that 'authentic' aboriginal peoples lived in total spiritual harmony with their land (see Smith 2001).

As well as being factually incorrect, academic and ostensibly authoritative arguments in support of popular views that 'living in harmony with the land' constitutes 'traditional' Indigenous ways have potentially dangerous political consequences. Such literature is widely used to demonstrate just how much of the original connection between 'real' Aborigines/Indians/natives and the land has been 'lost' with contact with Europeans or other dominant (often settler) groups and to justify arguments for why modern 'tainted' Indigenous peoples should not be granted special rights to land or its resources (Horton 2000; Langton 1996: 17).

Unfortunately, similar views can also be found in anthropological literature. In his paper entitled 'The Return of the Native' Adam Kuper (2003; see also Redford and Stearman 2003; Rowland 2004) argues forcefully that it is no longer valid to assert that Indigenous peoples, as the first settlers of many now-colonized lands, should have any greater rights to the land than recent settlers. He uses, as the basis of his argument, a rigorous rebuttal of claims that Indigenous peoples lived in harmony with the land. He rightly dismisses fictitious and erroneous statements that '[Indigenous] culture is associated with spiritual rather than with material values' (Kuper 2003: 390). He goes on to argue that the strong 'ecological thread' in the rhetoric about Indigenous hunters, and the 'dogma [that] hunters are in tune with nature', may never have been true and certainly is now lost to any Indigenous hunters who have been very much influenced by contact with others (2003: 390–391). While we agree with the *facts* of Kuper's assessment, we do not support his conclusions that 'with the best will in the world it may not be possible to return to a pre-Columbian state of nature' and that consequently 'land claims on behalf of former "nomads" typically raise very tricky questions' (2003: 391–391). Why should Indigenous peoples today conform to acknowledged inaccurate, inappropriate, and impossible expectations among settler communities or other dominant social groups regarding 'authentic' Indigenous behavior? As Omura points out in response to Kuper's arguments:

[I]ndigenous peoples are still sub-ordinate to Euro-American society because it is that society that defines indigenousness and controls decision making on indigenous problems. (2003: 396)

Most Indigenous peoples and their supporters make no claims that land rights will return the current colonial estates of North America, Australia, Africa, and Europe back to a native Utopia where all human beings live in total harmony with nature. Such expectations are not the result of assertions by Indigenous peoples, because Indigenous knowledge never did take this form, and few Indigenous peoples made such claims until encouraged to do so by well-meaning, but ill-informed, Euro-Americans (Brosius 2000; Horton 2000).

The evidence that Indigenous peoples modified the land in the distant past does not sit easily with some environmentalists who retain the stereotype, critiqued by several authors (for example, Brosius 2000; Perkins 2001; Ross and Pickering 2002), of aborigines as 'Children of Nature', the ultimate conservationists, who lived off the land without destroying it or doing anything with it. There is often, therefore, antagonism from environmentalists toward anthropologists and archaeologists who seek to change that stereotype and who point to evidence for substantial landscape change by Indigenous peoples in the past (Rowland 2004; cf. Head 1990).

Debunking the Ecologically Noble Savage Myth

Arguably the best known and most well-developed of the anthropological responses to the 'ecologically noble savage' view is that presented by Sheperd Krech III in his book *The Ecological Indian* (1999). Krech begins his anthropological and archaeological critique of this view by citing a common view of the romantics:

In their earliest embodiment they [Native Americans] were peaceful, carefree, unshackled, eloquent, wise people living innocent, naked lives in a golden world of nature'. (1991: 17)

Krech's book is an analysis of what he perceives to be inconsistencies between the notion of the Indian living in total harmony with the environment and Native American wastefulness of resources. Krech argues that these so-called wasteful actions had social bases, and, even though many had little effect on the sustainable production of the landscape, because human population densities were so low, they demonstrate that Native-American resource use practices were not underlain by any conservation ethic. Native Americans burned the land; performed impressive hunting drives that killed hundreds of buffalo, elk, deer, and beaver; and built massive irrigation systems that failed and left environmental degradation that exists into modern times. Yet 'their populations were too small to have made much of a difference' (1999: 99). Indians' 'few numbers trod so lightly as to leave bounty for European eyes almost everywhere' (1999: 78). The implications of Krech's book are that 'if there had just been more Indians they would have trashed the place' (Hunn 2002).

There have been a number of other critiques of 'the ecologically noble savage' (Alvard 1998; Brosius 2000; Diamond 2005; Flannery 1994; Horton 2000; Kuper 2003; Redford 1990; Redford and Stearman 1993; Rowland 2004; Upshal 2000), yet none has drawn the debate that Krech's book has. It is beyond the scope of this book to provide a detailed rebuttal of Krech's findings. An excellent analysis has already been provided by Hunn (2002; see also Hunn et al. 2003). Here we briefly review some of the central concerns that have been expressed by Hunn and others (for example, Feit 1987; Johannes 1987; McAnany and Yoffee 2009; Posey 1992; Snodgrass and Tiedje 2008; Tiedje and Snodgrass 2008) and analyze the implications of Krech's and others' approaches for Indigenous natural resource management opportunities.

Hunn (2002; Hunn et al. 2003) argues that the main problem with Krech's (and others') deconstruction of the ecologically noble savage is that the members of the 'new orthodoxy' (that small-scale societies did not conserve) have such a narrow definition of the word 'conservation' (for instance, Alvard 1998) that it would be impossible, or at least rare (see Tucker 2003), for any but the most romanticized 'savage' to meet the definition. For example, Smith and Wishnie define conservation as 'any action or practice . . . [to] prevent or mitigate resource overharvesting or environmental damage . . . [that is] *designed to do so*' (2000: 493, emphasis added). According to Smith and Wishnie, not only must conservation be the specific goal of resource management but also must there must be no other expected benefit of management, other than conservation of biodiversity (2000: 501). In small-scale societies, therefore, conservation can only ever be an involuntary or opportunistic by-product of natural resource management. Alvard (1998: 476, 477) agrees with Smith and Wishnie, arguing that conservation that is not 'by design' is 'epiphenomenal conservation' and not true ('altruistic') conservation.

There are two issues here: the first relates to the definition of 'conservation', and the second relates to the design of conservation action. Hunn (2002; Hunn et al. 2003) argues that 'conservation' must be distinguished from 'preservation'. Preservation of biodiversity and environment means complete protection of all resources. Clearly this is a virtually impossible goal for any society that needs to exploit (even sustainably) the resources of the earth. As Hunn notes, 'it is patently absurd to expect humans to live on this planet without impact' (2002). He goes on to acknowledge the consequences of this attitude for collaborative conservation between Indigenous and Western land and resource managers:

> [W]hile the preservationist ideal is clearly alien to indigenous peoples, a notion of conservation as 'caring for the earth' is widely recognized. To hold indigenous peoples to the preservationist standard undermines the possibility of an effective alliance between conservation biologists and indigenous communities in defense of the environment. (Hunn et al. 2003: S82)

Of course, even those authors advocating the 'noble ecologist' view would not admit to such a narrow definition of Indigenous conservation practices. But the problem is that when these proponents of the 'living in harmony' model *do* acknowledge that Indigenous peoples had an effect on the land, the impact is seen as 'natural', similar to the sorts of things animals do – like beavers building dams or platypus digging burrows. This attitude promotes a view of 'conservation' meaning 'preservation' – being in complete 'balance with nature' (Hughes 1983: 5).

The second issue regarding the definition of conservation – that relating to 'design' and 'intent' – is more problematic. How does one demonstrate the conservation 'design' of a particular action (Berkes 2003)? Feit (1987) argues that Waswanipi Cree had deliberate conservation goals in their hunting of moose. Using over two decades of qualitative and quantitative data, Feit demonstrates that, although it is easy and efficient to hunt moose, especially in winter months, Waswanipi chose to limit the numbers of these animals hunted using a variety of strategies ranging from monitoring populations, through stewardship, to rotating hunting territories. Feit argues that by choosing to limit harvest numbers, Waswanipi hunting law is *designed* to manage resource exploitation.

Hunn uses a similar argument to demonstrate that by *choosing* to limit favored resources, Tlingit also demonstrate the conservation intent of their actions. He provides a case study analysis of Tlingit gull-egg collection to illustrate this problem (Hunn et al. 2003). Tlingit deliberately avoid collecting eggs from 'complete' nests (those with three eggs). This ensures that nests where embryos in the eggs have begun to develop are not disturbed. According to Hunn and associates the intention and design of this practice is conservation of the gull. But scholars who have advocated that only 'altruistic conservation' can be considered true conservation (Alvard 1998, 2003; Smith and Wishnie 2000; Tucker 2003) have argued that, because developing eggs may not be preferred for taste reasons (Alvard 2003), the Tlingit collection law is not true conservation (Alvard 2003; Tucker 2003). Tucker argues that 'human behavioral ecology more easily accounts for self-centered, short-term behaviors' (2003: S98), and Alvard (1998) believes that optimal foraging theory can better predict human resources management than can Indigenous knowledge. They argue that the Tlingit egg-collection case is an example of 'epiphenomenal conservation', because the so-called conservation law is based on multiple motives. But Hunn asks 'why not allow multiple motives?' (2003). He points out that even in the modern world, present-day conservation goals are not devoid of 'other' motives, such as desires to protect specific species deemed valuable by our society (2003).

It is clear from the *Current Anthropology* debate about 'conservation' of gull-eggs that, just as extremist arguments in favor of the ecologically noble savage have led to political problems for Indigenous peoples, so, too, can extreme arguments about the 'destructive savage'. Alvard claims that '[t]he answer to the rhetorical question "Is one therefore *not* a conservationist for not conserving a resource that is abundant relative to the demands placed on it?" is yes' (2003: S93). If that is the case, Indigenous peoples can never be regarded as partners in present-day conservation (see Berkes 2003; Feit 1998; Hunn 2002, 2003; Hunn et al. 2003).

The arguments of those who require 'altruistic conservation' by Indigenous peoples to be demonstrated imply that evidence of environmental degradation by Indigenous peoples in the past denies modern Indigenous descendants any rights to be part of present-day resources management (cf. Broughton 2003). Diamond (1986, 1988, 2005), for example, argues that the failures of prehistoric hunter-gatherers to recognize environmental management mistakes (such as over-harvesting of moa in New Zealand and deforestation by Anasazi and on Easter Island) until it was too late is evidence of the difficulties people in small-scale societies have in identifying the impacts of their actions without some degree of abstract and objective (that is, scientific?) environmental management monitoring techniques. The failure of pre-industrial peoples to sustain their resources was due to incompetence and the inability to solve 'difficult ecological problems' (see also Smith 2001).

Johannes (1987) was quick to dispute Diamond's early position, and his brief rebuttal is often overlooked in more recent literature; yet his contribution was (and remains) important. Johannes agreed that Diamond's argument about the myth of people living in harmony with nature is 'unassailable' but pointed out that, if researchers document *only* counter-examples to the ecological savage, document *only* examples of environmental devastation caused by the actions of precolonial peoples, then we 'run the risk of perpetuating a counter-myth that sound environmental practices were absent in such civilizations' (1987: 478). He provides several (brief) counter-counter-examples, and concludes:

> The coexistence of wise and unsound environmental practices is a characterization of many, if not all civilizations. The danger of overemphasizing the weaknesses of environmental management in preindustrial cultures is that their strengths will be ignored. (1987: 478)

Recently Johannes's arguments have been taken up and expanded in a volume edited by McAnany and Yoffee (2009). Authors contributing to this volume demonstrate that claims for environmental 'mistakes' by small-scale societies ignore the various complex environmental situations in which the 'mistakes' occurred. In many cases, the environmental degradation described by Diamond (2005) occurred not as a primary result of human action at all.

So if extremist positions on either side of the debate succeed, present-day descendants of precolonial land managers are caught in an impossible double bind. According to the 'old orthodoxy' of the ecologically noble savage, the current knowledge of Indigenous peoples has been so altered by colonization that they wear shoes and hunt with rifles (Langton 1996), consequently demonstrating that the 'tide of history' has washed away their once close and harmonious connection with the land and its resources. Their failure to remain in harmony with the land denies their right to be involved in modern land-management conservation. But according to the 'new orthodoxy', even their ancestors had no ability to manage resources. The only reason moose and elk and buffalo and whales and kangaroos and dugong and turtles remain in abundance (or at least were in abundance until white settlers implemented unsustainable harvesting) was because there were too few Indigenous hunters to make a lasting impact. Once again, the sins of the fathers have been visited on the sons, and descendants of original land users are deemed, like their ancestors, to be too incompetent to be allowed to manage resources that clearly need scientific oversight (Diamond 2005).

CONCLUSION

The incorporation of Indigenous peoples into processes of colonization and state formation resulted in massive dispossession of Indigenous peoples from their lands and natural resources. Modern science served as the knowledge system to support this dispossession by privileging scientific practice and perspective as built on foundations of truth, and by creating a divide across which Indigenous ways of being could not pass. To this day, the scientifically constructed separation between Indigenous peoples and Western practice continues to mute the voices of Indigenous peoples.

A double bind of romanticized authenticity or degraded inauthenticity paralyzes any meaningful discussion of how Indigenous perspectives might be integrated into practical natural resource management regimes and brings into play a long list of obstacles, some subtle and unstated, to collaborative conservation approaches.

In the next chapter we document our argument that it is the lack of Indigenous voice outside the Western system that lies at the heart of many of the obstacles to incorporating Indigenous knowledge into practical natural resource management. We ask: How can Indigenous ways of knowing be recognized within mainstream bureaucratic structures? How can Indigenous peoples be heard within the cacophony of sound that is the scientific discourse on land and resource management? We identify the conceptual and practical barriers to integrating Indigenous participation into natural resource management that arise from the manner in which knowledge binds the Western perspective on Indigenousness.

In Chapter 4 we provide some examples of these obstacles, focusing on Indigenous experiences in Australia, the United States, India, and Thailand. Nevertheless, despite the numerous barriers that exist, there *are* examples of Indigenous peoples' involvement in land and resource management planning. These examples are discussed in the final chapters of the book, along with an assessment of experiences to construct recommendations for the future of Indigenous collaborative conservation and natural resource stewardship.

Chapter 3

BARRIERS TO INTEGRATING INDIGENOUS KNOWLEDGE INTO NATURAL RESOURCE MANAGEMENT

We demonstrated in Chapters 1 and 2 that many Indigenous peoples find themselves in a 'double bind' regarding the acceptance of the relevance of their knowledge by some in the West. The first bind is epistemological; the second is institutional.

At the epistemological level, Indigenous peoples' knowledge is often challenged as much for what it is *not* as for what it *is*. For those who believe that Indigenous peoples once lived in harmony with the land (see Chapter 2), changing nothing and trusting nature to make provisions for all aspects of their survival, modern aboriginal peoples have lost the knowledge that informed this ability, and therefore they and their knowledge have no place in modern natural resource management (Bolt 2004; Windschuttle and Gillin 2002). Alternatively, for those who believe that Indigenous peoples never had any understanding of conservation or the environmental consequences of their actions and, save for their low numbers, would have 'trashed the place', modern Indigenous peoples have no relevant knowledge that could help with resources management in a world where development pressures make any additional impact on natural resources likely to result in tragedy (Rowland 2004).

Despite these relatively widely held beliefs about the irrelevance of Indigenous knowledge in natural resource management, there are an increasing number of scientists and resource managers who recognize that Indigenous peoples do indeed have knowledge that is legitimate and relevant to modern natural resource management and who desire to work more closely with Indigenous peoples to improve resource management practices (Bowman 1998, 2000; Fernández-Giménez 2000; Head 2000; Kimmerer 2002; Sillitoe 1998, 2002; Weber, Butler, and Larson

2000). Although some of these joint management opportunities have been successful, others have failed (see Chapter 5). Failure is not necessarily a result of any contestation relating to knowledge but is a result of institutional barriers to integrating knowledge. Institutional barriers occur largely as a result of the political systems that have established narrowly defined government departments and compartmentalized legislative and bureaucratic processes.

In this chapter we review the specific nature of these two over-arching barriers to the integration of Indigenous and scientific resources management by analyzing a number of themes or 'strands' that come together under the headings of 'epistemological barriers' and 'institutional barriers' to Indigenous involvement in natural resource management. These barriers are summarized in Table 3.1. We discuss each of the barriers theoretically and empirically, using a literature review of the concepts involved. In the next chapter we provide illustrations of how these barriers apply to specific case studies from Australia, the United States, India, and Thailand.

TABLE 3.1   Summary of barriers to Indigenous involvement in NRM.

Barrier	Description
Epistemological Barriers	
A IK not recognized	There is lack of recognition that Indigenous knowledge once had a place in natural resource management.
B Narrow definitions	Narrow definitions of concepts of 'tradition' and 'custom' reduce opportunities for recognition of Indigenous knowledge in modern communities.
C Nonvalidation of IK	Indigenous peoples' expertise and connection to the land or seascape are not deemed to have been 'proven' to the satisfaction of scientists and resources management bureaucrats.
D Translation of IK	Indigenous peoples are required to translate their knowledge into frameworks that are widely understood by scientists and resource managers.
E Social/ spiritual expression	When knowledge is expressed in a social or spiritual, rather than a scientific, framework, scientists often find the relevance of such information challenging.
F Codification of IK	The need to write down information can lead to Indigenous concerns about codification and appropriation of knowledge.
G Ownership of knowledge	Barriers can arise when Western systems of property rights (including intellectual property rights) are imposed over Indigenous ways of controlling and managing ownership of knowledge.

Continued

TABLE 3.1 *Continued*

Barrier	Description
H Spatial/ temporal boundaries	Barriers may occur as a result of a system that requires land and water to be bounded spatially and temporally via the demarcation of areas on maps or within chronologically defined management planning systems.

Systemic or Institutional Barriers

Barrier	Description
I 'Outsiders' kept 'outside'	Bureaucratic arrangements such as meeting requirements and government institutional structures make the involvement of any 'outsiders' difficult.
J IK & management institutions	Barriers that occur when Indigenous knowledge cannot be accommodated within reductionist and formulaic approaches to management such as those found in management manuals.
K Decentralization	Barriers can arise as a result of the decentralized nature of Indigenous concepts of governance and decision making, which challenges bureaucratic systems of centralization.
L Racial/ cultural inferiority	Some 'races' or cultures are seen as being categorically inferior, practicing inherently destructive or under-productive forms of livelihood, and therefore incapable of possessing a complex knowledge of nature.
M State power	The State has more power than Indigenous people do and so has greater control. Indigenous people must strategize about how and when to assert their concerns.
N 'Benevolent' West	The State is assumed to act benignly, despite obvious resource degradation under the State's watch. Indigenous people must prove that State actions have been detrimental.
O Globalization	The State needs to meet global environmental challenges on global (often theoretical) scales, rather than on the local scale used in Indigenous knowledge systems.

EPISTEMOLOGICAL BARRIERS

In Chapter 1 we outlined the differences between scientific and Indigenous ways of knowing. We established that knowledge in scientific communities may be perceived to be constructed differently from knowledge in Indigenous communities, and the two knowledge systems are often applied differently. We demonstrated that science tends to favor knowledge that is developed by specialists and that is narrowly shared, compartmentalized, and acquired through rigorous, replicable experimentation in a reductionist and rational paradigm. Indigenous knowledge, although asymmetrically shared, is community-based, holistic, and founded on empirical observation over a long period of time. As a consequence, it is sometimes difficult for scientists and modern, university-trained resource managers, on the one hand, and Indigenous land managers, on the other, to recognize the value of each others' knowledge.

One of the main problems relates to the way in which Indigenous knowledge is often expressed. Indigenous knowledge may be articulated in ways that science-trained managers find difficult to understand and to access, because it exists in a social or even spiritual framework that scientists find unfamiliar. This unfamiliarity in the *presentation* of knowledge, often more than the knowledge itself, may be exacerbated by managers' perceptions about what constitutes the knowledge of 'traditional' peoples. There are concerns that modern Indigenous land-management agents, acting in outwardly modern ways (such as driving cars, wearing shoes, and hunting with rifles) may cause damage to sensitive and already abused environments through the application of poorly developed or even 'lost' understandings of traditional ways in a 21st-century world.

Epistemological barriers manifest themselves in a variety of subthemes of paradigmatic difference. We now present a number of these subthemes, which we identify as key to understanding the nature of epistemological barriers to the integration of Indigenous knowledge into 'mainstream' natural resource management.

A. Indigenous Knowledge (IK) Not Recognized

There is lack of recognition that Indigenous knowledge once had a place in natural resource management.

There is considerable debate in both anthropological and ecological literature regarding the *extent* of the effects that 'traditional' or 'precontact' Indigenous resource managers had on landscape evolution (Alvard 1998, 2003; Bowman 2000; Head 2000; Horton 2000). Nevertheless, apart from the authors of completely fanciful works, such as Morgan (1991), even the staunchest supporters of the ecological noble savage model recognize that Indigenous life had *some* impact on the environment (see Chapter 2).

The question is, therefore, not whether or not Indigenous land and water resources stewardship practices affected the environment but instead what was the nature and extent of that effect? As we outlined in Chapter 2, modern views occupy a continuum, from those (mostly ecologists) who see the pre-industrial world as essentially natural to those who have argued that the landscape seen at the time of the arrival of Europeans/colonists/other settlers was largely anthropogenic.

This issue is central to the debate about whether or not Indigenous peoples have a right to be invited to the present-day resources management negotiation table. For those who view landscape as anthropogenic, it is unarguable that Indigenous resource stewards should be part of the continued management of the environment they helped to create. But for those who perceive that nature was 'natural' until the arrival of civilization, there is little place for ancient customs and traditions in a modern world that has seen massive environmental change.

B. Narrow Definitions

Narrow definitions of concepts of 'tradition' and 'custom' reduce opportunities for recognition of Indigenous knowledge in modern communities.

In Chapters 1 and 2 we alluded to the problem of the concept of 'tradition' in debates about roles for Indigenous knowledge in modern resources management. Although in anthropological discourse it is widely recognized that custom and tradition are flexible, this is often not the view of the wider public and of ecologists. There has been much recent debate about what constitutes 'traditional' knowledge and 'traditional' resource management (for example, Berkes 2008; Hobsbawm 1983; Walsh and Mitchell 2002). The implications of this debate on barriers to incorporating 'traditional' knowledge into modern land and resource management practices are obvious. For those people (mostly anthropologists) who recognize that tradition changes over time and that 'in order to maintain tradition [Indigenous peoples] must reinterpret that tradition, thus introducing change to maintain continuity' (Mearns 1994: 263), there is little concern when modern Indigenous peoples introduce new technologies and new understandings to 'traditional' resource stewardship knowledge and practice (Chase 1989). But for those who desire to see Indigenous peoples conforming to an often Western-imposed stereotype of traditional resource management behaviors (see discussion in Bradley 1998a; Langton 1996; Sillitoe 2002; Stevenson 2006), such as hunting with spears and wearing virtually no clothes, the Indigenous 'accommodations to the colonizers are interpreted as the decay of a pristine culture rather than the creativity and flexibility of a dynamic one' (Head 2000: 207).

The disappointment that comes with Indigenous peoples' 'failure' to meet imposed stereotypes of 'traditional' actors in the environment often leads to the complete rejection of any overtures by Indigenous resource stewards to be involved in modern management planning and practice (Brosius 2000).

C. Nonvalidation of Indigenous Knowledge

Indigenous peoples' expertise and connection to the land or seascape are not deemed to have been 'proven' to the satisfaction of scientists and resources management bureaucrats.

The epistemological differences between Indigenous and scientific ways of demonstrating knowledge and expertise were documented and discussed in Chapter 1. In the West, an 'expert' is one who acquires data via the establishment of replicable experiments, interpreted through the application of verifiable laws of nature, and leading to independent recognition and accreditation of knowledge gained through promotion to prestigious positions and/or the awarding of certificates and medals. An expert is one who speaks with authority on the narrow field in which that individual has researched for many years (Schafersman 1997).

Indigenous ways of encoding authority lie within social and spiritual frameworks and are traced via kinship systems (Merlan 1998). Knowledge is communal, with no one person necessarily having all the relevant knowledge on a subject. As Ellen and Harris (2000) note, Indigenous knowledge is communal knowledge, shared asymmetrically (see Chapter 1). Authority to speak comes as much from social status as from a knowledge base, and accreditation is based on one's kinship and heritage rather than achieved via the awarding of externally recognized degrees.

It may, therefore, be difficult for scientists, or, more important, the bureaucratic and legal systems through which they operate, to recognize the authority of Indigenous resource stewards who cannot produce the degrees and accolades recognized today as the marks of the qualified expert. As Walsh and Mitchell (2002: 23–24) note, bureaucracies reward people for being good at things that modern society values. Indigenous knowledge of natural resource management is currently not valued, and therefore Indigenous peoples attract neither payment/reward for sharing their knowledge nor recognition that they have knowledge of relevance in the modern world (Stevenson 2006).

Similarly it may be difficult for Indigenous peoples to comprehend the narrowness of the knowledge of the scientific experts. Tight focus on particular elements of the natural system can result in some significant knowledge, but that same tight focus can seem ill-advised to Indigenous experts whose knowledge is marked by constant recognition of the interactions of land, water, and spirits that are the mark of Indigenous knowledge systems.

D. Translation of IK

Indigenous peoples are required to translate their knowledge into frameworks that are widely understood by scientists and resource managers. [and . . .]

E. Social/Spiritual Expression

When knowledge is expressed in a social or spiritual, rather than scientific, framework, scientists often find the relevance of such information challenging. [and . . .]

F. Codification of IK

The need to write down information can lead to Indigenous concerns about codification and appropriation of knowledge.

These three related points (D, E, F) follow logically from subtheme C. Because the modern resource management bureaucracy is based primarily on scientific ways of constructing knowledge, privileging science, and requiring the presentation of independently verifiable facts and credentials, Indigenous peoples must often 'translate' their knowledge into ways of understanding that are familiar to those trained in modern scientific ways of thinking (Stevenson 2006). Such translation leads to the compartmentalization of Indigenous knowledge, 'picking out the eyes' and ignoring those aspects that do not easily resonate with scientific ways of knowledge construction. This requirement often results in an overemphasis on *facts* and on 'what people know' (Agrawal 1995) rather than on 'how people know' (Phoenix-O'Brien 2002), and a consequent de-emphasis of the spiritual framework for knowledge that lies at the heart of much Indigenous knowledge.

Ellen and Harris (2000: 15) argue that 'once Indigenous knowledge is drawn within the boundaries of science, it is difficult to know where to draw the boundaries between it and science' (see also Agrawal 1995). Walsh and Mitchell (2002) concur, arguing that knowledge that is held in song and story, or maps that are encoded in art or seasonal calendars, lose important details and become muddied when translated onto paper (see also Basso 1996). Muddied boundaries quickly lead to essentialization and appropriation. Codifying Indigenous knowledge in this way defeats the objectives of participatory resource management and totally disempowers local knowledge holders. It would be interesting to watch the howl of resistance that would arise if scientists and bureaucrats were required to recast their own knowledge in Indigenous ways.

G. Ownership of Knowledge

Barriers can arise when Western systems of property rights (including intellectual property rights) are imposed over Indigenous ways of controlling and managing ownership of knowledge.

Through the constructs of colonial legal systems, property rights are vested in individuals or corporate entities, and the notion of property is expanded to include not only physical objects and land but also ideas, innovations, and techniques (Riley 2005; Shiva 1997, 1998). Property ownership is a fundamental basis from which capital accumulation can take place (Marx 1867: Chapter 26). Competition for property and ideas is viewed as an efficient mechanism for stimulating innovation and assigning value. As with political organization, property rights are centralized in clearly identified individuals or in entities with clearly defined chief executive officers:

> Knowledge is considered to be the product of individual creativity, based on Western scientific thought and systems of knowledge creation and gathering whereby the resource base is merely viewed as 'raw material'. (Shiva 1998; see also Posey 2000: 40–41)

Therefore, the process of obtaining rights of ownership or use is simply a matter of negotiating with the appropriate individual or corporate executive officer.

In Indigenous communities, however, where both authority and knowledge is dispersed across the community (Ellen and Harris 2000; Posey 2000), the process of obtaining rights is neither simply nor clearly defined. Indigenous knowledge belongs simultaneously to everyone and to no one (Basso 1996; Rigsby 1998). The success of a bureaucracy or corporation in obtaining the permission of one Indigenous individual to use their ideas and knowledge does not convey clear title to the property rights embedded in that knowledge. In fact, such an approach to negotiations of access to knowledge and/or resources – involving only individuals or 'leaders' – can be completely at odds with Indigenous constructs of property 'ownership'.

However, Western legal systems are notoriously silent on methods for recognizing and protecting group rights or for defining group processes to defend and enforce group rights (Riley 2005). Rigsby (1998) argues that failure by the West to recognize alternative ways of constructing ownership results from the major difference between Western and Indigenous approaches to property: the notion of 'exclusion'. In the West, 'the right to exclude others from entry and use is critical or diagnostic of property rights in land' (Rigsby 1998: 29). But such exclusivity is rare in Indigenous communities. As a result, Indigenous communities are placed in the awkward position of both asserting their own intellectual property rights in their cultural knowledge and practices and defending against the attempts of others to reduce their group rights into individually conveyed intellectual property rights (Kalland 2000).

This notion of group versus individual ownership of property is particularly pertinent in debates regarding access to marine resources. Sharp (1998) points out that debates over ownership of the sea have raged between traditional owners and outside users since the declaration of the *Magna Carta* in 1215, when tidal waters in Britain were recognized as publicly owned, thereby extinguishing the previously held rights of traditional coastal fishing villagers (Sharp 1998: 51). This 'common' ownership was overturned in 1663 by the English jurist John Seldon, who argued that 'the King of Great Britain is Lord of the sea flowing about' (Seldon 1663, cited in Sharp 1998: 52), a view that challenged a previous judicial ruling by the Dutch jurist, Hugo Grotius, who in 1603 had argued that the sea and its resources could not be 'owned'. Grotius's ruling followed a breakdown in the *Magna Carta* declaration, with illegal acts of the Crown allocating certain lease rights to private landowners (Sharp 1998: 51–52).

None of these British and European approaches to the sea and its resources meets the property rights asserted by many maritime Indigenous communities who claim ownership of the sea in the same way as others claim ownership of the land. For many Indigenous communities there are few differences between sea and land (see Bradley 1998b; Memmott and Trigger 1998; Palmer 1998; Peterson and Rigsby 1998; Sullivan 1998). For Aboriginal peoples in Australia, for example, land property and sea property are constructed into 'a seamless web of cultural landscape', and community-based ownership laws carry fluently from one to the other (Sharp 1998: 49ff).

H. Spatial/Temporal Boundaries

Barriers may occur as a result of a system that requires land and water to be bounded spatially and temporally via the demarcation of areas on maps or within chronologically defined management planning systems.

Maps in Indigenous societies do not contain the clearly separated frontiers that we see in modern cartographic constructions of the world (Byrne 2008; Fox 2002). In fact maps in Indigenous societies may take forms other than cartographic representations of physical geography; they may include songs, stories, memories, and other oral traditions. Such representations may be seen in Indigenous concepts of 'place'. As Casey (1996) has argued, 'place' is a concept that is defined by local knowledge. Place differs from 'space' in that place is a culturally and socially defined phenomenon. Different people view places in different ways:

> Rather than being one definite sort of thing – for example physical, spiritual, cultural, social – a given place takes on the qualities of its occupants [Bradley (2001, 2008) would argue that this includes the spiritual occupants of place], reflecting these qualities in its own constitution and description and expressing them in its occurrence as an event: places

not only are, they happen. (And it is because they happen that they lend themselves so well to narration, whether as history or story). (Casey 1996: 27)

There are many examples in anthropology of people's differing perceptions of place. Basso (1996), for example, explores the concept of wisdom as it is encoded in Apache understanding and naming of places. Gorring (2002) demonstrates that 'place' need not replicate 'site', for, unlike place, site is an entity that is easily defined and bounded and hence can be mapped (see Casey 1996: 26). Place, in contrast, cannot be so easily bounded and hence is difficult to map (Byrne 2008; Byrne and Nugent 2004; Fox 2002).

Bradley (in Yanyuwa families, Bradley, and Cameron 2003) has demonstrated the problems of mapping places in his work on the Yanyuwa Atlas, entitled *Forget about Flinders*. Flinders was an early 19th-century explorer who mapped much of Australia's coastline. But his maps of Yanyuwa country were utterly meaningless to Yanyuwa people. Flinders's maps ignored the things that *happen* – the songlines, the stories, the connectivity between one happening and the next, as played out in the location of particular sites within a complex panorama of a landscape of events (see also Nabokov 2002; Williams and Mununggurr 1989).

Because maps require the imposition of boundaries on places and spaces, they are often meaningless when used outside the cultural creation of the mapmakers. In modern societies dominated by European-derived management systems, bounded spaces are respected because they can be managed; boundaries denote legal ownership and therefore responsibilities. Bounding of space or even place may occur in Indigenous societies, but the construction of boundaries often results in bounded spaces that look nothing like those constructed by people from outside the landowning group.

Bounding time can cause the same sorts of problems as those created by bounding space. In Judeo-Christian belief, time is linear. Time can be divided (bounded) into measurable components – hours, days, months, years – and all these components follow one another sequentially. Many Indigenous cultures do not perceive time in this way. For them 'time calendars consist of multiple and simultaneously existing time categories such as "practical time", "social time", "religious time", "dream time", etc.' (Janca and Bullen 2003: S40; Pickering 2004). Time is often cyclical, or co-existing, with events from 'the past' recurring in the present as more than memory. Bradley (2001, 2008) explains that for the Yanyuwa Aboriginal peoples from northern Australia, the landscape is occupied by spirit beings and ancestors who once lived and acted on the earth and who still play a major role in people's lives today. Godwin (2005; Godwin and Weiner 2006) documents similar beliefs for Aboriginal people from central Queensland, who regularly discuss issues of law with long-dead ancestors who continue to appear in various forms in the present.

Dominant elites, who privilege a linear concept of time that denies the ongoing existence of deceased kin, view their own culture as 'progressing'. As Perkins (2001) argues, 'progress' is closely aligned with hegemony, with the ability to measure time deemed a mark of sophisticated scientific knowledge. The representation of Indigenous peoples as 'timeless' primitives implies a backwardness that has helped support the dispossession of Indigenous peoples.

Yet for many Indigenous peoples time and place intersect recursively, with ancient memories being kept alive in modern landscapes. Such 'memoryscapes' are constantly created and recreated through the performance of songs, dances, and rituals and through the retelling of stories and reallocation of place names (Nabokov 2002: 145).

Along with philosophical and epistemological challenges caused by these different constructions of space and time, practical problems also arise. This is often manifested when Indigenous peoples are required to speak about place while being physically removed from that place. For example, for many Indigenous peoples, attending planning meetings in District or Regional offices well away from native lands is a daunting experience that involves the purchase of airfares, accommodation in unfamiliar hotels, and unpaid time away from local employment. It means travel away from traditional lands and country into neighboring territories, and then speaking about distant homelands on someone else's country/land. Indigenous peoples often regard speaking *about* the needs of country while remaining *on* country as an essential component of good management planning (Bradley 2001; Ross and Coghill 2000). Bureaucratic systems that require Indigenous land managers to attend meetings away from country can cause unease and anxiety among people who believe that speaking on another's country is disrespectful to their own country and to that of the people responsible for the meeting place.

There may also be problems within the meeting environment itself. Western-style committee meetings, with formal chairpersons, agendas, minutes, and timeframes, may be incomprehensible to some Indigenous peoples, particularly those not educated in a Western-style system (Stevenson 2006). Even when Indigenous representatives are well versed in bureaucratic structures, a meeting in which that representative is the only non-European or the only local person can reduce even the most bombastic community member to a shy observer.

Most Indigenous people prefer meetings that are open-ended in terms of time and number of participants who can speak. In Aboriginal

Australia some community meetings may take days or weeks to allow speakers time to consult with family members (both living and spiritual). This kind of meeting environment is as foreign to Western bureaucrats as the Western meetings are to most local community people.

This last subtheme, under the umbrella category of barriers relating to epistemological knowledge constructs, demonstrates how epistemological barriers to knowledge sharing can generate other barriers that are more institutional or structural in nature. In many ways the problem of meeting location would also fit under subtheme I, which follows shortly. We now turn to an investigation of systemic or institutional barriers to incorporating Indigenous knowledge into 'mainstream' land and resources management.

SYSTEMIC OR INSTITUTIONAL BARRIERS

Indigenous concepts and beliefs about nature and resources have challenged, and continue to challenge, the hegemony of colonial and scientific constructs of 'power dominance and progress' over the untamed 'wilderness' of the uncolonized landscape (Langton 1996: 11; see also Byrne 1991; Ross and Pickering 2002; Sullivan 1993, 1996). Consequently, Indigenous perspectives on natural resource management are accommodated into land management policies only when they do not confront the dominance of scientifically based systems and practices that view nature as an economic resource, fragmented from social, spiritual, or cultural concerns. When Indigenous communities assert their interests in natural resource management in such a way that colonially constructed hierarchies of control are contested, suddenly collaboration becomes strained (Stevenson 2006). The implementation of collaborative conservation becomes problematic when differences in knowledge systems contradict the interests of power that are structurally embedded in resource-management regimes.

This observation is important. While epistemological barriers to the recognition of the validity and place of Indigenous knowledge in current land management policies are gradually being reduced with increasing examples of attempts by scientists and resource managers to overcome the hegemony of their disciplines and involve Indigenous peoples in management planning, institutional barriers, constructed by modern bureaucratic systems, remain important obstacles to co-operative management of natural resources. These are the institutional barriers erected by bureaucratic policies that lock scientists into a Western political system in which compartmentalization and demarcation of functions and even office structures serve to inhibit incipient partnerships.

We now turn to review the subthemes that we identify as key to understanding the nature of systemic or institutional barriers to the integration of Indigenous knowledge into 'mainstream' natural resource management.

I. 'Outsiders' Kept 'Outside'

Bureaucratic arrangements such as meeting requirements and government institutional structures make the involvement of any 'outsiders' difficult.

Continuing on from subtheme H (spatial/temporal boundaries), this subtheme extends the exploration of the concerns that arise within Indigenous communities when meeting arrangements adversely challenge Indigenous ways of speaking for country and its resources.

Natural resources management in most parts of the world is the responsibility of governments, through environment or natural resources programs. Bureaucracies have been established to oversee the development of legislation and policies on land, water, and resources management, with law and policy required to conform to political agendas set by governments.

Bureaucracies determine boundaries of operation. Not only is the knowledge compartmentalized through the establishment of bureaucratic branches comprising experts in a variety of different scientific areas (biologists, zoologists, chemists, pollution experts, and so forth), but the bureaucracies are divided into geographic regions, where experts have knowledge compartmentalized into ecosystems or particular habitats (coastal geomorphologists, wetlands biologists, grasslands ecologists, and so on).

For many Indigenous peoples such compartmentalization of knowledge and bounding of knowledge into artificially separated disciplines and regions is often incomprehensible (see Chapter 1).

J. IK and Management Institutions

Barriers occur when Indigenous knowledge cannot be accommodated within reductionist and formulaic approaches to management, such as those found in management manuals.

From the perspective of science, all knowledge should be reducible to individual component parts and neatly segregated into categories of similarity and difference (see Chapters 1 and 2). When this approach is applied to the integration of Indigenous knowledge into management plans or resource manuals, the result can be problematic. Indigenous peoples who are asked to add their knowledge or views to such documents under headings or columns labeled 'Traditional Indigenous

Practice', 'Use by Indigenous People', or 'Indigenous Name' often find insufficient space to record their ways of knowing about a species or landscape (King 1997). One problem is that no response to any category in a Management Plan is permitted to be more than a few sentences or even words long. When a category addresses rattlesnakes, for example, there is no scope for including information about creator beings, the relationship between those above and below the ground, or the obligations of humans to snakes generally (cf. Feit 1987; see Huntington 2000; Nabokov 2002). Yet, from an Indigenous perspective, the proper management of rattlesnakes cannot be taken out of this broader context; to isolate certain stewardship elements is to lose both meaning and efficacy. The bureaucrats and management officials may feel satisfied that all the boxes are neatly filled in, but from an Indigenous perspective, this does not even approach a collaborative management process.

K. Decentralization

Barriers can arise as a result of the decentralized nature of Indigenous concepts of governance and decision making, which challenges bureaucratic systems of centralization.

Bureaucratic systems established in modern states depend on the appointment of centralized leaders who then act independently as 'representatives' of their constituents. The assertions of these representatives are considered binding on the group as a whole, since such leaders are empowered to follow their own ideas in arriving at policies, programs, and negotiated settlements (Martin et al. 1997).

> The academic community is quite undemocratic, hierarchical and driven by competition, jealousy and power plays. The status and privileges of academics depend heavily on their position as professionals and their links with other professional groups and managers, all of whom help establish the framework for managing employees lower in the pecking order. The status and privileges of academics are based on claiming areas of knowledge as the exclusive preserve of professional experts. Academia is essentially a competition for power and status carried out using bodies of knowledge as bargaining chips. (Martin 1984: Chapter 8)

Within the scientific paradigm, actions of appointed leaders are considered to be perfectly legitimate and binding on the communities they represent. Indigenous communities with egalitarian, decentralized, and/or dispersed traditions of authority find the process of centralized leadership and decision making problematic, both in terms of the process for decision making and for the legitimacy of the decisions so reached (Ellen and Harris 2000; Posey 2000). Particularly for Indigenous communities that did not consider themselves a unified whole until after the colonial process identified them as such, the political unit that they are asked to represent is a complete construction of the colonial experience (Rowse 2000: 161; Wise 1985).

There was no such thing as a leader of 'the Lakota' or 'the Massai' or 'the Yanyuwa', because these bounded labels assigned by colonial administrators mask significant diversity and independence within a population that shared cultural attributes but not political unification (Coombs, Brandl, and Snowdon 1983). Furthermore, expertise, knowledge, and authority were also often dispersed across the community rather than centralized in one community member, resulting in multiple loci of power (Ellen and Harris 2000; Posey 2000). Particularly for egalitarian societies, it was unlikely that all the critical Indigenous knowledge of the community would be held by any one member of that community (see Chapter 1).

In the context of natural resource management, bureaucracies designed to make and implement management plans need to, or desire to, seek the input of Indigenous communities; however, this input is generally not through a dispersed process of consulting a wide number of individuals within relevant Indigenous communities but through an appointed leader or expert from each community who is expected to know everything and speak for everyone. Resource managers often feel that Indigenous collaboration has been accomplished when one tribal/community representative is included in one meeting in which natural resource management is discussed. From the perspective of the Indigenous community, however, such a superficial engagement with the community does not even amount to consultation, let alone collaboration.

L. Racial/Cultural Inferiority

Some 'races' or cultures are seen as being categorically inferior, practicing inherently destructive or under-productive forms of livelihood, and therefore incapable of possessing a complex knowledge of nature.

Colonial assumptions that inferior 'native races' use (or fail to use) resources, to the detriment of 'the national interest,' persist in many places. These assumptions can work in several ways. During the colonial period, the colonizers often saw Indigenous peoples as taking from the bounty of nature without any effort. These 'noble savages' were thus devoid of useful knowledge of nature and required outside help to be shown how to use resources more productively. In the postcolonial era, with the rise of modern conservation discourses, 'inferior' peoples are sometimes seen as engaged in inherently destructive livelihoods, such as swidden agriculture or hunting species that are now endangered as a result of modern land- and sea-management practices. Such peoples are perceived as having knowledge of how to ransack nature rather than manage it. Government land and resource managers perceive that such people and such knowledge require powerful, civilized outsiders, skilled in the use of science, to protect threatened resources (Stevenson 2006). The 'national interest' often looms large in these sorts of interventions.

The specifically racial element enters the picture when the purportedly ecologically destructive people are cast in terms of incommensurable difference. For example, in classical racist formulations, a biological inferiority leads to either indolent or destructive habits. In the contemporary world, race and culture are often conflated in more complex ways. Moore, Pandian, and Kosek (2003: 27–28) note that the apparently liberal recognition of cultural difference can amount to the portrayal of a hardwired culture, or the identification of race through cultural markers. Where cultural differences are seen as wholly or nearly immutable, culture takes on racial overtones. For example, when Thai foresters refer to the 'tribal characteristics' of upland minorities, or 'hilltribes', they speak not simply of cultural differences but of a hard and fast culture that either cannot be changed or can be changed only through the most forceful wrenching of people from land and resources. In such situations, so-called geographies of exclusion (Moore, Pandian, and Kosek 2003: 29) begin to make sense, with the offending groups either quarantined or evicted from such areas as national parks. Inevitably in such cases, the transfer of knowledge of how to better use or conserve nature is strictly a one-way street, from superior race-cultures (like 'the Thai') to inferior others (like the 'hilltribes').

M. State Power

The State has more power than Indigenous people do and so has greater control. Indigenous people must therefore strategize about how and when to assert their concerns.

Ultimately, all Indigenous peoples are incorporated into nation-states that have greater power under the current global political economy than do Indigenous groups, even those with some degree of recognized sovereignty (Hall and Fenelon 2009; Perry 1996). The State has the power to simply say 'No' to Indigenous involvement in natural resource management. As a result, Indigenous peoples have to approach co-management negotiations more carefully than do State resource agency personnel, creating strategies and plans that take into account the personalities involved, the overall political climate, the State fiscal situation, and the strength of the Indigenous request before ever approaching a

State agency. In contrast, State agencies can casually include a single Indigenous person in a meeting with virtually no preparation, have a self-satisfied sense of having included 'the Indigenous perspective', and then determine that involvement is no longer needed, with few or no political consequences (Stevenson 2006).

Anthropologists have long pointed to the role of power in masking oppressive colonial relationships with cheerful faces of voluntary assimilation and internalized domination (Cheater 1999; Fanon 1967; Foucault 1977; Ortner 2006). Those insights must be extended to the realms of Indigenous knowledge and natural resource co-management. To achieve a situation in which genuine collaboration is reached between the State and Indigenous peoples residing within the State's boundaries, these issues of power need to be explicit and transparent in the negotiation process. Otherwise, the likely outcome is the 'all or nothing' approach that so many Indigenous communities have experienced: either the State will allow Indigenous people to play no role in resource management, or the State will delegate the entire responsibility to an Indigenous entity with the understanding that the delegation will be retracted if the performance of that entity is disappointing to the State in any way. Genuine co-management cannot occur until some impediment is accepted by the State that prevents unilateral assertions of power such as these over the collaborative process.

N. Benevolent West

The State is assumed to act benignly, despite obvious resource degradation under the State's watch. Indigenous people must prove that State actions have been detrimental.

The colonial myth of the West bringing progress to backward natives is still deeply embedded in the modern psyche (Bodley 2008). In the context of natural resource management, the default assumption is that having Western involvement is an improvement over anything that Indigenous peoples had in place before, or at worst a neutral force on the landscape. As a result, Indigenous people have to make additional efforts and use political capital any time they want to assert that Western involvement has been detrimental to the natural resources in their region. Indigenous people have to divert energy away from the actual management of their resources into a justification to State entities and Western NGOs that the colonial status quo must be overturned. This burden of proof creates yet another barrier to Indigenous participation in Western-dominated natural resource co-management. When Indigenous people note the sudden decline in a local species, the first question in the Western mind is 'What are the Indigenous people doing wrong?' because the assumption is that, as a rule, Western natural resource management is working. Specific hunting practices, ceremonial resource uses, and new commercial market interests of the Indigenous people are immediately suspect. However, defects in Western use and management regimes over previous centuries are not considered as culprits unless and until Indigenous people assert that history, and even then the evidence is often discounted in favor of the colonial myth of progress.

O. Globalization

The State needs to meet global environmental challenges on global (often theoretical) scales, rather than on the local scale used in Indigenous knowledge systems.

Globalization provides an additional all-encompassing barrier to the incorporation of Indigenous knowledge in natural resource management. Economic globalization has connected geographically distinct ecosystems, and therefore environmental problems, creating a perceived need for natural resource management to be undertaken on a global scale. As a result of the global nature of environmental degradation, such as global climate change, Milton (1996: 153) points out that the breadth and complexity of environmental damage cuts across ecosystems and even nations. This makes local management 'in practical terms extremely difficult'. In fact, international conventions, such as the Kyoto Protocol, encourage solutions to environmental degradation that validate the Western styles of knowledge that privilege broad-scale, theoretical responses to ecosystem challenges and deny the relevance of local level interventions.

Conducting environmental research at the global scale reinforces the epistemological and institutional barriers faced by Indigenous peoples seeking a stronger voice in natural resource management. Because Indigenous knowledge is locally focused, and derived from direct interaction with the local environment, conceptualizing extra-local environment connections proves challenging to Indigenous peoples. According to Milton (1996: 154), because Western knowledge is created outside the local context, it therefore 'has to be legitimized with reference to independent principles and assumptions usually in terms of scientific rationality'.

DISCUSSION

There are, of course, many other kinds of barriers, but we believe that these are the barriers that occur most commonly in the areas where we work and are the ones that are often overlooked in academic and applied discourses, because they are the least visible. We turn next to a presentation of a series of case studies that explain each of these barriers. We demonstrate that although many of these barriers have their roots in the epistemological differences between the Indigenous and Western constructions of knowledge that we discussed in Chapter 1, the practical manifestation of the barrier is often institutional.

Once these epistemological barriers are understood to be as much institutional as methodological, then other areas of conflict and concern for Indigenous peoples also become apparent – for example, desires by Indigenous peoples for greater recognition of Indigenous ways of learning within Western education systems; the opportunity for Indigenous understandings of the medicinal qualities of resources or even spirits to be accepted as part of the treatment of Indigenous patients in a modern health care system; and the acknowledgement of Indigenous economic development aspirations within a global economic environment.

In Chapter 2 we discussed the problems that arise when Indigenous communities are required to use Western-style bureaucratic structures as vehicles for the achievement of self-determination goals, including desires for a re-establishment of traditional rights and responsibilities toward the management of country. In this way, arguments relating to institutional barriers to the recognition of Indigenous desires for involvement in natural resource management have far-reaching consequences for other aspects of Indigenous peoples' lives in the modern world, and although these wider implications are beyond the immediate scope of this book, we must realize that once the nature of such barriers is identified, mechanisms to overcome the problems may be far more widely applicable than just resources management.

In Chapter 4 we provide case studies that illustrate the barriers outlined above. These case studies demonstrate that simply appropriating Indigenous people's knowledge and adding it to scientific understandings of resource management is not enough. The people themselves must also be partners in resource-management endeavors.

Chapter 4

Exploring Obstacles in Action: Case Studies of Indigenous Knowledge and Protected-Areas Management

In the introductory chapters of this book we outlined some of the theoretical and practical factors that have underpinned a general reluctance by resource-management bureaucracies to allow Indigenous peoples to have a significant involvement in resource planning. In Chapters 1 and 2 we discussed the nature of Indigenous knowledge in comparison with Western ways of knowing and found that, although there are times when Indigenous peoples and Western-trained scientists think similarly, in the main there are historically constituted epistemological barriers to shared ways of knowing. These epistemological barriers have produced a range of practical obstacles to the development of collaboration between government land managers and traditional peoples, as outlined in Chapter 3. In this chapter we provide some case study materials to illustrate our earlier arguments and to provide the baseline data for analyses of similarities and differences in the construction and influence of obstacles to Indigenous involvement in natural resources management in different parts of the world.

Of course, the impediments to collaborative natural resources management are not isolated hurdles, to be overcome one by one. They largely act in concert, and at times they can combine to build a substantial obstacle to the creation of ways forward for the development of opportunities for shared custodianship of resources. Nevertheless, to meet the demands of the Western-trained mind, we have created the categories outlined in Chapter 3 as heuristic devices for investigating the specific phenomena we have observed in our case studies.

We recognize that our examples must, by necessity, separate the barriers and obstacles to collaboration into discreet elements; such is the nature of writing (Nabokov 2002). Indigenous history and knowledge are a multimedia production, involving imagery, song, story, dance, art, and symbol (Nabokov 2002: 40). To reduce such complexity to text, in which the writer or reader can present or absorb only one word at a time, is to reduce understanding to single, isolated components, presented in a linear progression, and to imprison our investigation within the limitations of our imposed medium of writing. Writing demands that ideas are subdivided into themes and subtexts that can be easily handled by both writer and reader. The consequence is a false separation of elements that, in reality, are inseparable.

In an effort to overcome at least some of the impositions of the written word on our examples – which we have, in reality, learned as a result of years of observation, engagement, and experience – we have organized the case studies presented in this chapter under the barrier headings from Chapter 3. The case studies have been segmented into individual illustrations of how single barriers, or small groups of barriers, operate; this arrangement will give the reader concrete examples of the concerns raised in Chapter 3. To bring our compartmentalized examples back together, we end each of our case studies with a brief overview of how our investigations combine to illustrate some of the larger issues identified in the first chapters of this book. We then end the chapter with an integrated analysis of the individual case studies, which provides a holistic overview of the connection between our case studies and the theoretical arguments we have raised so far.

Our case studies come from Australia (where Indigenous peoples make up a very small minority of the population and where Indigenous voice has few opportunities to be heard in any political activity); the United States of America (where there are political and historical similarities with Australia, although here Indigenous peoples can have a role in providing advice and input into protected-areas management where those protected areas are part of treaty rights or Reservations); India (where Adivasi – 'first inhabitants' – make up 8% of the population and are often regarded as primitives, badly in need of Hindu civilization); and Thailand (where local farmers are regarded as either good managers or poor managers based largely on racial and cultural identifiers).

AUSTRALIA – SOUTHEAST QUEENSLAND

Australia has been occupied by humans for at least 45,000 years (Allen and Holdaway 1995; O'Connell and Allen 1998). The first Aboriginal occupants of the continent were probably maritime fisher hunter-gatherers (Bowdler 1977), although occupation of all parts of the Australian landmass – from the coasts to the deserts, from the forests to the glacial uplands – by around 30,000 years ago (Ross, Donnelly, and Wasson 1992) indicates a relatively rapid adaptation to many different ecosystems. Throughout the entire period of human settlement across Australia there is evidence that Aboriginal peoples were developing strategies for managing the resources of the environments they encountered, particularly with fire (Bowman 1998, 2000).

The first Europeans to come to Australia did not recognize the complexity of the adaptive responses Aboriginal people had made to the environment (Horton 2000: 169). William Dampier, for example, who visited Australia's western coast in 1688, described the Aboriginal inhabitants as 'the miserablest people in the world', living only on what nature provided. Yet Aboriginal people lived in places where European explorers, such as Burke and Wills, died for want of food and water, and over time explorers' accounts of Aboriginal villages associated with worked gardens and irrigated landscapes challenged initial notions of Aboriginal people as 'noble savages' living off the meager provisions of the land (Lourandos 1997).

Australian Aboriginal Impact on Ecosystems

Barrier A – IK not recognized and Barrier C – nonvalidation of IK

Debate over the extent of the impact of Aboriginal land-management activities on the environment of Australia began in the early 19th century, soon after British settlement (Horton 2000: 14) but reached a crescendo during the late 20th century and still smolders today. The notion of the noble savage living in harmony with the land has continued alongside the 'man the destroyer' model for several decades (Rowland 2004).

One of the earliest papers to challenge the noble savage view was Rhys Jones's seminal work on 'fire-stick farming', a term he coined to characterize the effects of Aboriginal burning on the 'natural' landscape (Jones 1969). In this and subsequent papers on Aboriginal fire management (for example, Jones 1973, 1975, 1995), Jones argued that anthropogenic burning transformed native bushland into grassland (see also Bowman 1998, 2000; Bradley 1995; Dodson, Fullagar, and Head 1992; Rose 1995). According to Aboriginal oral testimony (for example, B. Coghill and S. Coghill in Ross 1998), the regular burning of grassland landscapes encourages new growth in plants and provides grazing areas for macropods and other animals, thereby ensuring a regular and predictable supply of both plant and animal foods for Aboriginal farmers.

Evidence in support of these claims comes not only from anthropological sources, such as archaeological research and ethnohistorical analyses, but also from palynological and geomorphic studies (for example, Ash 1988; Bowman 1998, 2000; Dodson, Fullagar, and Head

1992; Singh, Kershaw, and Clark 1981). Peter Kershaw's pollen studies from a deep sediment core from Lynch's Crater (Cape York Peninsula) (Kershaw 1976, 1985, 1986), for example, has demonstrated the coincidence of dramatic change in vegetation and charcoal particle counts at 38,000 years before present (BP). Kershaw argues that such a change could not have been natural:

> It is difficult to imagine that natural fires created by lightning strikes should suddenly become critical after having had little influence on any vegetation for many thousands of years without some kind of concomitant climate change. (1986: 184)

But 'fires made by man would be a different proposition', Kershaw (1985: 184) argues. Kershaw has proposed that the pollen data from Lynch's Crater have not only provided confirmation of archaeological indications of the early presence of humans on the Australian continent but also provide evidence for the virtually immediate use of fire by recently arrived humans (see also Flannery 1994).

The implication of this research is that these Aboriginal burning practices were deliberate, and the consequences were both predicted and realized (cf. Alvard 1998, 2003; Hunn et al. 2003; Sillitoe 2002).

But despite this scientific 'proof' of Aboriginal expertise in land management, obstacles still blocked an acceptance that Aboriginal peoples could ever have modified the vegetation enough to effect any lasting change that could be regarded as 'land management' (Horton 2000).

In 1982 ecologist David Horton argued that Aboriginal burning had had little impact on already fire-tolerant vegetation communities. Horton posited that the massive changes to the Australian environment wrought by the impact of global environmental and climatic changes throughout Quaternary glacial-interglacial cycles, coupled with natural fire events resulting from lightning strikes, were far more important in the transformation of vegetation communities than was Aboriginal burning.

Clark (1983) and Dodson, Fullagar, and Head (1992) partly agreed with Horton, although these authors took a more moderate view that recognized that the major transformations to Australia's vegetation were environmental/climatic *and* anthropogenic (see Lewis 1982, 1991 for a similar view from North America). Climate change caused the *direction* of change to vegetation, Clark and Dodson and associates argued, but Aboriginal burning affected the *extent* and the *duration* of change.

This moderate view was rapidly overtaken by a popular work on Australian Aboriginal impacts on the landscape (including Pleistocene megafaunal extinctions), written by another ecologist, Tim Flannery. In *The Future Eaters* (1994), Flannery argued that, as in North America, megafaunal extinctions occurred rapidly after first human arrival.

Flannery linked megafaunal extinctions directly to Aboriginal hunting and indirectly to burning, arguing that the sudden removal of so many grazers from the ecological system as a result of overkill by naive hunters meant that a new mechanism was required to maintain grasslands. Flannery proposed that Aboriginal burning filled this vacant ecological niche, and this supported Flannery's argument that Aboriginal peoples acted as destroyers of the natural environment and its resources.

Horton (2000) has vigorously disagreed with Flannery's thesis. The blitzkrieg model of overhunting of megafauna, Horton and others argue, is totally unsupported in Australia because of the long period of overlap between megafauna and Aboriginal occupation (at least 15,000 years, with megafauna surviving until 25,000 BP at Lancefield Swamp [Gillespie et al. 1978; see also Dortch 2004] and 30,000 years at Cuddie Springs [Field, Fillios, and Wroe 2008; Field and Fullagar 2001]). So Flannery's model of destructive hunting practices by Aboriginal Australians falters at the archaeological evidence hurdle.

In 2000 Horton returned to his 1982 argument that Aboriginal land-management activities were so minor as to leave no visible imprint on the Australian ecosystem and landscape. He argued that those who continue to advocate that Aboriginal land use created the environment encountered by the first European settlers do so for purely political purposes (Horton 2000: 7–19):

> For many years it was both politically correct, and anthropologically sound, to argue against the proposition that Aborigines had made no impact on the Australian environment. Politically correct because it supported the proposition, still heard today in the native title 'debate', that if you don't use it you lose it – if you owned a whole continent and you weren't using it productively, you deserved to have it taken away from you. (Horton 2000: 7)

Flannery and Horton provide two extremes of this academic argument about Australian Aboriginal influences on the environment over time, and consequently two extreme interpretations of scientific evidence about the long-term role Aboriginal Australians played in the shaping of Australia's landscape. Another ecologist, Lesley Head, provides some balance in this debate. Head (2000) examines the role of Aboriginal land-management practices in a number of areas. With respect to fire, Head points out that, indeed as Horton has argued, it has been a part of the Australian ecosystem for hundreds of thousands of years – long before any human presence on the continent. Why then, she ponders (Head 2000: 96–97), did natural fire produce only massive vegetation changes following the arrival of people? Like Clark (1983) and Dodson, Fullagar, and Head (1992), Head acknowledges that climate changes produced the continent-wide landforms and vegetation patterns seen in Australia today (that is, the *direction* of vegetation change over time) but recognizes that the smaller-scale changes in vegetation seen in palynological records following the arrival of Aboriginal humans are due to anthropogenic influences (the *extent* and the *duration* of change) (Head 2000: 124–130). Furthermore, contra Alvard (1998, 2003), Head (2000: 128) argues that such anthropogenically induced changes were deliberate and provided a 'conservation impact' on fire-sensitive plant communities such as *Callitris* (native Cyprus pine – see Bowman and Panton 1993; cf. Hunn et al. 2003; Sillitoe 2002). It is, therefore, authors such as Head, Jones, and Bowman who have compiled the scientific evidence required to 'prove' the existence of Indigenous fire-management knowledge in Australia, as known by Indigenous land and resource managers (Figure 4.1).

'Proof' that Australian 'hunter-gatherers' practiced other forms of environmental management also relies on scientific data. There is now abundant archaeological and geomorphic evidence to support Aboriginal claims for a long history of natural resource stewardship, including gardening (Balme and Beck 1996); irrigation (Lourandos 1980, 1997; Williams 1987); fish, shellfish, and eel farming (Barker and Ross 2003; Lourandos 1997; Meehan 1988; Ross and Quandamoooka 1996a, 1996b); plant cultivation and vegetation modification (Gott 1983; Head 2000); and dugong and turtle custodianship (Bradley 1997, 1998a, 1998b; McNiven 2008; McNiven and Bedingfield 2008; Ross and Bigge 2009).

In short, there is now scientific evidence to support Aboriginal Australians' claims that their ecological knowledge comes from long-held land stewardship customs practiced over tens of thousands of years. To deny the existence of such practices is equally as political as the blind acceptance that so concerned Horton (2000). Rigid denial provides an irrational and unsupported rejection of Aboriginal peoples' roles in the custodianship of land and sea, and stewardship of the country's resources, and sustains a refusal to allow a role for Aboriginal Australians in modern land, water, and natural resource management. Denial of Indigenous evidence – or acceptance of such evidence but only with scientific proof – ignores Aboriginal demands for traditional land, sea, and resource stewardship strategies to be incorporated into current mainstream resource-management principles.

Dugong Management

Barrier C – nonvalidation of IK, Barrier D – translation of IK, Barrier E – social/spiritual expression, and Barrier J – IK and management institutions

The evidence for Aboriginal stewardship of Australia's land and the sea countries, and their resources, is overwhelming yet is often not well recognized beyond the relevant Aboriginal communities and the particular

FIGURE 4.1 *Xanthorrhoea* (grass trees) reshooting after fire on North Stradbroke Island. In precontact times, regular Aboriginal burning would ensure the frequent regeneration of this and other important resource species (photograph by A. Ross).

researchers who have studied them. Part of the problem here relates to the need for Indigenous peoples to translate their knowledge from spiritually or socially constructed knowledge into more scientific frameworks that are understood by scientists and resource managers. An excellent example of this relates to the management of the dugong.

The dugong (*Dugong dugon*), or sea cow, is an endangered marine mammal that lives in the warm waters off northern Australia (EPA 1999). In 1999 the Queensland Parks and Wildlife Service (QPWS) and the Environmental Protection Agency (EPA – now the Department of Environment and Resources Management, or DERM) – developed and implemented a species recovery strategy to plan for the management of the endangered dugong (EPA 1999). The plan has been updated (EPA 2007), although with few management changes incorporated.

Dugong numbers have been declining for many years as a result of a range of factors, including entrapment in fishing nets, power boat strikes, decline in sea grass habitat (the only food of this animal), and Indigenous hunting, a traditional activity often associated with ceremonial times in most parts of northern coastal Australia (Bradley 1997, 1998b; Bradley et al. 2006; McNiven 2008; McNiven and Bedingfield 2008; Ross and Bigge 2009).

Many researchers have blamed hunting by Aboriginal and Torres Strait Islander Australians for the most significant declines in this species (Heinsohn et al. 2004; Marsh et al. 2004; Smith 1987, largely because Indigenous hunting has a very visible impact on the animal. Bradley (1997) has countered these claims by the provision of very detailed observations of dugong catch numbers over more than a century. His research has documented that the numbers of dugongs taken by Yanyuwa hunters in the Gulf of Carpentaria, northern Australia, have declined from 20 per hunter per year in the 1880s to 4 per hunter per year in the 1990s. Dandrubin Gorenpul hunters in Moreton Bay, southeast Queensland (see Figure 4.2), have also taken only very few animals in recent years and have recently imposed a moratorium on any dugong hunting at all (Ross and Moreton In press).

Despite increasing anthropological evidence and Aboriginal documentation of their knowledge of and laws for the sustainable hunting of dugongs, scientists and resource managers have continued to blame Indigenous hunting as a principal cause for the species decline. The Queensland *Dugong Species Conservation Plan* (EPA 1999), and the subsequent document on the *Conservation and Management of Dugongs in Queensland* (EPA 2007), although recognizing the wide range of impacts on this mammal, have developed management controls for only two activities – fishing and Aboriginal hunting. Several areas of the Great Barrier Reef Marine Park (northeast coastal Queensland – see Figure 4.2) are now off limits to all fishing; they have been designated as 'Dugong Conservation Areas', and Aboriginal hunting is permitted in these areas only under a permit issued by QPWS and following data-monitoring by QPWS scientists.

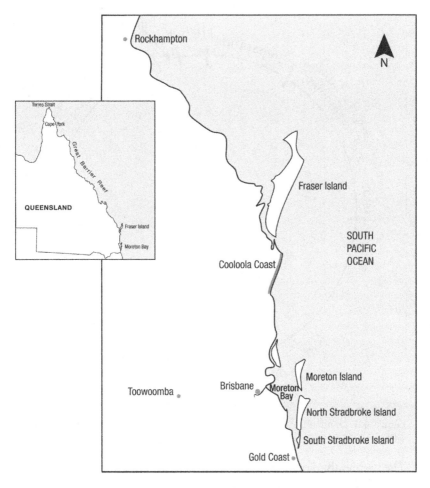

Figure 4.2 Map of southeast Queensland showing places mentioned in text.

The planning documents also include recommendations for the 'education' of Aboriginal hunters in the scientific management of dugongs, and they offer to provide Aboriginal communities with dead dugongs (those struck by power boats or caught in fishing nets) to obviate the need for hunting. According to Dandrubin Gorenpul dugong hunters from Moreton Bay, Mark Jones, Brian Coghill, and Shane Coghill, these recommendations are offensive to people who have been monitoring and caring for this resource for thousands of years and who are required by their traditional law to perform a range of rituals, songs, and ceremonies during all phases of the hunt, including preparation, hunting, butchering, and distribution of meat (Figure 4.3; see also Bradley 1997, 1998b).

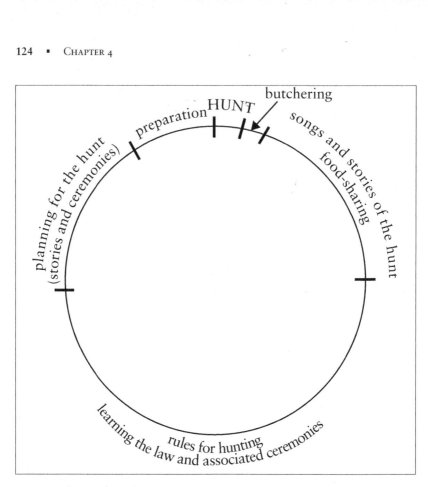

Figure 4.3 Dandrubin Gorenpul hunting cycle, showing the social framework within which hunting occurs.

The presentation of a dead dugong to a group would cause the complete breakdown of the social and spiritual elements of the dugong hunt, and the recommendation in the plan demonstrates a complete failure by scientists to listen to the knowledge provided by Aboriginal hunters and custodians of this species.

Archaeological evidence demonstrates that dugongs have been hunted by Indigenous Australians for at least 2,000 years (McNiven and Bedingfield 2008). Ethnographically, dugongs occupied a significant place in Aboriginal cultural traditions (Bradley 1997, 1998b; McNiven 2008). In many parts of northern Australia the dugong is an animal associated with creator beings, and it therefore requires great respect and correct treatment if it is to survive and remain available to Aboriginal hunters. Hunting was and is undertaken within strict social and cultural customs and controls. According to Dandrubin Gorenpul dugong hunter Shane Coghill, preparation for a dugong hunt requires the sanction of senior members of the community who have knowledge of dugong life cycles. Not only do these elders dictate where and when a dugong can be taken, they also set conditions on the age and the sex of the animal to be taken. No hunt can be conducted without the permission of these senior knowledge-holders. The preparation for the hunt involves checking and maintenance of equipment and the repetition of stories, songs, and law to reinforce correct hunting behavior (see Figure 4.3). The hunt itself is restricted to skilled men; the ability to hunt dugong was and continues to be a status marker in many dugong hunting communities (as whale hunting is among many North American communities [Freeman et al. 1998]). Once caught, the dugong is butchered and its meat and oil shared in accordance with kinship and other obligations, all determined by law. Therefore, dugong hunting is not simply a subsistence activity – it is strongly controlled and is based on generations of law and knowledge relating to its stewardship.

Aboriginal control of dugong hunting was interrupted in Moreton Bay soon after first European settlement of the area in 1828. From the mid-19th century to the 1940s a commercial dugong oil industry operated, largely managed by the missions on North Stradbroke Island (Lanyon 2003: 405). Dugong harvesting increased dramatically during this period, and dugongs were taken in ways that contradicted Aboriginal law. But following the demise of the dugong oil market and the enactment of the Queensland Aboriginals Protection and Restriction of the Sale of Opium Act of 1897, which discouraged any 'traditional' behaviors, dugong hunting all but ceased. Nevertheless, Coghill told Ross that knowledge of dugong life histories and of Dandrubin Gorenpul law relating to dugong stewardship continued to be passed down, usually in secret (see Ross and Moreton In press). By 1990 dugong numbers in Moreton Bay had returned to more sustainable levels, and dugong hunting recommenced briefly, only to be stopped again early this century as a result of a directive from senior Dandrubin Gorenpul men who have perceived new threats to this species.

For many years scientists have monitored the varying numbers of dugong all along the east coast of Queensland using mainly fixed-wing aircraft to fly over known feeding grounds (Marsh and Sinclair 1989; Marsh et al. 2004). Scientific management of dugongs is firmly based on the results of these surveys, with any decline in dugong numbers triggering the closure of certain dugong conservation zones to restrict commercial fishing (which can entangle and drown dugongs in fishing nets) and Indigenous hunting. Aboriginal concerns that scientific data are flawed and consequent management decisions defective are rarely heeded.

In Moreton Bay, dugong monitoring and count activities are carried out by QPWS staff via aerial surveys. On one such flight, QPWS staff included a local Quandamooka Aboriginal Ranger, Dandrubin Gorenpul dugong hunter Mark Jones, as a participant in the aerial count. Jones was surprised that the flight path commenced on the western side of the bay. He informed the QPWS staff that Aboriginal people in Moreton Bay had a great deal of knowledge about the habits of dugong, acquired as a result of a long history of regular (almost daily) observation and monitoring of dugong feeding patterns and movements. Such knowledge, he explained, was a requirement of all dugong hunters living in accordance with Dandrubin Gorenpul law, which dictates that any decisions about dugong hunting must be based on a careful reading of a variety of signs identifying the health of dugong populations (cf. Bradley 1997, 1998b; McNiven 2008; Sillitoe 2002). As a consequence of this knowledge and long-term monitoring, Jones knew that at this time of year dugongs always fed on sea grass beds off the southwestern coast of Moreton Island (Figure 4.2). He proposed to the aerial survey crew that a lot of time and money could be saved by flying straight to the eastern barrier islands and commencing the count there. The senior scientific officer, however, informed Jones that, as this was a *scientific* exercise, the flight path had to be the same every time the aerial survey was conducted, to ensure comparability of results from one count session to the next and to provide data that would be comparative with aerial surveys conducted elsewhere in the dugong range (Heinsohn et al. 2004; Marsh et al. 2004). Jones protested that this logic was irrational; time was being wasted, and the results would not represent reality. Why fly over an area when it was well known there would not be any dugongs there and risk running out of good light before reaching the area where dugongs were known to occur? The flight, however, continued as planned by the scientist in charge of the project.

Toward the end of the flight, few dugongs had been sighted, much to the consternation of the QPWS staff. Jones persuaded the flight crew to circle over the Moreton Island sea grass banks on the way back to base in the fading light. As the team flew high over these banks, hundreds of dugongs were sighted, but it was too late to count them. Although the aerial survey continued on the next and subsequent days, Jones remained perplexed that so much time and money could be 'wasted' on an aerial survey that was so seemingly inefficient. To further complicate matters, Jones and other Dandrubin Gorenpul dugong hunters have told Ross that dugongs have acute hearing and are easily 'spooked' by noise (information supported by Janet Lanyon [2003], a dugong scientist at The University of Queensland). Power boats and low-flying aircraft cause dugongs to panic and dive. In the highly turbid waters of Moreton Bay it is impossible to see dugongs that are not near the surface. Aerial surveys that disturb dugongs are therefore unlikely to produce accurate population counts.

Lanyon (2003: 405) has confirmed Aboriginal concerns of inaccurate aerial survey data from Moreton Bay. She records that 'previous surveys underestimated the dugong population resident within the bay through irregular and/or unrepresentative survey designs', and she particularly notes the marked seasonal variation in dugong numbers and distribution in the bay. Yet these count data form the primary source of information on which dugong conservation and management (including permitting of dugong hunting) occurs in Queensland (EPA 1999, 2007).

Pressure on Indigenous hunting of dugongs by conservation groups and governments has increased since 1999, when Aboriginal activist Murandoo Yanner won an Australian High Court Appeal that resulted in the recognition of Indigenous rights to hunt traditional animals without a government permit (Yanner 1999). Scientific evidence for a decrease in dugong numbers since 1999 based on aerial survey data, and recent scientific studies of dugong 'life histories' that show a decline in dugong birth rates, have been interpreted by scientists as a direct result of increased hunting of dugongs by Aboriginal and Torres Strait Islander hunters (Heinsohn et al. 2004; Marsh et al. 2004). Analyses of these data, however, suggest that scientists' interpretations could be insecure (Bigge 2008; McNiven and Bedingfield 2008; Ross and Bigge 2009).

Scientists are well aware of the inaccuracies of aerial survey data (Marsh et al. 2004), admitting that 'recent trends detected by aerial surveys are not a reliable index of the status of the . . . dugong population' (Heinsohn et al. 2004: 442; cf. Lanyon 2003: 405). Problems include water turbidity and the rarity of data collection points (for surveys in Torres Strait and the Great Barrier Reef [see Figure 4.2], surveys have been conducted only during three to four weeks in November and December of just four years between 1985 and 2001). Yet despite these problems, aerial survey records provide the baseline data for development of dugong population modeling and consequent species management (Heinsohn et al. 2004; Marsh et al. 2004).

Population modeling provides the basis for calculating sustainable dugong hunting levels or 'potential biological removal (PBR)' (Heinsohn et al. 2004):

$$PBR = N_{min} \times 0.5R_{max} \times RF$$

where

N_{min} = minimum population estimates based on aerial survey data,

R_{max} = maximum natural rate of population increase based on studies of dugong life history,

RF = recovery factor – a constant based on known recovery rates of cetaceans generally.

Given that this formula is used as the primary basis for calculating (scientifically) acceptable dugong harvesting rates by Indigenous hunters, and given that correct calculations for both N (population size) and R (rate of population increase) are based on the results of aerial survey data, the accurate counting of dugong population numbers is vital to the development of meaningful policies on the control of Indigenous hunting. Unfortunately, it appears that this has not been the case. Not only are aerial survey data problematic, but 'most information about dugong *life* history has been obtained indirectly from retrieved *carcasses*' (Heinsohn et al. 2004: 418, emphasis added), making R a poorly known quantity, too. With no specific RF (recovery factor) for dugongs (Heinsohn et al. 2004), we clearly see that calculations of PBR do not give Indigenous people confidence that conclusions of 'overharvesting' are supported.

Another problem with the scientific studies of Indigenous dugong take relates to the actual count of dugong harvesting. Bradley (1997) has demonstrated that dugong hunting rates in the Gulf of Carpentaria have declined by more than 80% since 1920, yet recent counts of dugong take-rates in the nearby Torres Strait suggest a massive increase in dugong hunting to unsustainable levels (Kwan 2002 in Marsh et al. 2004: 442). Kwan estimated that some 1,000 dugongs are taken each year from the Torres Strait, an unsustainable take-rate based on PBR calculations. As a consequence, Marsh and her research team (Heinsohn et al. 2004; Marsh et al. 2004) called for a major reduction or even a cessation of dugong hunting throughout the Torres Strait and Great Barrier Reef.

The problem here is that the calls for a moratorium on Indigenous harvesting are predicated on scientific data that Indigenous people cannot accept. Not only are aerial survey data problematic, as outlined above, but take estimates can also be flawed. In this case, Kwan's data were collected from April to September of 1998 and 1999 and then compared to aerial survey counts conducted during November and December of other years (Kwan 2002 in Marsh et al. 2004: 442). Given Lanyon's (2003) confirmation of Dandrubin Gorenpul knowledge that Moreton Bay dugongs are highly seasonal in their movements, and Bradley's records over some 20 years of highly seasonal behavior of dugongs in the Gulf of Carpentaria (Bradley 1997, 1998), we can clearly see that data relating to dugong numbers collected at different times of the year are not necessarily comparable.

McNiven and Bedingfield's analysis of archaeological evidence of dugong take rates in the Torres Strait over thousands of years is further confirmation of the problems of drawing management conclusions from limited data. McNiven and Bedingfield (2008) analyzed dugong bones from an archaeological mound on Mabuiag Island in the Torres Strait and discovered that during precontact times, dugong hunting rates were between 80 and 100 dugongs per year for that small island alone. If these data are extrapolated across the whole of the Torres Strait, then an annual harvest of 1,000 dugongs has been a sustainable practice in the Torres Strait for at least 400 years. From this analysis it is clear that scientific conclusions about the viability of dugong populations and the sustainability of Indigenous hunting must be questioned.

Interestingly, in these recent studies specifically dealing with Indigenous hunting of dugongs, Indigenous peoples were at no time asked by the scientists to provide their own input into the data collection, nor were anthropologists such as Bradley, who have lived with and worked with dugong hunters for over 20 years, asked for their input. Scientists have made it clear that Indigenous peoples need to be trained in monitoring techniques before their knowledge can be considered (EPA 1999, 2007). Given the inaccuracies of the scientific data collection methods, one wonders who should be training whom in monitoring and who should be teaching whom about data collection and species management!

This case study emphasizes the disconnect between scientific and Indigenous ways of knowing, in this case, data collection and interpretation versus spiritual framing of management requirements, as well as the divisions between Western and Indigenous management institutions – one a scientifically supported bureaucracy and the other a socially constituted institution of hierarchical knowledge based on kinship and Indigenous law. A similar discontinuity exists in fisheries and sea management more generally.

Fisheries Management

Barrier C – nonvalidation of IK, Barrier D – translation of IK, Barrier E – social/spiritual expression, Barrier H – spatial-temporal boundaries, and Barrier K – decentralization

The barriers to Indigenous involvement in dugong management are duplicated in other forms of marine resources management. In Moreton Bay, Dandrubin Gorenpul people have fished for sea mullet (*Mugil cephalus*) for generations; the remains of mullet have been found in shell midden deposits dating to more than 2,000 years before present (Ross and Tomkins In press; Ulm 1995; see Figure 4.4). Mullet feed in the rivers in the south of Moreton Bay before moving into the open sea to spawn and then commence their migration northward, following a set route (Barker and Ross 2003). This route takes the fish out to sea, following the east coasts of South Stradbroke, North Stradbroke, and Moreton Islands. The school turns west into the bay at the northern tip of North Stradbroke Island or at Cape Moreton, the northeastern point of Moreton Island (Figure 4.5).

Figure 4.4 Dandrubin Gorenpul traditional owners and other members of the Quandamooka community participate in the excavation of a shell midden that demonstrates the longevity of the Moreton Bay fishery (photograph by A. Ross).

According to Dandrubin Gorenpul knowledge, mullet have a social structure similar to that of Dandrubin Gorenpul people. The mullet elders show the young fish the ways of the school and lead the mullet migration. Dandrubin Gorenpul tradition states that elder mullet must not be taken while the school is migrating. This ensures that large numbers of mullet come into Moreton Bay, following the elders who know the route (Barker and Ross 2003; Ross and Pickering 2002; Ross and Quandamooka 1996b). It is only then that fish can be caught.

Before European domination of the landscape, the bulk of mullet fishing by Dandrubin Gorenpul people occurred once the mullet came into Moreton Bay. Aboriginal fisherfolk called on dolphins to help drive large quantities of fish toward the shore, where groups of men and women would wait to scoop up the fish in nets. The dolphins would be rewarded for their part in the fishing activity with a portion of the catch. The remainder would be shared among the wider Quandamooka community and their guests (Barker and Ross 2003; Hall 1984; Ross and Quandamooka 1996b; Ross and Moreton In press).

Dandrubin Gorenpul people are today not able to be involved in mullet fishing. A large commercial industry and an increasing number of recreational fishers now enjoy the vast majority of the catch (Barker and

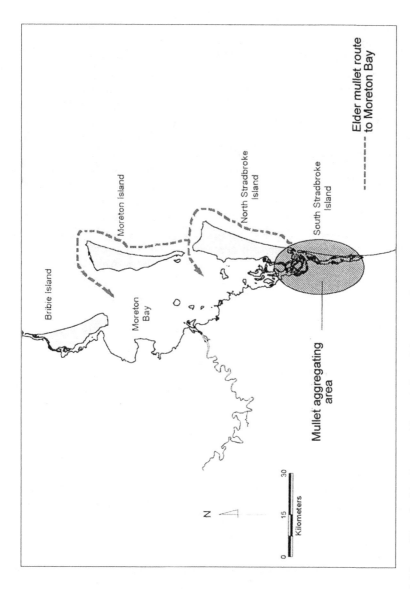

Figure 4.5 Map of Dandrubin Gorenpul knowledge of the sea mullet migration route into Moreton Bay.

Ross 2003). Today, many mullet are caught by commercial fishermen off the east coast of the islands before the fish enter the bay. Some Dandrubin Gorenpul fisherfolk believe that the failure of commercial fishing ventures to allow the mullet elders to teach their young the ways of the mullet social group is the primary cause of the decline in the mullet fishery in Moreton Bay in recent years.

Today, fishing activities in Moreton Bay are controlled and managed by the Queensland Fisheries Service (QFS, within the Department of Employment, Economic Development and Innovation [DEEDI] – formerly the Queensland Fisheries Management Authority [QFMA]), a Queensland state government authority. This scientifically based organization finds the Dandrubin Gorenpul arguments about fish social life alien to their knowledge base, and therefore no notice is paid to Aboriginal theories of fish decline (Barker and Ross 2003). Unlike Dandrubin Gorenpul knowledge of sea mullet stewardship, which emphasizes both input and output controls on the fishery, scientific management is via a system of input controls only. The input controls imposed by the QFS limit the number of commercial operators, restrict gear and boat size, provide for closure of certain areas to fishing, impose bag limits, and establish size (the larger the better) and sex criteria for marine animals permitted to be taken (QFMA 1997: 26–27). Emphasis is on the species, rather than on habitat; this is due to:

1. the definition of 'Moreton Bay' adopted by the QFS in its planning policies, and
2. the legislative limits on QFS responsibilities.

Legislative provisions limit the QFS definition of 'Moreton Bay' to the *waters* of the bay. Coastal lands, the islands of the bay, and hinterland catchments are not included. The limited perspective by QFS on what constitutes fish habitat prevents the integrated management approach of the Dandrubin Gorenpul fishers who understand the synergies between marine *and* terrestrial signals that inform an understanding of species and habitat health (Baker and Ross 2003). Furthermore, the QFS is 'responsible for the management, use, development and protection of the State's naturally occurring *fisheries resources*' (QFMA 1997: iii, emphasis added). This means that the QFS must manage *species* but not the entire ecosystem within which the resource occurs.

Wider ecosystem management is the responsibility of other government agencies. In Moreton Bay there are 14 separate pieces of legislation, administered by five different State government departments and four local government authorities, which relate to the management of the bay (QFMA 1997: 16–20). Each department and authority has a different responsibility toward the management of the resources of the bay. Consequently, demarcation and compartmentalization of responsibilities under legislation and government structure ensure that holistic management of the waters and resources of the bay, such as are demanded by the traditional owners, is institutionally impossible, however desirable it might be.

Fraser Island Dingoes

Barriers A – IK not recognized, Barrier C – nonvalidation of IK, Barrier E – social/spiritual expression, Barrier H – spatial/temporal boundaries, Barrier I – 'outsiders' kept 'outside', Barrier J – IK and management institutions, and Barrier K – decentralization

The institutional barriers that have confounded an integrated approach to the management of the sea mullet fishery in Moreton Bay are seen elsewhere in coastal Australia. Butchella (Badtjala) Aboriginal people have lived on Fraser Island and the adjacent Cooloola coast (see Figure 4.2) for over 4,000 years, according to archaeological records. Today Fraser Island is famous as a tourist destination and for its dingoes. Dingoes are a 'native dog', introduced to Australia about 3,500 years ago and considered by many Aboriginal communities to be an integral part of human society (Rose 1992). Dingoes on Fraser Island are a particularly pure breed and are therefore of great scientific significance (Phoenix-O'Brien 2002).

Until the late 1990s visitors to Fraser Island fed the dingoes, and the dogs became seemingly tame. On April 30, 2001, a nine-year-old boy was killed by two aggressive and hungry 'lone' dingoes, and there was a demand for urgent action to be taken. The loudest voices came from local residents, tour operators, park managers, and scientists. Aboriginal traditional owners were barely heard.

Scientific knowledge about dingoes focuses on their biology and behavior (Baker 2005). Scientists construct the dingo as 'natural', and its management therefore falls under the jurisdiction of the Scientific Section of the Queensland Parks and Wildlife Service. A Dingo Management Plan was written without any input from social scientists, anthropologists, or traditional owners (Phoenix-O'Brien 2002: 54), and, apart from a brief statement at the commencement of the plan that dingoes are important to Butchella people, there is no other mention of Aboriginal people or their relationship to dingoes in the plan. The management strategies that the scientists proposed for the management of dingoes focus on putting dingoes back into their 'natural' setting (Hytten and Burns 2007). These strategies are quite different from the Aboriginal approach to the animal.

Throughout mainland Australia, dingoes have a central place in Aboriginal society. Rose (1992) documents that knowledge of dingoes is linked to knowledge of country by the placing of dingoes in both nature and culture. The Yarralin Aboriginal people of the Northern Territory have linked dingoes inextricably to their law, and the dingo forms part of kinship and totemic systems and community identity:

> In Dreaming, only the dingo walked then as he does now. He was shaped like a dog, he behaved like a dog, and the dingo and human were one. It was the dingo who gave us our characteristic shape with respect to head and genitals, and our upright stance. Ancestors and contemporaries, dingoes are thought still to be very close to humans: they are what we would be if we were not what we are. (Rose 1992: 47)

For the Butchella on Fraser Island also, dingoes were, and continue to be, closely associated with people (Phoenix-O'Brien 2002). Butchella people wish to continue to interact with the dingoes on Fraser Island, to feed them and talk with them. Butchella knowledge constructs the dingo as part of the human world and not as wild.

Nevertheless, despite the differences between scientific and Indigenous constructs of Fraser Island dingoes, it would be wrong to assume that QPWS scientists had no interest in finding out about Butchella knowledge. The chief scientist on the project had a great interest in and respect for Aboriginal knowledge and wanted to include research into Aboriginal dingo-stewardship knowledge in the preparation of the plan but was thwarted by a number of political and institutional barriers to the recognition and incorporation of Indigenous knowledge into planning.

The most significant of these barriers relates to Queensland's geography and bureaucratic responses to the tyranny of distance in a large state. Most government departments in Queensland have their head offices in Brisbane, the capital city in the southeastern corner of the state. Policy is determined here, but most on-the-ground management occurs in regional offices based in various large regional towns, or in local offices based in smaller rural centers or on government protected area estate. In QPWS, scientists who work on Fraser Island are based in the Southern Region Office in Toowoomba, approximately 200 km west of Brisbane (see Figure 4.2). There are no cultural heritage officers or social scientists linked to the QPWS in this office, but within the same government building there are other DERM staff, including cultural heritage staff. The DERM cultural heritage manager sits some 30 m away from the dingo researchers. Despite this proximity of personnel, the DERM cultural heritage officer is unable to work with the QPWS zoologist, because, although Fraser Island is within the QPWS Southern Region, Fraser Island is not in the DERM Southern Region; DERM has regional boundaries different from those in QPWS. In the wider DERM structure, Fraser Island is in the Central Region, which has its cultural heritage officer in Rockhampton – 600 km north of Toowoomba (Figure 4.2). The Southern Region cultural heritage officer has no jurisdiction over Fraser Island and therefore no knowledge of the Aboriginal politics and interests of this area. The Southern Region QPWS scientist was not able to work closely with the Central Region cultural heritage manger because of the tyranny of distance and lack of funding for travel.

Discussion

Barrier B – narrow definitions

These case studies demonstrate the intersection of epistemological and institutional barriers to the incorporation of Indigenous knowledge into the bureaucratic structures that manage natural resources in Queensland, Australia. It is clear that the institutional barriers are the result of the privileging of a scientific paradigm that compartmentalizes both knowledge and management systems. Indigenous knowledge does not suffer from this division between types of knowledge and between the resource and its ecosystem but is caught up in these paradigms because of the institutions within which management knowledge is constructed.

Although the principal barriers to the genuine co-management of natural resources in Australia are seemingly institutional, the underlying problems remain epistemological. While scientists continue to be trained in positivist paradigms, there can never be an understanding by Western bureaucrats of an authentic 'one stop shop' approach to the management of country, such as advocated by Aboriginal peoples.

At the heart of all these barriers lies the most significant of all barriers to recognizing the relevance of Indigenous knowledge of land and resource management in mainstream bureaucratic structures: the view, held by some, that 'traditional' Indigenous knowledge from the past has been altered irrevocably owing to colonization and that the knowledge recorded today bears no resemblance to that held in precontact times. This barrier is most clearly seen in the Yorta Yorta High Court Native Title decision of December 2002 (Yorta Yorta 2002).

The Yorta Yorta Aboriginal people of the Murray Valley, along the border between the current states of New South Wales and Victoria, claimed native title rights over lands along the Murray River based on their unbroken connection to this land as demonstrated by their retention and maintenance of traditional land management activities. Citing archaeological evidence of campsites along the Murray River from over 20,000 years ago to the present, along with ethnohistorical accounts of Aboriginal people living on these same sites well after first European contact, and anthropological evidence of a continued attachment to these sites, the Yorta Yorta believed they had a water-tight case for native title, which requires the demonstration of a continued connection to country, in accordance with traditional laws and customs, from the time of British sovereignty (Yorta Yorta 2002). The Yorta Yorta claimed that their connection to country had survived in their modern-day desires to continue 'traditional' hunting and gathering activities and to protect midden sites and other cultural heritage places. Among many lines of evidence used as demonstration of traditional laws of traditional protection of heritage places was the Yorta Yorta's long battle to regain access to human skeletal remains illegally removed from the Murray River in the late 19th and early 20th centuries. The Yorta Yorta have been one of the pioneering Aboriginal communities in Australia to seek, successfully, the repatriation of these skeletal remains for reburial in accordance with traditional burial practices, demonstrated by archaeological evidence to date back thousands of years (Pardoe 1988).

Despite the seeming strength of these claims, the High Court ruled that none of these modern activities relating to heritage maintenance was 'traditional'. Cultural heritage management and repatriation of human remains disturbed by development and research, the Full Bench of the court found, are not 'traditional' activities, since Aboriginal people have demonstrated an active interest in the protection of heritage places only in relatively recent times. The ruling argued that 'traditional' activities, such as hunting and gathering, were desired by the Yorta Yorta only for recreational purposes. Because most members of the community were living in towns and employed, none practiced these 'traditional' ways for 'traditional' subsistence purposes. In short, the court ruled that:

> the tide of history has washed away any real acknowledgement of their traditional laws and any real observance of their traditional customs. (Justice Olney, Federal Court Judge in Yorta Yorta Native Title claim hearing, 1998, upheld in a 5-2 majority decision of the Full Bench of the High Court, December 2002; see Crawford and Cavanagh 2002)

This view arises, in part, as a result of perceptions of 'traditional' knowledge held by many in the Western world today. 'Traditional' is often regarded as 'pertaining to the past' or to 'original' belief structures. Modern expressions of Indigenous knowledge, perhaps supported by modern scientific evidence or couched in Western language, are often regarded as being so different from Western constructs and stereotypes of Indigenous 'tradition' as to be totally removed from any reality (Figure 4.6).

Although anthropologists are well aware of the changing nature of 'tradition' (for example, Ellen and Harris 2000; Gorring In prep.;

Figure 4.6 Dandrubin Gorenpul clan members attend a community information day to share knowledge about the management of resources in Moreton Bay, past and present (photograph by A. Ross).

Hunn 1993; Perkins 2001; Posey 2000), this is not the perception of most people or of the Western legal system (Gorring and Ross 2004). This is surprising given the many years of government policy that have not only encouraged and rewarded the modern manifestation of Indigenous ways but also have punished retention of the old ways.

The Australian case studies provided here demonstrate many of the barriers presented in Chapter 3. At the level of the epistemological divide, Indigenous knowledge, especially when constructed in social or spiritual terms, is rarely recognized unless translated into expressions that meet scientific requirements or unless supported by scientific proof (Barriers A, C, D, and E); and at the more practical level, Indigenous management institutions are too foreign to Western bureaucratic agencies to be easily accommodated into collaborative ventures (Barriers H, I, J, and K; see also Chapter 5).

UNITED STATES OF AMERICA – PINE RIDGE, SOUTH DAKOTA

American Indian resources were appropriated despite treaty rights by virtue of the federal trust status of Indian lands. To 'protect' Indian lands from the unscrupulous dealings of whites, the federal government defined Indian people as their wards and held all tribal lands and lands allotted to individual Indians in trust (Getches, Wilkinson, and

Williams 1998). Trust status meant that title to Indian lands could not be sold or otherwise transferred without the permission of the federal government (Prucha 1992: 344–345). It also meant that the federal government possessed a 'trust responsibility' to manage those lands in a manner that the government viewed to be in the best interest of its Indian wards.

When the U.S. government was trying to foster small-scale agricultural production, the 'best' use of Indian lands was to lease them out to white farmers and ranchers (Hurt 1987: 158–161). When the U.S. government was confronted with an energy crisis, the 'best' use of mineral-rich Indian lands was to lease them to mining companies to extract coal, uranium, and natural gas (Ambler 1990; Eichstaedt 1994). In virtually every instance, an objective review of the contractual terms of these leases would lead one to the conclusion that it was mainstream economic interests that the federal government was responsible for protecting, rather than the lands and economic interests of their Indian wards (Hall and Fenelon 2009).

The legal status of trust lands was therefore effectively used to remove Indian people from decisions about their own lands, unless Indians chose to adopt Western land management practices. The Dawes Act of 1887 was ostensibly designed to reward those American Indians who demonstrated the willingness and ability to practice 'acceptable' land-use practices, such as farming (Carlson 1981).

The establishment of reservations by treaty allowed some nominal continuation of traditional forms of political organization (Figure 4.7), although in the early years the federal government, through the Bureau of Indian Affairs (BIA), acted as the de facto source of authority on reservations (Taylor 1980: 92–96). It was not until the Indian Reorganization Act of 1934 (IRA) that the BIA began to recognize the importance of more institutionalized forms of tribal self-governance. However, the longevity of tribal self-governance was severely called into question with the advent of the Termination Policy of the 1940s and 1950s. The mission of termination was the complete integration of American Indians into the mainstream population as tax-paying citizens and the removal of tribal governments from federal tutelage to complete submission to state and local governments (Castile 1998: xxii–xxvii, 10–12). After more than two decades of disastrous outcomes from termination policies, the federal government began to swing back toward more genuine forms of tribal self-governance in the 1960s (Fixico 1998).

The approach of the Clinton administration was to respect a government-to-government relationship with tribes, directing all federal agencies and departments to implement their programs in a 'sensitive manner respectful of tribal sovereignty' (Wolfley 1998: 5). This approach was

Figure 4.7 The Pine Ridge Indian Reservation provides some degree of Indigenous control, as this sign indicates (photograph by R. Sherman).

not continued by the Bush administration. By executive order, President George W. Bush terminated three tribes in the State of Texas that had been his legal and political opponents since he was Governor of that state (Indian Country Tomorrow 2001). This attitude was carried throughout his Presidency. A more favorable approach is being implemented by the Obama administration (Capriccioso 2009; Indigenous Peoples 2010).

Dispossessing the Lakota: State Power and the Land

Barrier A – IK not recognized, Barrier B – narrow definitions, Barrier M – state power, and Barrier N – 'benevolent' West

Lakota lands (Figure 4.8) were appropriated by the U.S. government at the end of the 19th century through a series of treaties, and later through negotiated Agreements then legislated as Acts. While ceded lands were redistributed to white settlers and major business interests in what would become the state of South Dakota, reserved lands were ostensibly for the lives and livelihood of Lakota people. However, while Lakota people remained the nominal owners of reservation lands, they were legislatively dispossessed from real control over the land through the construct of the federal government holding these lands in trust for Indian people

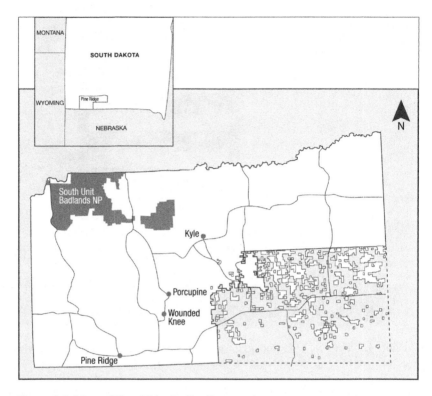

Figure 4.8 Map of Pine Ridge Indian Reservation.

(see above). This empowered the government to decide what was 'in the best interests' of their Indian wards, which from the federal perspective was rapid assimilation into white social and economic practice. This legal land status was used effectively to remove Indian people from making decisions about their own lands.

There was a synergy between assimilating Lakota people into white cultural practices and asserting governmental authority over land-management practices. From the federal point of view, agency personnel superficially assumed that Lakota ecological knowledge and conservation values 'died with the buffalo'. The government consciously turned traditional hunter-gatherer families into sedentary farmers to strip them of their Lakota culture in favor of more 'progressive civilization'. The government equated removing Lakota people's culture with removing them from nature. As General Warner noted in his 1889 address at the Pine Ridge Agency:

> You can no longer live as you did in the past. The Buffalo has disappeared from the plains. There is no longer any room for the genius of the

fisherman or the energy of the huntsman by which you can obtain a living. The white man by plowing up the soil and cultivating it and raising the flocks and herds gets the money with which to educate and clothe his children, build houses and make himself happy and comfortable. We want the time to come when your rich lands shall bud and blossom with wheat, corn and other productions. When the grass upon your boundless acres shall go to fattening your cattle, your horses and your sheep, instead of as now, left for the fire to consume it in the Spring. (Report of the Sioux Commission of 1890, Council meeting between The Commission and Chiefs, Pine Ridge Agency, June 15, 1889, p. 29 [RG 75, Entry 310, Item 40 - Report of the Sioux Commission of 1890, 4505 - 1890, Box 22, Pine Ridge Folder 3, 11E2/28/4/10])

One element of assimilation was to eradicate the tribal commons by dividing all reserved lands into individually owned land allotments, where nuclear Lakota families would become yeoman farmers as envisioned by Thomas Jefferson, instilled with the inherent value of individual property rights. Under the provisions of the Dawes Act, tribally held lands reserved by treaty were divided up into 160-acre plots and were then distributed to individual Indian households (Carlson 1981; Hurt 1987: 231). The stated motivation for this Act was embedded in the policy of assimilation: to help free Indian people from the bonds of tribalism by giving them individually held lands that they could farm as entrepreneurs in the model of white commodity agriculturalists (Taylor 1980: 41). In addition, those Indians who received allotments to engage in 'acceptable' land-use practices, such as farming, were granted U.S. citizenship, which was otherwise withheld from Indian tribal members until 1924 (Carlson 1981: 10, 24 n.19).

The reality of the Dawes Act was very different from that outlined in government propaganda. In truth, any tribal lands that exceeded the total acreage that was needed to make individual allotments to tribal members were declared 'surplus' and opened up for white settlers, often before land distributions to tribal households were complete (Hurt 1987: 168–169; McChesney 1992). The allotment process began on Pine Ridge in 1904, with a total of 2,789,309.81 acres allotted to 8,269 Indians in parcels of 640 acres to heads of families, 320 acres to wives, and 160 acres to children (1919 Annual Report, Pine Ridge Indian Agency, by Superintendent Henry Tidwell, Dec. 20, 1919 [MC 1011, Roll 106, NARS 8]). By the time the policies underlying the Dawes Act were repealed in 1934, nationally some 83 million acres of tribal lands had been taken, representing an appropriation of 60% of the total tribal lands held when the Dawes Act was initially passed (Carlson 1981; Hurt 1987: 172–173). Nearly half the remaining tribal lands were located in the semiarid or arid West.

Ultimately, government policy swayed from changing Lakota people into farmers to leasing out allotted lands to white farmers and ranchers. Any lands that were not being grazed or cultivated were viewed as wasted. Superintendent Henry Tidwell, in his 1919 Annual Report on the Pine Ridge Indian Agency, reported:

> In the past, the vast possibility of the reservation as a grazing country has never been utilized by either the Indians or whites. While Stockmen never were aware that it was possible to lease the Indian lands until a few of them made inquiry with regard thererto, but such inquiry was only made after the stockmen became cramped for pasture in other stock raising localities, due to the fact that the original homestead law was amended to permit of the homesteading of a section of grazing land where heretofore only a half section was allowed. In that way, the great open range was soon broken up for the cattlemen and pasturage had to be sought somewhere else. They therefore turned to the Indian reservation. Prior to the time that the homestead law was amended the stockmen could also obtain a great area of land for grazing at a very reasonable price, but with the influx of the homestead the price increased and this also aided materially in bringing the white stockmen to the Indian reservation. . . . [A]s a result this entire reservation has been leased by both large and small white ranchers. About three-fourths of the reservation was applied for and leased within the past two years. For the first time, therefore, in the history of the reservation, all of the grass is being utilized in the production of beef and mutton, bringing a revenue to the Indians never heretofore obtained by them. (Dec. 20, 1919, p.2 [MC 1011, Roll 106, NARS 8])

However, the lion's share of the benefits of farming and ranching was not going to Lakota landowners. As one Lakota man reported in 1938: 'These grangers, their [sic] buy Indian land and living on it and beside always leasing the other Indian land, just pay .05 or .07 or 10¢ an acre, and they making a biggest profit, and poor Indians just they get 6 or 16 dollars a year' (letter from Jacob White Eyes to John Collier, dated May 13, 1938, Kyle [Entry 121, Box 23, CCF Decimal 066, 58586-37 PR 066]). Lakota landowners lost both the economic benefits and resource management authority over their lands.

This historical overview illustrates the narrow understandings of previous governments with respect to Indian attachment to land and Indigenous knowledge about the management needs of their lands, and it also demonstrates the institutional barriers of state power and authority that existed in these times, when government control over people and their resources was wielded as benevolence but in practice had little empathy with Indian needs and desires. The response of the Lakota to the resulting dispossession further emphasizes the differences between Lakota knowledge and the ways of the bureaucracy.

Lakota Responses: The Authority of Connection

Barrier A – IK not recognized, Barrier C – nonvalidation o
D – translating IK, and Barrier H – spatial/temporal bound.

Conflicting views on Lakota ecological knowledge begin wi
history of how and when the landscape was first settled. The ..itorial
landscapes of Indigenous peoples in North America have been drawn by
Euro-Americans. The sources of information they have for native inhabi-
tation are the accounts of early explorers and the archaeological record,
which cannot be easily attached to any particular contemporary cultural
group. Furthermore, the multigenerational contours of a nomadic lifestyle have been elusive for the staunchly sedentary Euro-American. As
a result, the standard history texts assert that the Lakota people moved
into the Plains region in the early 1700s, because that is when Euro-
Americans first saw them as they moved across Minnesota and crossed
the Missouri River.

Lakota tribal histories tell a different story, one with a considerably
longer time line. Lakota oral histories describe an extended cyclical connection to the Black Hills since their emergence as a people out of Wind
Cave. The cultural knowledge of the position of constellations has been
used to establish Lakota presence in the region of the Black Hills long
before Euro-Americans place them there. As a result, Lakota people view
Euro-Americans as recent and inexperienced arrivals onto the landscape.
One Lakota man explained:

> Your society, the greater society, is basically less than 500 years old. And
> the concepts of this land – North America – how they first came here –
> their worldview. We have totally different worldviews. Our origin stories
> are different. Look at your origin stories. What do you know about man-
> kind and evolution? You know God made man in 6 days and on the 7th
> day he rested. If you look at the book of Genesis and read that, what do
> you know about your beginnings? We as Lakota people believe we came
> out of Wind Cave. Okay, so what does that attach us to? We're attached to
> the land. We have this great affinity that we're part of the land – we're not
> above it, below it, we're part of it. So if you look at the ideals of Genesis,
> that man's a creation and how the book of Genesis gives man dominance
> over the world, that's the difference that you see. We don't believe that.
> We're part of the food chain. Yeah, we do have a way of seeing the world
> differently than animals, but we believe animals to be on par. Our lan-
> guage gives credence to respect the animal nations into their own.

The mobility of the traditional Lakota lifeway is explained in relation
to its ecological impacts, designed to never overuse a particular area. As
one old man explained:

We never used or exhausted all the resources on any place we went. We'd move to a certain spot, they'd set up camp, and hunt, get our berries, hunt, and follow the year, and then they would pick a place to winter, they called it, where there was water, etcetera, and they would camp there all winter. They never get in the same place twice, and by doing so they allowed the grass, the animals, to replenish themselves. Renewable they call it today, renewable energy.

In the face of nearly a century of dispossession from their lands, Lakota people articulate their conservation values in an integrative and complex discourse (Figure 4.9). While Western ecology divides the world into living and nonliving things, Lakota conservation values infuse all aspects of the earth, the universe, with spirit, kinship, and respect. Rather than privileging certain species over others, a balance is maintained within which all creatures are valued. For example, eagles are viewed as sacred messengers, but not exclusively. Other birds and coyotes are also described as messengers. Maintaining healthy grasslands

Figure 4.9 Lakota elder Pete Helper and his daughter Darlene explain Lakota perspectives on the relationship between humans and animals (photograph by K. Pickering Sherman).

becomes a method of maintaining communication between the animal and spirit worlds.

Lakota Nomenclature: We Are All Related – Mitakuye Oyasin

Barrier E – social/spiritual expression

There is also an epistemological difference in how animals and plants are identified. For Western science, it is the material manifestations of a species that lead to identification. If the bird has a wingspan of 1.5 to 2.5 m, has talons, a yellow beak, and golden brown feathers, it is an eagle. In contrast, traditional Lakota concepts of identification turn on the behavior and talents of the animal, the internal characteristics rather than the physical manifestations. As one elder explained: 'A long time ago, the Indians claimed the eagle as holy. So whoever has the name, they consider themselves as above everyone else. So the eagle knows when something happens. They fly around the house. They know it. That's why they call them eagles'.

Another Lakota man explained that the Western distinction between living and nonliving things is inapplicable within Lakota nomenclature.

> We've always believed we come from the stars. We have our own notions of science embedded in our beliefs and the way we live. And we have that connection to stars and constellations. We never believed that the earth was flat. It was always round to us. Everything in nature was a circle. . . . We connect with every living creature, every blade of grass has a life. Even the rocks have a life, and the spirit of the wood that we burn represents god in itself. It's a light, you know. So all these things you see, that's to think about the Lakota ways. A lot of people don't articulate it. . . . And one of the greater notions in Lakota is something called *wolakota*, and that's to live in peace and harmony. You'll see that in certain elders who in retrospect know what it is to live in peace and harmony.

Animals are relatives of humans in every sense of the word. A Lakota woman recalled her father instructing her: 'I guess he said my grandpa said that when somebody passes away, so many days later [the eagles] come and how do you call that? They whistle around and I guess that's their spirit. Or a deer. They also say if a deer comes near your house after so many days after a loved one dies, that would be that loved one. The spirit would go in there, they said'. As relatives do, humans and animals look out for each other, and make sacrifices for each other's well-being. As one woman explained: 'I was taught the elk and the deer, they're like my brothers and my sisters. And on my Mom's side that's the clan they come from. And then on my Dad's side they come from the bear and the buffalo. They watch us, so every time we go out and hunt, we put out tobacco for them, thank them for giving up their lives for us to survive'.

In an interview outdoors when Pickering Sherman and members of the Lakota tribe were discussing eagles, they suddenly heard something that sounded like a man out in the trees by the creek. A middle-aged daughter said to her 93-year-old father: '*Lecala wicasa naungap*. [We just heard a man.]. *Eagle ewunglakapi ukan wicasa hotayaneche* [We were talking about an eagle, and here we heard a man]'. The father replied: '*Grave wanhehel. Hetanhe eteke* [There is a grave there. It must be from there]'. The daughter then explained: 'We talked about the eagle, and here somebody made a sound. I had a brother that died eleven months ago. The year is not even up. It's going to be up next month in June. So maybe that's him. He's come back. He really liked to talk, yeah, so maybe that's him. . . . *Tuew ecanyan hoganaeciye* [Someone really did clear their throat]'.

Lakota stewardship traditions are born of mutual respect between humans and other life forms, not out of dominion or superiority of humans over other life forms. As a result, the most common assertion in relation to Western notions of wildlife management is that the wildlife should be left alone with what they need and should be allowed to provide for their own needs. As expressed by one Lakota man in relation to traditional uses of prairie dogs:

> You see, the Lakota people are nomadic by nature. So they are not going to go and camp on a prairie dog mound and try to make sure that the prairie dogs don't spread or whatever. They are gonna camp close to them and then move on. So you know actual hands-on management was at a minimum, but they did use the prairie dog for subsistence. At that time [when Lakota people were nomadic] everything was in its place without the intrusion of man itself, everything was at a balance. So they insure that. You can practice it by leaving it well enough alone. They go to Africa, Africa alone, I think the wildlife there will manage itself. But you know you have man there studying and doing all this research and whatever and it creates problems. And they feel there is a weak portion of it they want to instill that they work on that area, and it throws it all out of balance.

Similarly, in relation to plants, like *tinpsila* or wild turnip, the man confirmed 'there is no management, but it takes care of itself'.

When another old man was asked how Lakota people managed wildlife, he replied:

> Well we didn't. I guess all the natural resources that were here at the time, they weren't like cared for the way it's kind of defined by the European

people. The best thing that we could do is to let them roam wild and not wipe out what they got to eat. If the buffalo berries, buffalos ate them things, and if we went and we destroyed everything that they ate then we wouldn't have buffalo. So probably the best thing that we could do is to let them live. . . .

The same elder was asked to compare Western and Lakota management methods. 'It's totally different, man. Because the federal people think that they've gotta pen everything up, and feed them and make sure they don't get disease and etcetera, where the Lakota people felt that the best thing that you could do for like the buffalo, the prairie dog, or whatever, is to leave them alone, and let them live, and don't take what they need'. Lakota people consistently replaced the term 'management' with the concept of 'stewardship', implying a duty of care, accountability, and spiritual obligation toward nature and emphasizing service to the land over self-interest (Carpenter , Katyal, and Riley 2009: 1067–1074; see Chapter 6).

From a Lakota perspective, when there are problems with species health, the source of the problem is seen in failed relationships, not in numbers or graphs. As one Lakota woman observed:

> Well this goes hand in hand with everything. It's a living being. All living beings are sacred. Same thing about animals. Same thing about trees. Same thing about the land. Same thing about the waters. Same thing about the air that we breathe. Same thing about the rock. They're all just related. We're just all related, I don't know how to explain it any other way. Just like you don't, like now a days, you look at kids and they just go out and kills ants. Ok why are you killing these ants? You know I mean they're killing things that they don't need to be killing because they're losing that relationship. There's just no need to be killing animals and to be going out and cutting down the tree for no reason. I mean there's just no other way to explain it.

Excessive killing is difficult to understand within a framework of relationship, as observed by one old Lakota man: 'I've known guys go out and shoot wild turkeys, we got a lot of wild turkeys, they shoot twenty, thirty wild turkeys. What for, you know? I never understood that. Why would they kill thirty turkeys? And I seen them do it, but you know the strange thing is that the turkeys outlasted the hunters'.

Those most connected to the land are identified as the best stewards of the lands, with all Lakota people encouraged to increase the connections they have to the land. The traditional ecological knowledge is not asserted or separated from people directly engaged in practical knowledge applications. The knowledge cannot be catalogued and extracted for its 'usefulness' to development, since it is situated, embedded, and particular (Pickering Sherman, Van Lanen, and Sherman 2010).

The source of knowledge is not abstracted from the resource but is born of experience with the resource:

> The buffalo nation, in our own education and observations, we have learned from the buffalo that they have a particular way of living. They're the ones that we received the concept of surrogate motherhood, because they take in orphans and they do travel in families. So observations of nature are time proven by other animals and how they survive. They taught us. That's where we went to college and got our education. It all comes with the experience of living with the land and having the respect to see the animals, to see them as nations on their own and how they all complement one another.

Lakota stewardship principles, therefore, are embedded within social and moral precepts of respect, kinship, reciprocal obligation, and sustainability, not simply utilitarian use (Figure 4.10). It is not salvage conservation focused on particular species, or the privileging of certain species over others, but an integrative and holistic view of the landscape populated with relatives, each deserving of respect. The notion of limits is integral to this perspective. As one elder noted:

> I know that there isn't really any possibility of going back to the way that the Great Spirit intended for the land to be used, but I think that they should take a very serious look at what they're doing to the land. Once they do they're going to realize what's causing it, and once they find the cause they better look for an answer how to fix it, because you know and I know that there's an end to everything. Once you use up everything that Mother Earth's got to offer, you ain't got nowhere else to go.

Fundamentally, they are reasserting Lakota identity and the fact of Lakota cultural survival. In their subjective perceptions of wildlife populations based on experience, they present a direct challenge to scientific models that set harvest limits without physical reference to the animals themselves. Ultimately, though, there is a sense that white people will eventually understand that they don't know what they are doing and will finally ask Lakota people to share what they have always known. 'Then once . . . our culture is healed and you'll see it come back and . . . eventually it'll really, you know, help people around them. Like Sitting Bull once said that the *Wasicu* or country is going to come to us and ask us how we do this . . . , or come for our help and he said what we're going to tell them is that it's the Pipe. That Pipe is what lead us'. By reference to the *Canunpa,* or sacred pipe, a symbol for prayer and healing within Lakota traditions, the implication is that the only way to understand Indigenous knowledge is to understand Indigenous spirituality.

Figure 4.10 Members of the Lakota Buffalo Caretakers Cooperative implement their Lakota perspectives on economy, culture, spirituality, governance, and land conservation through their stewardship of bison (photograph by D. Bartecchi).

The Source of Ecological Decline

Barrier A – IK not recognized, Barrier C - nonvalidation of IK, Barrier J – IK and management institutions, Barrier M – state power, and Barrier N - 'benevolent' West

In contrast to the social and spiritual context for knowledge outlined above, the Western approach to resource management has been to dominate and change nature for human purposes alone. One early Indian Agent working with the Lakota at Whetstone Agency in South Dakota from 1869 to 1870 exemplified this perspective when he reported:

> Nature seems to resent the first attempts to cultivate the soil in this far-off land, and turns upon the hardy intruder her whole battery of weapons. Terrible rain storms deluging the land, and often mixed with hail of sufficient size to destroy vegetation and endanger animal life; the waterspout and wild tornado; the scourge of the locust, the grasshopper and the beetle. But if he be patient, and continue to turn aside the water-shed of nature formed by the close-matted roots and grass of the broad prairie, uncovering the rich black mold, *he will be rewarded by a gradual change in climate*; for the rain absorbed by the cultivated soil will be

given back into the air, again returning in dews and gentle showers. But this is a lesson not easily taught the Indian, who has a childlike interest in the present and small care for the future. (Poole 1881 [1988]: 38–39, emphasis added)

Given our current experiences with global climate change, this early assertion of the impacts of Western agricultural practices is ironically prophetic.

Far from admiration for the marvels that scientific management regimes brought to the reservation, Lakota people bemoan the negative effects that Western management have had for native species of plants and animals on the reservation. From these view points, the government management has been at the helm of natural resource management during a period of incredible ecological degradation and species loss, beginning with the demise of the buffalo: 'Most people don't even know American history because I guess the conquerors write the history. But yeah, there was a great effort to wipe out the buffalo. It was one of the greatest ecological disasters in this country'.

Other local extinctions include the grizzly bear, grey wolf, and Audubon bighorn sheep. As late as the 1950s, three species of grouse flourished on the reservation; now only one remains. Many species of plants, such as Barr's milkvetch and the western prairie fringed orchid, have also been lost, as have species of fishes, reptiles, and amphibians. A small species of fox (*vulpes velox*), commonly known as the swift fox, was nearly extirpated during the campaign to eliminate prairie dogs by chemical means (Sherman 2007).

The assumption that 'the government knows best' is not one made by Lakota naturalists. When asked about reservation lands, an elder man responded:

Well, they're being managed by the United States government, and anything managed by them couldn't be good. Because you know if you drive across, through here, you look out and you see that a lot of the land is white spots that are in these fields and stuff. They don't grow nothing, in the fall of the year, that'll be the only bald spot. They're killing the land and that's by overplanting and that type of stuff. I think they're not doing a real good job, and they're expecting too much out of a small parcel of land. They're trying to get millions, and what it boils down to, instead of caring for the land, it's 'we're going to make millions, hell with the land, we'll kill the land, so what, we got our money'. What they don't understand, the old 'give a man a fish' routine comes back into play. They keep doing that, pretty soon they ain't going to have any land.

An elder woman concurred: 'I have noticed like there is less antelopes. We used to see them all over. Now there is hardly any, and like for some reason the deer all get disease, certain kinds of disease, so we are even worried about killing deer now'.

A Lakota elder described how the government approached eagle management, oblivious to the religious and spiritual significance of eagles to Lakota people (omitting the past tense which is not a feature of Lakota language apart from the context):

> The Indians, you know, old days, this. They kill them [eagles] and make a costume for themselves, the Indians. Like, you know, dance. Put everything on his body and dance. And but now they [the government] know that. They know that, and they make a law on them, and if anybody shoot them, the eagle, they're going to punish them, right now. You see war dance any place. There's a war, you know, use the feathers all over his body and dance. Pow-wow. And they call them a really high place.

His daughter added: 'I guess what he is saying is the eagle is real high. It's highly, what you call it, respected by us. . . . Eagles really have power to us'. The spiritual implications of misusing or mistreating eagles are so profound that the idea of the government claiming some higher authority to punish people for their spiritual appeal to the power of eagles is ludicrous. In this context, then, Western techniques for species protection are absurdly black and white, born of a mentality of use value rather than spiritual value or balanced relationships between humans and nature.

Lakota people discuss the impact of Western economic practices on the land in terms of holistic ecosystems and species interaction that contemporary environmental scientists claim to be 'bringing to management'. There is a strong interest in returning buffalo to the lands, in part because of their more adapted integration into and co-existence with the other natural resources of the Plains. Prairie dogs, living symbiotically with buffalo and providing food for the eagle, are also important. The government practice of poisoning prairie dogs was opposed, because this 'management' technique was hurting eagles, particularly since the real long-term solution was to stop overgrazing.

Similarly, *tinpsila,* or wild turnips, also viewed as a special Lakota food, are threatened by cattle. Cattle are an invasive species at the forefront of degrading reservation natural resources. As one Lakota man explained: 'The cattle are genetically engineered animals that aren't a compliment to the ecosystem. The buffalo created the Plains and now cattle are pretty destructive environmentally and they're destroying a lot of the Plains – if you look at the images from space there are a lot of bare areas. And it doesn't improve the quality of the water in the Plains'. The species in decline are those threatened by cattle grazing, road development, and fencing.

In contrast, buffalo figure in Lakota discourse as a return to traditional Lakota identity and to the qualities of self-sufficiency, hard work, and connection to nature that are the most desired aspects of earlier Lakota life (Figure 4.11). Another man added: 'Traditionally they said the buffalo is the one that managed the prairie dogs. They're the ones that actually covered the holes if they were getting too bad, and they covered the holes of the prairie dogs, so that's how they were controlled that way, through the bison. But, cows they don't do that. They add to the overgrazing of the land, whereas the buffalo was kind of a more intelligent animal too'. A woman noted the social benefits of raising buffalo on your own land: 'If they don't have a regular job, there's always other things to do, like the garden, the children, the horses. My brother raises buffalo out in the country out there, and he's really, really busy all the time. He always has his kids working, which I think is good'.

There is more at stake than philosophy in the decision about land-use policies. Three-quarters of all households, and more than 80% of traditional households, continue to use wild resources (Pickering and

Figure 4.11 Butchering a buffalo on Pine Ridge Indian Reservation. Skills in buffalo field processing, which had been lost over the last century, are now taught through actual involvement and practice rather than through books or classrooms (photograph by A. Ross).

Jewell 2008). The destructive practices of overgrazing, and the great impact cattle have on the health of the land, are directly affecting wild plant species on the reservation.

More destructive uses, like mining, are opposed for similar reasons: 'I grew up in the Badlands', one Lakota man explained, 'and there's a lot of wildlife out there, and it's a beautiful, beautiful place. I'd rather see buffalo herds and ecotourism, rather than destroy the Badlands. We have some people here trying to promote that zeolite mining [in the Badlands]. . . . As long as the resource is there, they'll do it. It may not be in my lifetime, but . . .'

It is clear from this range of examples that there is a pronounced disconnect between Lakota knowledge and land stewardship, on the one hand, and Western natural resource management systems, on the other. Lakota knowledge is based on kinship relations between people and resources, and stewardship practices must recognize the complex interaction between humans and plants and animals. State authorities rarely recognize or understand such reasoning, and conflicts between bureaucratic decision makers and Indian knowledge holders have been a regular consequence of this epistemological and institutional divide.

Institutions and Land Management

Barrier G – ownership of knowledge, Barrier J – IK and management institutions, Barrier K – decentralization, and Barrier O – globalization

Given the connected view between humans and nature that Lakota people express, the practices of commodity agriculture, and cattle ranching in particular, are seen as ecologically damaging by many Lakota residents. However, because of a combination of the trust status of the land, and the subordinate authority of the IRA tribal government, land-management policies continue to be skewed toward the needs of cattle.

Initially, federal agencies responsible for reservation lands, centralized within the Bureau of Indian Affairs, were structured to privilege Western economic views of nature as use values. With the advent of the Indian Reorganization Act in 1934 and the Indian Education and Self-Determination Act of 1975, some of this responsibility has been returned to formally recognized tribal governments. However, these tribal governments are themselves a structure created by the federal government to emulate the ideals of Western constitutional governance. Centralization was imposed through the creation of constitutional tribal reservation governments in the 1930s. In the United States the establishment of reservations by treaty allowed some nominal continuation of traditional forms of political organization, although in the early years the federal government, through the Bureau of Indian Affairs, acted as the de facto source of authority on reservations (Taylor 1980: 92–96). It was not until the Indian Reorganization Act of 1934 (IRA) that the BIA, under the leadership of John Collier, began to recognize the importance of more institutionalized forms of tribal self-governance. 'Collier succeeded in preserving Indian identity from complete absorption within the "melting pot" by creating a system of autonomous tribal entities *within* the political and economic superstructure of American society as a whole' (Castile 1998: xix). Unfortunately, the approach of the IRA had less to do with restoring traditional forms of tribal political organization than with standardizing tribal governments to reflect U.S. Constitutional form and inject the oversight authority of the U.S. Secretary of the Interior (Castile 1998: xviii–xx; Taylor 1980: 97–107).

Tribal constitutional governments remain beholden to the revenues and fiscal oversight of Washington, D.C. The cost of running a tribal government in compliance with federal standards creates pressure to generate tribal revenues. In the absence of any industrial or other private sector economic base, the main areas of revenue generation have been leasing tribal lands out for agricultural uses, along with some limited revenues from a remote and modest tribal casino. The tribal government has run up millions of dollars of debt, primarily from salaries for government employees building the tribal government institutions that ultimately facilitate economic appropriations from the outside. To offset these debts, the tribal government floats bonds that are secured by the pledge of future income streams from tribal land leases. Therefore, the interests of commodity agriculture continue to take priority from the perspective of the tribal government, regardless of priorities of tribal members. The BIA then manages and regulates the lease arrangements for tribal lands, since they are leased under federal trust oversight. As in the developing world, debt for infrastructure becomes the trap for inducing and then indenturing local governments to act in favor of global capital interests rather than in their own local interests. The result is a highly compromised form of self-governance, vulnerable to simultaneous disavowal from both the federal government and the Lakota people. When asked how effective tribal government is, more than 55% of the reservation replied it was ineffective or very ineffective (Pickering and Jewell 2008).

For the average Lakota tribal member, outside cattle interests have more power over tribal government than they do. The conflicts between cattle operators and Lakota people dominate discussions of nature, land, and economics, and Lakota concerns are consistently subordinated. As one Lakota man explained: 'It's supposed to be open range, but that's a big issue here. There's a guy that's part White and [part] Indian who leases land off the Indians to put his cattle on, and now four people have died on this road 'coz of his cattle. Now it looks like the animals have more rights than humans. . . . That didn't give the rancher the right to let his animals roam the land and let people die because of his animals'. To this day, there are stories of white leasers acting like landowners, denying access to and even physically assaulting the actual Lakota landowners who attempt to utilize the wild resources on their own land. An elder woman observed: 'The full bloods are always still struggling to get into housing or we have problems with our leasers, yeah white ranchers, they even chase us off of our own land, so that is kind of hard'.

The feeling of subordination continues into the political realm as well. As one Lakota man said:

> If I had my way, the buffalo would be top priority over cattle, and that's how it used to be on our reservation. [The land] used to be just one solid color. But the Stock Grower's Association all around the Pine Ridge Reservation, they pushed the Congressmen to start giving these allotments to Indians, like the head of household got six-hundred forty acres, and then the eighteen-year-old or the wife got a hundred and eighty, and then the next kid, the eighteen-year-old got eighty acres, then it went down forty acres. And so when they had Congress do that to these reservations, then the Stock Growers were able to come in and say who can lease the land or not. And it took the power away from the tribal government, at that time. Otherwise the tribal government wouldn't even let the Stock Growers come into our reservation. So once they did that now, you got Stock Growers.

When Lakota people observe natural resources in stress, they have to hope the federal government will act, because Lakota people have been disempowered as stewards of the land. Lakota narratives of land management often involve waiting for the government to finally discover what Lakota people knew all along, as one man explained in relation to the recovery of bald eagles:

> I would say that the United States wanted to put that Endangered Species Act on bald eagle, and many eagles and hawks, I think that kind of deteriorated the economic development of the eagle feather. I would say that was good, I'd say. Otherwise, they might have become extinct. Our people knew about this, but we couldn't do nothing. . . . We did put a stop to that strychnine, that's what they were using against these prairie dogs, and the eagles come down and eat the poisoned prairie dogs and they got killed, so we put a stop to that use of strychnine. There's a lot of them [eagles] coming back now, but I would say it's due to the prairie dog population.

One might argue that the most direct solution to the problem of reservation resource management would be to demand an end to the federal trust status of land and a removal of the artificially imposed institutions of the constitutional tribal government. However, the pitfall in this logic is that without federal trust status, lands are no longer governable by the tribe and revert to the jurisdiction of the state where they are located. Furthermore, tribal self-governance is a political status conferred over the land base held by tribes. Without that federally defined land base, there is no claim to tribal self-government. The politically defined solution to federal trust status is the loss of tribal sovereignty and the social, cultural, and political protection that implies. So how are Lakota conservation values to fair between this rock and a hard place?

Managing from the Grassroots Up: Collective Action without Institutions

Barrier K – decentralization and Barrier O – globalization

The answer lies in the methods Lakota people have had for surviving within the context of domination. Lakota people have become adept at keeping their agendas moving forward despite government interference. They have found that using indirect methods that do not trigger assertions of federal authority are more successful than directly challenging the dominance of the federal government. Indirect methods of action become equivalent to a kind of political adverse possession, that after having been involved in a practice long enough, the government loses its authority to stop the practice, since if the practice were a real challenge to government authority, the government should have noticed the activity before now and acted on it.

As a result of the Lakota grassroots action to ensure that their own cultural practices remain intact, the impetus for greater conservation measures within Indian country can be seen to be coming from Indian communities themselves, not from government institutions or NGOs. These communities are witnessing the loss of their natural resources through the management of their lands exclusively for commercial agriculture and are poised to make a change.

Part of the success of this grassroots movement is that it lacks centralization or utilization of processes recognized by the state and therefore is going forward largely unobserved. One bison operator characterized the participants in this grassroots movement thus: 'Human beings, common guys, that's what we are, *ikce wicasa* (common man)'. This same strategy was used successfully by Lakota people to maintain their language, religion, and social customs during the darkest days of forced assimilation policy by the government. The Western need for rapid progress runs directly counter to Lakota patience in pursuing a strategy that is intended to be so gradual as to go unnoticed. The visibility that reinforces a sense of accomplishment for the Western mind violates the basic premise of how this movement can succeed. Fundamentally, the physical move back onto the land will accomplish a political move of regaining control and stewardship of the land for Lakota purposes, rather than for the purposes of commercial agriculture. In their visualization of a subsistence base for land use, Lakota people are presenting an alternative to global market domination. One Lakota man articulated this altèrnative future:

> Have our own food, let the bison roam openly like they did a couple hundred years ago. On this two million acre piece of land here? Oh yeah! Everybody just live in common. Self-sustaining, through bison, through our own food, doing our own renewable energy and just get back to the simple way. . . . Just go back to the natural way, 100%, and get away from the feds and everybody else. We can do that, we are nation . . . right on, man! We can do it! . . . [Then] we won't even think about any kind of political problems. Just imagine yourself in that world. You don't even deal with that [politics].

Questioning the authority of the BIA to act in their best interests, some Lakota landowners have decided to negotiate directly with their lessees, despite the assertion of the BIA that they (the BIA) should be involved. If the Lakota are successful in displacing white ranchers from the reservation, despite bureaucratic obstacles, the question remains whether 'conservation' will become a future strategy for displacing the Lakota once again. Internationally, Indigenous communities are portrayed as opposing conservation, because of their traditional uses of wild species that are now vulnerable in large part because of globalized appropriation of Indigenous resources. By fighting 'what is best', as defined by the government, Lakota people run the risk of being labeled anti-environmental.

A growing number of Lakota households are using the expiration of a lease term to regain beneficial use of their lands, for housing, for subsistence, and for cultural expression. Land consolidation is another growing phenomenon. A full 62% of households said they would like to live on their own land, and another 20% expressed a preference for living in a rural isolated home. However, currently only 23% of households are living on their own land (Pickering and Jewell 2008).

These family-based efforts to recover the land by turning to traditional forms of governance are grounded in Lakota conceptions of decentralized decision making and virtually complete local authority. They are working independently, discovering through social networks how others have succeeded in implementing a new land regime. Here we see the very type of experimentation, sharing results, testing new methods that are the hallmarks of science. As one bison operator envisioned: 'Bring everything back in a sacred motion, hey-ya. . . . Everybody happy, the ol' IRA thrown out the door, everybody looking toward the future excitedly, kids happy, everybody, old people'. The content and organization of this revolution defies Western expectations, however, and therefore is going essentially unnoticed by the powers that be. The movement is decentralized, disbursed across a broad array of individual landowners, both those in possession and those dispossessed from their lands.

The strength of decentralization, however, highlights the greatest obstacle to collaborative conservation. To work collaboratively, partner organizations need to recognize what the project entails. For academics and environmental activists, the Western epistemological approach is obscuring the object of their collaborative efforts. Without a centralized entity, outsiders interested in collaboration are frustrated, looking for leadership. The efficiency so prized by a market paradigm becomes a barrier to working in a context of disbursed individuals moving an often unstated vision forward within their own time and place.

The Boundaries of Management Authority

Barrier H – spatial/temporal boundaries

Reservations themselves were the first imposition of artificial boundaries onto a historically fluid landscape. As one Lakota man explained:

> Upon the changing of the complexity of our land here, being put on this reservation and having its boundaries, people used to practice a variety of different cultural activities anywhere in this land that comes from way down the eastern end of Nebraska, southeastern end all the way to Montana in the mountains. So what we did was, when they made these boundaries here, it created that isolation for the ceremonies. So people had to go to that Badlands, the northern part [of the reservation], and what they did is they did the ceremonies, the *Hanbleciya*, the eagle catches, the variety of different aspects of culture in seclusion, away from mainstream society. People over here, they had a lot of traffic. Pine Ridge was the hub of everything even then. So what they did in order to get away from everybody, they took the ceremonies out that way.

From a Lakota perspective, it is not of great consequence whether land is park land, tribal land, or private land, the significance comes in the relationships of respect that are shown for the land. Lands themselves are to be treated with respect. Land is associated with intergenerational care and training, the physical location through which knowledge and spirituality is transmitted.

This view of land runs counter to the typical approach of Western park management, which emphasizes compromise to accommodate competing uses. For example, places such as Bear Butte, in the Black Hills, are areas of special significance for prayer for Lakota people. The perspective of Western state and federal land managers has been to determine which week Lakota people need access or want the access of competing tourists restricted. Bear Butte has even been proposed as the site for a shooting range and biker bar by non-Indian interests. These conceptions, from a Lakota perspective, imply that somehow the sacred nature of places can be turned up or down, like the heat on a furnace, and radiates to some artificially determined boundary line but no farther. For those immersed in Lakota cosmology, this view of the sacred is unthinkably limited.

The Lakota concept of individualism is strong and supported in the realm of wildlife, where each person has animals of special significance only to them, born of various ceremonies and rituals. As an elder Lakota woman explained: 'For other people it comes to them as a dream, certain animals that they dream about, they go on vision quests for, the bear, and the spider, there are people that do have the characteristics of these animals. [But that would be] individual, yeah, to certain people'.

In sharp contrast to developing countries around the world, there are no local environmental organizations to speak of on the Pine Ridge Reservation. Yet, the individual responses of Lakota household participants indicate that there is a strategic agenda in place that it designed to recover control and conservation of nature as it is defined by Lakota ecological knowledge.

Discussion

The Lakota case study demonstrates the salience of the barriers to genuine co-management outlined in Chapter 3. Lakota natural resource stewardship practices were either ignored or disparaged, as Western ideals of agricultural land use were imposed within the newly defined Reservation boundaries. The concept of land as a commodity to be owned was forced onto the Lakota through an allotment system, and then beneficial ownership of those lands was removed from the Lakota through the fiction of the government holding those lands 'in trust' for the Lakota people. Structurally, the existing Lakota system of resource knowledge, spread throughout the tribe, was dismantled as federal agents took charge of the administration and management of Lakota resources 'for the good' of the Lakota. Indigenous knowledge holders were excluded from the process of land and resource management, and only those who embraced cattle ranching or farming were deemed 'progressive'.

In the contemporary reservation setting, conflicts between the Lakota and Western knowledge systems continue unchecked. Lakota conceptions of nature as instilled with spiritual and social significance are trampled by the narrow economic interpretations of land by the federal and tribal structures dedicated to supporting the cattle industry. The hierarchical and centralized tribal government, which was created in the image of the U.S. government, bears no resemblance to the decentralized concepts of governance and decision making that are comfortable for grassroots Lakota people. Ironically, those with the greatest knowledge of the lands and resources on the Reservation have the least power to influence management decisions about those resources. Wild plants and animals continue to play a significant role in the nonmarket based economic practices of Lakota households but are given little or no weight in the management regimes imposed by federal agencies and the Westernized tribal government. The Lakota are poised to create change within the power constraints of the federal Reservation system, however. By exercising their rights to obtain beneficial use of their allotted lands when cattle leases expire, Lakota families are slowly moving back onto the resource and revitalizing their ancestral traditions of self-sufficiency through integration with nature. Rather than a Western form of revolution, however, a more subtle and culturally appropriate Lakota response to these co-management barriers has begun, through individual and family-based determination to continue their hunting and gathering practices, to transfer their Lakota knowledge to the next generation, and, when possible and effective, to confront the governmental structures with concrete alternatives that allow for collaboration between the best of Lakota and Western management approaches.

The Lakota examples, therefore, clearly demonstrate the epistemological barriers regarding the recognition of Indigenous knowledge; the socially and spiritually constituted knowledge that links people and animals as kin cannot be accommodated in Western ways of knowing and consequently Lakota have been required to establish a common language with the West to demonstrate their connection with land and nature (Barriers A, B, C, D, and E). As well as a common language, Lakota people have had to adopt Western governance structures that have displaced traditional law and even imposed Western species on the land, which have subsequently imposed a Western debt structure on the whole community (Barriers G, J, and K), while all the while the state continues to exercise ultimate control over all aspects of Lakota life, ostensibly for the good of the people, but in reality to the detriment of traditional systems of stewardship and knowledge (Barriers M and N).

India – Southwest Rajasthan

India's tribal groups (usually referred to as 'Adivasi') often inhabit isolated hills and forests that they worship 'animistically' (Snodgrass, Lacy, et al. 2008; Snodgrass, Sharma, et al. 2007, 2008; Snodgrass and Tiedje 2008; Tiedje and Snodgrass 2008). They are foragers and swidden agriculturalists and thus generally semi-independent of the dominant settled society that surrounds them. Indigenous peoples in India also continue to inhabit protected and reserved forests, parks, and wildlife sanctuaries.

Phulwari ki Nal, in the Indian state of Rajasthan, is the largest nonfragmented forest tract remaining in the Aravalli Mountains (Figure 4.12). It is seen as a key to local 'ecological security' in the way its lush greenery checks the advance of the Thar desert from the western regions of the state, protects the watershed of the entire region, and provides for local livelihoods in so many diverse ways. Local tribals, mainly Bhils, Girasias, and Kathodias, continue to inhabit this park.

In 1988 Phulwari ki Nal was passed to the Wildlife Wing of the Rajasthan Forest Department (RFD) as a Wildlife Sanctuary, and most of the RFD's management activities now center on the protection and restoration of wildlife and wildlife habitat. In the precolonial, colonial, and more recent postcolonial past, the forests of Phulwari ki Nal were valued primarily for their *economic* benefits to larger state political formations, rather than for their usefulness to locals or to the Indian people as a whole. Today, tree felling is not allowed within the sanctuary, either by the state or by locals, except when necessary to protect wildlife. Nevertheless this rule is regularly violated.

Other economic activities by Adivasi are permitted (if sometimes only informally by the RFD and not specifically in law). These include open grazing of animals in those degraded woods not closed off for recovery or planting of saplings; taking of dead wood for fuel; collection of fruits and tubers for food; extraction of gum from trees for consumption and for sale; and the use of certain plants for medicinal purposes.

The Adivasi communities living in and adjacent to the park are impoverished and growing in numbers. They place a growing pressure on natural areas such as Phulwari ki Nal, and these pressures bring conflict over resource use in this protected area.

Conflicts over Conservation Goals

Barrier A – IK not recognized, Barrier C – nonvalidation of IK, and Barrier J – IK and management institutions

A significant barrier to collaborative management in Phulwari ki Nal is the perception by many RFD employees of local tribal communities as their main opponents in the battle to save Phulwari, not as potential conservation partners. Many RFD employees perceive tribal communities as 'enemies' of the forest as a result of their harvesting and other natural resources extraction activities in the park.

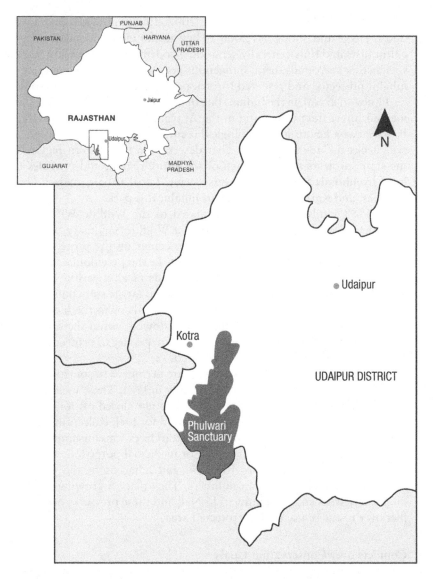

Figure 4.12 Map of Udaipur district and Phulwari ki Nal Wildlife Sanctuary.

Despite this perception, however, most RFD officials have admitted that locals possess a deep and rich knowledge of the local flora and fauna. Adivasis, from children to elders, can easily name and identify hundreds of useful trees, plants, roots, and other forest products, and they are respected for their 'ethnoforestry' knowledge. Adivasis are, in fact, sometimes consulted by the RFD regarding tree management (as in the case of RFD ranger, Dr. Satish Kumar Sharma, one of Snodgrass's research collaborators).

RFD officials (such as Dr. Sharma) also recognize that tribals have a deep knowledge of ecology, in the sense that they are seen to grasp the holistic interrelationships between the different elements of an ecosystem. Yet some officials believe that all this Adivasi knowledge, however deep, is typically used to *exploit* the forest, rather than to protect it for long-term sustainable use. Locals are seen to use their superior knowledge of the woods of Phulwari to exploit local forest resources before others are able to do so. Because locals are believed to possess knowledge of how to exploit the forest, but not knowledge of how to conserve it, members of the RFD are reluctant to turn over control of this sanctuary, even in limited form, to local tribals.

In this sense, then, the barrier to Indigenous involvement in land management is not so much a failure by managers to recognize the existence of Indigenous knowledge per se but a failure to recognize that this knowledge is relevant to land management, because the Indigenous knowledge does not clearly relate to government paradigms of conservation or forest management; paradigms that inform government management institutions, like the RFD.

Religious Expressions of Resource Values

Barrier E – social/spiritual expression

The previous barrier, at first glance, relates to the perception by the state that locals are primarily nonsustainable users of the forest and thus not true managers and certainly not conservationists. But this would not be an entirely accurate conclusion, because the RFD has blamed the local failure to conserve less on knowledge per se and more on local religious values that failed to guide the deployment of this knowledge (Snodgrass, Lacy, et al. 2008; Snodgrass, Sharma, et al. 2007, 2008).

An example of this is the way that Bhil tribals promised their mountain gods 'gifts of fires'. If certain boons, such as gifts of health, wealth, and prosperity, are granted to Adivasi supplicants, tribal believers reward the giving deity by setting an entire mountaintop aflame. Such ritual practices are described by Bhils as 'fire baths' or 'black skirts' for the way they can leave an entire slope darkened.

RFD rangers acknowledge that locals are, at times, ahead of modern resource managers in their recognition of the way fire can promote forest health. Nevertheless, the ritual practice of 'fire baths' is not recognized as an attempt to promote healthy forests; these religiously motivated fires often burn very hot and do great damage to the jungle. Foresters thus cited these religious rites, and other similar practices, as evidence of the narrow-minded and even irrational nature of local Adivasis. In the state's eyes, local tribals practice rites that are meant to ensure *human* prosperity, but not nature's. Such practices, foresters explain, demonstrate the local view of the forest as divine and thus a potentially limitless source of power and welfare. Such views are not compatible with the RFD's conception of the park as a fragile and potentially exhaustible natural resource. Overall, the RFD does not think that traditional ecological knowledge of the forest, no matter how old and how deep, could be effectively guided by an irrational religious system of exchanges between hungry humans and their superhuman gods who demand violent recognition of human love and respect. What are needed, the foresters argue, are the sound principles of modern forest management.

This example supports the ideas raised in the first discussion presented – the RFD does generally recognize the existence of Indigenous knowledge but cannot see the value of such knowledge in scientifically informed land management practices.

Lack of Indigenous Institutions

Barrier A – IK not recognized, Barrier K – decentralization, and Barrier L – racial/cultural inferiority

Another barrier to potential forest co-management efforts in Phulwari is the perception by some members of the RFD that locals do not have the institutional wherewithal to manage the resources of the sanctuary. RFD employees sometimes comment on the social fragmentation – on individual, household, clan, and tribal levels – within the communities inhabiting Phulwari. Many rangers argue that, on individual psychological levels, locals are unable to think beyond their own immediate self-interests. Any management institutions that demand individual and household restraint in the service of larger social interests have disappeared, and any remaining collective efforts at joint management and defense of local forests, however feeble, are perceived to be simply overwhelmed by tribal poverty, overpopulation, the allure of markets for forest products, and the overall complexities of modernity (Figure 4.13). Many RFD staff believe that tribals are unable to manage their own communities as a result of their illiteracy, poverty, lack of family planning, and general 'backwardness'. To expect them to be able to manage the natural resources around them, and certainly to rely exclusively on them to do so, would be to invite disaster, many RFD staff believe.

We disagree, in part, with these assessments of local knowledge, values, and institutional potential. The small Kathodia population seems to use the forest in a largely sustainable manner. Most Kathodias are

Figure 4.13 Bhil laborers are paid by the RFD to build roads, 'check-dams', wild animal watering holes, and other structures within the sanctuary (photograph by J. Snodgrass).

generally landless and as such do not have the same impact on the forests as other tribals in the area. In addition, in our opinion, Kathodias maintain closer cultural ties to the forest itself than do other tribal communities, such as the Bhils; for example, they are known for their unique form of worship of snakes, monkeys, and leopards. Though landless and thus heavily dependent on the forest for their survival, they seem to recognize, through a combination of religious respect and enlightened self-interest, the need to treat the forest well.

Bhils in Phulwari, too, are especially careful to protect and tend to the various useful and economically valuable trees in the area. For example, most fruiting trees are not generally cut and nor are a variety of religiously significant trees, such as banyan, peepal, and others, which are either worshipped or provide products such as flowers that are used in the worship of the gods. Some trees are also seen as ancestors to certain tribal clans in the area, and these, too, were not cut but instead worshipped. Also, many of Snodgrass's Bhil tribal research collaborators have been known to stand toe to toe with poachers and the various timber mafias at work in the area, to prevent illicit cutting of resources that were meant for local use. Some also plant trees next to their homes and fields, and these provide resources for home building, burning the dead, building corrals and fences, as well as for many other uses, thus taking stress off the forest.

Nevertheless, many Bhils of Phulwari do not act in ways that promote the sustainable use of their resources. And when they *do* do so, it is often only to promote species that are economically valuable. Similarly, local Bhils do not seem to possess the institutional will or organization to protect the woods and wildlife around them effectively. In short, despite the fact that many individual Bhils strive to use their resources in a sustainable way, others are directly responsible for the deforestation and continued degradation of the local jungle. And, of even greater concern for the RFD, many Bhils are directly responsible for the declining numbers of leopards, hyenas, jackals, and other predators within the park. These are poisoned, hunted, and generally harassed within Phulwari, largely because they are seen as a threat to local herd animals. Clearly there is considerable contestation about the nature of Indigenous conservation knowledge and its application in Phulwari.

Illegal Harvesting 'In Their Blood'

Barrier J – IK and management institutions and Barrier L – racial/ cultural inferiority

The biggest environmental problem in the area is the illicit harvesting of timber. Some tribal villagers do everything in their power to stop such harvesting. Others turn a blind eye to it, and still others are directly involved in this illegal activity, sometimes in cahoots with the timber mafia or even with certain individually corrupt RFD employees. Many Adivasis seem little concerned when their goats, who eat almost anything in sight, devour saplings newly planted by the RFD and theoretically protected behind 'cattle barriers'. They are more concerned for the economic well-being of their resource – in this case, goats.

Local Indigenous peoples are also encroaching on the forest in greater and greater numbers every year. Their families continue to grow, eight or nine children being preferred if not the norm. Large families mean more power and influence within the local clans and tribes, but, of course, they put pressure on dwindling agricultural land and on forest resources.

Population growth brings increased construction of houses. Although most tribals prefer tin roofs and cement homes, they are usually not in an economic position to acquire them, and so each home requires hundreds of trees, creating a very real stress on the forest (Figure 4.14). Bhils, Kathodias, and other tribals also illicitly cut bamboo planted by the RFD, even those lathis that were to be harvested in such a way that the village as a whole would share in the profits. Often bamboo is harvested

Figure 4.14 Bhil tribal home within Phulwari ki Nal (photograph by J. Snodgrass).

hastily, to discourage detection by the authorities, and this encourages harvesting that does not allow for efficient regrowth.

In this respect, we would not dismiss all RFD assessments of local environmental knowledge, values, and institutional practice – or, in this case, the lack thereof. After all, local populations often do seem to use their knowledge to maximize the exploitation of the jungle around them rather than to conserve the forest for future or sustained use. Similarly, local institutions, when they exist, seem largely incapable of preventing such overuse and degradation.

Some foresters even suggest that such thought and practice, and such lack of conservation and sound management, are intrinsic to these tribal communities and constitute even a deep and abiding racial or ethnic quality of Adivasis. It is in their religion, if not in the blood that runs in their veins, they argue. Here, however, we would suggest something different. Tribals would seem traditionally to have been good conservationists and sound custodians of the woods. But historical processes and the circumstances of modernity have made it difficult for such values and practices to manifest themselves. We believe that the right circumstances could reverse this state of affairs. Tribal peoples, tapping into different potentials within their knowledge and institutions, could become powerful stewards and guardians of their jungle homes and thus powerful allies in the Indian state's newfound concern with conservation.

Indigenous Inability to Manage the Land

Barrier L – racial/cultural inferiority

The examples provided above demonstrate that the main barrier to successful joint management in Phulwari is not simply the perception by the Rajasthan Forest Department that tribal peoples are exploiters rather than sustainable users of the forests but is also a result of the state's failure to recognize, or at least to properly account for, history. In some cases, members of Hindu caste society as well as employees of the RFD tend to think of Adivasis as backward and superstitious children who cannot think sensibly and thus cannot rationally manage their lands on their own. At times, such traits are even racialized, and seen to be at the core of tribal blood and being. Such sentiments must be considered alongside more general tribal feelings of exclusion from Indian caste society. Such feelings are experienced daily as a condescension from certain Indian foresters who perceive locals as primitives badly in need of Hindu civilization and badly in need of education on how to take care of themselves properly, as well as their forests.

Such perspectives are not only ill-informed but are dangerous for locals as well as for the jungles of Phulwari. Such a point of view fails to account for the fact that the local lack of conservation thought and behavior is historically contingent, emerging as it has from an erosion of local ownership of forests and a general feeling of exclusion from mainstream society. As such, this perception fails to ask the more important questions of why exactly local peoples do not treat their lands better, whether and how current environmental practices might be reversed, and what new circumstances might be necessary to effect such a reversal. As a result, it fails to imagine the way that local Adivasis might be transformed from Phulwari's greatest enemies to its staunchest defenders.

Discussion

Barrier O – globalization

Adivasi communities, then, have experienced a historical erosion of their tenure rights over lands they consider rightfully theirs. To clarify these points, we need to provide a brief local history, which allows us to understand the present-day Adivasi expression of their relationship with the Phulwari forest in terms of global historical influences.

India's tribals have experienced oppression and marginalization from India's and Rajasthan's various states – precolonial, colonial, and postcolonial – as well as from the various citizens inhabiting dominant settled caste society. In Rajasthan, tribal power was eroded in the precolonial period first by emerging Rajput kingdoms and then by the Marathas of Maharashtra. The British pushed these tribals further into isolated forests that were oftentimes subsequently appropriated by the British in their empire's hunger for lumber for ships and railways. And British commodity-extraction policies continued in post-Independence India as the newly formed Indian state sold clear-cutting and mining contracts to outside groups and pursued national 'development' projects such as dams that alienated tribals from their increasingly degraded forest homes (on tribal histories in India, see Arnold and Guha 1995; Baviskar 1995; Breman 1985; Gadgil and Guha 1992, 1995; Guha 1999, 2000 [1989]; Hardiman 1987; Rangarajan 1996; Sivaramakrishnan 1999; Skaria 1999; Sundar 1997).

At the local level, Phulwari was officially a hunting ground of the Maharajas, not tribal property. In many Bhil people's eyes, the state was seen as responsible for dispossessing Indigenous peoples from their lands and then ruining such lands through their destructive clear-cutting practices. They describe the Indian state, and the Forest Department especially, as corrupt and interest-driven and thus not competent to manage local forests. Given this state of affairs, many tribals vote Communist. This party has promised that, if elected, they will abolish the sanctuary and return the lands to their rightful Indigenous owners.

This brief historical narrative helps to explain why the Indigenous peoples of Phulwari do not manage their resources sustainably and why they are not currently conservationists. Tribal institutions associated with the regulation of natural resources in the area in and around Phulwari have vanished from the local landscape. Ritual gatherings of clan leaders – where religious commitments were connected not just to individual needs and desires but to joint resource management rules and sanctions through mechanisms of debate, compromise, consensus-building, and simple bullying – are no more. Institutions for the joint management of collective resources withered with these tribal communities' dispossession from their lands. With no real authority or ownership over the lands on which they forage and reside, there is little reason for clan leaders to meet and discuss joint land management, and little reason for local families, clans, and tribes to curtail their uses of the land for the 'greater good'. After all, any such sensible management of these lands could simply result in the lands being used by other user groups.

This has resulted in a kind of 'tragedy of the commons' at work in Phulwari (but see Chapter 1). Locals, who might in other contexts be responsible stewards of the land, have been transformed into users rushing to exploit resources before others get to them. In such a situation, the

Indian state is not seen as a potential management partner but rather as a competitor for scarce resources and, based on past clear-cutting practices, a rapacious destroyer of local livelihoods.

Phulwari, then, has been transformed into what we might call a de facto 'open access' commons. Phulwari is theoretically owned and managed by the state, but locals suggest that the state does not really own the forests. Likewise, the state is not seen to manage and protect the forests effectively, and certainly not with the level of love and connection that local Adivasis might display in other contexts. As a result, from local perspectives, there is a power vacuum, given that there is perceived to be no legitimate authority managing the forests of Phulwari. The forest is owned by no one and thus is managed by no one. On paper, the forests of Phulwari, as a wildlife sanctuary, are closed to use by both the state as well as by locals. In actuality, the forest is used by whoever can get away with it and whoever is willing to run the risks associated with the illegal harvesting of forest produce.

The barriers here are clearly complex and are strongly linked to the historical context of the specific situation pertaining to this forest. Although local tribals clearly have knowledge about forest management, that knowledge is often not expressed in ways RFD staff can access (being spiritual in conceptualization) or has been obscured by racial and cultural differences or the effects of recent local and global history.

THAILAND – NAN PROVINCE

Doi Phukha National Park (DPNP) lies in Nan Province of northern Thailand (Figure 4.15). The different communities that live in the vicinity of the park have accommodated new state conservation regimes and expanding protected areas, such as DPNP, in different ways. The predominantly Thai-Lue villages of the lowlands, situated on the edge of DPNP, have worked out effective informal co-management arrangements with park officials, in part because they have been able to decrease the area of their swidden fields and fall back on their lowland paddies and other sources of livelihood. They have also been able to garner allies among local NGOs who have helped them present themselves as people with valuable Indigenous knowledge and a functioning community forest; they have thus gained the grudging respect of the park for their own resource management efforts.

The Lua people of the uplands, whose communities and lands are completely encompassed by the park, have been less successful. The Lua and their swidden farming system have been designated in national policy and popular thinking as ecologically malignant.

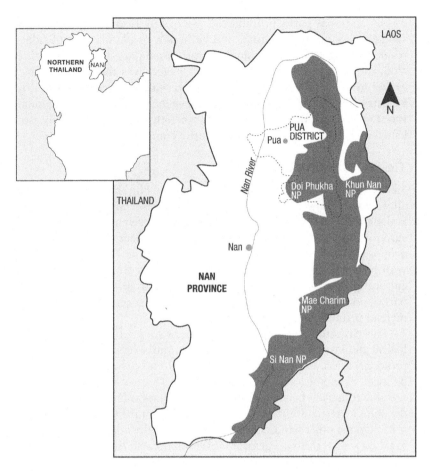

Figure 4.15 Map of Nan Province and Doi Phukha National Park.

The Thai-Lue of Silalaeng

Silalaeng subdistrict is located in a valley occupied by seven mostly Thai-Lue villages. The 1960s saw widespread deforestation in the area, resulting from state-sanctioned logging and cutting of firewood for a nearby tobacco-curing plant. But the major cause was the spread of swidden cash-cropping. In response to the situation, the Silalaeng subdistrict head, a well-respected Thai-Lue leader, prevailed on local farmers to decrease the area of their swiddens in the hills above the valley and work toward creation of a forest preserve (*paa sanguan*). Traditional hunting and gathering activities were allowed in the preserve, but only for domestic consumption.

In 1983 a national park in the area around Doi (Mount) Phukha was proposed, with an area that would encompass the Silalaeng community

172 • Chapter 4

forest. National parks prohibit the use of any resources, including via swidden agriculture, hunting, and gathering of plants. Some Silalaeng residents were still swiddening in the proposed park area, but the threat from the park that touched the most villagers was the loss of rights to gather forest products. The community repeatedly petitioned the Royal Forestry Department and other relevant agencies to leave the community forest area out of the park. However, when the park was formally established in 1999, it encompassed the entire community forest.

The Lua of Doi Phukha

Silalaeng subdistrict is bordered to the east by Phukha subdistrict, where all 12 Lua villages are completely within DPNP. Since DPNP was formally established in 1999, park officials have been applying heavy pressure on the Lua to limit the area of their swiddens. Park officials have proposed several agricultural changes to bring the Lua into compliance with park objectives. The main proposal is that the Lua intensify agricultural production by planting fruit tree orchards. This proposal is also part of an implicit park effort to reorient the Lua economy toward commercial production and wage labor.

This case study highlights the salience of some of the major epistemological and institutional obstacles to collaborative resource management in protected areas. On the one hand, the Thai-Lue occupy a position in the political, economic, and racial hierarchy of Thai society from which they are able to make effective alliances and put forward arguments that force the state to recognize their knowledge and resource management institutions. On the other hand, other groups, such as the Lua, have largely failed to take a seat at the management table both because their lands fall entirely within a state-designated protected area and because they do not fit externally imposed criteria of knowledgeable and capable resource managers.

Indigenous Knowledge: Recognition, Misrecognition, and Denial in a Racialized Landscape

Barrier A – IK not recognized, Barrier C – nonvalidation of IK, and Barrier L – racial/cultural inferiority

The term 'Indigenous knowledge' (*phuumpanyaa chaw baan*) has entered the Thai lexicon as some NGOs and peoples' organizations have sought to argue that people in and around protected areas possess important knowledge that is relevant to resource management. However, struggles over collaborative resource management and the status of Indigenous knowledge in Thailand must be understood against the back drop of Thai internal colonialism, the authority of bureaucratic state institutions, and the resulting disadvantages imposed on upland minorities living in and around protected areas and forest reserves. Some upland communities have benefited from the growing currency of the concept, but the results have been uneven at best. The contrast between the situations of the Thai-Lue of Silalaeng and the Lua of Doi Phukha highlights the tenuous status of Indigenous knowledge in Thailand. For example, the Lua fit into the Thai category of 'hilltribe', which is part of a racialized discourse in which hilltribe people are assumed to be backward and stubborn and practitioners of environmentally destructive 'shifting agriculture' (*rai luan loy*). The persistence of such stubborn racial and epistemological hierarchies hinders collaboration between state institutions and many rural communities.

Recognition of Indigenous Knowledge: The Thai-Lue of Silalaeng

Barrier J – IK and management institutions and Barrier M – state power

With the proposed establishment of DPNP in 1983, the Thai-Lue villagers of Silalaeng were threatened with loss of access to the forest preserve that they had managed for local use since 1975. The park, which was formally established in 1999, did eventually encompass the forest preserve despite appeals by Silalaeng residents to leave it out of the park. This action by the state struck the residents of Silalaeng as fundamentally unjust. Tawin, a Silalaeng leader involved in forest issues, told Delcore in 2003: 'We conserved that [forest] area starting in 1975, and then the national park came in and wanted to control the whole thing. It's as if someone raised a chicken until it was big and fat, and then someone else came and grabbed it like it were their own'.

During the 1990s leaders such as Tawin made alliances with local small-scale Thai NGOs, including one led by a Silalaeng native. The NGOs helped Silalaeng residents link their struggle for rights to manage their forest reserve to the larger national struggle for increased local rights to resources. Since the early 1990s local NGOs have used their institutional networks to help bring sympathetic visitors to Silalaeng to talk to local leaders and tour the forest preserve. NGO activists, villagers, and some state officials from around the country have visited the area, and it has also served as the site for Kasetsart University's Regional Community Forest Training Center (RECOFTC) field school, which brings foresters from around Asia to Thailand for social forestry education. At the same time, Silalaeng forest leaders have joined with larger national efforts by NGOs and peoples' organizations, such as the Assembly of the Poor, to dramatize rural land and resource use issues. During major Assembly of the Poor protests in Bangkok in early 1997 representatives from Silalaeng traveled to Bangkok to express their solidarity with those engaged in similar battles in other parts of the country.

Silalaeng leaders have also thrown their support behind a proposed version of community forest legislation that would allow community forests and national parks to co-exist. Finally, in 1997, Silalaeng joined an effort by peoples' organizations and NGOs to ordain community forests in northern Thailand in honor of King Rama IX's 50th anniversary on the throne, in part an effort to send the message that community forestry was not only ecologically sound but also patriotic (Delcore 2004; see Chapter 5). These efforts combined have transformed Silalaeng into a celebrated case of effective local resource management (Figure 4.16).

This review of the place of Silalaeng in local historical and political perspective would appear to negate the existence of any barriers to the involvement of local peoples in land management. However, it also provides the framework for further analyses (see below) that suggest that any such management partnership is less robust than would, at first glance, appear. Nevertheless, there are some positive opportunities that have been generated by these local/NGO relationships, and in some situations there have even been occasions when barriers have been overcome.

Coinciding Conservation Goals

Barrier D – translation of IK

The following analysis demonstrates one way in which Thai-Lue people have *overcome* barriers that result from different languages of

Figure 4.16 The Thai Lue ritual for river spirits at the onset of the rainy season (photograph by H. Delcore).

conservation. Thai-Lue community leaders have successfully pressed the case that their forest reserve is in fact a 'community forest' (*paa chumchon*). The idea of 'community forest' is part of an NGO-inspired counter-discourse to scientific forestry in Thailand. The idea behind community forestry is that rural communities have long practiced forest conservation by designating certain forest areas for specific non-agricultural uses, including hunting, gathering, and limited logging for domestic use. The discourse of community forestry explicitly aims to break down the perceived monopoly of scientific forestry on knowledge relevant to forest management and conservation. It is here that community forestry links up with 'Indigenous knowledge', as promoted by various peoples' organizations and some NGOs. In Thailand, the concept of Indigenous knowledge includes the general idea that the local knowledge and institutions of rural populations have long been the basis for wise rural resource management, and that such knowledge and practices deserve inclusion in the state's resource management strategy. Importantly, local people such as the Thai-Lue of Silalaeng have not been passive recipients of community forest and Indigenous knowledge discourses but have actively engaged with NGO allies to strengthen their discursive hand against such state institutions as national parks and their epistemological backing in scientific forestry.

It is in fact true that many Tai and non-Tai ethnic groups have traditions that roughly fit the notion of 'community forest', although there is legitimate debate about the extent of such practices in specific times and places. The important point here is that the Thai-Lue of Silalaeng are an example of a group that has been relatively successful at making its case as a nature-friendly community whose culture and institutional arrangements justify its continued control over resources. At this point, Silalaeng community forest leaders are able to point to at least a 30-year history of active forest conservation in the community forest area, with attendant claims that this management has a basis in a more generalized, ecologically sound culture, at least until state-led development skewed incentives toward such unsustainable resource use as the large-scale swidden cash cropping that swept Silalaeng in the 1960s and early 1970s.

DPNP officials have credited the Thai-Lue with significant conservation achievements, and this has led to a variety of co-management efforts in the community forest. DPNP and RFD officials sometimes hire Silalaeng community forest leaders to speak to various gatherings to share their insights. Silalaeng leaders have spoken to audiences of foresters as well as the Lua of Doi Phukha; to the former, they emphasize the credibility of local management, whereas to the latter they speak about the benefits of conservation to a presumably recalcitrant and ecologically destructive audience. While some Thai-Lue leaders are anxious to see their community forest granted more formal legitimacy by the passing of a friendly Community Forest Bill (which has been repeatedly stymied in the Thai Parliament), many are satisfied that they have gained a relatively secure status for their community forest.

Why have the Thai-Lue been able to work out a relatively positive relationship with DPNP? First, the conservation successes achieved in the community forest must indeed be recognized. Through painstaking effort, a long series of Thai-Lue leaders have been able to forge community consensus about the advantages of community forestry. Of course, the fact that many farmers in Silalaeng have lowland fields in the valley made their abandonment of swidden activities in the hills easier, though some remain bitter at the loss of agricultural land there. Supplementary income from labor migration and, to some extent, weaving and selling naturally dyed cloth (with dyes made from leaves and bark gathered in the community forest; Figure 4.17) have also mitigated the effects of lost income from swidden agriculture.

However, the Thai-Lue have also benefited from the fact that they share a similar cultural base with the Thai majority. While they may undertake activities deemed by the state and urban people as 'environmentally harmful' (such as swidden agriculture and logging), these activities are not seen as inherent to their culture. Like other Tai-speakers, they are perceived as lowlanders, despite their proximity to and many

Figure 4.17 A Thai Lue man boils bark he gathered in the Doi Phukha National Park to make dye for his wife, a local weaver (photograph by H. Delcore).

activities in the hills and forests, and so their resource use practices are granted de facto legitimacy. Indeed, the fact they practice lowland paddy agriculture abets a general sense of conflicting interests between them and all uplanders, because swidden agriculture is often framed as a threat to the water supply for lowland agriculture. In short, in contrast to the hilltribes, they are not seen as inherently recalcitrant and ecologically destructive. In a sense, then, their conservation initiatives, while notable, are, from the perspective of state officials, not terribly surprising. They are Thais (in both the current legal and ideological sense), and so they must love the Thai nation and its resources and can be expected to (eventually) see the value of forest conservation. Such is not the view of Lua hilltribes.

Misrecognition and Denial: The Lua of Doi Phukha

Barrier D - translation of IK and Barrier L – racial/cultural inferiority

In the case of DPNP, the Thai-Lue have clearly benefited from the increased currency of the concept of 'Indigenous knowledge' in Thailand. Working with their local NGO allies, Thai-Lue community leaders have successfully promoted themselves as exemplars of the potentials for sound resource management by rural people. Thailand's upland minorities are in a very different situation. Lumped together as backward and primitive, they are assumed to be 'ecologically malignant' (Pinkaew 2002), disrupting the possibility of healthy forests – defined as free from human activity.

Note that the popular Thai conception of 'hilltribe' is essentially a racial formulation. Thais tend to conceive of hilltribe culture as so radically and stubbornly different from their own as to verge on a hard-wired set of dispositions and behaviors only just barely open to change. (On the point of radical Thai-hilltribe difference, there is of course much evidence to the contrary, not least the fact that many Tai-speakers who live near or in the uplands have long practised swidden agriculture). A Thai-Lue villager living on the edge of DPNP, commenting on the conflict between the park and the Lua people who live within its borders, said: 'The Lua have low education, and they need training and development to get them to come out of the forest. Oh! This is a hard thing to do, to get them to change their form of livelihood'. The invocation of how hard it is to get the hilltribes to change their ways is a constant feature of the Thai discourse on hilltribes. A DPNP official put it this way:

> Silalaeng has been caring for the forest [in the community forest area] to a point, but there might be some things which they can't handle themselves. As for the hilltribes [that is, the Lua], they have low education,

and their livelihood is swidden agriculture. They think mainly about their stomachs [*paak thong*] and not about caring for the forest. They can't get this through their heads. They're hard-headed.

In addition to the invocation of 'hard-headedness', the official also conjures up another common impression of the Lua in particular, that they only think from day to day, and once their stomachs are full they are happy. The implicit contrast here is between the Lua and the more progressive Thais, who have moved away from subsistence rice farming and into commercial agriculture (Figure 4.18). The park promotes a similar move by the Lua – intensification of agriculture in certain (smaller) land areas to earn income from cash crops, obviating the need for swidden rice farming. As Moore, Pandian, and Kosek (2003) point out, these speakers need not articulate a full-blown argument for biological racial inferiority to nonetheless convey a sense of cultural difference so hard as to be racial in connotation.

In 1997 a Thai forester who was participating in the RECOFTC field school recounted the following to Delcore. A recent lesson had dealt with the livelihood strategies of different upland groups in the area, and the forester was commenting on the tendency for

Figure 4.18 Dancers at Ban Toey's annual feast for the rice spirits (photograph by H. Delcore).

the Hmong (settlers of the uplands from outside the area) to move more readily into commercial production than some other groups. She asserted that the commercial orientation of the Hmong was a 'tribal characteristic' (*laksana pracam phaw*). Delcore argued that this ought to be viewed less as a cultural feature and more as a product of the historical fact that the Hmong have been involved in commercial production of opium for some time, perhaps making the move into other cash crops easier for them. The forester was non-plussed, and a Thai professor working with RECOFTC explained to Delcore that when the forester used the term 'tribal characteristic', she was not talking about a mere ethnic trait but a racial notion of why Hmong behave the way they do (to which the forester readily agreed). From there, of course, the conversation had to take an entirely different turn.

As implied by the mention of 'tribal characteristics', Thais do in fact recognize some differences between hilltribe groups. The Karen, for example, have been able to build for themselves a reputation as relatively ecologically friendly. Karen peoples' organizations and their NGO allies have pressed the case of the Karen to the state and public, via the media, highlighting the rotational nature of Karen swidden practices and the spirit beliefs that foster conservation of particular forest areas (see Pinkaew 2002). On the other end of the spectrum, the Hmong have long been seen as the most ecologically destructive group, often (sometimes erroneously) portrayed as pioneer swiddeners who senselessly degrade, beyond rehabilitation, large forest areas before moving on. Recently, however, the Hmong reputation has begun to improve. Hmong farmers in many parts of northern Thailand have converted field crop areas into fruit tree orchards, an activity sometimes recognized as preferable to outright swiddening, although fruit orchards have also been at the center of some upland-lowland water-use conflicts in northern Thailand. In addition, the Hmong affinity for commercialized production is often met with ambivalence by lowlanders, who sometimes credit the Hmong as hardworking and ambitious, while also criticizing them as greedy and grasping.

The official and lowlander perception of the Lua is also somewhat ambivalent. On the one hand, they are widely recognized as one of northern Thailand's autochthonous peoples, and so they are not typically criticized as interlopers. On the other hand, they are also seen as quite primitive and both 'uneducated' and 'hard-headed'. They do practice swidden agriculture and so bear the burden of the 'ecologically malign savage' as well, which has acted as a significant barrier to the recognition of their legitimate place in forest management.

Discourse and Counter-Discourse: The 'Shifting Agriculture' Concept

Barrier A – IK not recognized, Barrier C – nonvalidation of IK, and Barrier D – translation of IK

The Lua communities in DPNP are completely encompassed by the park, and park officials are in the process of pressuring the Lua to decrease the amount of land under swidden cultivation. The dominant Thai conception of hilltribe agriculture centers on the term 'shifting agriculture' (*rai luan loy*). The image implied by this term is one of constant movement and severe deforestation of successive forest areas, almost without reason. Some upland peoples, such as the Hmong, Lisu, Akha and Mien, have in fact practised a form of swidden agriculture that can be characterized as 'long cultivation-long fallow' (Yos 2003: 16–22). In this model, the farmer cultivates a swidden plot for several years until productivity declines, the plot is abandoned, and a new plot is opened elsewhere. In some cases in the past, this method meant that communities moved when the land around the settlement was no longer suitable for cultivation. However, the Lua practice a form of swidden cultivation known as 'short cultivation-long fallow' (Yos 2003: 25–26). In this system, a field is cultivated for one season, followed by cultivation of other plots for up to 10 years or so, with eventual return to the original plot. Under such a system, settlements are typically permanent or semipermanent, and new fields are opened up only to accommodate new households.

To talk about this kind of swiddening more effectively, some Thai NGOs have promoted the use of the term 'rotational swidden agriculture' (*rai munwian*) as part of an attempt to institute a counter-discourse that recognizes the diversity and sustainability of swidden systems (see Pinkaew 2002). Proponents of rotational swiddening point out that it is both sustainable *and* consistent with forest conservation. Lua villages are surrounded not by denuded hills but by swiddens in various states of regrowth, as well as forests that have been designated by the community for non-swidden uses. Further, several studies have shown that rotational swidden systems promote greater biodiversity, because different plants and animals thrive in forests in different states of regeneration (Yos 2003: 14). In this reconceptualization, fallow swiddens are not 'degraded forests' (as the RFD would have it) but forests of different kinds, often with their own classification terms in local languages. Thus, the Lua rotational swidden system could plausibly be adapted to facilitate both the conservation goals of the national park and the livelihood of the inhabitants.

Nevertheless, park policy does not recognize the sustainability or ecological benefits of Lua agriculture. Indeed, from the start, the Lua, as a 'hilltribe' group, are defined as ecologically destructive, and their agriculture is classified as 'shifting agriculture' and therefore incompatible with a national park. The idea that the Lua have knowledge of upland resources that might be helpful to park planners is very foreign to the worldview of most Thai foresters. In 2003 Delcore discussed the concept of Indigenous knowledge of the environment with the director of DPNP, who admitted that such knowledge exists. However, when asked for examples, he cited Hmong Indigenous knowledge: 'I have a pick-up truck, so my younger brother needs a pick-up truck, too', a critical reference to the perceived Hmong energy for commercial activities and implied ecological malignancy. Asked specifically if the Lua have any such knowledge, he replied: 'Oh, there is very little', while making a hand gesture with thumb and forefinger pinched together, almost shut. Later, the Director credited the Karen with possessing Indigenous knowledge while also delivering this criticism:

> The Karen in Chiang Mai, they point to the map and say, 'We want this area [under our control]'. But if you ask them where they plan to cut [swiddens], they don't know! This isn't 'wisdom' [*phuumpanyaa*] and it's not 'a culture of forest management' [*watthanatham kaan catkaan paa*].

Later, Delcore learned that this director had been transferred to DPNP from an area in Chiang Mai Province where he came into sharp conflict with Karen villagers in his jurisdiction. Clearly this forester does not recognize that Lua, or other hilltribes, have any Indigenous knowledge relevant to resource management and holds a view that scientific ways of knowing are far superior to any knowledge held by traditional peoples.

Management Policy to Change Traditional Land Use

Barrier G – ownership of knowledge, Barrier H – spatial/temporal boundaries, and Barrier M – state power

The current informal policy of the park is that 'swidden is swidden, forest is forest'. In other words, areas devoted to swidden can continue as such, but new fields cannot be cleared. This situation is considered by the Lua as unworkable for several reasons. First, foresters tend to look on fallow swiddens as 'degraded forest', and they pressure the Lua to abandon some of their more mature fallows and intensify production elsewhere. Second, a cap on new swiddens, plus natural population growth in the villages, would mean forced out-migration for the younger Lua as land becomes scarce – barring of course the development of new agricultural methods.

In place of swidden agriculture, park officials have been promoting the commercialization and intensification of Lua agriculture on specific plots of land, hoping that Lua farmers will eventually abandon their multiple fields and instead focus production on one or two. Proposals from the park include the development of fruit tree orchards and terraced rice fields. The Lua raise a number of objections to such proposals, including concerns that commercial production would hinge on having lowland merchants willing to actually travel into the park to buy their produce. Perceiving commercialized agriculture as risky, most Lua farmers therefore prefer to stay with their subsistence-first strategy of swidden rice production, augmented by cash income from collection and sale of forest products. Unfortunately, then, there is little common discursive ground between the park officials and most Lua; the officials see traditional Lua livelihood as a threat to the environment, while the Lua consider park pressure on their agricultural practices unfair, and so they continue to stonewall.

Advocacy and the Role of NGOs as Mediators

Barrier I – 'outsiders' kept 'outside', Barrier J – IK and management institutions, and Barrier M – state power

Institutional barriers to more effective Lua engagement with park officials are also present. Until recently, the Pua District head, an appointed official of the Ministry of the Interior, chose an influential Silalaeng Subdistrict resident to serve as *kamnan* (subdistrict head) of Phukha Subdistrict. The last such appointee was a construction contractor engaged in extensive road-building activities using Lua laborers paid at less than half the going day-labor rate. The first locally elected Lua *kamnan* took office in 2002, but his assistant was a Silalaeng resident and a holdover from the old appointee system. This assistant *kamnan* was also a construction contractor and business partner with the Silalaeng *kamnan* at that time, who in turn has reportedly been involved in illegal logging activities in and around the park. Needless to say, such leaders have had little interest in organizing the Lua of Doi Phukha as an effective political force to confront park policy. If anything, such powerful lowlanders stand to benefit from any infrastructural development, agricultural commercialization, and increased tourist traffic generated by the park.

Alternatively, since the late 1990s some lowland NGOs have had increased contact with the Lua of Doi Phukha. Some of these activists were involved in the earlier campaign to highlight the success of the Silalaeng community forest. The NGO activists are explicitly sympathetic to the Lua and have helped advocate for them to forestry officials. In one case, a lowland NGO activist helped organize a demonstration at the RFD office in Nan Town to protest the arrest of three Lua farmers captured while clearing a swidden in DPNP in 1999. Yet, while they actively engage in the discourses of Indigenous knowledge, community forestry, and rotational swiddening, some of the NGO activists share the basic contention of the park officials that the Lua should move toward a more intensive form of agricultural production in order to accommodate the park. The Lua are clearly perceived as 'outside' the mainstream management system that is locked in a trope of institutional authority supported by state systems.

Indigenous Counter-Discourses

Barrier D – translating IK and Barrier E – social/spiritual expression

The Lua have yet to make productive use of the counter-discourses of Indigenous knowledge and rotational swiddening. They have been involved with these discourses and their NGO proponents for a shorter time than the people of Silalaeng. Also, until recently, there have been few Lua leaders with the lowland education and experience that facilitates the complex negotiation of discourse and counter-discourse in the Thai language. This is changing. As of 2003 there was one college graduate from among the Lua of Doi Phukha who was working for the local watershed unit of the RFD, which was then led by a progressive Thai forester who was often at loggerheads with the park administration. Another, named Somsak, was nearing graduation, actively involved with local NGOs, and an outspoken critic of park administration. He was ready and able to begin to press the argument for Lua Indigenous knowledge. Describing Lua opposition to the park in 2003, he noted both overt and covert strategies:

> Villagers in Ban Toey [Somsak's home village] have moved the large concrete boundary markers laid down by the park [see Figure 4.19]. It's the power of the villagers. . . . And on August 11, we'll have a festival for the rice spirits, to express the fact that people can plant rice and co-exist with the forest at the same time.

Somsak's comment reveals a self-conscious awareness that ritual can be made to represent to the outside world the fact that people and forests can co-exist and that the Lua, too, have Indigenous knowledge of the environment.

Discussion

The idea of Indigenous knowledge in Thailand, with its component discourses of community forestry and rotational swiddening, certainly has gained legitimacy in the last decade. However, the argument for local rights to resource use and management on the basis of previous achievements and cultural attributes has some important pitfalls. The achievements of some groups can be recognized and validated while

Figure 4.19 A Doi Phukha National Park boundary marker, like the one Lua villagers physically moved farther into the park to protest the enclosure of their farm lands by the park (photograph by H. Delcore).

those of others can be misrecognized or ignored. The cultural attribute of 'Indigenous knowledge' can be granted to some groups but denied to others. These pitfalls may loom in any ethnically diverse area, particularly where one ethnic group occupies the dominant political and economic positions. In the case of Thailand, the racialization of ethnicity further promotes the position that some groups, like the Lua, possess inherently inferior and 'hardened' cultures that can be ameliorated only through coercive conservation measures such as the imposition of national park regimes. Until there is more recognition by state officials that groups such as the Lua are capable of complex and useful knowledge of the environment, there is little chance that effective collaborative efforts will arise.

The case study presented here from northern Thailand demonstrates a complex web of knowledge relating to the place of Indigenous peoples in mainstream resources management. Some local peoples' knowledge is valorized while others' knowledge is demonized. Discourses of racial inferiority and cultural difference underlie the different constructs that exist in government approaches to local knowledge. The existence of barriers in this case study cannot be easily categorized and supported, illustrating the interwoven nature of much of the debate about the place of Indigenous people in resource stewardship.

DISCUSSION AND CONCLUSION

These case studies, coming as they do from very different geographical and political situations, demonstrate the wide range of barriers to the incorporation of Indigenous peoples and their knowledge into natural resource management decision making. Nevertheless, these case studies also demonstrate that there are some broad similarities across the distinctly different geographic, social and political examples presented, with shared epistemological and systemic/institutional differences between local peoples, on the one hand, and government bureaucrats, often supported by Western trained scientists, on the other. The range of barriers presented in our case studies is summarized in Table 4.1.

There were four barriers that were identified in all four case studies. We all identified that Indigenous knowledge is socially and/or spiritually constituted (Barrier E). In all case studies the Indigenous knowledge tended to be holistic, incorporating social, ritual, and spiritual aspects, while government land managers' knowledge was largely scientifically constructed. This epistemological barrier was often the basis for government managers' nonrecognition that Indigenous knowledge was once, or is now, part of resource knowledge and stewardship (Barrier A). Where Indigenous knowledge *is* recognized, its relevance to modern resources management is often regarded as insufficiently proven (Barrier C). Closely linked to these three barriers is a fourth – Barrier J, in which barriers occur when Indigenous knowledge cannot be easily accommodated into scientific reductionism or formulaic approaches such as are found in management manuals. We all found examples of this in our case studies.

Interestingly, none of us explicitly identified the problem of codifying Indigenous knowledge. Nevertheless, we all feel that, because most of the Indigenous knowledge of which we are aware is an oral tradition, usually linked to the social and spiritual format within which knowledge is encoded, translating such knowledge into a written document does often introduce the problems we discussed under the Barrier C heading in Chapter 3. In fact, we have all identified codification concerns in the form of a discussion of Barrier D (translating Indigenous knowledge into a Western format), Barrier H (the imposition of Western-defined temporal or spatial barriers), and/or Barrier K (barriers that arise as a result of decentralization of decision making). All these barriers, we would argue, are visible and practical representations of the problems that occur when Indigenous knowledge is required to be presented in formats foreign to those people or communities holding the knowledge.

Barriers relating to perceptions of racial inferiority were articulated by Snodgrass and Delcore for India and Thailand. Such racial and social constructs have led modern managers to perceive Indigenous land use in

TABLE 4.1 Barriers

Barrier	Australia	United States	India	Thailand
Epistemological Barriers				
A IK not recognized	Poor understanding of relevance of Aboriginal NRM knowledge to management	Lakota knowledge misrepresented by history and ignored as part of dispossession	IK perceived as being based on self-interest	Racial denigration of Lua limits recognition of NRM
B Narrow definitions	Narrow definitions of 'tradition' reduce recognition of Aboriginal NRM abilities	Lakota traditions deemed to have died with assimilation		
C Nonvalidation of IK	Dugong, dingo, and fisheries knowledge deemed irrelevant to Western NRM requirements	European history misrepresented Lakota connections to land	Adivasi goals of forestry management fall outside RFD perspectives	Perceived racial inferiority of Lua blinds state managers to relevance of Lua IK
D Translation of IK	Aboriginal hunters and fishers need 'education' in Western ways	Lakota required to develop a common language with West to demonstrate connections to land and resources		Successful introduction of IK into NRM followed common language of management, but without common language, IK ignored
E Social/spiritual expression	Dugong, fisheries, and dingo management set in social and spiritual knowledge	Lakota knowledge sees people and animals as related	Adivasi knowledge set in social and spiritual frameworks	Lua, in particular, express association with land in social and spiritual ways
F Codification of IK				

TABLE 4.1 *Continued*

Barrier	Australia	United States	India	Thailand
G Ownership of knowledge		Tribal government debt constrains decision making over retained lands		Lua forced into new land management, outside knowledge base
H Spatial/temporal boundaries	Bureaucratic boundaries disadvantage Aboriginal NRM implementation	Archaeological timeframes and reservation boundaries limit Lakota connections to resources		Park boundaries limit Lua land management practices
Systemic/Institutional Barriers				
I 'Outsiders' kept 'outside'	Aboriginal approaches to dingo management fall outside Western constructs of the resource			Government appointments ensure Lua kept outside decision making in the park
J IK and management institutions	Aboriginal institutions for dugong and dingo management foreign to Western managers	Government institutions and cattle ranching management fail to recognize interconnections between people and natural resources, causing resource decline	Forestry institutions unable to accommodate Adivasi management strategies, often based in social institutions or historical impositions	NGOs used to support Indigenous protests against state control of resources; park institutions used to limit Lua access to resources

continued

TABLE 4.1 *Continued*

Barrier	Australia	United States	India	Thailand
K Decentralization	Aboriginal NRM knowledge centralized, while bureaucracy is compartmentalized	Tribal government, based on Western models, interferes with traditional Lakota institutions	Adivasi management institutions not recognized by RFD	
L Racial/ cultural inferiority			Adivasi perceived as unable to manage NRM owing to 'backwardness' or innate selfishness	Hilltribes perceived as too stubborn and backward to manage natural resources
M State power		State control of land denied Lakota access to resources		State overrides traditional Indigenous access to forests and forces land use change
N 'Benevolent' West		Government policies ostensibly aimed to protect Lakota		
O Globalization		Global commodities require cattle ranching, which reduces viability of Lakota resources	Oppression and historical appropriation of resources limits ability of Adivasi to practice 'traditional' NRM	

these two case studies as unproductive or even an anathema to current conservation requirements or to Western requirements for a productive resource landscape. Although a racially structured barrier was not explicitly noted by Ross or Pickering Sherman and Sherman, we would argue that there are elements of this barrier that exist in Australia and the United States; perhaps they are not as overtly articulated by natural resources managers as they are in India and Thailand. This barrier has been self-consciously sanitized, because in Australia and the United States overt racism is not legally accepted, even if it may be socially tolerated, often surviving as an undercurrent of a white discourse on superiority or advancement. Conversely, we recognized Barrier B – narrow definition of such concepts as 'tradition' and 'custom' – only in our Australian and United States case studies. Perhaps external definitions of 'tradition' are issues relating more to colonial situations in which assimilation was forced onto Indigenous peoples as part of the colonization process (Ross and Pickering 2002).

It is interesting that the barriers relating to the ownership of knowledge and property rights disputes (Barrier G) have been explicitly recognized only for Thailand and the United States. Once again, this is possibly not so much due to an absence of such disputes in Australia and India as to the manifestation of these barriers in other forms in these case studies. For example, in Australia, much of the current natural resources debate is now undertaken in the context of native title discourse. Under the provisions of the Native Title Act of 1993, Aboriginal traditional owners are able to claim native title rights over any lands or waters where such rights have not been extinguished by historical land or resource acquisition activities. National parks are technically deemed to be claimable lands (although successful native title claims over such categories of land are rare). Property rights issues, therefore, underlie all natural resource management disputes in Australia. All the barriers identified for the Australian case studies, therefore, incorporate Barrier G as a basic and underlying premise.

Furthermore, we all recognize that modern property rights disallow or at least make no provision for the recognition of alternative (for example, Indigenous) land ownership structures (Barrier A). These differences in property rights relate to government oversight of land use and land management, and they reflect the overarching power imbalance that exists between Indigenous resource users/stewards, on the one hand, and state authorities, on the other (Barrier M). Failures by Western resource managers to recognize Indigenous property rights are exacerbated by modern boundary constructions, both temporal and spatial, that create problems for the incorporation of Indigenous ownership systems into planning mechanisms that are designed at totally different temporal and/or geographic scales (Barrier H). This barrier was expressly identified by all but the Indian case study.

Of the remaining barriers, there are a variety of different systemic and institutional barriers that have been identified in our case studies. Given the very different social, historical, and political contexts within which our research has been conducted, a wide variation in the institutional barriers is unremarkable. On the contrary, a great deal of overlap here would be highly surprising. However, what is important is that such barriers do indeed exist in all our case studies, supporting the arguments presented in Chapter 3 that the barriers to the incorporation of Indigenous peoples and their knowledge into resources management is not necessarily a purely hypothetical debate.

The consequences of the existence of these barriers vary in each of the case studies but include some of the following:

- Increased sedentism (often in towns)
- Enforced changes to land-management strategies (with this being a recent problem in Thailand and India)
- A reduction in the amount of land available to Indigenous peoples for traditional resource stewardship practices
- Centralization of power and management authority out of the hands of traditional resource authorities
- Increased opportunities for commercial exploitation of resources (especially in India and the United States)
- Valorization of the hegemony of science
- An increase in mono-species management (especially in India and the United States) – which introduces a range of other problems
- Continued removal of traditional resource knowledge holders from the resource management decision-making table.

Overall, our case studies demonstrate that there is a vast range of ways of knowing about the environment. We have demonstrated practical, forthright know-how, in which Indigenous people think in ways that are very like scientific paradigms, such as in Australia, where some aspects of Indigenous knowledge have been supported by strong empirical data gathering on the part of Indigenous traditional resource custodians, and in Rajasthan, where some Adivasi stewardship institutions resemble Western institutional management structures. We have also demonstrated numerous examples of the great disparity between Western and Indigenous knowledge, particularly in situations in which Indigenous knowledge is couched in social or spiritual terms that cannot be easily assimilated into Western management paradigms. Examples of the spiritual expression of knowledge that we have outlined include

Lakota knowledge of human/animal relationships, which informs management decisions, and Thailand's Lua spiritual knowledge of forest resources. Both examples demonstrate how Indigenous knowledge falls outside government managers' knowledge frameworks. These examples, then, demonstrate the similarities and differences between Indigenous and Western ways of knowing that we discussed in Chapter 1, and they illustrate the epistemological barriers that were consequently identified in Chapter 3.

We have also demonstrated some of the practical or institutional barriers that result from these different ways of knowing that we outlined in Chapter 3. We have seen that Indigenous and Western resources institutions are often based on very different pragmatic systems – with Indigenous resource stewardship often having a social context that is completely foreign in most government bureaucracies, such as the disputes over dingo and buffalo management in Australia and the United States (respectively) and conflicts over access to forest resources in Thailand and Rajasthan.

In the next chapter we examine ways in which some of these barriers have begun to be overcome. We introduce some of the advances in co-management arrangements, particularly those developed in Australia. Co-management has the potential to go a considerable distance in recognizing a role for both Indigenous knowledge and Indigenous people to be involved in natural resources decision making.

Chapter 5

JOINT MANAGEMENT AND CO-MANAGEMENT AS STRATEGIES FOR INDIGENOUS INVOLVEMENT IN PROTECTED-AREAS MANAGEMENT

Given the unexpected commonality in the identification of barriers to incorporating Indigenous knowledge into mainstream natural resource management seen across the different case studies presented in the previous chapter, we should not be surprised that there has also been a degree of consensus in attempts to overcome these barriers. Over the past three decades management agencies, particularly those charged with the management of protected areas, have become increasingly interested in developing institutional arrangements that provide opportunities to promote a role for Indigenous involvement in natural resource management decision making.

In this chapter we review the growth of a number of strategies that have been adopted by resource management regulators around the world to provide an opportunity for sharing Western and Indigenous management knowledge and practice. We focus on various models of co-operative or collaborative management (usually termed 'co-management'), a shared approach to protected-areas management used in a range of different formats.

Australia has been at the forefront of international developments in the area of joint management and co-management between modern states and Indigenous peoples. Indeed, many of the approaches to land management discussed in this chapter were originally developed in Australia but are now also found elsewhere. We thus begin the chapter with Australian examples, and indeed the bulk of the chapter deals with case studies from this island nation.

For comparative purposes we then move to India and Thailand. Readers will see there both parallels and differences between natural resource management in Australia and these two nations. In part, the differences relate to the fact that India and Thailand are run by local elites who sometimes claim if not 'Indigenous' origins at least long histories, centuries and even millennia in fact, of contact with the land and its Indigenous groups. For example, in the Indian state of Rajasthan, local Rajputs ruled over, and sometimes with, Adivasis. This complicates management issues, because locals from non-Indigenous groups make competing claims for historical rights over the land. Management regimes in these two states are heavily Westernized, as are the elites. The issues are thus continuous with the Australian example. Nevertheless, joint management and co-management take specific forms in India and Thailand, and Indigenous peoples try to resuscitate centuries-old relationships, often framed in religious terms, between historical rulers and local Indigenous peoples.

Overall, we believe the models explored in this chapter represent important advancements over the exclusion of Indigenous peoples and their knowledge practices from resource management. However, these advancements are far from perfect. Many of the arrangements we discuss continue to reproduce the inequalities that keep scientific knowledge and Indigenous knowledge relatively separate and unequal. The Lakota Indigenous Stewardship Model presented in the next chapter, we believe, solves some of the problems raised in this chapter.

BEFORE CO-MANAGEMENT

'Ayers Rock' in central Australia was 'discovered' and named by William Gosse in 1873. The area has been occupied by Pitjantjatjara and Yankunytjatjara Aboriginal people, who call themselves 'Anangu', for over 35,000 years (Smith, Prescott, and Head 1997). The rock (known to Anangu as *Uluru*) is a place of special significance as a result of creation stories associated with the formation of the landform and its manifestation of the *Tjukurpa* (Anangu law and knowledge, handed down from creator beings in the distant past).

In the early 1900s the area around Uluru and another nearby rock outcrop, known as *Kata Tjuta* to Anangu but Mt. Olga to the Australian population, was declared an Aboriginal Reserve; Anangu were forcibly relocated to the reserve while the rest of their land was taken up by pastoralists. In 1950 'Ayers Rock' was declared a national park, and in 1958 Uluru and Kata Tjuta were excised from the Aboriginal Reserve to form Ayers Rock–Mt. Olga National Park. Title was vested in the Director of the Australian National Parks and Wildlife Service – an Australian federal agency – and Anangu were removed from the park into other parts of the reserve. Ayers Rock–Mt. Olga National Park was managed in accordance with Western park-management principles until 1985, and during this period Anangu had no involvement at all in the management of one of their most sacred and significant places.

Removal of Indigenous peoples from national parks is not just an Australian phenomenon. In 1999 Mark Spence wrote his seminal work on the American wilderness, entitled *Dispossessing the Wilderness*. In this book Spence argued that the deliberate removal of American Indians from national parks, especially in western parts of America, was a result of 18th- and 19th-century European visions of parks as the embodiment of the Garden of Eden. Removal of Indigenous peoples from parks was designed to assist with the reclamation of Eden by European settlers and park users.

George Catlin was one of the first Europeans to see Yellowstone, which he described in 1832. He marveled at the 'untouched' lands of the American west, although at this time he recognized that Indians were an integral part of this wild country. He and other patriarchs of the environmental movement, such as Thoreau, Muir, and Leopold, all argued that Indians, practicing culture, had been and continued to be integral to the construction of the wild lands of the United States. They even used the term 'Indian Wilderness' to describe such places as Yellowstone and Yosemite. In the 19th century, Americans were keen to portray America, now independent of Britain following the American War of Independence and the War of 1812, as different from Europe in as many ways as possible. Art and literature of the time all emphasized an Indian Wilderness, as we can see in the works of Ralph Waldo Emerson, Washington Irving, Henry Wadsworth Longfellow, Herman Melville, and others (Cronon 1995; Spence 1999). But by the end of the 19th century these views of an inhabited wilderness were 'superseded by the idealization of uninhabited landscapes' (Spence 1999: 11).

In the 1860s and 1870s there was an increasing vision that the correct place for Indians was on reservations rather than in wilderness. Yellowstone had originally been declared 'Indian territory' and set aside for the protection of Indians, forcibly removed to Yellowstone from throughout the American west. But by the late 19th century Yellowstone had been legislated as the first national park in the world (then termed 'nation's park'), and its role as a place for the protection of Indians changed quickly and dramatically.

Park managers began to assert that wilderness lands such as Yellowstone were far too untamed and wild to have ever been places conducive to human use and occupation (Spence 1999: 5). Indians may have passed through such lands, they argued, but only rarely. It was clear, they declared, that Indians never liked such places (those moved there forcibly certainly were unhappy), and therefore their role in the creation of the landscape must have been minimal, the managers argued (Spence 1999: 4). Geysers like those in Yellowstone were regarded by Indians as 'sacred to Satan' and were therefore avoided, park managers assumed, ignoring the abundant evidence for Indian campsites throughout the geyser basin as well as the evidence for Indian burning and other land-use practices that had shaped the area over thousands of years (Spence 1999: 43).

Despite such unfounded claims, people were soon persuaded that wild and pristine lands were evidence that Indians had never lived in these areas (Spence 1999: 33–42). If they had, then they had failed to follow God's instructions to Adam to till the earth and make it productive (Cronon 1995; see Chapter 2), and they therefore did not deserve them. These 'unspoiled' lands were as close to the natural Garden of Eden as Europeans could imagine, and, although wild, they were clearly part of 'unspoiled nature'. In this way people convinced themselves that Yellowstone and other wild places (including Yosemite, Glacier National Park, and the Sierras) had always been empty and uninhabited wildernesses, and the removal of Indians was therefore fully justified.

Unfortunately there are many examples of the removal of Indigenous people from parks and protected areas, even today, although in the 21st century 'removal' is not a physical expulsion of people from their lands. Today, 'removal' of people from lands and waters that are now protected areas occurs in the form of deleting any reference to original owners and occupiers of land in park-management literature or interpretive information about the place. We provide an example here.

For the Lakota Sioux of South Dakota, Wind Cave in the Black Hills is one of their most sacred creation places. It is from out of the cave that humans and buffalo were born. They emerged from the living, breathing cave that protects the lungs of the Black Hills. Wind Cave does, literally, breathe. When air pressure outside the cave is higher than the air pressure inside the cave, air is pulled into the cave. When the outside air pressure is lower than that inside the cave, air is drawn from the cave. Consequently the cave breathes in and out, and on an out breath in the Creation time, life was breathed into humans and buffalo.

Lakota have cared for the sacred Black Hills for generations. They raised and hunted buffalo here, along with deer, pronged horn antelope, and other game. They also harvested many wild plants and, after Spanish contact, rode horses across the adjacent plains that are still their homeland.

Wind Cave is now a national park. A visitor to the park cannot enter the cave without first passing through the Visitor Center – which is typical of visitor management in U.S. parks – beautifully developed with excellent explanations and a variety of interpretive elements. The first interpretive element the visitor to Wind Cave meets is the 20-minute introductory film. Here the ecology of the park is presented and the science of the cave explained. The visitor is told of the 'discovery' of the cave by Jesse and Tom Bingham in 1881, which marked the beginning of the long history of exploration and mapping of this amazing site. There are just two minutes in this film dedicated to Lakota knowledge of buffalo (but nothing on human creation).

In the large interpretation hall downstairs (and en route to the visitors' entrance to the cave – via an elevator) there is more information about the history and geology of the cave. Indigenous knowledge of the existence of the cave (but not knowledge of its meaning or place in Lakota ontology) is mentioned in a single panel at the beginning of a time line that extends along over 60 m of wall; this time line presents only European history and exploration of the cave, apart from the initial board acknowledging that Indians, too, knew of the existence of the cave.

There is, therefore, no mention of the significance of the cave to Lakota in either the introductory video or on the time line, or anywhere else in the Interpretation Center. There is no indication anywhere that Indigenous people may have had a long association with the place. There is no role for Indigenous involvement in the management of the park, despite the fact that one of the aims of the park and the adjacent wildlife preserve is to re-establish the buffalo herd decimated by overhunting in the 17th and 18th centuries.

Luckily such a complete removal of Indigenous people from a protected area is now rare, and there is an increasing recognition by governments and regulators that traditional land and water users and stewards should have a role in decision making about the management of protected areas. One of the best known models for shared management between representatives of government and traditional owners is the shared management model initially developed for Uluru–Kata Tjuta National Park.

AUSTRALIA

Shared Management Models

Shared management models are based on 'a power-sharing exercise of resource management between a government agency and a community or organization of stakeholders' (Pinkerton 1992: 331). Shared management takes many forms, including formal joint management (supported by legislation), less formal co-management (supported by policy arrangements but not legislation), and Indigenous Protected Areas.

In Australia, 'joint management' differs from 'co-management'. Co-management in Australia is a formal *agreement* between Indigenous people and land/resource managers, whereas joint management is a legal principle, enshrined in legislation, that recognizes the rights, interests, and obligations of both traditional owners and relevant government agencies acting on behalf of the rest of the population (Smyth 2001: 75). Joint management is, therefore, a *legal* arrangement for knowledge-sharing, power-sharing, and co-operative management outcomes. Joint management aims to combine Western approaches to conservation with Indigenous knowledge approaches to management (Craig 1992: 135). It is based on four principles:

1. the lease or other legal transfer of Indigenous-owned land to the government as a national park;
2. the integration of natural and cultural resource conservation;
3. the integration of social and cultural perspectives within a broader management framework; and
4. the development of mechanisms to ensure co-operative management between Indigenous land owners and park managers, largely through the development of Boards of Management. (Smyth 2001: 75)

Most protected areas in Australia that are managed under a formal joint management agreement adopt these four principles, although there are variations to this model (Smyth 2001).

Joint Management: The Uluṟu Model

The best-known model for joint management in Australia is that adopted in the Northern Territory for Uluṟu–Kata Tjuṯa National Park, in Central Australia, and Kakadu National Park in the 'top end' of the Northern Territory. It is commonly known as 'the Uluṟu model' (Smyth 2001: 83). The advantage of the Uluṟu model of joint management is that it offers opportunities for scientists and Aboriginal people to work together to achieve effective natural resource management (Baker, Woenne-Green, and the Mutitjulu community 1992; Walsh 1990, 1992).

The legislation under which joint management operates in the Northern Territory generally, and at Uluṟu and Kakadu specifically, is the Northern Territory National Parks and Wildlife Conservation Act of 1975. The Act provides for the establishment of Boards of Management with majority Aboriginal membership (Press 1995: 8; Smyth 2001: 78–80; Wellings 1995: 244; Willis 1992: 161). Although on the surface the existence of a majority Indigenous Board would seem to allow for Aboriginal control of the management of the park and its resources – because 'these Boards have functions and powers equal to that of the

Director of National Parks and Wildlife' (Press 1995: 8) – Aboriginal control does not and cannot occur in practice. Section 14D of the Act outlines the functions of the Boards:

- prepare Plans of Management, *in conjunction with the Director*;
- make decisions *consistent with the Plan of Management*;
- monitor management within the Park, *in conjunction with the Director*;
- formulate advice on future directions for management of the Park for the government Minister responsible for national parks, *in conjunction with the Director*. (Wellings 1995: 238; Willis 1992: 161, emphasis added)

It is clear from these provisions that authority for decision making in the park rests ultimately with the Director. Although the Director must 'consult' with traditional Aboriginal owners and have 'due regard' for the needs of traditional owners with respect to their needs to hunt and gather in the park and otherwise practice cultural activities (Press 1995: 8), any dispute between the Board majority and the Director as representative of the managers is resolved by the government or through the courts (Wellings 1995: 242) and not within principles and practices of Aboriginal law and knowledge. In short, primacy in decision making rests in the legislative provisions and bureaucratic structures of the arrangement, not in Aboriginal obligations regarding access to land and resources, their rights to be asked permission about management of owned resources, or traditional responsibilities to make decisions about the management of country.

There are a number of examples that illustrate this point. The most obvious example witnessed by visitors relates to climbing Uluṟu.

The Climb

According to the *Tjukurpa*, Uluṟu was created in the Dreaming by a number of creator beings: *Mala*, the hare-wallaby; *Kuniya*, the python; *Liru*, the poisonous snake; *Lungkata*, the blue-tongue lizard; *Panpanpalala*, the bellbird; *Itjaritjari*, the marsupial mole; *Luunpa*, the kingfisher; and *Tjintirtjintirpa*, the willie wagtail (Breeden 1997: 15–21). All these beings are embodied in various parts of the rock, and all parts of the rock are thereby associated with the *Tjukurpa* through the creation stories.

The *Tjukurpa* is more than a set of stories.

> The *Tjukurpa* is the foundation of Aṉangu. It provides the rules for behaviour and for living together. It is the Law for caring for one another and for the land that supports our existence. . . . *Life and Land Are One.* . . . The *Tjukurpa* is all around us in the landscape itself. . . . To see

Uluru through Anangu eyes is to see a complex religious and ceremonial stage. Uluru's many features are very important because they are evidence that the ancestral beings of the *Tjukurpa* are still with us. Their Law is kept strong in our hearts and minds every day we live here. This is why we have a responsibility to keep our land and our cultural traditions alive. Our past, our present and our future depend upon it. (Mutitjulu Community 1990, emphasis in original)

Part of the *Tjukurpa* relates to the climb up to the top of the rock. This route is sacred to the Anangu people. According to the *Tjukurpa*, only initiated men may climb this route to the top of the rock, because the climb requires a certain level of knowledge within the Mala tradition. 'To travel the path in ignorance is inappropriate behaviour' (Doherty 1996: 38).

The Anangu and the national parks staff who jointly manage Uluru-Kata Tjuta National Park have, until recently, agreed not to close the climb to visitors, because so many come to Uluru expressly to undertake this activity. But a sign in English, Japanese, and German at the foot of the climb expresses Anangu wishes:

Nganana Tatintja Wiya – 'We Never Climb'

The traditional owners of Uluru-Kata Tjuta National Park ask visitors not to climb Uluru because of its spiritual significance as the traditional route of the ancestral Mala men on their arrival at Uluru. We prefer that visitors explore Uluru through the wide range of guided walks and interpretive attractions on offer in the Park. At the Cultural Centre you will learn more about these and the significance of Uluru in Anangu culture.

Anangu have not closed the climb. They prefer that you – out of education and understanding – choose to respect their law and culture by not climbing. Remember that you are a guest on Anangu land. Anangu traditionally have a duty to safeguard visitors to their land. They feel great sadness when a person dies or is hurt. (Department of Environment, Water, Heritage and the Arts 2009; see also Breeden 1997: 189)

Despite this request, more than 100,000 tourists climb Uluru each year (ABC News 2009a). For many of these people, the climb is the only activity they undertake while on a one-day trip to Uluru from Alice Springs (Breeden 1997: 189–190). The Anangu call these tourists *minga* ('ants'), because this is what they look like as they crawl up the rock.

One of the major reasons for the large number of climbers is that brochures of Uluru written by travel agents and tour operators advertise climbing Uluru as a 'must do' activity (Doherty 1996). Jacobs and Gale (1994: 115) demonstrate that visitors generally develop their itineraries from information gained before departing for their holiday. Consequently the nature of information about Uluru provided by tour companies is vital in informing visitor behavior.

Doherty's analysis of tourist previsit literature about Uluru found that:

> 50% of operators openly promote climbing Uluru, and 10% publish photographs of people undertaking this activity. 50% of operators ignore the issue of [whether or not to undertake] the climb altogether; they offer no information on the Traditional Owners' cultural concerns regarding this culturally inappropriate visitor behaviour. Only 8% of operators provide alternative activities to climbing Uluru. These alternatives are to watch the sunrise or join a base tour. (Doherty 1996: 77)

Tour operators do not acknowledge that Uluru is a culturally sensitive landscape, where certain behaviors are not acceptable. In fact, Uluru is promoted largely as the climb, with the nearby Yulara tourist resort 'promoted as the reward for the feat of climbing' (Jacobs and Gale 1994: 116). Alternatives to the very arduous climb, such as viewing the nearby rock art sites on the Mala Walk, are not only ignored in most of the literature but also are sometimes actively discouraged as being 'too strenuous' (Jacobs and Gale 1994: 37).

Many tourists, therefore, do not realize that climbing Uluru is inappropriate until they arrive at the Uluru Visitors' Centre or read the Anangu sign at the base of the climb. Although Anangu wishes are made clear in the sign, by this stage many people have already made their plans to climb the rock. When they are on an organized tour there are often no other activities provided for those who change their minds at the last minute (Jacobs and Gale 1994).

Despite the very strong co-operation between Anangu and rangers regarding this issue, Anangu have been powerless to impose their law on visitor behavior because of the institutional structures that allow tour operators to exercise primary control over visitor activities.

Recently Anangu decided to more formally exercise their desires regarding the closure of the climb. On July 8, 2009, the new Draft Management Plan for Uluru-Kata Tjuta National Park was released for public comment. The draft plan recommended closing the climb 'for cultural and environmental reasons' (ABC 2009a). Strong reaction to the plan was immediately received, including from the then Prime Minister, the Hon. Kevin Rudd (MP), who, on July 10, 2009, said: 'I think it would be very sad if we got to a stage, though, where Australians and frankly our guests from abroad weren't able to enjoy that experience. . . to climb it' (*The Australian* 2009). Other immediate criticism came from the Federal Opposition – who called on the Prime Minister to veto the proposal (ABC 2009b) – the Northern Territory government, and from a number of tourists:

> 'This is a secular country. Dictating access to a popular tourist destination based on religious beliefs is unacceptable'. ('Jim')

> 'By all means close the rock to climbers in adverse weather conditions, but to permanently close it would a denial of the rights of all Australians'. ('Saint Mike')

> 'The decision to climb or not to climb should remain with the individual, not the park management (white or black)'. (Anon)

> 'I understand the opposition to people climbing it. But at this point, it is a pilgrimage to travel to Uluru and climb it. I suggest that it is as important to Australia in general as it is to the traditional owners, and that should be considered'. ('Si')

> 'It is not as if anyone built it. It was always there. Climb on it if you want. It is like saying you can't swim in Sydney Harbour or walk around the Grand Canyon'. ('Ron Rat') (ABC News 2009a)

For Anangu there was relief that a ban of climbing the rock was in sight:

> You can't go climb on top of the Vatican, you can't go climb on top of the Buddhist temples and so on and so forth. . . . Obviously you have to respect our religious attachment to the land, too, so we're saying please do not climb Uluru – we've said it in all languages. (Vince Forrester, ABC News 2009a)

However, it now appears that the ban may not be implemented. ABC News on October 20, 2009, reported that a 'plan to ban tourists from climbing Uluru could be scuttled after the wording of a draft management plan was altered following strong submissions from the tourism industry' (ABC News 2009c). A final decision on the wording of the Plan of Management is still to be made, with that decision resting with the Federal Environment Minister. As with all aspects of 'joint management' at Uluru, decisions about Aboriginal heritage and cultural matters are not the responsibility of the traditional owners.

Training

Another example of the primacy of Western management systems in the joint management arrangements at Uluru and Kakadu relates to training (Press 1995: 9; Wellings 1995: 245; Willis 1992: 163; cf. Stevenson 2006). At Kakadu there are no requirements or opportunities for Western scientists and the (mostly white) rangers who manage the parks on a day-to-day basis to be 'trained' in Aboriginal stewardship techniques. At Uluru the lease agreement does allow for management staff 'to utilise the traditional skills of Aboriginal individuals and groups in the management of the park' and for non-Aboriginal staff to be given 'appropriate instruction' about the 'traditions, languages, culture, customs, and skills of the relevant Aboriginals . . .' (Willis 1992: 163); nevertheless, the emphasis of training in both parks is on Aboriginal rangers learning scientific ways of management (Willis 1992).

Living in the Park

There is one aspect of the Uluru model that does allow some elements of Indigenous law and knowledge to have primacy over Western legal systems. In both Uluru and Kakadu, some traditional Aboriginal owners live in the parks under the provisions of the parks' Plans of Management and the lease-back agreement. Those people living on 'outstations' in the parks are able to maintain a traditional relationship with the land on which they live. Here Aboriginal law dominates certain limited aspects of daily life, although establishment of the outstation in the first place must be within the provisions of the Plan of Management, and Western laws have supremacy over Indigenous law in terms of criminal acts and a large number of social matters.

At Uluru the provisions of the original lease-back of Aboriginal land to the government reserved certain rights to the Aboriginal people living on the park, including rights to enter and to use the park in accordance with Aboriginal tradition, the right to hunt and gather in the park, and the right to practice ceremonial and other cultural activities in the park (Willis 1992: 160). But once again, these rights are subject to Western legal strictures:

> The lessor [that is, the nominated agent of the government, usually the Director of National Parks] reserves in favour of relevant Aboriginals and groups of relevant Aboriginals the following rights, which shall operate *subject to the direction or decisions of the Uluru-Kata Tjuta Board with respect to health, safety or privacy.* (Willis 1992: 160, emphasis added)

Overall, the Uluru model of joint management brings some advantages to Anangu people. Nevertheless, in spite of the fact that this land is Anangu land that has been leased to the Australian government, Anangu knowledge plays a consistently minor role in most aspects of park management.

Other Joint Management Models

As well as the Uluru and Kakadu model, there are other joint management models for protected-areas management in Australia. Smyth summarizes the four main models of joint management that exist in different parts of the country; see Table 5.1.

In practice, each of these models is very different from other joint management models, and each provides very different rights to Aboriginal owners. All these models recognize Aboriginal rights to occupy and use the parks, and these rights are protected either by law, the lease-back agreement, or via the Plan of Management (Smyth 2001: 84). But all these protections are based in Western bureaucratic systems and, from the wording of protections placed in lease-back agreements, require only a change in government or a change in attitude within the bureaucracy to change the arrangement.

An example of the problems that arise from the situation of Indigenous rights in a Western bureaucratic system can be seen in recent legal battles over Aboriginal access to hunting rights in national parks. Aboriginal rights to hunt and gather are recognized as essential to cultural identity (Smyth

TABLE 5.1 Joint-management models in operation in protected areas in Australia (Smyth 2001: 83).

Gurig Model (NT)	Uluṟu Model (NT & NSW)	Queensland Model* (QLD)	Witjira Model (SA)
Aboriginal ownership	Aboriginal ownership	Aboriginal ownership	Lease of park to TOs
Equal representation on Management Board	Aboriginal majority on Management Board	No guarantee of Aboriginal majority on Board	Aboriginal majority on Management Board
No lease-back to govt. (i.e., Aboriginal ownership)	Lease-back to govt. required for long period	Lease-back to govt. required in perpetuity	Ownership of land rests with govt.
Annual fee to TOs	Annual fee to TOs, community council, or Board	No annual fee paid	No annual fee paid
e.g., Gurig National Park	e.g., Uluṟu, Kakadu, Nitmiluk, Booderee [NSW], Mutawintji [NSW]	e.g., None finalized	e.g., Witjira National Park

*In 2007/2008 Queensland developed an Indigenous Protected Area (IPA) model that this state has labeled a 'joint-management' model. However, the new IPA model is not technically 'joint management'; the Queensland IPA model is discussed later in this chapter.

2001: 85) and are therefore enshrined in most joint management agreements (Press 1995; Wellings 1995; Willis 1992). But as these rights to hunt and gather need to meet Western perspectives of conservation and biodiversity, as well as Western concepts of hunting and gathering and Indigenous 'conservation', they are regularly open to challenge. This was demonstrated clearly in the wake of the Yanner High Court decision.

Hunting Rights and the Yanner Decision

Although the Native Title Act of 1993 and the subsequent Native Title Amendments of 1998 both included recognition of native title rights for native title owners and claimants to hunt and gather over native title owned or claimed lands and waters, not until November 1999 were these rights clarified. In a High Court action, which is binding on all parties and cannot be appealed, an Aboriginal man, Murrandoo Yanner, appealed against an earlier ruling in the Supreme Court of Australia that he was guilty under the Queensland Fauna Conservation Act of 1974 of illegally taking two crocodiles for his own family's use. Yanner successfully argued in the High Court that section 211 of the Native Title Act of 1993 applied and that in taking the crocodiles he was exercising his native title rights to the resources of his country (*Yanner vs. Eaton* 1999).

Between October 31 and December 1, 1994, Murandoo Yanner used a traditional form of harpoon and a dingy (aluminum boat) with an outboard motor to hunt and kill two juvenile saltwater crocodiles on a pastoral lease that was part of his native title lands. Under the Queensland Fauna Conservation Act of 1974, this action was illegal, as Yanner had neither applied for nor received a permit or license from the Queensland environment department (the then Environmental Protection Agency) to take these protected animals.

In the initial hearing in the local Magistrate's Court, Yanner argued that, although his actions may have been illegal under Queensland state law, under Section 211 of the federal Native Title Act of 1993 his actions were legal, because he was exercising his native title right to hunt these animals. In Australia, in accordance with Section 109 of the Australian Constitution, federal law supersedes state law if there is any contradiction between the two. The Magistrate's Court supported Yanner's arguments, but the Queensland government appealed the decision in the higher Supreme Court, which overturned the Magistrate court's decision. The arguments in the Supreme Court were that crocodiles are an endangered species, protected by the state of Queensland, and that the protection provided to endangered species by the Fauna Conservation Act of 1974 was effectively a form of state 'ownership' of the crocodile, and 'ownership' by the state extinguishes native title rights under the provisions of the Native Title Act of 1993.

Yanner appealed to the High Court (Australia's highest court of appeal). On October 7, 1999 the High Court ruled in a majority decision that:

1. The method of capture of the crocodiles was irrelevant to the native title rights Yanner was claiming (that is, the use of a motorized boat and a metal harpoon was immaterial to the case);
2. The land over which Yanner was hunting was indeed part of his native title lands (and therefore the provisions of the Native Title Act of 1993 applied);
3. Hunting juvenile crocodiles was an integral part of Yanner's traditional law (as recognized by the Native Title Act of 1993);
4. State control of endangered animals is not 'ownership', so the provisions of the Fauna Conservation Act of 1974 do not extinguish native title.

Consequences for Aboriginal Involvement in Protected-Areas Management

Aboriginal people throughout Australia heralded this case as a victory for Aboriginal hunting rights, including rights to hunt in protected areas both with and without joint management arrangements. Many Aboriginal groups commenced hunting a range of animals deemed by national parks staff and conservationists to be conservation icons – animals such as dugongs and turtles in particular.

To hunt endangered species in this way, especially using 'modern' weapons, did not meet Western perceptions of what constituted 'caring for country' and 'stewardship', and many conservationists and scientists have recently withdrawn their support, not only for Indigenous hunting activities in protected areas but also for the concept of joint management of protected areas generally. One of the most noticeable shifts in support for Aboriginal people's rights has occurred with respect to scientific support for dugong hunting (Marsh et al. 2004; see Chapter 4).

So, although joint management agreements might recognize that traditional hunting, fishing, and gathering practices are integral to the maintenance of cultural identity (Smyth 2001: 85), Aboriginal rights in this area are limited in several ways. The most significant imposition is that Aboriginal rights to access resources will always be secondary to the rights of scientists and managers to protect biodiversity and species conservation in accordance with legislation, lease agreements, or plans of management. Hunting and gathering must be sustainable in order to be supported (Smyth 2001: 85), but who determines sustainability? We have already seen that recent scientific research has claimed that Indigenous hunting of dugong is unsustainable (see Chapter 4) but that their scientific methods for collecting their baseline data are flawed. Yet scientific evidence, even if based on data collected using flawed methods, will always be privileged over seemingly 'unproven' Aboriginal knowledge.

In short, joint management:

> is a concept rather than a fixed model, and there is significant variation in the 'models' applied across Australia and subsequently the provisions for Aboriginal involvement and the inclusion of their knowledge. (Phoenix-O'Brien 2002: 63)

Co-Management

Co-management occurs where formal but not legally binding arrangements regarding land and resources management are negotiated between Indigenous owners and protected-area managers. According to George, Innes, and Ross (2004: 9), co-management is a constantly negotiated process between stakeholders in an area (but especially between park managers and traditional owners) that leads to a partnership between stakeholders with shared and equitable responsibility for management (see also Berkes 2009). The aim of co-management is to allow government agencies and traditional owners to develop agreements about land and sea management – at both species and habitat levels – with agreements based on shared knowledge and shared decision-making structures as the basis for the implementation of management regimes (Berkes 2009: 1693; George, Innes, and Ross 2004: 5).

Despite the good intentions that come with the negotiation of co-management agreements, as with joint management arrangements, most co-management outcomes privilege Western knowledge and Western bureaucratic structures. One example of this imbalance in co-management comes from the development of a co-management agreement for the Great Barrier Reef Marine Park (GBRMP) and the Great Barrier Reef World Heritage Area (GBRWHA) in Queensland (George, Innes, and Ross 2004) (see Figure 4.2).

Co-Management in the Great Barrier Reef Marine Park and World Heritage Area

A role for Indigenous involvement in the management of GBRMP was an initiative of the Aboriginal organization 'Sea Forum', established during the 1990s and continuing into the 21st century. The aim was to facilitate the incorporation of Indigenous knowledge and management practices into everyday management activities in the GBRMP. Despite a good working relationship between the Great Barrier Reef Marine Park Authority (GBRMPA) and the traditional owners, a number of problems in the implementation of co-management arrangements in GBRMP have arisen, with the majority of problems relating to epistemological and institutional disconnects between Western land managers and traditional land owners.

An underlying systemic problem that informs many subsequent organizational issues for Indigenous land managers is that traditional owners are regarded by governments as just one stakeholder in a multi-stakeholder environment. Although traditional owners (and many GBRMPA staff) argue that Indigenous people are very different stakeholders from other park users, the bureaucratic system finds it difficult to separate the special needs and rights of Indigenous park users from the rights of others. As a consequence GBRMPA finds it difficult to recognize that there are many different Aboriginal cultural groups, with different knowledge relating to marine resource use, in the area covered by the GBRMP and GBRWHA. The marine park covers 345,950 km^2; it is the largest marine protected area in the world. The Great Barrier Reef World Heritage Area is the largest World Heritage Area on earth, covering 348,000 km^2. Given this vast extent, the protected area incorporates a large number of different traditional owner groups. It is inappropriate to consider all these culturally, linguistically, and socially diverse Aboriginal and Torres Strait Islander parties as a single stakeholder entity.

Despite its huge size, the protected area that is the GBRMP and GBRWHA does not cover the entire reef. The national park and the world heritage area include few land masses. Some reef islands are incorporated into the zoning, but little of the mainland is represented. Aboriginal estates, in contrast, include both land and sea territory (McNiven 2008), and many Aboriginal groups do not recognize the excision of the GBRMP and GBRWHA from the remainder of their traditional country. Nevertheless, traditional owners are required to negotiate with GBRMPA only over those areas where there is intersection between traditional owner country and GBRMPA legal boundaries. There are no opportunities for management to be developed on the basis of traditional owners' legal tenure frameworks. Management is entirely built on Western boundary constructions.

Another barrier to Indigenous approaches to management of the protected reef area is a further corollary of the bureaucratically recognized boundaries of the protected area: GBRMP and GBRWHA are managed by the highly centralized GBRMPA, which is a structure completely different from Indigenous decentralized social systems and management structures:

> The challenge for GBRMPA and for the Indigenous parties to co-management is that GBRMPA (like most non-Indigenous authorities) is a centralized body with authority over a very large spatial area of sea and reefs, while Indigenous authority (under customary law) is decentralized, with prime authority being invested in the traditional owners of many clan estates. (George, Innes, and Ross 2004: 40)

Because of these Western-imposed management systems, to be heard in co-management agreement-making ventures, Aboriginal groups find it necessary to form into organizations based on Western notions of representation. The fact that such organizations rely on government funding to remain viable further forces traditional owner groups to operate outside their traditional governance structures.

Increasingly, Indigenous groups are rebelling against organizations, including Aboriginal organizations, that are formulated on Western governance models and are re-asserting 'Indigenous governance' (Smith 2005). One such governance model that is currently being developed in GBRMP is the TUMRA (Traditional Use of Marine Resource Agreements) scheme.

Traditional Use of Marine Resource Agreements

Traditional Use of Marine Resource Agreements, or TUMRAs, are co-operative marine resource management initiatives that grew out of earlier failed co-management exercises in GBRMP. The TUMRA scheme is a legislative document proposed by traditional owners in accordance with the Great Barrier Reef Marine Park Regulation of 1983 (QLD) and is recognized by the Environment Protection and Biodiversity Conservation Act of 1999 (Federal) as a statutory document that allows the harvesting of marine resources from the GBRMP (Cullen 2007). Havermann and associates (2005: 260) describe TUMRAs as having the ability to 'empower' traditional owners in their role as 'guardians of sea-country', as traditional owners will fulfill an 'invaluable' conservation role for GBRMPA. Many Indigenous owners do not agree, however, as Cullen's (2007) research demonstrates.

In 2007 Michelle Cullen interviewed representatives of Indigenous groups, GBRMPA staff, and marine scientists working in GBRMP to discover their views on how well they thought TUMRAs were working with respect to the management of dugongs in the GBRMP. All interviewees agreed that TUMRAs were an improvement on previous co-management arrangements between Aboriginal communities and the GBRMPA, but all interviewees also felt that several aspects of the agreements remained problematic.

Indigenous communities view the TUMRA scheme with caution. Indigenous knowledge relating to marine resources stewardship includes knowledge of land dwelling spirits and other coastal resources, and consequently Indigenous goals for co-management of a marine environment such as the Great Barrier Reef reflect a more holistic and ongoing strategy for management than is allowed in the TUMRA scheme; traditional owners want to be involved in the management of the *whole* of sea-country:

> [I] would like to see Traditional Owners in full control of their saltwater country, managing all their resources, not only turtles and dugongs but having the power and authority to make decisions about management in all areas. (Indigenous community representative, cited in Cullen 2007: 22; see also Bradley 1998; McNiven 2008; Nursey-Bray 2005)

Indigenous representatives were also disappointed that, despite expectations of a genuine partnership between scientists, managers, and Indigenous peoples, the TUMRA scheme privileges scientific knowledge, especially with respect to endangered species such as turtles and dugongs. This has led to barriers in cross-cultural communication between Indigenous turtle and dugong hunters, who see hunting as an integral part of species conservation (Bradley 1998; Ross and Bigge 2009; cf. Sillitoe 2002), and Western managers, who cannot see a connection between resource extraction and species preservation:

> co-management initiatives will be condemned to failure if Western parties continue to come to the [management] table with a belief in the superiority of their knowledge over that of all others, and a view to 'educate' the Traditional Owners, rather than to understand them. (Cullen 2007: 35)

All interviewees raised their concern that lack of communication had resulted in limited trust between Indigenous resource stewards and Western scientists and GBRMPA staff, which has, in turn, limited the effectiveness of the TUMRA scheme.

Another shared concern of interviewees related to the 'top down' nature of the management of TUMRAs, despite its being an initiative of a former Indigenous institution (Sea Forum). Management processes in the scheme are entirely based in Western governance structures and Western timeframes for negotiation, largely because of the political imbalance between other stakeholder groups, such as commercial and recreational fishers, and traditional owners:

> Indigenous hunting is a very sensational [cause of dugong mortality] and it's easy [for management agencies] to target. . . . It's much harder to

target boat owners [who also cause dugong deaths] because the electorate is going to be much more sympathetic to boat owners than they are to Indigenous people. (Cullen 2007: 31)

Cullen concludes:

there are a number of epistemological and systemic barriers to successful co-management of natural resources, including dugongs, in the GBRWHA. Epistemological barriers include the different knowledge contexts of Western managers and Traditional Owners, and the creation of trust relationships. These barriers are tempered by past practices, political perceptions and are underlain by the different constructions and use of knowledge. Systemic barriers include timeframes for management, funding, and the differing goals and objectives for dugong management that emerge from Western managers and Traditional Owners. (2007: 32)

Robinson, Ross, and Hockings (2006) agree with Cullen's analysis. They argue that the TUMRA scheme is a form of *partnership* between GBRMPA and traditional owners but is not a true co-management initiative. True co-management recognizes Indigenous people's rights to have a say in environmental and resource management, to be involved in decisions about resource use, and to be permitted to use the country to benefit the environment as well as the people's social, economic, and cultural requirements (Carlsson and Berkes 2005; Robinson, Ross, and Hockings 2006; Stevenson 2006). If Indigenous resources and stewardship knowledge are limited by Western knowledge systems and Western governance structures, then true co-management has not been achieved. However, the TUMRA scheme *is* an advance on previous co-management arrangements between Indigenous communities and GBRMPA and may be considered to be a 'first step' toward genuine co-management arrangements in this part of Australia.

Indigenous Protected Areas

There is a view in some co-management literature that genuine co-management has been achieved in the establishment of 'Indigenous Protected Areas' (IPAs) (Gilligan 2006; Smyth 2001, 2006). However, in practice, IPAs – like joint and co-management – often reproduce epistemological inequalities.

IPAs are based on IUCN (International Union for Conservation of Nature) guidelines that define an Indigenous Protected Area as: 'An area of land and/or sea especially dedicated to the protection and maintenance of biological diversity and associated cultural resources, and managed through legal or other effective means' (cited in Smyth 2006: 15). IPAs provide for the recognition of Indigenous ownership and use of resources and management of land as being comparable to Western ownership and management systems. They are established through formal conservation agreements under state law, but if developed in accordance with IUCN principles, IPAs will provide for a primary role for Indigenous law in management.

In Australia IPAs are funded by governments, and, to continue to receive such funding, Aboriginal IPA managers must develop a Plan of Management for the IPA that involves 'expertise from government conservation agencies' and be 'endorsed by indigenous landowners' (Smyth 2006: 16); it is, therefore, a plan that must meet scientific principles of biodiversity conservation as its primary objective. Management of the IPA must be in accordance with the biodiversity conservation goals established in the Plan of Management (Smyth 2006).

In Australia more than 20 IPAs have been declared since 1988. According to Smyth, IPAs bring a range of benefits to Indigenous IPA managers:

- they allow Indigenous people to live on their traditional lands;
- they encourage the transference of traditional knowledge from 'elders' to young people;
- they facilitate the implementation of traditional land and cultural resources management practices, such as fire management and maintenance of cultural sites;
- they provide training and employment in the management of traditional country; and
- they promote economic opportunities (for example, tourism). (2006: 19).

Despite these positive advantages of IPAs to Indigenous peoples, community conserved areas such as IPAs 'are not a panacea for all conservation problems' (Kothari 2006: 9–10). Kothari lists a range of problems that arise from the establishment and implementation of community conserved areas (CCAs):

- weakened traditional governance and management institutions because of the need to operate within colonial or centralized political systems, and/or as a result of strong commercial forces;
- a consequent undermining of traditional forms of authority over resources management;
- general lack of governmental and funding support;
- 'straight-jacketed' approaches to CCAs by governments, 'often taking over key community functions, or establishing uniform and parallel institutional bodies based on representative politics, rather than facilitation and improving upon an existing [Indigenous or local] system';

- internal inequalities as a result of power imbalances within local management systems;
- subsequent lack of interest in CCAs from younger generations; and
- some perceptions of 'over-harvesting' as traditional resource use now competes with other forms of commercial and recreational exploitation; which
- can lead to lack of support for CCAs by conservation groups who perceive that traditional resource managers are not operating in accordance with conservationists' expectations of 'ecologically noble savages'. (Kothari 2006; cf. Brosius 2000; Head 1990, 2000).

In a recent review of IPAs in Australia, Gilligan noted a similar list of issues plaguing Australian Indigenous community conservation areas. Gilligan found that:

- funding for IPAs is low – less than $0.18 per hectare per annum; this has reduced the long-term security for IPAs;
- there is poor credibility of IPAs as public accountability for funding is poorly executed by Indigenous communities who are required to perform Western-style accountability with limited training;
- Indigenous communities are often required to juggle a range of government programs, of which IPAs are only one component, in order to maximize overall community benefits; Indigenous communities see all these programs as interrelated, but Western governments compartmentalize programs and do not understand why IPA projects may be linked by Indigenous communities to health, aging, welfare, or other social programs;
- Indigenous IPA managers are increasingly required to meet government imposed management outcomes which do not always accord with Indigenous aspirations for resources and land management;
- there is, at times, inadequate recognition of the primacy of Indigenous decision making and governance regimes; and
- there needs to be a recognition that Aboriginal country does not end at the shoreline – many Indigenous communities desire to see their IPAs extend to incorporate sea estates. (2006: 46–56).

From these reviews it would seem that many CCAs and IPAs – both in Australia and elsewhere – are little different from joint managed or co-managed parks. Although these lands are Indigenous-owned lands and not government lands, and although IPAs can be created without any requirement for lease-back of land, they are still very much controlled by Western bureaucratic and knowledge structures.

Dhimurru IPA and Epistemological Barriers

Robinson and Munumgguritj (2001) provide an example of an IPA established close to Yirrkala, Northern Territory, on Yolngu lands. Management of this Aboriginal land is largely under the control of Dhimurru (traditional) rangers who receive their instructions from Yolngu elders. Yet Dhimurru rangers must collaborate with the Northern Territory Parks and Wildlife Commission staff to develop the formal Plan of Management for the area (Robinson and Munumgguritj 2001: 101). Furthermore,

> work on this project [the IPA] has involved quantifying indigenous harvesting and identifying the effects of commercial and recreational fishing activities, *to help Yolngu make informed decisions about future management.* (Robinson and Munumgguritj 2001: 101, emphasis added)

and

> Scientific researchers [assisting with the preparation of the Plan of Management] have also shown Yolngu people that, *in contradiction to Yolngu knowledge and law,* loggerhead turtles are not born in Yolngu territories but in areas of southern Queensland. (Robinson and Munumgguritj 2001: 101, emphasis added)

This latter example of the dominion of Western knowledge over Indigenous knowledge and law has been elaborated by Kennett and associates (2004). When Yolngu knowledge about turtle migration to Arnhem Land differed from that known to scientists advising the Dhimurru Land Management Aboriginal Corporation, scientists felt that it was important to 'correct' the 'misinformation' that underpinned Yolngu cosmology. Scientists took Yolngu senior law makers to see baby turtles on the beaches of central Queensland, which challenged Yolngu law:

> [This visit] led Yolngu to wonder about these animals which their Law held to live, forage and nest in local [that is, Northern Territory] coastal-marine waters. Discussions that revealed that Western knowledge held a different view of Dhalwatpu [Green Turtle] and Garun [Loggerhead Turtle] biology and migratory behaviour led to Dhimurru's interest in working with Western scientists to research migration patterns. (Kennett et al. 2004:162)

Kennett and associates argue that this sort of knowledge exchange is an example of 'two-way' learning, yet all the learning seems to have been demanded of Indigenous peoples; there have been few epistemological challenges for scientists (cf. Stevenson 2006).

IPAs in Queensland and Institutional Barriers

In 2007 the Queensland government developed a form of jointly managed protected area for Cape York, in far northern Queensland, that is an amalgam of joint management and IPA principles. This new protected area category is called 'National Park (Cape York Peninsula Aboriginal Land – CYPAL)' and is created over Aboriginal land, although management incorporates both Indigenous and Western systems.

In July 2008 the first of these new types of protected area was declared as 'Lama Lama National Park (Cape York Peninsula Aboriginal Land)', to be known as 'KULLA National Park (CYPAL)'. The then Queensland Minister for Natural Resources and Water, the Hon. Craig Wallace, MP, claimed that this new national park type would have an underlying tenure of Aboriginal freehold land managed as a national park under joint arrangements between the Queensland state and Indigenous owners of the land (Hansard, Queensland Legislative Assembly, May 15, 2008).

The creation of KULLA National Park (CYPAL) is indeed a historic and important development in Queensland. It is the first jointly managed national park in the state, and the move signals that the Queensland government recognizes the Indigenous connection to country that is so important in Indigenous cultures. Yet, as with joint management and IPAs elsewhere in Australia, there remain a series of epistemological and institutional barriers to genuine Indigenous management of Indigenous lands in KULLA National Park (CYPAL).

Under the provisions of the (QLD) Cape York Peninsula Heritage Act of 2007, KULLA National Park (CYPAL) is to be managed via the establishment of two Advisory Committees, the *Cape York Peninsula Regional Advisory Committee* and the *Cape York Peninsula Region Scientific and Cultural Advisory Committee*. Although the *Cape York Peninsula Regional Advisory Committee* is to have at least 50% Aboriginal representation, and it *may* have an advisory role relating to land management (Cape York Peninsula Heritage Act of 2007, Section 20[b]), the primary management functions under the Act lie with the *Cape York Peninsula Region Scientific and Cultural Advisory Committee*. This is an expert committee, with members chosen by government ministers (Cape York Peninsula Heritage Act of 2007, Section 22). 'Indigenous community use areas' are subject to approval by both the Advisory Committees (Cape York Peninsula Heritage Act of 2007, Section 15) and even then cannot be approved unless other (non-Indigenous) stakeholders agree (Cape York Peninsula Heritage Act of 2007, Section 16), and the Aboriginal community submits business and management plans that meet Western bureaucratic requirements (Cape York Peninsula Heritage Act of 2007, Sections 18–19).

Despite the rhetoric that National Parks (Cape York Peninsula Aboriginal Land) will be 'a new class of protected area to enable national parks to be created over Aboriginal land without the need for lease-back arrangements' (Department of Natural Resources and Water Fact Sheet 2008), implying that Aboriginal people will have control over their traditional lands, it is clear that management of these national parks will be dominated by Western land managers.

Discussion

The situation described above is not peculiar to Australia. Stevenson (2006) has discussed a similar situation regarding inequalities in Canadian co-management arrangements and consequent contestations between government resource managers and Indigenous resource users. Stevenson demonstrates that Canadian Indigenous resource users must speak the language of the scientists and organize themselves into Western-style bureaucracies to have their voices heard at the management table (2006: 167, 169–171). The need for Indigenous people in Australia to submit to formal Plans of Management, developed using scientific knowledge, is a similar 'language' requirement. Furthermore, Stevenson documents that in Canada Indigenous people are expected to meet Western stereotypes of Indigenous resource use, which often involve notions of 'Mother Earth' and sustainable management: '[W]hen Aboriginal peoples do not act, in the eyes of the conservation bureaucracy, in the best interests of "conserving wildlife", their "Indianness" and their rights to "manage resources" are questioned' (Stevenson 2006: 168). This is similar to the conservationists' response to the Yanner legal decision regarding Indigenous hunting. And although co-management provides First Nations Canadians with a means to express their knowledge about resources and their uses, Indigenous ways of relating to the environment are regularly challenged and even dismissed by Western resource managers, and state-based power relationships and structures dominate all aspects of supposedly co-operative, shared management (Stevenson 2006: 173). In Australia, this occurs even on Aboriginal-owned IPAs. The objectives of co-management are set by the state, Stevenson observes, and these objectives are rarely varied or negotiated, even when Indigenous people demonstrate flaws in the management structures.

Consequently, the failures of co-operative management arrangements are not unique to Australia. To further explore the various ways in which co-management principles operate outside Australia, we now turn to a review of co-management in two of our other case study regions – first in India and then in Thailand.

INDIA

Joint Forest Management (JFM) in India: Harnessing Adivasi Religion

Exploitation of naturally recurring resources in the British colonial period reduced forest cover on the Indian subcontinent to around 40% by 1854. This fell to less than 20% in post-independence (1947) India. Currently, nondegraded forests cover only 10% of India; national forest policies dictate that this number should stand at 33%.

In the early 1980s, to avert an environmental catastrophe and salvage the economic viability of communities dependent on hundreds of forest products for their survival, India reversed its commodity-extraction policies and initiated 'social forestry' programs. These farm forestry schemes – typically plantings of fast-growing trees such as eucalypts on privately and communally owned plantations – were meant to provide income and forest produce to local groups and to reduce pressure on national primary and secondary forests. However, India's forests continued to degrade, and the state decided to manage forests to better serve local needs, traditions, and sensibilities and to better respect local values, knowledge, and practice. As such, in the early 1990s India began to transfer limited control of protected 'degraded' national forests – that is, forests with less than 40% crown cover – to local communities. The state and locally constituted forest councils would now collaboratively manage these lands in a new scheme dubbed 'Joint Forest Management' (JFM).

JFM is being tested in forests bordering the Phulwari ki Nal Wildlife Sanctuary (see Chapter 4). Officially, JFM is not allowed in the sanctuary itself. National laws forbid local harvest of *any* forest produce from wildlife sanctuaries, which prevents the Rajasthan Forest Department (RFD) from offering the kinds of incentives that usually motivate locals to co-operate with official management plans on state-owned lands such as Phulwari. However, Forest Protection Councils (FPCs) comprising Indigenous members are being set up in villages falling within the sanctuary's boundaries (Figure 5.1). The RFD and local NGOs hope this and other forms of state-local co-operation will alleviate pressure on the sanctuary by encouraging Indigenous peoples inhabiting these villages to harvest forest produce from lands outside the sanctuary and also, unofficially, from the forests and grasslands of the Phulwari ki Nal itself in a more sustainable fashion.

To build support for state activities in Phulwari, forest rangers in the employ of the RFD, such as Dr. Satish Kumar Sharma, who has long-term experience in Phulwari ki nal and other Rajasthani contexts and who has also been collaborating with Snodgrass in his research, have communicated participatory forest-management schemes in local

Figure 5.1 Council of village Bhils discuss forest management (photograph by J. Snodgrass).

idioms. For example, Dr. Sharma has experimented with promoting wildlife and forest conservation through a local Bhil tribal rite referred to as 'distributing saffron' (*kesar bantna*). In this rite Bhil leaders decide that a forest is degraded. There follows a summoning of local shamans, who beat drums, call local gods, and spread saffron along the boundaries of the degraded forest land. Subsequently, these shamans, along with elders and other clan members, pronounce these patches of forest land as closed to further use for a given period of time, generally five years. Anyone who attempts to use the land before that time risks bringing on themselves the displeasure of local deities.

The forest department hoped to use this traditional blessing to further motivate Indigenous Bhils to protect recently restored forest plots. These were patches of 50–100 hectares on the boundaries of Phulwari ki Nal, which were planted with as many as 10,000 saplings of bamboo (*bans*) (*Dendrocalamus strictus*), hardwoods, such as teak (*sagwan*) (*Tectona grandis*), sisam (*Dalbergia latifolia*), and neem (*Azadirachta indica*), and fruiting species such as amla (*Emblica officinalis*) and ratna jyot (*Jatropha carcus*). The hardwoods, Bhils and other Indigenous inhabitants of Phulwari were told, would be harvested and sold in such a way that locals would split profits with the state. For example, profits from 1-hectare plots would be allotted to single families inhabiting nearby villages. Likewise, the seeds, fruits, and useful parts of other trees and plants were to be harvested seasonally, providing permanent income for locals. For example, the *neem* trees' leaves, bitter bark, and seed oil could be sold for medicines and soaps, the *amla* trees' fruits were to be earmarked for medicines and chutneys, and *ratna jyot*'s fruits would be used in the production of biodiesel. In many cases, NGOs active in the area participated in these income-generation 'eco-development' schemes.

Despite Dr. Sharma's and the RFD's efforts, this version of JFM has had limited success in Phulwari ki Nal, as assessed by Dr. Sharma himself as well as others. As to why this is the case – and in order to assess more generally the potential of similar co-management efforts to use religion to promote conservation and sustainable forest management (Figure 5.2) – we must examine local history and politics.

As Snodgrass learned through many hours of interviews, the lands that are now the Phulwari ki Nal Wildlife Sanctuary were, through the 17th and 18th centuries, maintained as hunting grounds by Rajput

Figure 5.2 Bhil herbalist, Kalaji, sits near clay horses, which, in order to bring prosperity, have been 'sacrificed' to the gods of the mountain (photograph by J. Snodgrass).

rulers of the independent kingdom of Bhumat. During the 19th century, however, control of these lands shifted to the *Maharanas* (great kings) of Mewar (centered in their capital city of Udaipur), who were subordinate to the British. The ancestors of Snodgrass's Adivasis research collaborators, he was told, were not independent resource managers of the lands they occupied but even as late as Indian independence (1947) were subordinate to the natural resource management regime of local (Bhumat) rulers, who were *jagirdars* (feudal lords) owing allegiance to the king of Mewar, himself beholden to the British Raj.

The Rajputs dominated forest management, because the British left most actual land management in local lords' hands, demanding only tax payments from them based on the total revenue of agricultural and forest lands. However, Bhil research collaborators said that tribal headmen (*patels*) and councils (*pancayats*) did take an active role in forest management. Patels, who were typically appointed by Rajput lords, for example, helped to resolve disputes over the ownership of valuable eucalyptus and *mahua* trees. Local Bhils described mechanisms by which natural resource disputes could be taken to ever higher levels of tribal councils. Heads of *pancayats*, for example, could meet in higher-level councils when disputes could not be resolved locally. Similarly, oral histories suggest that Bhils then also served on forest patrols and as lower-level managers for their feudal lords. Tribal headmen and other local leaders often had the responsibility of ensuring that royal forest dictates were carried out in Indigenous villages. Adivasis from the area were also known as valuable Rajput foot soldiers (Kolff 1990).

In this historical and political context, tribal Bhils explained the meaning of the rite of 'distributing saffron'. As previously described, Bhil shamans gather, beat drums, summon local deities, and spread saffron along the edges of degraded forests to announce that tribals and others could not use or access these forest lands, typically for five years. But respondents explicitly disclaimed that the rite per se led to successful forest management. Rather, it provided a vehicle to announce and render public the decisions of shamans and tribal *pancayat* councils. These leaders – along with the lords of Bhumat, the king of Mewar, and ultimately the British Raj – stood behind and enforced the management decisions made public by this rite. Successful forest conservation in these instances, therefore, rested on the perceived authority and power of tribal councils and kingly mandates. To interpret these words: More important than the will of the gods or spirits invoked by this rite was the will and the political power of the various collectivities behind the rituals.

The RFD's current sponsorship of the rite of distributing saffron might seem to be a return to a traditional form of forest management, joining the state with tribals to manage local natural resources. However, interviews with tribals about Dr. Sharma's performance of this rite revealed a different perception. Indigenous Bhils generally appreciated this effort to respect local values and practices, but they doubted that it alone would substantially change Bhil forest practices. As to why, Bhil respondents repeatedly and energetically pointed to the noticeboards demarcating the RFD's ownership of the lands of Phulwari, noting the omission of village names from the placard. Because they were not considered even shared owners of these forests, they asked us (to summarize responses heard repeatedly): Why should they protect the lands of Phulwari when they did not even have the legal right to do so?

Indeed, in all discussions about the current rite of distributing saffron, Bhil respondents repeatedly lectured Snodgrass about history and politics. The RFD, or *Janglat* in local parlance, could sometimes be 'thieves' (*cor*) and for that reason the Bhil's enemy (*dusman*) (cf. Robbins 2000). Many tribals described the Indian state and the RFD as responsible for dispossessing them from their land and then, to boot, ruining the lands through clear-cutting practices. Informants often spoke of how Rajput lords had first pushed their ancestors from the rich lowland valleys into the hills, with the independent State of India subsequently robbing even these lands by designating them as national forests, parks, and sanctuaries. Local tribals spoke especially of the new India's destructive development policies, with valuable eucalypts and indeed entire mountainsides of fruit, medicine, and timber trees sold in charcoal contracts to Hindu merchants. How these contracts and resulting clear-cuts ruined local economies were the first stories encountered by Snodgrass in inquiring about the rite of spreading saffron and its role in the newly emerging local-state collaborative management of natural resources.

In these interviews Bhil respondents emphasized the disappearance of traditional Indigenous natural resource management institutions and other radical transformations of local peoples' connections to state land-management regimes. In pre-1947 Rajasthan, as Snodgrass pieced together from oral histories, Indigenous tribals played an important though indirect role in forest management. They strained against Rajput forest laws but often helped kings and lords manage and patrol forest lands, which they considered partly their own (see Gold and Gujar 2002). The new RFD, as the arm of the independent nation of India, however, reversed tribals' historical rights of use and shared ownership of forest lands. The *pancayat* gatherings, where shamans, headmen, Bhil elders, and other clan leaders discussed forest management, are no longer connected to legitimate land-management regimes and thus are now powerless. Post-Independence India, then, has progressively disconnected Rajasthani tribals from the state's land-management decisions and policies; a situation about which respondents repeatedly complained, having been rendered trespassers and squatters on lands they historically considered (at least partly) their own.

The new *pancayat* raj system – a form of village rule that largely displaced the old caste and tribal councils (*pancayats*) – does include Indigenous Bhils in political processes related to many important issues. However, these modern village councils are generally powerless regarding natural resource management, with generally *no* authority over forest lands such as wildlife sanctuaries, which are managed by the RFD. Moreover, typically illiterate and tradition-bound Bhil shamans, headmen, and others often complained of feeling excluded from these bodies. Likewise, they suggested that this new system of 'local' rule, under the guiding paradigm of 'development', commonly favored outside interests and did not better the economic situations of tribals (see Unnithan-Kumar 1997).

For these reasons Bhils repeatedly and forcefully said that the RFD's sponsoring of the rite of distributing saffron could not itself ensure successful forest conservation. The ritual can be performed, Snodgrass was told, but local peoples had no rights to enforce its mandates, with all such rights now in the *Janglat's* (as mentioned, the RFD in local parlance) hands. While Bhils historically defended forest lands they considered partly their own, they now had no legal right to extract naturally occurring resources from such lands, even if they defended them. So what might be the point of such a defense, especially when it might mean risking one's life in the dead of night against armed men from one of the many local 'timber mafia'?

These details might suggest that the RFD's sponsoring of the rite of spreading saffron was inconsequential and irrelevant with respect to Bhil thought and practice related to the forest. However, Snodgrass feels such a conclusion is wrong, a point he defends by returning to material heard repeatedly in ethnographic interviews:

Despite typical Bhil vitriol regarding the RFD and the Indian state, research collaborators nevertheless sometimes spoke of these bodies as necessary and beneficial. They often said that they did *not* want the Indian state to abandon the sanctuary, despite their voting for Communist leaders who often ran on such a platform. In fact, both interviews and surveys reveal that many Bhils favor higher fines for illicit cutting and harvesting of forest resources, with an overwhelming 90.3% of survey respondents agreeing that the government should more heavily fine individuals who illegally cut forest trees. Bhils in the survey also generally thought that the RFD should forcefully close off damaged sections of the forest from human and domesticated animal use (81.5%), and a majority (62.2%) thought more guards were needed to protect the forests of Phulwari effectively. The latter statistic is especially significant given certain local views of RFD guards as legendarily corrupt. Even more perplexing were respondents who themselves had been fined, yet called for higher penalties for illegal harvesting of forest resource. And those calling for more guards were sometimes those who had needed to bribe an RFD official to avoid such fines and who had railed vociferously against the injustice of such levies.

Over time, the logic of these representations of the RFD began to make sense. Informants were saying that successful forest management needed power, authority, and even out-and-out force. In an ideal world, tribal people would be recognized owners of the park, able to enforce their own laws and regulate access to its resources. By voting Communist, research collaborators chased this dream. However, most residents of this sanctuary, despite their frequently fiery rhetoric and publicly professed political optimism, held out no real hope that the sanctuary would be abolished or that they would be given total authority over the land now encompassed by this sanctuary. Their next best alternative was to keep at least some remnants of state power, especially if in a form that could be checked by local institutions such as the emerging FPCs.

Some tribals did say that too much collaboration with the RFD might lead to, as Nadasdy (1999) warns, a further appropriation of their last remaining resources, such as their Traditional Environmental Knowledge (TEK). For this reason tribals were reluctant at first to speak to members of Snodgrass's research team, including Dr. Sharma, about their knowledge of healing plants and the forest. Nevertheless, as real as such a fear was, many seemed to fear even more an absence of institutional power that could enforce forest laws, which would leave the forest open to exploitation by every timber mafia and entrepreneurial poacher, tribal or non-tribal, from here to Ahmedabad. Power and enforcement had to come from somewhere, they argued – better from an imperfect and partially corrupt source than from nowhere at all.

These counter representations of the RFD and the Indian state help explain why locals did not totally dismiss this sponsorship of distributing saffron as irrelevant and meaningless. In fact, on the contrary, Bhils told Snodgrass how they energetically joined Dr. Sharma in this activity. Their energy, enthusiasm, and laughter, in their own words, pointed to their joy in enacting and revamping this traditional Bhil rite. Their puffed-out chests and smiles, as Dr. Sharma described it, communicated as deeply as their words that they valued the respect proffered by the RFD, and Dr. Sharma in particular. They were pleasantly astonished that Dr. Sharma and other members of the research team took such an interest in Bhil tradition. Pride mixed with astonishment as they enthusiastically recounted details of this rite and related dimensions of their history. Indeed, such interactions clarified that sponsoring this rite importantly showed goodwill, and thus formed a bridge between the RFD and local peoples. It demonstrated mutual respect and co-operation. This helped repair recent distrust between Bhils and the state and potentially re-established historical relations of joint local-state forest management that had fallen into disrepair but that locals considered critical to the protection of naturally occurring forest resources in the jungles of Phulwari.

However, the renewed trust relationship between Bhils and RFD does not mean that simple sponsorship of the saffron distribution rite alone would lead to successful Bhil conservation and sustainable forest management. Respondents were very clear on this point, demonstrated by their repeated return to the themes of history, politics, and their community's unjust exclusion from forest lands, in interviews that began with discussions of Bhil religious rites.

This leads Snodgrass to the conclusion that the RFD's sponsorship of religious rites such as distributing saffron, *in combination with striving to involve Bhils and other communities in actual forest management decisions and processes,* can play an important role in promoting sustainable forest use in these contexts. Referencing Indigenous sacred beliefs, values, and practices can help to create the social bonds and trust between the state and local communities that is necessary to making 'joint' forest management actually succeed. Snodgrass learned that, historically, such bonds, and to a certain degree such trust, existed. Sacred exchanges of symbols between kings and tribal leaders and councils supported these relationships of trust and respect: for example, Bhil *patels* might be allowed to wear certain styles of turbans and ornamentation that linked them to the sacred and political universe of the Rajput *rajas* and *maharajas*. However, it was learned that such trust gained significance only where Bhils also had actual rights over forest lands and resources. Divorced from rights, these sacred symbols lost their meaning and significance.

To rephrase, religion can play important roles in these contexts, especially when it reinforces and is reinforced by other conservation-relevant institutions and practices. Rites such as distributing saffron signal the will and desires of tribal collectivities that communicate and make public the decisions of Bhil *pancayat* councils as well as the potential sanctions associated with those decisions. However, to affect behavior meaningfully, these rituals must connect to collective bodies with real rights and authority over forest lands and resources, which back and enforce the decisions of religious leaders and even of the gods. But, as revealed by ethnographic and ethnohistorical interviews, present-day *pancayat* gatherings of clan leaders – where religious values, beliefs, and commitments can connect powerfully with resource-management decisions, rules, and sanctions through complex mechanisms of debate, compromise, consensus-building, and simple bullying – are largely powerless. Consequently, such traditional religiously imbued councils cannot connect local peoples to legitimate regimes of land management such as the RFD. Disconnected from actual power and authority, distributing saffron maintains its bark but not its bite.

Based on these research findings, a practical recommendation to the RFD and NGOs working on forest issues in this area is that they should pay attention to the potential for religion to stimulate pro-environmental thinking and practice. Collective rites such as distributing saffron are important, because the institutionalized values they enact provide a blueprint for collective commitment. While the particulars of how this can be implemented depend on cultural and social context, the principle should apply to many other conservation regimes among Indigenous peoples around the world. However, Snodgrass stresses that even a strategy attuned to sacred personal and institutionalized values will fail to affect behavior if not rooted in material and political realities. The ritual of distributing saffron may have great potential to activate local commitment and emotion for conservation, as suggested by respondents' smiles and laughter as they recounted participation in such revamped rites, but the *rite*, without a connection to political *rights*, will almost certainly fail to affect actual resource use and management.

This case study clearly shows that religion and belief are key framing elements of co-management in Rajasthan. In the following example from Thailand, religion also forms a central theme to understanding the mechanics of co-management.

THAILAND

Ordination of Trees

As noted in Chapter 4, the Thai-Lue of Silalaeng have worked out some effective co-management structures with the administration of Doi Phukha National Park. Thai-Lue leaders and their allies in the local NGO movement have established their co-management position through a long process of political advocacy, including participation in a nationwide 'tree- ordination' effort. Communities across Thailand have used tree-ordinations to maneuver the Royal Forestry Department and other state institutions to recognize local rights to manage resources on national forest reserve and national park lands. The link between ritual innovation and co-management in Thailand provides a case in the possibilities as well as limitations inherent to co-management.

Tree-ordinations involve the adaptation of the Buddhist monk ordination ritual for use of trees. The practice of ordaining trees originated in northern Thailand in the late 1980s as a response to widespread deforestation from logging and the expansion of farmland. The first formally organized and public tree-ordination ritual was apparently held by a monk named Phra Khru Manas in Phayao Province in 1988 (Montree et al. 1992; see also Darlington 1998, 2000; Isager and Ivarsson 2002). Phra Khru Manas, concerned about deforestation, reasoned that ordaining trees would help people see the value of forests and discourage logging by achieving a symbolic association between trees and monks. The practice soon spread to other provinces, including Nan, where Delcore conducted field research from 1996 to 1998. A socially active monk from Nan named Phra Khru Phithak Nanthakhun traveled to Phayao in 1990 to visit Phra Khru Manas. He returned to Nan to hold the first tree-ordination there in 1990, in his home village of Kiw Muang, followed by a larger ordination in 1991 with participation from 10 different villages in Sanamchay District (see Darlington 1998). Since then, environmentalist monks, farmers, and NGO activists have held over 20 tree-ordinations in Nan, as well as dozens in other provinces around Thailand (Isager and Ivarsson 2002; Tannenbaum 2000). The rituals have aided in the conservation of ordained areas and bolstered the legitimacy of rural peoples' efforts to manage and conserve natural resources in the face of state preferences for centralized control.

In 1996–1997 the Thai-Lue villagers of Silalaeng were part of a major round of tree-ordinations dedicated to King Rama IX. The Silalaeng ordination of its community forest, which is enclosed by DPNP, was one of 12 tree-ordinations performed in 1996–1997 in honor of the King's 50th anniversary on the throne (Figure 5.3). Like the first two tree-ordinations in Nan in 1990–1991, those in 1996–1997 were explicitly aimed not only at conservation but also at the formation of community forests in the ordained areas. Leading up to each ritual, ordaining communities would revise and strengthen, or create outright, village-level community forest committees and rules. Typically, after a tree-ordination, community forest committees forbid felling any trees in the ordained areas, since the trees have gained the symbolic status of monks. The committees do allow a range of other uses by local people, including hunting, gathering, and collecting firewood, though the rules vary from place to place. The local community forest committee then becomes the institution that works with local forestry and administrative officials to manage the forest. In the case of the Silalaeng community forest, DPNP officials allow some activities in the ordained community forest – such as gathering medicinal and edible plants and leaves and bark for domestic textile dyeing – which would not otherwise be allowed in a national park.

Figure 5.3 A tree-ordination in Nan Province, December 1996. The cloth announces the ordination as part of the celebration of the 50th anniversary of the reign of King Phumiphol Adulydej (photograph by H. Delcore).

Community forests in Thailand have no legal standing, and attempts to pass a Community Forest Bill through Parliament have repeatedly foundered. Indeed, the existence of community forests runs counter to principles of Thai administration, whereby all management of natural resources is centralized in the bureaucracy, with its apex in Bangkok. However, when tree-ordination organizers ordain a community forest, they bring the symbolic weight of Buddhism and, in 1997, respect for the monarchy to their side. The rituals have resulted in the acquiescence of local officials to limited forms of local management in national forest reserves and national park areas. Community forest establishment via tree-ordination in effect does an 'end run' around this centralized system and represents a de facto (if legally precarious) victory for local resource management.

Elsewhere, Delcore (2004) has critically assessed some of the cultural processes involved in planning and executing tree-ordinations. There are three problematic aspects to the rituals, particularly the ones conducted in 1996–1997: reinforcement of political and social hierarchies that work against co-management; manipulative aspects of the rituals; and continued lack of formal legitimacy for many co-management arrangements on Thai forest land.

The tree-ordinations of 1996–1997 were organized to celebrate the 50th anniversary of the reign of King Phumiphol Adulydej (King Rama IX) in 1996. State and private organizations marked the Golden Jubilee with a variety of public celebrations and fundraising drives for the king's various charities and development projects, and the Royal Forestry Department launched a major reforestation campaign in the King's name. To join in the celebration, Peoples Organizations and NGOs in northern Thailand spearheaded the foundation of the 'Program for the Community Forest Ordination of 50 Million Trees in Honor of the King's Golden Jubilee' (*Khrongkaan Buat Paa Chumchon 50 Laan Ton Phua Chalerm Phrakiat*: PCFO). The 12 tree-ordinations performed in 1996–1997 in Nan were part of this effort.

Rama IX, a constitutional monarch, is a popular figure in Thailand, but he also fulfills a central role in the construction of Thai nationalism. Since the early 1900s the slogan 'Nation, Religion, and King' has been at the heart of Thai nationalism (see Keyes 1987; Reynolds 1993; Vella 1978; Wyatt 1984). This symbolic trilogy – which invokes the unity of the Thai nation, Buddhism as the national religion, and the monarchy – has become deeply rooted in Thai political culture. All Thais who aspire to political goals must wrestle with how to position themselves vis-à-vis these three key symbols of Thai national identity.

The idea of ordaining community forest areas for the King's Golden Jubilee in 1996 originated with Joni Odashao, a nationally recognized leader of the Karen upland minority group. In October 1995 Joni Odashao addressed a major meeting of northern Thai NGO activists and farmer leaders in which he outlined a plan to ordain a large number of community forests 'for the King' during the course of 1996. His plan gained support in national NGO circles. NGO activists and their local allies hoped the tree-ordination plan would facilitate alliance building between interests in the government and the broader public sphere and deliver the powerful symbolism of the monarchy to their cause. One national Thai NGO leader argued that the plan provided a chance to take local tree-ordination efforts like those in Nan to the national stage. He noted that with Buddhism and the King both in the picture, no one would dare oppose the plan. Indeed, the actual rituals (see Delcore 2004) incorporated a great deal of national-ist and royalist symbolism, as if daring opponents of community forestry and its co-management goals to oppose the ordination efforts.

Although ritual manipulation in the service of grassroots causes could be taken as a hopeful sign, we stress here the ambivalent implications. The establishment of community forests via tree-ordinations could be seen as a method of establishing a category of customary rights, which have been notably absent from Thailand (Peluso and Vandergeest 2001: 778). Yet, in spite of these challenges to state claims of control over resources, the tree-ordination rituals for the King in 1996–1997 were also potent displays of hierarchy and inequality in Thai society. The rituals symbolically bolster the legitimacy of the state, its functionaries, and their symbolic head, the King. Any political benefits the rituals deliver to the cause of grassroots environmentalism will have to be weighed against this contradictory and somewhat unintended outcome.

Tree-ordination rituals also enact the inequalities that exist within the grassroots environmentalist movement. Although tree-ordinations originated with monks and village-based environmental activists, the main agents of their elaboration and spread were middle-class NGO activists. Given their goal of achieving political legitimacy for community forestry, the NGO organizers sought to frame what is in fact a multivocal ritual event with complex symbolic elements as a fairly straightforward statement of local commitment to and proficiency at forest conservation. The ordinations and the various Thai religious symbols and rituals involved in them were thus essentialized as general examples of local wisdom in a way that made them comprehensible to extra-local actors (state officials, the media, and the urban middle-class people). In the hands of the NGO activists, the ordination was an expression of rural peoples' love and respect for the forest; Buddhism is a conservationist religion, the animist rituals called the local spirits to help protect the forest, and so on. As Delcore (2004) has shown in the analysis of an actual ritual, such representations flatten out significant complexity in the ways participants actually experienced and interpreted the ritual.

Another problematic aspect of the rituals involves their use of the threat of spiritual consequences to those who break the rules. Through the ritual, the trees obtain the symbolic status of monks, so felling them would result in severe demerit. The rituals also call on the local spirits to watch over the forest and guard against felling trees. The main objects of these prohibitions are illegal logging interests. However, the local villagers themselves are also subject to the prohibitions established through ordination. In the village of Kiw Muang, where the first forest in Nan Province was ordained, a rich lore has arisen that describes the consequences of breaking community forest rules. One story recounts how a man entered the ordained forest and shot a wild boar, breaking the rules against hunting in that area. As he carried the boar home, another man mistook him for a boar and shot him dead. Villagers understand such accidents as the work of spirits who bring misfortune to those who break the rules, and they repeat such stories to warn one another. But some Thai observers have criticized the use of spiritual fear to produce compliance with community forest rules in place of voluntary commitment.

Ideally, tree-ordinations are preceded by an extensive period of consensus-building in the ordaining community. The monks and the

NGO activists involved never intended to impose ordained forest prohibitions on locals; indeed, they were hoping for the opposite: fully empowered community forest committees that can co-manage the forests with local officials. In Kiw Muang, the local consensus for ordination and community forestry was quite strong. Yet, in other cases that Delcore witnessed, the consensus-building process at the local level was incomplete, especially in the rush to ordain forests in honor of the King in 1996–1997. Unfortunately, weak local consensus regarding ordaining community forests can result in a resource management regime that follows the logic of state resource management in which management regimes are imposed on an ambivalent population.

Finally, in the absence of a Community Forest Bill that grants legal standing to the ordained community forests, local resource managers have to rely on the continued forbearance of local officials for the work of community forest committees. In Silalaeng this means that the co-management arrangements with DPNP remain the goodwill of national park officials, who continue to claim the last word in the management of the Silalaeng community forest.

DISCUSSION

Many have argued that there are a number of advantages to joint management, co-management, and Indigenous Protected Areas. For example, George, Innes, and Ross have listed eight advantages of co-management:

1. reduction in social and cultural consequences of protected area declaration;
2. collaboration between Western and Indigenous knowledge systems;
3. efficient and equitable management of wildlife;
4. mechanisms for conflict resolution;
5. recognition of Indigenous systems of tenure, management, harvesting, and use;
6. enhancement of the collection and exchange of information relating to resource management;
7. development of mutual trust between Indigenous communities and government representatives; and
8. increased respect and understanding between Indigenous communities and government representatives. (2004: 30)

Our comparative case studies show that collaborative resource management is indeed a step forward in breaking down some of the obstacles to the involvement of Indigenous peoples in natural resources management. Nevertheless, a careful analysis of the information presented in this chapter also demonstrates that a number of barriers have continued into the various co-management systems.

The social and cultural consequences of the declaration of protected areas remain a concern for most Indigenous communities who are not able to continue to live on their land or who, if they are, must do so in accordance with plans of management that are designed by the state and that privilege the scientific focus on management of wildlife over the rights of Indigenous resource users. Collaborative integration of Indigenous and Western knowledge systems, or between Indigenous and state management structures, and the collection and exchange of information relating to resource management still create challenges if the Indigenous and Western knowledge systems are different, particularly if they lead to different management goals. Indigenous systems of tenure, resources stewardship, and wildlife harvesting and use are often not recognized by the state if Indigenous knowledge or management institutions are likely to cause a perceived decline in species abundance, as measured by scientific monitoring devices. Alternatively, where there *is* recognition of Indigenous knowledge and management ways, such as occurred with the saffron ritual in Rajasthan and the tree-ordination rituals in Thailand, the complex social and political contexts in which the knowledge and resource management practice occur are sometimes poorly understood. As a consequence, there may be little trust between Indigenous resource users and resource-management bureaucrats, and limited respect and understanding between Indigenous communities and government representatives.

Nevertheless, some advances have been made, especially in situations in which interested bureaucrats take the time to listen to Indigenous peoples and, with the support of the traditional land managers, incorporate elements of traditional ecological knowledge into management planning. Dr. Sharma's use of the saffron ritual in forest management in Rajasthan, in harmony with the involvement of Bhil knowledge holders, demonstrates that, with good will, there can be small successes in collaborative management of resources.

A conscientious and charismatic manager, keen to learn and involve Indigenous knowledge holders, in many ways can be more important to the co-management process than the structure of the process itself, at least in the short term. Where such interest is absent, and where understanding of Indigenous protocols is deficient, co-management arrangements can be flawed and can even cause offence. An example of this problem can be seen in the current (2007) plan for the Conservation and Management of Dugongs in Queensland (EPA 2007). In this plan, the importance of dugongs to Aboriginal peoples and Torres Strait Islanders is recognized in theory but not in practice. As was demonstrated in Chapter 4, the initial 1999 Dugong Conservation and Management Plan recommends the 'education' of Indigenous Australians in the conservation needs of dugongs and offers to donate dead dugongs to Indigenous communities to obviate the need for hunting, thereby demonstrating a lack of appreciation for the role that hunting dugongs plays in Australian Indigenous society. These offensive management strategies are repeated in the current plan, signed in December 2007. A review of Queensland's marine mammal conservation plans is being undertaken in early 2010, and it will be interesting to see whether revised TUMRAs (Traditional Use of Marine Resources Agreements) will provide the effective mechanism, proposed by the discussion papers associated with the review, to reduce such inappropriate responses to Indigenous needs.

Conclusion

In this chapter we have seen that many of the barriers to the recognition of a role for Indigenous knowledge in the management of natural resources (Chapter 3) have carried over into the co-management system. This, we argue, is largely because co-management in most of its applied forms remains dominated by Western epistemologies and institutions. Berkes (2009) argues that co-management is not just a tool for managing resources. The key to successful co-management is the management of human relationships. Equitable power-sharing – two-way knowledge sharing that does not privilege one form of knowledge over another – the development of trust between partners, a focus on process rather than institutions, and the direct involvement of Indigenous people in management decisions need to form the bases of the co-management relationship (Berkes 2009: 1693–1694). '[C]o-management that does not learn often becomes a failed experiment. . . . Successful co-management is a knowledge partnership' (Berkes 2009: 1699).

Stevenson (2006) makes similar points. When co-management is dominated by technical experts and reductionist scientific paradigms that focus only on management of resources, the effects of management decisions on the social, cultural, and political frameworks of Indigenous societies are ignored to the detriment of the traditional resource users. Stevenson proposes an alternative form of co-management that emphasizes genuine two-way knowledge sharing. Called the 'Two Row Wampum Approach to Co-management', this model is based on the design of an Iroquois belt, with two parallel rows of color representing canoes on the rivers of life, which are a metaphor for nation-to-nation relationships built on respect, shared authority, and autonomy. This form of co-management relationship building recognizes Indigenous knowledge and scientific knowledge as parallel pathways to the achievement of a balance between resource-management requirements and human user needs (Stevenson 2006: 176–177). Stevenson's model, although challenging, provides a significant new direction for the advancement of co-management opportunities.

Nevertheless, we are concerned that the Two Row Wampum Approach will retain the current separation between scientific knowledge constructs and Indigenous ways of knowing, with the parallel canoes never meeting. As another alternative to current co-management arrangements we provide a different model, also based on Indigenous metaphors of shared relationships. The Lakota Stewardship Model differs from current co-management systems not only by being an initiative of Indigenous people but also by having been designed and implemented by Indigenous people. It differs from the Two Row Wampum Approach because the Stewardship Model emphasizes the intermingling of Western and Indigenous knowledge systems. In the next chapter we outline and analyze this Indigenous model of protected areas and natural resource stewardship.

Chapter 6

THE INDIGENOUS STEWARDSHIP MODEL

> At the level of application is found the arrogance of practice, which is still rife in formal institutions that are confidently and without qualms determined to continue with the monochromic logic of Western epistemology.
>
> (Odora Hoppers 2002b: vii)

Imagine, if you will, a scenario in which colonial governments and Indigenous peoples sit down together in good faith to develop a co-management system in which both sides are truly equal in their contributions and willing to make concessions to arrive at a balanced plan of land and resource stewardship. Imagine, too, a society in which all knowledge systems are respected, and the insights from each system are applied for the benefit of wild resources and the people who subsist on them. Imagine a co-management system in which Indigenous people are integrated into the entire spectrum of management policy, design, and implementation, from field work to setting harvest limits and seasons, to adopting administrative regulations. It was with this vision that Richard Sherman initiated the collaborative process that culminated in the Indigenous Stewardship Model.

Up to now we have demonstrated that the barriers to genuine collaborative management in natural resource management are epistemological, methodological, and systemic. Even when co-management policies are developed and implemented, the Indigenous intellectual property is often either marginalized or appropriated. As Odora Hoppers (2002a) notes, people's knowledge in the co-management system is eroded because of the low value attached to that knowledge. She argues that in sharing and recognizing different knowledge systems, science needs to be prepared for the 'visions that collide' with generally accepted scientific principles (2002a: 7–8). We have demonstrated that the visions that collide tend to lead to the abandonment of knowledge that counters scientific understandings rather than to compromise.

In this chapter we provide an outline of the Indigenous Stewardship Model as a different approach to co-management that has the potential to lead to genuine compromise. The Indigenous Stewardship Model has addressed many of the visions that collide between Indigenous perceptions and scientific perceptions of natural resources and their management. This stewardship model started with a member of the Oglala Sioux Tribe, Richard Sherman, and during its development became a collaborative effort of many Native and non-Native people working with Indigenous communities in the United States and abroad. The development of the Indigenous Stewardship Model for the Pine Ridge Reservation in South Dakota gave people ideas and avenues for natural resource management that they could explore. People knew a change was needed but didn't know which direction to take. Even though they have sensed the need to integrate local cultural values into their management planning, many tribes have adopted purely Western methods of management because they did not have an available alternative. Also, it is easier for tribes to procure federal money for programs when they agree to adopt the Western model of management as opposed to the Indigenous model.

Within the Indigenous Stewardship Model, reference is made to preliminary work done on the Pine Ridge Indian Reservation in South Dakota. On Pine Ridge, over one hundred years of land appropriation, cultural suppression, and imposition of livestock monoculture has resulted in the reduction and extirpation of many plant and animal species native to the area. Element 1 of the Model began when Richard Sherman, Executive Director of Oglala Sioux Parks and Recreation Authority (OSPRA), developed the first comprehensive Tribal Fish and Wildlife Code for the Pine Ridge Indian Reservation, enacted by ordinance of the Oglala Sioux Tribe in 1986. Sherman grew up as a hunter-gatherer on the Pine Ridge Reservation and therefore was intimately familiar with subsistence practices and resources on the reservation. In the 1990s Sherman implemented the Model as lead biologist of OSPRA in conjunction with the creation of the Stewardship Division, designated to integrate Western biological and Indigenous knowledge into Oglala Sioux Tribal operations, and the creation of the Tribal Ranger Program. The Model articulated and instilled the guiding principles for developing stewardship systems for fisheries, wildlife, and buffalo resources across the Pine Ridge Reservation, and it also provided a foundation for pursuing a professional, constructive working relationship with the National Park Service.

During the formulation of the Indigenous Stewardship Model, whenever workshops were held or inquiries were received from other tribes, the interest and enthusiasm were profound. The Oglala Sioux Tribal government adopted the model in full and other tribes have also adopted concepts from the model. During the formation of the Indigenous Stewardship Model, a number of other tribes contacted OSPRA and indicated that they did not know where to begin their own process. So the model provided them with a starting point. Following recommendations from a study by Professor Terry McCabe of the University of Colorado-Boulder in the late 1990s, the National Park Service expressed interest in adopting the Indigenous Stewardship Model as a way of guiding its relationship with the Oglala Sioux Tribe in the South Unit of Badlands National Park. The South Unit comprises half of the entire Badlands National Park and is a protected area within the boundaries of the Reservation, where management authority is shared by the National Park Service and the Oglala Sioux Tribe (see Chapter 4).

The Indigenous Stewardship Model reflects a difference from Western management in that it is a *guideline* for a process rather than a dictated linear set of provisions to be universally adopted. By highlighting pitfalls and opportunities that tribal communities face, the Indigenous Stewardship Model gives a starting point for integrating culturally appropriate solutions to issues of management and conflict resolution. Depending on the needs of a particular Indigenous group, the model may be used in part or in total.

Because of the long history of outside agencies trying to assert power over tribal authority and tribal resources, tribal agencies are often reluctant to collaborate. The tribe, like the state, has to deal with the vagaries of the political climate at any given time. Historically this situation has caused the relationship between the tribe and the state, as well as that of the tribe and federal agencies, to run hot and cold over time. There is also a remarkable lack of awareness about the political status of tribes as sovereign nations within the United States. This history has also produced a tendency for tribal officials to mimic the intolerance they have experienced at the hands of scientists and to dismiss completely the perspectives of scientific approaches to management in favor of traditional Indigenous values and perspectives. The Indigenous Stewardship Model recognizes the ongoing nature of these political difficulties and focuses on methods for both raising awareness and resolving or coping with conflict. In this way the model will benefit tribes and the agencies that work with tribes, and it will have clear applications beyond the United States.

Despite the aims of the Indigenous Stewardship Model to alleviate discord between tribes and non-tribal governmental entities, the differences between these two entities are made apparent even in the difficulty of how to present the model. Resource agency personnel and academics have expected the Indigenous Stewardship Model to be a linear, proscriptive, and definitive text for how to work with tribal communities.

Tribal members, in contrast, are looking for a guideline that provides relevance to the cultural and natural heritage of the tribe and comfort for the people's own cultural perspectives that are embedded in the history, spirituality, and long-term commitments of the tribe. These two needs are often diametrically opposed and cannot be satisfied by deferring to one or the other in a single document. The deep underlying differences are too great to bridge implicitly. Compromise, sensitivity, and parallel efforts are all necessary to construct a bridge between the tribal and non-tribal knowledge systems. As a result, the key contribution of the Indigenous Stewardship Model is the construction of a common language that respects both Indigenous and scientific perspectives rather than allowing one to dominate the other. The effort is not to change but to accept the other. In this way the Indigenous Stewardship Model moves the role for Indigenous people and Indigenous knowledge out of the back seat and into the forefront of management.

BACKGROUND

The social, economic, and political context of the Pine Ridge Reservation defines and constrains the environment in which natural resource management and conservation attempt to operate. On the reservation, the market economy is weak, with limited opportunities for Lakota residents to be fully employed in wage work or to develop small businesses in the mainstream model. Social relationships are the dominant organizational principle for Lakota communities on Pine Ridge. Reservation residents rely in large part on culturally and historically based non-market systems, such as familial labor organization, extended kinship networks, and community-based support systems, to satisfy their basic needs.

Lakota emphasis on the extended family (*tiospaye*) is a central principle of reservation economic life. Generosity is still valued highly today as it was in the traditional life-way of the Lakota (Pickering 2001). Sharing food resources among kin, whether purchased or harvested through hunting and gathering, is still an operative force for reservation residents. Natural resources figure squarely within the ideal of self-sufficiency for many Lakota households (Pickering and Jewell 2008; Pickering, Van Lanen, and Sherman 2010).

Spiritual beliefs, including the conceptualization of natural resources, play a critical, albeit understated, role in shaping the Pine Ridge economy (Pickering and Jewell 2008). Traditionally, Lakota beliefs conceived of the natural world as imbued with *wakan*, or power; all beings, and even inanimate objects, possess this force (DeMallie and Parks 1987: 28). This force was also believed to guide human actions and was to be revered as potentially harmful if not respected (DeMallie and Parks

1987). The world was conceived as existing in a state of unity where humans are merely another member of the natural world. The land was more than a base of resources for nutritive survival; the land was the birthplace of the Lakota people and the source of all power (Young Bear and Theisz 1994: 27–28; see Chapter 5). Disrespect toward the land or the natural world constitutes an affront to the very core of the spirituality that guides Lakota belief and action. Survival for the Lakota has meant judiciously using the resources surrounding them (Deloria 1944). Thus, for the Lakota, '[s]cience and religion were not separate – they were one' (Hassrick 1964: 246).

There is a fundamental epistemological divide between grassroots conceptions of nature as co-equal relatives and structural conceptions of natural resources as merely an input in the generation of wealth through global capitalism. This divide lies at the heart of why Lakota Indigenous knowledge and ethics, which revolve around nature and the environment, have not been implemented in relation to reservation lands, or within Badlands National Park, until the development of the Indigenous Stewardship Model. Proponents of the Western scientific approach often claim that too much of the Indigenous knowledge system practiced in traditional times has been lost for people to be able to piece together a meaningful management system. Two things come to mind. First, traditions and knowledge are not static but ever-changing to meet the vagaries of changing times. Second, Indigenous peoples are not limited by the loss of old knowledge, because they apply their own unique values and philosophies to their grounded interactions with their local landscape, creating an orderly system of natural resource stewardship during contemporary times.

The Indigenous Stewardship Model was developed by Lakota people to help overcome the epistemological disconnect between natural resource use and conservation. Because this model is the product of Lakota knowledge, we do not wish to appropriate the intellectual property of the model, and hence the remainder of this chapter is written by Richard Sherman, the Oglala Sioux Tribal member who has played the major role in developing the Model (Figure 6.1).

OVERVIEW OF THE INDIGENOUS STEWARDSHIP MODEL

The primary goal of the Indigenous Stewardship Model is to create a comprehensive Indigenous approach that enables tribes and other Indigenous communities to steward their natural and cultural resources on an integrated, stable, and continuous basis at a minimum of cost and maintenance. The Indigenous Stewardship Model advances efforts to revive and implement the ecological values and practices of Indigenous

Figure 6.1 Richard Sherman on an ethnobotanical excursion with university students (photograph by K. Pickering Sherman).

knowledge systems. Generally speaking, during the centuries before Western colonial expansion, Indigenous peoples were profoundly connected with their natural surroundings. Indigenous cultures were based on a wide variety of beliefs about the intricate balance of life, integrating all beings, human and non-human, living and non-living, into complex relationships of interdependence and mutual respect. Native peoples approached the natural world with an attitude of reverence and stewardship rather than dominion. Indigenous ecological practices reflected an intensive, first-hand knowledge of local environments, knowledge that was acquired and passed on over countless generations. These unique knowledge systems, together with the Indigenous cultures and values that supported them, are being actively suppressed in the contemporary context of Western-dominated natural resource management. The inflicted government policies and land-management practices that destroyed subsistence lifestyles and seriously damaged ecosystems around the globe continue unabated. Government agencies are reluctant to recognize the legitimacy of Indigenous environmental practices or to include Indigenous perspectives in natural resource planning and management. As a result, American Indian tribes continually find themselves in conflict with federal and state resource agencies.

Through its design and implementation, the Indigenous Stewardship Model acknowledges the effectiveness of Indigenous ecological practices and advocates for policy reform so that these practices are recognized and accepted. In addition, the Indigenous Stewardship Model proposes means to evaluate and apply those Western practices that are in accordance with Indigenous laws and values. The Indigenous Stewardship Model outlines several key elements in a process by which other Indigenous communities might develop their own systems and approaches to land stewardship in their areas, thereby serving as a model of ecological stewardship for Indigenous communities worldwide. Each element of the Indigenous Stewardship Model may be pursued either separately or as part of a comprehensive natural resource stewardship plan. The Indigenous Stewardship Model is not a rigid proscription but rather is intended to permit flexibility and change as conditions dictate and to offer suggestions of things to be aware of – recommendations, alternatives, potential solutions, cautionary tales, and encouragement – and to warn of pitfalls.

Over time, the Indigenous Stewardship Model strives to permanently alter the way in which colonial governments view their relationships with Indigenous governments and peoples. Co-management strategies for lands and natural resources between tribal and non-tribal government agencies need to be developed, and conflict-resolution methods institutionalized, to help prevent the bitter disputes that have long characterized tribal/governmental relations.

Equally important, the Indigenous Stewardship Model seeks to transform the lives of Indigenous communities. Equitable systems of sharing the natural wealth of native lands will expand opportunities for Indigenous communities to reinvigorate subsistence practices and self-sufficiency within the context of international boundaries and economic globalization. Indigenous pedagogy transfers knowledge from elders to children, in turn empowering the children to become the real stewards of the environment in the future. To the extent possible, the damage inflicted on native biological diversity and ecosystems needs to be mitigated and remedied, so that viable populations of plants and animals are maintained, fragile habitats are protected, and culturally significant medicinal, ceremonial, and food practices involving wild plants and animals are preserved (Figure 6.2).

The Indigenous Stewardship Model recognizes, adheres to, and promotes policies that support Indigenous nations. The primary and ultimate policy is sovereignty. Sovereignty infers the right to culturally appropriate self-governance, economic self-sufficiency, and lifestyles. Sovereignty also infers the right to a clean and healthy environment and the right to steward, or manage, natural and cultural resources according to each nation's knowledge system.

Efforts to reform both the content and the process of reconciliation between tribes and outside agencies culminated in the development of the initial Lakota Ecology Stewardship Model, starting in the 1980s. The hope for that model was to steward tribal lands based on the values and philosophies of Indigenous peoples while acknowledging some contribution from Western management practice. The Lakota philosophy,

Figure 6.2 An abundant variety of wild food plants important to the Plains Indian tribes, including three types of wild turnips, wild onions, and Sego lily bulbs (photograph by C. Voormann).

that all aspects of life are connected, provided the premise on which to build a natural resource stewardship system. Integrating Lakota perspectives into the management approach not only enhanced the resources but served the people better as well. One of the differences between the Oglala Sioux Tribe and the State of South Dakota is that the tribe must accommodate a population with high levels of unemployment. There are cultural and spiritual reasons for needing access to natural resources and to community healing that flows from restoring the connection between Lakota identity and the wild resources of the land. Therefore, the stewardship system needed to be configured to accommodate these differences. Despite the fact that the knowledge system of Lakota people has been suppressed by government policies, the values underlying Lakota culture continue to provide a strong foundation for a natural resource stewardship system.

The Indigenous Stewardship Model aims to provide Indigenous communities and outside agencies with a common language by which to communicate, a template for working together effectively. It looks at some of the pitfalls and caveats common to other collaborative or co-management approaches and provides methods for finding a road forward together. The Indigenous Stewardship Model is meant for other Indigenous communities as well, beyond Pine Ridge. Pine Ridge was the place where much of the model was initiated and explored, and it was adopted by Oglala Sioux Parks and Recreation Authority and the Oglala Sioux Tribe in 1986. However, politics must always be addressed; the political climate at any given time may prove to be either a blessing or an impediment. A solid educational component is needed as well, for tribal councils, natural resource agency staff, tribal members, and the general public, so that those who are beyond the initial development of an Indigenous stewardship system have the opportunity to understand the model and continue to share the model with young people and other communities with new ideas and opportunities for implementation.

Model Elements

The Elements of the Indigenous Stewardship Model are summarized in Table 6.1 and displayed as an operational diagram in Figure 6.3. We now briefly describe the basic principles in each Element of the model.

Category A. Active Indigenous Stewardship on Tribally Controlled Lands.
   Element 1: Indigenous ecology: Land and habitat maintenance, restoration, reserve
   The Indigenous Ecology component of the model proposes to establish, operate, maintain, and promote a responsible system of stewardship that provides for the harvesting and processing of wild resources based on Indigenous knowledge systems and the underlying values of those systems. This component includes many typical biological activities and endeavors with wildlife, fisheries, plant and wildlife habitat, rehabilitation and mitigation, and co-operative projects with other entities (tribal, private, state, and federal). One way of integrating Western and Indigenous approaches is to always leave an unexploited capacity so that the plants, animals, and the land itself can rest. Maximum sustainable yield must be avoided to better sustain the ecosystem holistically. As stated previously, survival for the Lakota means using the resources surrounding them judiciously (Deloria 1944). On the reservation the unemployment rate is currently (2005 figures) approaching 50%, while the state unemployment rate is only 5%. Therefore, resource management on the reservation must be configured differently from state resource management. Reservation management needs to accommodate the subsistence practices and home-based enterprise alternatives that depend on having access to wild resources, whereas state management is not required to consider subsistence practices. Because the reservation consists of a

Table 6.1 Indigenous Stewardship Model

Category	Element	Description
A		*Active Indigenous Stewardship on Tribally Controlled Lands*
	1	Indigenous ecology: Land and habitat maintenance, restoration, reserve
	2	Subsistence lifestyles: Access to and equitable distribution of resources
	3	Promoting economic self-sufficiency (sustainable harvesting and ecologically sustainable micro-enterprise development)
	4	Connections to the land: Community monitoring and reporting
B		*Community Outreach to Support Indigenous Stewardship*
	5	Indigenous ethnobotany: Identifying, restoring, disseminating Indigenous knowledge
	6	Community input: Synergies between Indigenous knowledge and management systems
	7	Indigenous pedagogy: Intergenerational transfer of Indigenous knowledge
C		*Co-Management: Advocating for Indigenous Stewardship on Land Where Authority Is Shared or Absent*
	8	Validating Indigenous knowledge systems: Policy advocacy and reform
	9	Strategies for genuine collaboration: Avoiding appropriation and dominance
D		*Consensus Building and Conflict Management*
	10	Indigenous processes for decision making: Resolving internal differences
	11	Indigenous collaboration in decision making: Resolving external differences

hunter-gatherer population, the natural resource management system must accommodate that aspect of reservation life. State management is dictated by market economic interests of maximizing agency revenue from sports hunters, whereas on the reservation subsistence activities take precedence. On the reservation, wildlife management includes accommodating the desire of tribal members to put food on the table over the longest period of time to provide for the unemployed, elderly,

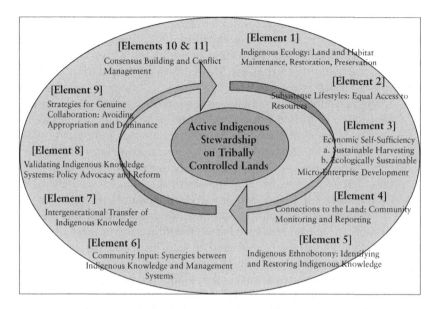

Figure 6.3 Elements of the Indigenous Stewardship Model (from Pickering Sherman, Van Lanen, and Sherman 2010).

and single parents who may need wild game and other wild resources to supplement their subsistence. Others may lack hunting equipment or may need someone to hunt for them. A mechanism that addresses all these concerns is integral to any meaningful plan implemented to serve the people of the reservation.

The state believes that the tribe does not manage natural resources well enough, and therefore the state prefers to manage all the wildlife and fisheries. The state's interest is in amassing power over reservation lands to the detriment of the political and cultural sovereignty of the Lakota Tribes within the state's boundaries; it has no understanding of the way the tribe manages its natural resources and assumes that no management is in place unless the state institutes it. The state needs to understand that there *is* a tribal management system in place, as well as motivations for why tribal agencies manage resources the way they do. For example, the tribe has been criticized in the past by outside management agencies for having low wildlife populations, without the benefit of any studies to substantiate those criticisms. When the tribal Stewardship Division of OSPRA designed wildlife population studies within the reservation's boundaries, a National Park Service biologist was invited to participate in the deer counts and to process the numbers. The results of the study revealed that there were more deer per square mile on the reservation than on adjacent state-managed lands. Another example: Visiting officials from the National Wild Turkey Federation during the early 1990s determined, following an empirical survey, that the Pine Ridge Reservation had the best Merriam turkey population density in the entire United States.

Inadequate livestock management practices, including the policies of the Bureau of Indian Affairs and illegal overstocking by certain cattle operators, have damaged land to the extent that some native plants no longer exist or exist only in low numbers. Poor land management has resulted in desirable plant species being replaced by undesirable species. Therefore, one of the purposes of the Indigenous Stewardship Model is to develop practices that will restore plant biodiversity, including wild foods, to the land. In addition, the model advocates practices that ensure an optimal balance between wildlife and domestic livestock production, as should be reflected in land-use stocking rates. There would be better land practices that do not deplete the land – margins would be left to ensure the survival of plants. Lighter stocking of cattle, once again, would also facilitate greater biodiversity. Greater biodiversity, in turn, would help to restore traditional harvesting from the land and help to alleviate diabetes and other diet-related problems on the reservation.

Because the model originated from the values and philosophies of Lakota people and their unique cosmology, implementation of the model would be more apt to maintain the land in as pristine a state as possible. The tribal buffalo herd, for example, is maintained in as wild a state as possible. The Western approach treats bison more as domestic animals. The healthy aspect of buffalo, being grassfed on the open range, is lost when bison are moved through the feed lot system and 'finished' for marketing purposes as if they were domestic livestock. The Lakota believe that, because buffalo provided for our needs for such a long time, it is now time for us to reciprocate (Sherman 2005). Government policies of bison extermination were used to subdue the Lakota rather than being a consequence of Lakota management practices.

Furthermore, tribes would be most apt to try to restore and retain what they had in earlier times when they lived a more traditional life. In the past all life was respected in such a way that one could not look at a tree in terms of board feet or animals in terms of the cost of their meat or trophy potential. The management system developed by tribes would be to plan for the worst-case scenario, so that in the event of calamities, natural or otherwise, the land would not become depleted, and the people would always have sufficient bounty to sustain themselves. A margin of safety would always be maintained to prevent over-depletion from occurring.

Element 2: Subsistence lifestyles: Access to and equitable distribution of resources

The Indigenous Stewardship Model encourages resource management to include all the needs of all the people: subsistence resource users, hunters, tourists, and conservationists. Tribal members need to have access to all parts of the reservation. If the area you live on is closed to hunting or gathering, you should still have access to every other stewardship unit. No one family or group of families can monopolize the resources closest to them. In the old way, the extended families (*tiospaye*) would know the needs of each family and could take into consideration emergencies, economic collapse, and other contingencies. Those who ignored the will of the people would ultimately be denied access to the resources. Subsistence practices are a vitally important part of reservation economics, and hence of the model.

Element 3: Promoting economic self-sufficiency (sustainable harvesting and ecologically sustainable micro-enterprise development)

The Indigenous Stewardship Model promotes the development of a system that considers a balance of market activities (such as hunting and fishing permits and tourism) and non-market activities (such as subsistence lifestyles and restoration efforts). Each Indigenous community should be able to influence how much market-based activity to engage in. For many Indigenous communities, alternative economic activities continue to be a significant part of their daily practice. The Western model seems to dwell on the maximum sustainable yield of resources, beyond which the land and resources become depleted. To optimize the resources, tribes would manage at a level below that. Tribes realize that they have to work with the Western managers as well, so there will always be elements of the Western method within tribal systems, as a means of maintaining communication between the two systems. For example, the fiscal realities of tribal government dictate that cattle will continue to be grazed on Lakota land. In contrast, under the Indigenous Stewardship Model, stocking rates would be determined to make allowances for wildlife and other resources beyond the simple commodity value of cattle on the market. Furthermore, the alternative economic value of natural resources to Lakota people who continue to live with the land are acknowledged and protected rather than ignored in an exclusively market-based economic view (Figure 6.4).

Tribal members should have the option of creating their own employment through micro-enterprise activities that use natural resources, such as porcupine quilling, wild plant gathering, and fashioning animal hides. The Indigenous Stewardship Model provides opportunities for Indigenous people to develop a means whereby crafters and harvesters might co-ordinate activities. A hunter, for example, may be interested only in the meat of

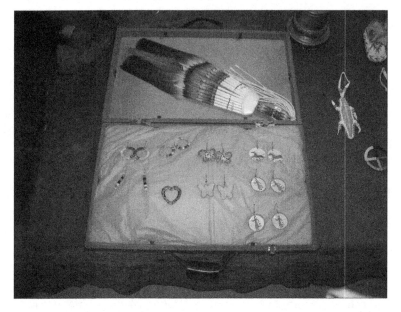

Figure 6.4 Examples of wild animal and plant products used by native artists in their micro-enterprises, including porcupine quills, bird feathers, sweet grass, deer hide, sinew, and vegetable dyes (photograph by Kathleen Pickering Sherman).

a deer but not the hide. However, that hide would be useful to a micro-enterprise artisan. A means needs to be devised to collect the items obtained but not needed by hunters, such as hides, feathers, bones, and sinew, and hold them in a repository for artisans and ceremonial practitioners.

With implementation of the model, other activities, such as eco-tourism, would be available for tribal members. Hunting, fishing, and wildlife viewing by tourists would lead to areas set aside from cattle to be used solely for wildlife production. More people on the reservation benefit from wildlife production than from cattle production (Pickering 2000; Sherman 1988). Ecotourism visitors would also spend money on the reservation, purchasing goods and services from other tribal enterprises, creating a multiplier effect for other local activities.

Element 4: Connections to the land: Community monitoring and reporting

Individuals who are intimately connected to the land and natural resources play a role in implementing the Indigenous Stewardship Model. In contrast, Western ideals hold that only professionals can adequately monitor the health of natural resources. However, natural resource professionals are limited by time and money in the degree to which they can become familiar with the resource. As a result, Western management decisions are often made from a remote location, often with little or no knowledge of the local area.

For Indigenous communities there are cultural benefits from having local people, particularly youth and elders, get outside onto the landscape again, in terms of positive self-esteem, intergenerational interactions, and restoring traditional values. Combinations of Western and traditional methods of monitoring can be employed, such as a database of oral histories and quantitative counts. Monitoring kits and training from Western approaches may be helpful to Indigenous land stewards. For example, on Pine Ridge, the entire reservation has been divided into 10 stewardship units. Tribal stewards can then be assigned to each stewardship unit to keep journals of their observations and provide these to tribal land managers. By living on the land, these stewards are able to provide a more detailed and continuous observation of the resources and the issues that affect their health than could a Western scientific professional living off the reservation. In the event natural resources funding is reduced, the stewards who already live on the land are able to continue monitoring and protecting resources.

The people dwelling on the land have an intimate knowledge of the land from being right there. Stewards would be selected by location in strategic areas, such as biosystems (open prairie, badlands, ponderosa pines, and so on), critical habitats, riparian areas, or wildlife corridors. Stewards should also be selected based on their own interests, whether it be in plants, birds or other types of wildlife, rivers, trees, or other elements of the ecosystem. Finally, stewards should be selected based on a cross-section of the people on the reservation, including traditional self-sufficient people, wage workers, ranchers and farmers, and representatives of all age groups and genders.

Stewards would be involved in the management decision-making process. Based on their field findings, they would make recommendations and share information with other stewards and tribal land managers and even with outsiders, such as researchers and students (Figure 6.5). Decision making, such as setting goals for the next seasonal round or setting harvest limits, would be improved because of the greater observational detail and experience provided by the local stewards.

Category B. Community Outreach to Support Indigenous Stewardship
Element 5: Indigenous ethnobotany: Identifying, restoring, disseminating Indigenous knowledge

In addition to economic values, there are cultural, community, and health benefits of implementing the Indigenous Stewardship Model. For example, the impact of soaring rates of diabetes on the Pine Ridge

Figure 6.5 Ethnobotanical excursions provide opportunities to document and disseminate the cultural and historical importance of Indigenous plants to both tribal members and Western scientists (photograph by K. Pickering Sherman).

Reservation population can be combated with increased outdoor activities around stewardship monitoring. A return to wild foods will also provide a healthier diet. In addition, reservation residents will experience greater self-esteem and personal motivation generated by a return to traditional hunting and gathering activities.

There are many major projects and long-term activities that might be used to implement Indigenous ethnobotany. For example, the nutritional value of local food plants may need to be determined, so that comparisons can be made with current processed foods that have contributed to the high percentage of diet-related diseases, such as diabetes. Field work may be needed to determine the location and status of specific plants of cultural and nutritional significance. Rehabilitation or restoration projects may be needed to return local lands to their original state of biodiversity. Long-term protection may also be needed for the collecting sites of plant species that are in heavy demand, so depletion of that resource may be avoided. Certain medicinal plants may be harvested and administered only by spiritual practitioners according to local Indigenous precepts. If documentation is culturally appropriate, elders or spiritual practitioners might be interviewed about the plants of cultural significance and how they were used in the past, to help educate youth and others. With the death of each elder some of the knowledge dies, too. To achieve the goal of resurrecting the ethnobotanical knowledge from the past, tribes need to document and disseminate the Indigenous knowledge that survives and help culturally relevant plants to survive. A native botanical garden based on local Indigenous knowledge of species of cultural and histori-cal importance might be established. A repository of culturally relevant seeds may be instituted as well. Protection of intellectual property should also be instituted so that Indigenous knowledge and information about sacred places and resource uses cannot be exploited by non-members for commercial purposes.

Element 6: Community input: Synergies between indigenous knowledge and management systems

People must be included in decision making. Indigenous knowledge needs to be incorporated with Western knowledge to describe what is sustainable and to provide information on what a healthy ecosystem looks like. As mentioned earlier, certain plants can be harvested only by spiritual practitioners and must be approached in a particular way, out of respect for the power of the plant. During the development of the Indigenous Stewardship Model, a project was created to study all the local plants on the Pine Ridge Reservation, from both traditional and Western perspectives. While scientific techniques were being used to learn about the medicinal qualities of one particular plant, the chemical elements that made this plant effective could not be determined. Advice was sought from a group of Lakota elders. One tribal elder pointed out that the researchers had overlooked Lakota knowledge of the spiritual aspects of the plant. According to this Lakota knowledge, every plant has a spirit, and the ability of the plant to heal depends on the interaction between the spirit of the plant and the spirit of the patient. The Lakota elder reminded the researchers that certain plants cannot be picked by just anyone. To harvest a plant in an inappropriate way could lead to dire consequences for the collector. There are a series of actions that must be performed before a plant can be collected. The plant must be approached in the proper way, and often a particular song must be sung to the plant by a medicine man before it can be gathered. Consequently, certain plants require a form of reverence to ensure that the collector is protected and that the medicinal qualities of the plant are efficacious.

One particular example of such a requirement is the Bush Morning Glory plant (*Ipomoea leptophylla*), known by Lakota people as *pezuta nige tanka* or 'big stomach medicine' (Figure 6.6). This member of the sweet potato family has large roots (often weighing as much as 45 kg) that often take the shape of a human being. If one of the 'limbs' of that root is broken during extraction from the ground, the corresponding part of the collector's body will also break (as this author discovered

Figure 6.6 Example of a young Bush Morning Glory plant (*left*), next to wild turnip plants (*tinpsila*) to indicate scale (photograph by K. Pickering Sherman).

to his discomfort when he broke the foot of one of these roots). This plant root is used to treat recurrent bad dreams. A knowledgeable medicine man is required to powder the root and to dust the powder onto the patient's body with a feather. The medicine man, however, is often reluctant to collect the root himself because of the consequences of damaging the root during its harvest. But although anyone can collect the plant (providing they are very careful and respectful of the root), only a medicine man with the requisite knowledge can successfully perform the medicinal application.

The Lakota belief that all of life is interconnected, prevents the Lakota people from managing in a way that is intrusive to natural resources. The same is not always true of methods utilized by Western scientists. Tribal biologists expressed concerns over population inventory methods proposed by Western scientists that they believed would unduly endanger wildlife. For example, scientists argued that the best way to count bighorn sheep (*Ovis cannadensis*) was to herd them onto a local butte using helicopters and land vehicles and to corral them into one small area. Unfortunately, Lakota managers' concerns went unheeded over the years, resulting in the unnecessary deaths of several bighorn sheep that fell from cliffs when chased or that succumbed to stress engendered by the counting methods. On one occasion, a young ram had been found dead, his death apparently due to strangulation by a non-expanding radio collar that the sheep had outgrown. Unobtrusive methods are especially critical when the animal population is still small and struggling for survival.

The preceding examples demonstrate the problems that can arise when policy decisions are taken away from the people living where the issues occur. The Indigenous Stewardship Model helps to resolve such problems through the system of appointing local stewards to monitor wildlife and other resources virtually on a daily basis.

Information about land management needs to be disseminated to the local population in order to gain everyone's input. According to Lakota tradition, everyone is afforded a say in all matters concerning the people. In the past, because resources were limited, extended family groups (*tiospayes*) could not all dwell in the same areas. Instead they dispersed across large areas according to resources availability. Each group had an intimate knowledge of their area and what was required to maintain it and to keep it in such a way as to support the people. As a result, everybody had to be educated as to what was happening to the land. In turn, each *tiospaye* realized the needs and abilities of each person in its group. In total, everyone was involved. During modern times, some of this inclusiveness has been lost. Bringing in the Stewardship Model will help bring everybody back into the decision-making process. Remaining vestiges of knowledge may be brought back, and the knowledge can once again be shared and perhaps even expanded. That remaining knowledge, once restored, can be brought back into use and transferred to future generations. Once the authority of the Indigenous knowledge system has been restored, Western knowledge may be incorporated to a degree to improve on the traditional system operating in modern times, so that the best elements of both systems may be used to manage the land. The best elements from the knowledge systems of other Indigenous groups may also be integrated to further improve the modern implementation of a traditional system. The more options that Indigenous peoples have available to them to select from in changing times, the better they can cope with those changes.

Element 7: Indigenous pedagogy: Intergenerational transfer of Indigenous knowledge

The key component of the Indigenous Stewardship Model is the transfer of knowledge to the youth. Traditionally, elders were the teachers providing a comprehensive and simultaneous education about all aspects of the Lakota body of knowledge in a way that was completely appropriate for the ability level of each child. Today the dominant education system does not allow for any deviation from the standard learning process and punishes those who do not learn in this way. As a result, many Lakota youth are labeled as 'special needs' children and end up with very low self-esteem regarding their scholastic abilities. In contrast to Western concepts of education, the Lakota approach infuses all of life with the opportunity to learn and grow. The term 'pedagogy', therefore, must be interpreted as a part of everyday life, with interactions between knowledge holders and community members, between elders and youth, between Indigenous people and Western people, and fundamentally between nature and human life.

The action words for an Indigenous pedagogy involve listening, observing, sharing, and emulating in all varieties of settings. This pedagogy, then, is part of the way elders teach Lakota youth. Chief Luther Standing Bear of the Oglala Sioux said, when referring to his people: 'Knowledge was inherent in all things. The world was a library. . . .' In the past, such knowledge was part of children's learning. Children learned by doing. Indigenous communities now have to include this form of learning along with classroom training. On the subject of ethnobotany, for example, if students are unable to do the practical learning, they will never develop an intimate knowledge of the plant community, an important prerequisite to maintaining the resource for the following generations. The ideal would be to have the children learn about plants from both Lakota and Western scientific perspectives and to understand the differences. Ultimately, children will become the stewards of the land, so they need to be trained correctly. By focusing educational efforts on youth within the schools, one obtains a secondary benefit: the youth often take these messages back into their homes. When tribal conservation rangers made presentations to classroom students on issues of wildlife conservation, the students later chastised their fathers and uncles for illegal hunting, because it endangered the resource and ultimately the welfare of future generations.

Category C. Co-Management: Advocating for Indigenous Stewardship on Land Where Indigenous Authority Is Shared with Western Managers or Is Absent

Building awareness of alternative approaches for co-managed lands or lands of cultural heritage without formal tribal control requires special attention. In situations where authority is shared or Indigenous authority is absent, neither Western scientists nor Indigenous knowledge holders should be in a position to claim exclusive authority or dismiss the perspectives of the other.

Element 8: Validating Indigenous knowledge systems: Policy advocacy and reform

This element of the model respectfully opposes any policy that diminishes sovereignty and associated rights for Indigenous peoples, foremost being the strict and sole reliance on Western-based approaches to land and resource management by colonial governments. Other policies that need scrutiny are those that allow exploitation of Indigenous natural, cultural, and intellectual resources. Opposition from colonial governments or those adopting a Western-based approach will result in conflict, and thus conflict resolution is a necessary part of this component of the model. In relation to policy, reforms are needed so that the tribe has a greater voice in participation, decision making, and policy implementation. Indigenous peoples need to have more control over their natural resources and land. When policy is made in areas far removed from agency offices, the real concerns and knowledge of the Indigenous peoples are lost. Policy becomes dis-embedded from the practical implications of the policies' consequences.

The differences between knowledge systems have to do with values and philosophies, so these need to be examined explicitly to determine where the conflicts are likely to arise. For example, the Western approach seems to be driven most often by economic interests, to the exclusion of spiritual, aesthetic, or cultural priorities. Because the land on the Pine Ridge Reservation is checker-boarded with non-Indian lands (see Figure 4.7), the State is able to mandate what is able to happen within the reservation boundaries. Nowhere is this clearer than in wildlife management. Before each hunting season, the South Dakota Game, Fish, and Parks agency announces that it will be issuing a certain number of hunting permits in Shannon County, one of three counties within the Pine Ridge Reservation boundaries. The number of permits it issues is derived arbitrarily, without meeting with tribal officials to determine population numbers, tribally established harvest limits, or local social and economic conditions.

An example of the disjuncture between policy developed in a remote office and policy formulated as a result of on-the-ground monitoring occurred during the 1990s, when Big Horn Sheep (*Ovis canadensis*) were being re-introduced into Badlands National Park. Audubon Sheep (*Ovis canadensis auduboni*, a subspecies of Rocky Mountain Big Horn Sheep), had originally inhabited this area, but over-hunting in the late 19th and early 20th centuries, with the arrival of European settlers, had caused their extinction by the early 1920s. The last herd was seen on Sheep Mountain Table in the South Unit of the Badlands National Park. In the 1960s Rocky Mountain Big Horn Sheep were introduced into the North Unit of Badlands National Park in an attempt to re-establish the population. The sheep had been penned and had not settled well. Several sheep died, so national parks officers decided to release the remaining population to pioneer out as they could. Over the following years the sheep established themselves in both the North Unit of the park, which adjoins the reservation, and the South Unit, which falls within the boundaries of the reservation (Figure 4.7). The sheep began migrating between the two areas and establishing breeding grounds in both the North and the South Units. Lakota people were well aware of the sheep movements, because they monitored them and saw them regularly.

The populations were doing so well that national parks staff decided to re-introduce more animals in the 1990s. A management strategy was needed, and a meeting was held to develop ways to count and monitor the existing population, to work out how to introduce the new animals, and to develop a species management plan. The meeting occurred at the Regional Office of the National Parks Service in Denver (Colorado) rather than in the area in which the sheep are found. A Lakota representative from OSPRA was invited to participate in the meeting because of his local knowledge of the animals. At the meeting, scientists dominated the discussion. None of these scientists had seen the sheep in Badlands National Park, and most did not realize that the sheep had established a regular migration route between the North and the South Units. The views and experiences of the tribal representative were not invited until the end of the meeting, after the management plans had been finalized. When the tribal representative spoke of his first-hand knowledge of the extent of the current population, he was required to provide documentary evidence for the claims of sighting in the South Unit. Luckily he was able to produce maps of sightings to provide the scientific proof required. The species management plan had not, at this stage, taken account of the total extent of the sheep population. Even after Lakota knowledge was provided, few changes to the final plan were made.

Element 9: Strategies for genuine collaboration: Avoiding appropriation and dominance

Co-management strategies in the Stewardship Model include mechanisms for tribal peoples and park managers to work together without tribal people being exploited or having park managers insist on the domination of the Western or scientific model. Indigenous people will always have to interact with non-Indigenous agencies. History shows that, because of the differences between the Western approach and Indigenous knowledge systems, there will inevitably be conflict. If Indigenous peoples and government resource agencies are ultimately going to work together, a common language must be developed that will allow both sides to get along. The way to do that is to combine the best elements of both systems to create a new system that respects both types of knowledge.

Federal agencies could support training programs and workshops that involve all the stakeholders, so the agencies and people train together in stewardship; in this way both are more adaptive and effective. Tribal members would participate in long- and short-term planning, monitoring and inventory projects for species of particular importance to the natural ecosystem. Ecological drivers such as fire, flood, and overgrazing could be observed and discussed by the land stewards in a detailed way rather than via abstracted computer models. The real impact of such events on the resources would then be better understood. Daily observation would replace fly-overs once every five years. Community institutions could be supported to implement the observations, execute the restoration projects, and interpret the results.

For example, the National Park Service (NPS) expressed a desire both to understand and to interpret native values in the Badlands National Park. Through genuine co-management, traditional forms of social, economic, and political organization would contribute to NPS understanding of ecologically sustainable societies. The more Lakota people are drawn away from land-based livelihoods, the more they will be drawn into unemployment and be deskilled from their traditional life-ways. The park could be a place where Lakota youth come to be trained in Lakota conservation practice. The sense of the role of nature in life would be reinforced with Lakota youth through internships, community service for troubled youth, and school programs. Restoration projects could be staffed with Lakota youth in this manner – for example, trail building and native plant restoration.

Another problem occurs when Western managers invite native peoples to join them in so-called collaborative approaches; agency staff tend to appropriate components of Indigenous knowledge for Western ends, without compensation or acknowledgement of the Indigenous contribution. For example, the NPS likes to designate certain areas as sacred, whereas from the Lakota perspective *all* the lands are sacred and interconnected, with a spirit and a relationship to humans that need to be respected. The linear approach of Western thinking runs contrary to the Lakota viewpoint. Federal agencies should perhaps not operate in a linear way and should not impose the categorization of Western thought onto Lakota views of the landscape.

The NPS and OSPRA had a good professional working relationship when there was a Stewardship Division at OSPRA, because they had a point of contact. Once the Stewardship Division was dismantled, that avenue for communication was lost. Different organizational structures and chains of command often accompany new leadership in an agency. New personnel in the federal system may not be sensitive to the collaborative and co-equal relationship between NPS and the Oglala Sioux Tribe. With the Indigenous Stewardship Model in place, the process of collaboration would be inherent in the orientation of new personnel. A model is more sensitive than a management plan, because it includes the values of the local people. To have genuine collaboration with outside entities, that sensitivity is essential.

Category D: Consensus Building and Conflict Management

Natural resource stewardship and conservation are inherently conflicted processes; typically a variety of people with diverging interests have multiple claims on land and resources. Because natural resource stewardship and conservation affect so many people's lives, decision making and conflict management must be addressed by these projects. Doing so will alleviate negative impacts and ensure that people realize the benefits of stewardship and conservation of their resources.

Element 10: Indigenous processes for decision making: Resolving internal differences

This element involves getting tribal members and tribal governments to work together and get along. Use of Indigenous ways is more culturally appropriate for Indigenous peoples. Making decisions and managing conflicts according to the Indigenous values of a culture, framing issues within a paradigm that 'makes sense' to those involved, and using a process specific to the local context provides sustained, satisfactory decisions and resolutions that do not induce additional conflict. For example, traditional Lakota decision-making practices rest on the values of interconnectedness, respect, humility, equality, and autonomy. Many Indigenous systems have a nested decision-making structure rather than one that is hierarchical. Indigenous decision-making bodies tend to be more flexible and meet based on need rather than on a schedule. Decisions are made based on what is good for the community rather than on individual interests, while respect for individual autonomy is maintained. A wider range of information is taken into consideration, and more time is allocated for the process. Community involvement and women's participation are often integral to the process, ensuring that all people are equally represented.

Unfortunately, many of these Indigenous methods for decision making and conflict resolution have been erased from modern tribal political processes, and inappropriate Western practices have been put in their place. Significant time and effort are needed to restore more balanced, inclusive, and flexible systems of decision making and conflict resolution to modern Indigenous populations. The Indigenous Stewardship Model encourages the integration of traditional values and philosophies into the process of developing and implementing a local stewardship system.

Element 11: Indigenous collaboration in decision making: Resolving external differences

This element is the corollary of Element 10 and involves getting tribal and non-tribal agencies to work together in more harmonious ways. Western methods of decision making, which are often top-down and fail to consult with Indigenous peoples before implementing conservation projects, have resulted in conservation areas abutting and absorbing

Indigenous territory. Western conflict-resolution models on their own have been unsuccessful in alleviating the resulting conflicts. By constructing a common language between Indigenous communities and Western scientists and resource managers, alternative forms of dispute resolution emerge that meld the best of both systems, avoid cultural inequality in favor of unstated Western perspectives, and produce decisions that are meaningful and satisfying to all the parties involved.

One of the greatest problems that Indigenous people face with the Western view is having it imposed on them. On the Pine Ridge Reservation, since there are checker-boarded acres within the Reservation (see Chapter 4; Figure 4.7), Western managers do not interact with Lakota people but simply impose bureaucracy on the tribe. Under the Stewardship Model, there would be communication between these Western managers and tribal members in every element of management, so the tribal voice would be heard and the management policies would reflect Lakota cultural and economic values. For example, tribal members need to be involved not simply at the point of receiving dictated harvest limits; equal decision making needs to take place from the earliest planning phases, through regulatory formulation and into the implementation of the final regulations. Communication between local stewards and the Western and tribal resource agencies would occur, and both western and tribal managers would interact, sharing in a common language.

The relationship between agencies and the tribal communities varies tremendously with the personnel assigned to the tribal areas. Without continuity, the progress in establishing genuine processes for collaboration remains sporadic and uncertain. Resistance can develop on the tribal side as well. For example, when an interagency team of fire experts was brought together to collaborate in a discussion of fire management on the Pine Ridge Reservation, the Bureau of Indian Affairs official went off on his own and began implementing his own methods, without paying attention or respect to the other participating tribal and federal agencies. As long as one knowledge system insists on dominance, no possibility exists for genuine collaboration. Common respect and a common language are necessary to obtain the benefits of both systems.

Everything changes with politics, whether external state and federal politics or internal politics within tribal government and tribal organizations. For example, some limited co-management arrangements have existed between tribes and the South Dakota Game, Fish, and Parks agency, whereby there was collaboration on hunting issues. But with the change of just one politician, years of negotiations and good will were lost. One of the reasons for the lack of continuity is the absence of mechanisms to deal with conflict resolution in the context of political change. The Oglala Sioux Tribe has been chided by outsiders for having a lack of political continuity, with a two-year term for tribal government. At the same time, when a new superintendent is brought into a federal park, continuity is also lost, so the effect occurs on both sides.

CONCLUSION

The Indigenous Stewardship Model is a comprehensive and dynamic effort to re-establish and promote Indigenous methods of ecology and land stewardship throughout the globe. Indigenous ecological practices and values have been ignored and suppressed, at great cost to the environment and the people. The combination of colonial and state policies, loss of historical homelands, and over-emphasis on commodity production has devastated both the biological diversity of ecosystems and the lifestyles of Indigenous peoples. The Indigenous Stewardship Model is representative of efforts and desires by Indigenous peoples worldwide to revitalize their own unique knowledge systems. It provides a process for constructing a culturally appropriate alternative with which to care for land and natural resources. While recognizing the potential contribution of Western models of resource management, the Indigenous Stewardship Model supports the holistic, locally embedded, and culturally significant role of natural resources in Indigenous worldviews. It promotes sovereignty by explicitly addressing methods for asserting the inherent right of Indigenous peoples to govern themselves with respect to natural resources. By exploring the best elements of both systems, the Indigenous Stewardship Model is intended to establish a method for communication between Indigenous communities and Western resource managers without the dominance and intrusion that often characterizes relationships between Indigenous peoples and proponents of the Western model. By empowering local people to act as the stewards of their immediate resources, the Indigenous Stewardship Model also offers methods for minimizing the costs and maximizing the outcomes of resource monitoring and maintenance.

Chapter 7

CONCLUSION

> I suggest [that] the terms for genuine participation have hardly been
> glimpsed, let alone put in place. (Campbell 2004: 164)

We commenced this volume with this pessimistic quotation from
Campbell (2004), relating to his work on co-management in Langtang
National Park in Nepal. Campbell argues that Indigenous knowledge,
which sees an inseparable connection between nature and culture, provides
an ontology that is incommensurable with scientific conservation, which
emphasizes the distinction between nature and society. He points out that
co-management arrangements in Langtang National Park struggle with
conflicting attitudes toward wildlife. Local Tamang peoples, who have a
strong social and cultural connection to the resources of the protected area,
construct wildlife as a resource for exploitation. For them, wild animals
interfere with subsistence farming practices and need to be managed to ensure
a balance between animal needs and human needs. However, government
managers are funded by Western (conservationist) financial donors who
require a conservation ethic for all aspects of park management.

The Tamangs' 'Indigenous' symbolic and practical phenomenologi-
cal unity of humans, territory, and species diversity runs counter to the
primary feature of the environmentalist worldview, which holds that
global biodiversity can be saved only by formalizing boundaries between
humanity and non-human nature (Campbell 2004: 163).

Campbell concludes that:

> Advocating participation with local communities in biodiversity conser-
> vation . . . can throw up issues of profound power differences in even
> establishing what there is to participate about. (2004: 163)

Our research discussed in this volume resonates well with the ideas
raised by Campbell. Yet we would not be quite as pessimistic about the

future as is Campbell. Although we have demonstrated that there are numerous barriers to the effective incorporation of Indigenous people and Indigenous knowledge in protected-areas management, we are confident that there are mechanisms in place that are gradually changing the power imbalance between traditional resource users and modern resource managers.

In this volume we have explored the theoretical structures that inform the constructs of Indigenous knowledge. We have demonstrated that epistemological barriers to the recognition of the worth of Indigenous knowledge arose from the historical trajectory of the evolution of science. Our case studies have demonstrated that barriers to resource management partnerships exist and that the epistemological barriers, in particular, have a strong degree of commonality between geographically and politically diverse situations.

Co-management arrangements have provided some impetus to overcoming these barriers to resource-management partnerships, but we agree with Campbell that such arrangements still have some distance to travel before equitable partnerships between Indigenous resource stewards and government resource-management agencies can occur. We have demonstrated that, although co-management arrangements are far superior to protected-area management models that make no provision for Indigenous peoples whatsoever, there are still many imposed bureaucratic restraints on genuine management partnerships arising from the institutions within which co-management is framed. Indigenous Protected Areas are yet a further improvement on co-managed areas, since IPAs allow Indigenous people and their knowledge to be at the forefront of day-to-day management, even if government agencies retain an over-arching control via the provisions of funding that bind management to bureaucratic requirements of scientific review. The Indigenous Stewardship Model currently being used by Lakota resource stewards on the Pine Ridge Indian Reservation, and in particular in the South Unit of Badlands National Park, South Dakota, is the model that best facilitates genuine partnerships between Western resource managers and Indigenous peoples. Under this model, there is recognition that Indigenous knowledge forms a legitimate basis for management but that Indigenous knowledge can incorporate scientific knowledge, especially with respect to lands that have been recently degraded in ways unknown in traditional Indigenous knowledge systems.

We conclude this volume with a detailed assessment of the ways in which co-management, Indigenous Protected Areas (IPAs), and the Indigenous Stewardship Model address (or don't address) the barriers to co-operation identified in Chapter 3 and grounded in the case studies of Chapter 4. We then reflect on how our analysis moves this debate forward, and we conclude with our visions for a genuinely co-managed future.

Co-Management, IPAs, and the Indigenous Stewardship Model: Opportunities for Breaking Down the Barriers

Most protected areas in the world, particularly national parks and forests, have little place for local peoples to be involved in management. Co-managed areas are the exception, rather than the rule, and therefore offer an important perspective on how resource management could operate. In the following discussion we review each of the barriers we identified in Chapter 3 and consider how co-management, IPAs, and the Indigenous Stewardship Model may or may not help to overcome each barrier. Table 7.1 provides a summary of our findings.

Epistemological Barriers

Barrier A: IK Not Recognized

Indigenous knowledge is explicitly recognized as part of the overall data gathering for co-management, but it is not necessarily internalized by managers on the ground and is often not appreciated by upper-level agency officers. Co-management is often a political decision, and therefore Indigenous knowledge is forced onto management agency staff as a result of decisions based on politics rather than what scientists see as good resource-management decision making.

In Indigenous Protected Areas (IPAs), Indigenous knowledge theoretically forms the basis for management planning, although in reality essential government funding to support an IPA is often conditional on independent scientific review of management plans, and this requirement generally ensures that scientific knowledge provides a major platform for management, even in these areas.

The Indigenous Stewardship Model starts from the premise that Indigenous knowledge survives and natural resources are dependent on the implementation of long-held knowledge about the needs of the environment. As a consequence, Indigenous knowledge underpins all management planning and activities. It simply cannot be ignored or discarded.

Barrier B: Narrow Definitions

In co-management there are opportunities for managers to see Indigenous people incorporating both Indigenous knowledge and modern science in their approaches to resources management, because the managers work with contemporary Indigenous people, living and working in contemporary settings. Nevertheless, there remains an impression in

TABLE 7.1 Summary of findings

Barrier	Co-Management	Indigenous Protected Areas (IPAs)	Indigenous Stewardship Model
Epistemological Barriers			
A IK not recognized	IK explicitly recognized, but not necessarily internalized or adopted by protected-area managers.	IK is the basis for management planning, although it may be superseded by scientific knowledge for funding purposes.	IK underpins all management planning and activities. It cannot be ignored or discarded.
B Narrow definitions	Practice demonstrates that IK is dynamic, although romantic notions of 'primitive ecological wisdom' can dominate scientific expectations.	As Indigenous people implement management schemes, narrow constructs of IK rarely occur.	Indigenous Stewardship Model recognizes that both Indigenous knowledge and scientific knowledge are dynamic, and both can work together in management.
C Non-validation of IK	Co-management may validate IK, but it is often regarded as inferior to science.	Validation of IK is not required; Indigenous resource managers are responsible for management.	Indigenous people are at the centre of management decision making, and IK does not require validation.
D Translation of IK	Requires that IK is understood by scientists, often in scientific forums.	Formal presentation of IK may be needed for funding support.	A common language of communication is required.
E Social/spiritual expression	IK needs to be removed from social/spiritual expression if it is to be accepted by managers.	IK can be retained in social/spiritual format except when required for funding or review.	All ways of knowing are respected through a common language of understanding.
F Codification of IK	Protected-area management requires management plans and other written documents. To be included in plans, IK must be codified.	IK needs to be written only when required for government purposes.	Indigenous people can choose which IK will be incorporated into management plans.

Table 7.1 Continued

G Ownership of knowledge	Indigenous people's ownership of knowledge is recognized but often appropriated.	IK is implemented in management by the owners themselves.	IK is implemented in management by the owners themselves.
H Spatial/temporal boundaries	Co-management occurs in Western-defined parks, and management is undertaken in Western time frames.	IPAs are declared over Indigenous lands and managed in Indigenous time frames.	Indigenous Stewardship Model applies over any land and can operate in any time frame.
Institutional/Systemic Barriers			
I 'Outsiders' kept 'outside'	Indigenous people are included in co-management as 'stakeholders'.	Indigenous people are 'insiders' in IPAs.	All resource stewards are equal partners, with Indigenous owners given special status.
J IK and management institutions	Western management institutions and knowledge structures completely dominate in co-management arrangements.	Indigenous social and knowledge institutions form the framework for most aspects of planning and day-to-day management.	The aim of the Indigenous Stewardship Model is for a common language of management to be developed, which requires compromise by all involved.
K Decentralization	Co-management cannot accommodate the decentralized nature of Indigenous knowledge systems.	IPAs can accommodate Indigenous frameworks relating to the social construction of knowledge.	The Indigenous Stewardship Model is designed to be implemented in accordance with Indigenous social institutions of knowledge.
L Racial/cultural inferiority	IK is often perceived as inferior to Western knowledge.	Where IK differs from science it is considered inferior.	The model is based on a shared language of communication, with no notion of inferiority or superiority of views.
M State power	Co-management requires state control of the management process.	Because IPAs rely on government funding, the State can control much of the activity.	To be effective, the Indigenous Stewardship Model needs to be adopted by the State.

Continued

TABLE 7.1 *Continued*

Barrier	Co-Management	Indigenous Protected Areas (IPAs)	Indigenous Stewardship Model
N Benevolent West	Incorporation of IK requires the goodwill of Western governments, bureaucrats, and land managers.	Funding for IPAs relies on support from scientists and the State.	The Indigenous Stewardship Model can operate with or without Western cooperation, but is most effective when there is equal support and responsibility.
O Globalization	Protected areas are often created in response to global environmental crises, so international agencies evaluate state management activities.	IPAs are usually declared in response to local community aspirations for protected-area management. There are therefore fewer global interventions in their management than occurs in co-management areas.	The Indigenous Stewardship Model has been developed to deal with local community aspirations for the protection and management of local resources. It is therefore the least likely of all these protected-area partnership models to be influenced by global issues. The advantage of the Indigenous Stewardship Model over other partnership models is that addressing economic issues is one of the functions of the model itself – it is not an institution imposed on the model by external government officers.

many co-management agreements that Indigenous knowledge is *only* that knowledge from the deep past. There is also the temptation to call on one Indigenous representative to be the token spokesperson for all Indigenous knowledge. In addition, some co-management sponsors continue to hold romantic notions of 'primitive ecological wisdom' and become disillusioned when Indigenous ways incorporate 'destructive' management elements, such as hunting endangered species or burning sensitive ecosystems.

This situation is not as problematic in IPAs. Here Indigenous peoples themselves implement the management schemes and consequently are able to call on all available knowledge, regardless of its 'traditions'.

The Indigenous Stewardship Model explicitly recognizes that both Indigenous knowledge and scientific knowledge need to be combined to produce effective resource management strategies in a world where modern society has brought about significant changes to the environment. It recognizes that all knowledge is dynamic and that there therefore needs to be a recognition of change built into the process of management.

Barrier C: Nonvalidation of IK

In theory, co-management is specifically designed to address this barrier to the incorporation of Indigenous people in resources management. However, in reality, Indigenous knowledge is generally regarded as inferior to science (see Barrier L, below), particularly if there are significant differences between what scientists know and what Indigenous people know. 'Working together' and 'sharing information' is usually a one-way process, in which scientists 'educate' Indigenous people about 'the truth' of particular management requirements.

In IPAs, validation of Indigenous knowledge is not required, because the Indigenous resource managers are primarily responsible for day-to-day management. Validation of knowledge becomes a problem only when government funding requires independent assessment of Indigenous management plans.

In the Indigenous Stewardship Model, Indigenous people are at the center of management decision making, and consequently their knowledge does not require validation by scientists. Indigenous knowledge and science are conceived as equal partners, and the model is designed to ensure that the hegemony of science does not dominate management planning or practice.

Barrier D: Translation of IK

This barrier remains firmly in place in most co-management arrangements, which means not only that knowledge is often taken out of its spiritual context (see Barrier E below) and expressed in formal language that is supported by empirical evidence but also that individual Indigenous people are expected to present the knowledge of an entire community, often contrary to community norms on ownership of knowledge (see Barrier G below).

This barrier applies even to IPAs, because funding and government support require formal funding applications to be developed. Indigenous people must always translate their knowledge into a language understood by scientists.

A key platform of the Indigenous Stewardship Model is that all participants in resources stewardship/management will work to develop a common language of communication. Neither Indigenous ways of sharing knowledge nor scientific preferences for knowledge formulation will dominate. The development of a shared, common language for communication ensures that all resource partners are equally respectful of one another and of the nature of the knowledge presented.

Barrier E: Social/Spiritual Expression

As indicated in relation to Barrier D, although in co-management agreements Indigenous people continue to hold their knowledge in accordance with social and cultural norms, such ways of knowing are sometimes repudiated as 'primitive' or 'backward' by the scientists involved in incorporating alternative forms of knowledge into formal management plans. As a consequence, Indigenous knowledge must often be removed from its spiritual expression to accommodate publication standards.

Another problem with co-management relates to the fact that Indigenous knowledge is shared asymmetrically in many Indigenous societies. It is inappropriate to ignore all those who have the right to speak on particular resources. Yet most co-management systems employ only a few members of an Indigenous community and expect these employees to be able to speak on all aspects of management planning of concern to an entire Indigenous community.

The value of IPAs is that Indigenous people are able to retain far more of their knowledge in its social format. Only those elements needed for funding applications or government reviews need to be removed into a more Western framework. The issue of having only one or a few individuals to speak on behalf of the ecosystem is not a problem in IPAs, since here all members of the community are able to participate in the compilation of information on which management plans are based.

Because of the different ways of knowing between science and Indigenous communities, allowing Indigenous knowledge to be presented in social or spiritual forms is a challenge for the Indigenous Stewardship Model. Nevertheless, with the goal of respecting others' views and the desire to develop a common language of understanding, the Indigenous Stewardship Model goes much farther in allowing Indigenous knowledge to remain in its social and spiritual form than do most other co-management models.

Furthermore, approaches such as the Indigenous Stewardship Model encourage the participation of the whole community in resource management decision making. In this way, those with the authority to speak on a particular species or ecosystem can do so. There is no requirement for spokespersons to represent others, or their knowledge.

Barrier F: Codification of IK

Most Indigenous knowledge comes from an oral tradition. Most scientific knowledge has been developed in a written tradition. All modern resources management requires the preparation of management plans based on legislation and government policy. Management implementation requires formal reviews of planning activities, with documented monitoring of results, and scientific review of outcomes, published in peer-reviewed journals or government reports. Indigenous knowledge can be incorporated in such a system *only* if it, too, is written down and scrutinized by external reviewers.

Codification of Indigenous knowledge applies only to IPAs when government funding applications need to be written and when formal reviews are undertaken. In day-to-day management the oral traditions of Indigenous knowledge can remain intact in these Indigenous managed areas.

The Indigenous Stewardship Model is based on respect for the knowledge of others and on recognition that all knowledge changes with time. Under this model some Indigenous knowledge is incorporated into written management plans. The difference from most other co-management arrangements is that Indigenous people can choose which data will be presented in written form and which will remain as an oral dataset.

Barrier G: Ownership of Knowledge

One of the major advantages of co-management is that this system recognizes that Indigenous people own their knowledge, and formal agreements are developed that acknowledge that Indigenous people's knowledge remains their property, even once that knowledge is incorporated into bureaucratic documents.

One problem with this system, however, is that sometimes Indigenous knowledge is acquired by resource managers without due compensation to the Indigenous knowledge holders. Indigenous people are often told: 'Well, if you want your knowledge used in managing your land, you have to tell us what you know'.

Where Indigenous people are employed to implement resource co-management programs that include their knowledge, they rarely hold senior positions in the management organization, and this situation can further increase Indigenous people's feelings that their ownership of knowledge is insufficiently recognized.

In IPAs Indigenous people are responsible for developing management plans based on Indigenous knowledge. The vast majority of the staff are Indigenous people who come from the community from which the knowledge also comes. The issue of appropriation is therefore not a concern, unless Indigenous knowledge must be given to scientists or bureaucrats as part of the funding application or external review process.

Because the Indigenous Stewardship Model was developed by Indigenous peoples, the model ensures that traditional custodians not only own the knowledge on which much of the management decision making is based, but they also own the management framework within which management planning occurs. This ensures that Indigenous ownership of knowledge is recognized and that adequate compensation for use of knowledge is made. It also integrates Indigenous knowledge holders into every aspect of the stewardship process, including employment as directors, wildlife managers, and public outreach specialists, rather than limiting Indigenous employment to menial, sporadic, advisory, or field support roles.

Barrier H: Spatial/Temporal Boundaries

Co-management arrangements are initiated by Western-trained management planners, and they generally relate to protected areas that have been declared over land or waters deemed by the state to have conservation value. The boundaries of these areas rarely coincide with Indigenous territories. As a consequence, Indigenous peoples may find that they have only cultural authority to be involved only in parts of co-managed areas, yet decisions made throughout the area may adversely affect adjacent parts of the ecosystems – not always incorporated into the protected area – areas for which traditional custodians are responsible.

Co-management is also run on Western timeframes, which often fall outside Indigenous temporal understandings. For example, planning for seasonal events such as school holidays or large fishing competitions has no basis in Indigenous seasonal conceptions.

IPAs are declared over lands within the territorial boundaries of one Indigenous group or a number of related groups. As a consequence, spatial boundaries of IPAs are usually within the social and cultural purview of Indigenous communities, rather than Western land-title arrangements. Temporal planning is also usually relevant to Indigenous seasons, rather than externally imposed holidays.

The Indigenous Stewardship Model generally falls between the confines of the co-management model and the Indigenous frameworks of IPAs. The Indigenous Stewardship Model may apply to all Indigenous lands, which may have a variety of different Western titles. The model is designed to apply equally to Indigenous owned land and national parks or other protected areas. It is a holistic model that manages ecosystems on Indigenous lands and takes little account of geographical boundaries, land title, and seasonal events.

Institutional/Systemic Barriers

Barrier I: 'Outsiders' Kept 'Outside'

Co-management is designed to ensure that all 'stakeholders' are included in resource-management decision making. One concern, however, is that Indigenous people are more than 'stakeholders' in the management of the resources on which their livelihoods have been based for generations. Indigenous people are concerned that, in many co-management arrangements, they are just one of many groups from 'outside' the state bureaucracy, when they should be given significant 'insider' status.

Meetings tend to be arranged on bureaucratic timeframes, with Indigenous resource managers required to travel to central offices and to meet at times that suit workers in Western bureaucracies.

Indigenous people are very much 'insiders' in IPAs. Meetings are held on Indigenous land at times and for periods that suit Indigenous communities. Nevertheless, despite the rhetoric that these resource management arrangements are on Indigenous land, managed by Indigenous people, for Indigenous people, there are few opportunities to ensure that scientists, bureaucrats, and other 'outsiders' remain 'outside'. Interference from government agencies continues.

There are neither 'insiders' nor 'outsiders' in the Indigenous Stewardship Model. The aim of the Indigenous Stewardship Model is genuine partnerships between all stakeholders, with Indigenous owners given special status in accordance with their traditional connections to place. Meetings are held on Indigenous land at times and for periods that suit Indigenous communities, although there are compromises for bureaucratic requirements, where appropriate and where agreed to by Indigenous resource stewards.

Barrier J: IK and Management Institutions

Western management institutions and knowledge structures completely dominate in co-management arrangements. Bureaucratic boundaries form the basis of management arrangements, governments remain the holders of land title, government agencies provide the legal and policy institutions within which co-management is constituted, and science provides the framework within which knowledge must be integrated. There are few opportunities for Indigenous social, cultural, or knowledge institutions to frame any aspect of the management process.

Indigenous social and knowledge institutions form the framework for most aspects of planning and day-to-day management in IPAs. Nevertheless, government funding dictates that IPAs meet government requirements for financial reporting and management planning, and government scientists require Indigenous knowledge to meet independent review. In this way elements of Western institutions impose themselves even on Indigenous-controlled resource management structures such as IPAs.

The Indigenous Stewardship Model can operate in either Western or Indigenous institutions. The aim of the Indigenous Stewardship Model is for a common language of management to be developed, and this requires compromises by all involved. As a consequence, Indigenous resource managers working under the Indigenous Stewardship Model may continue to present knowledge in accordance with social and cultural Indigenous institutions and yet incorporate scientific knowledge that is constructed in accordance with scientific ways of knowing. Institutions of management are also an amalgam of Indigenous and Western bureaucracies, with neither being privileged over the other.

Barrier K: Decentralization

Following from Barrier J, co-management cannot accommodate the decentralized nature of Indigenous knowledge systems. The asymmetrically shared nature of Indigenous knowledge is problematic for Western bureaucracies that require single, or at most, small group representation on committees. Where multiple Indigenous groups have an interest in a single co-managed area (such as when protected areas extend across several different tribal boundaries), the requirement of Western bureaucracies for individuals or small groups to represent entire sociocultural entities creates additional problems, especially if bureaucracies do not have the capacity to develop multiple management outcomes to meet the dissimilar needs of several different Indigenous communities, with different knowledges and different requirements for resource management.

IPAs are generally based within single Indigenous social units and are able to accommodate Indigenous frameworks relating to the social construction of knowledge. The decentralized nature of Indigenous knowledge arises only when IPAs need to deal with Western bureaucracies as part of the funding process.

Also following from Barrier J, the Indigenous Stewardship Model, having been developed by Indigenous people, is designed to be implemented in accordance with Indigenous social institutions of knowledge. This means that issues of management and conservation are discussed, formulated, and evaluated by everyday people engaged with the land rather than limited to individuals with titles, degrees, or positions in the hierarchy of Western management.

Barrier L: Racial/Cultural Inferiority

Although rarely overt, notions of the racial or cultural inferiority of Indigenous partners in co-management underpin many of the barriers that remain, despite the stated objectives of integrated management. Indigenous knowledge is rarely privileged, and scientists often feel that Indigenous partners need to be 'educated' about the 'truth' that only scientists know about resources.

In IPAs, although Indigenous knowledge dominates in theory, in practice most IPAs require scientists to review their management plans as a prerequisite for government funding. In reviewing management plans, scientists insist on 'accurate' knowledge as the basis of management. Where there are differences of fact between Indigenous knowledge and what scientists know, there is never any thought that scientific knowledge will give way to what Indigenous people know. Indigenous knowledge, where it differs from science, is regarded as inferior.

Based as it is on a shared language of communication, the Indigenous Stewardship Model provides an opportunity for genuine two-way sharing of knowledge. Neither Indigenous knowledge nor science is regarded as inferior to the other. The knowledge is different, but difference is valorized. This reduces opportunities for racial or cultural denigration of either form of knowledge.

Barrier M: State Power

Co-management requires state control of the management process. Although the state may perceive that co-management is based on its benevolence, the state remains all powerful in the process. Any dispute is resolved in favor of state law and policy and state political requirements. Where there is too much conflict, the state can simply withdraw from the co-management process and take over management completely.

In theory, IPAs can operate independently of the state. They are Indigenous natural areas that have been set aside by Indigenous title holders for conservation and management in accordance with Indigenous aspirations. In reality, because IPAs rely on government funding for the majority of their operating requirements, the state is able to control much of the activity on IPAs through the impositions of conditions on funding.

To be effective, the Indigenous Stewardship Model needs to be adopted by the state. This does give the state the opportunity to impose conditions on the adoption of the model and thereby to retain a privileged position of dominance over the process. Nevertheless, because the Indigenous Stewardship Model is designed to ensure the development of genuine partnerships, the prospect of a state's assuming total authority over stewardship management projects is less than occurs in co-management.

Barrier N: Benevolent West

In all collaborative management ventures presented here, the good will of the scientists in land-management bureaucracies, and their governments, is needed for successful implementation of collaborative programs. This is most obvious in co-management arrangements, which cannot succeed at all without government and bureaucratic support. Such benevolence is less essential in IPAs, although without government funding IPAs are unlikely to be maintained. The Indigenous Stewardship Model can operate independently of government support but is more likely to be successful with the good will of local managers, and the State, than without such support.

Barrier O: Globalization

Issues of globalization lie at the heart of Western dominance in co-management arrangements. Ecosystems management, and the creation of such protected areas as forests and national parks, have been largely in response to global environmental crises, especially in the previous two decades. National managers of protected areas need to meet international standards of best management practice, as defined by science, to avoid global condemnation for any failures. International conferences on protected-areas management, and international agencies such as the IUCN, constantly review achievements made by nation-states in environmental conservation. There are, therefore, few opportunities for governments to 'experiment' in conservation by allowing 'primitive' conservation ideals to dominate management decision making, even in co-managed areas.

IPAs are usually declared in response to local community aspirations for the protection and management of local resources. There are therefore fewer global interventions in the management of IPAs in comparison with co-managed areas. Nevertheless, national governments that are called on to provide funds for IPAs *are* required to meet international conventions of protected-areas management, and this requirement imposes a modicum of global influence over IPAs.

Like IPAs, the Indigenous Stewardship Model has been developed to deal with local community aspirations for the protection and management of local resources. Because the Indigenous Stewardship Model can also operate outside the need for substantial government funding and because this model operates on *all* lands and waters managed by Indigenous resources owners, the need for international scrutiny of management outcomes is far less than in either co-management arrangements or IPAs. The Indigenous Stewardship Model is therefore the least likely of all these protected-area partnership models to be influenced by global issues.

Nevertheless, because the Indigenous Stewardship Model does need to take account of economic and political circumstances on lands and resources incorporated into the Indigenous Stewardship Model, national and global economic issues do need to be addressed. The advantage of the Indigenous Stewardship Model over other partnership models, however, is that addressing economic issues is one of the functions of the model itself – it is not an institution imposed on the model by external government officers.

FINAL REFLECTIONS

Reflections on the Lua (Hank Delcore)

The Lua people of Ban Toey, in DPNP, held their annual rice spirit festival in August 2003. Although several lowlanders and two foreign anthropologists were present, no state officials were there to witness an event that the young Lua activist, Somsak, thought might serve as an expression of Lua ecological wisdom. On return to Silalaeng, however, I found that a Thai NGO activist friend was hosting a visit by the national Director of the Department of Environmental Quality Promotion (DEQP). Mere hours after coming from Ban Toey, I found myself describing the situation to the Director. She was not impressed by the Lua preference for subsistence rice production in their swidden fields, and instead described a national park in Chiang Mai Province. There, local people were working as masseuses and masseurs for tourists in the park, with a portion of their salary going to a community development fund that was being used for agricultural development projects for the wider community.

The next morning she and I both attended a ritual in Silalaeng, in which Thai-Lue people from several villages sacrificed a pig to a water spirit that inhabits a major stream that waters some of their rice fields. Although never explicitly stated, the Director's presence at the ritual was clearly part of my NGO activist friend's ongoing campaign to highlight the ecological base of Silalaeng's culture.

This episode has come to symbolize to me the distribution of racial privilege in and around the park. The very fact that the DEQP Director was in Silalaeng for the water spirit ritual, and not in Ban Toey for their festival just the day before, represents the power of the barriers we have discussed to promote recognition of Thai-Lue Indigenous knowledge and denial of similar value to Lua culture.

Yet I am also struck by the power of goodwill among concerned individuals to make a difference in breaking down epistemological and institutional barriers to cooperation among state resource managers and Indigenous peoples. In 2005 DPNP received a new director. I visited in 2006 to solicit his support for a proposed period of long-term fieldwork in the park focusing on ethnic relations among Thai-Lue, Hmong, and Lua people. The Director immediately agreed to provide his co-operation. He said clearly that there were things that he hoped I could help clear up for him. For example, he wondered why it seemed that he and his team were able to sometimes reach agreements with Lua representatives, but when these representatives returned to their communities, the agreements were scuttled. He sincerely hoped that my research would shed light on the processes within Lua communities that inhibited communication between officials and Lua leaders. I took his hope as recognition that institutional and cultural differences were real but that barriers could be overcome with more study and mutual understanding. At least he was not willing to fall back on time-worn characterizations of the Lua as backward and stubborn.

Further, several Lua residents noted that previous grievances with the park administration had ameliorated somewhat. Notably, Somsak – who had been at loggerheads with the previous director – said the new director was a reasonable person and that pressure on him and his fellow villagers to change their livelihoods had abated somewhat.

Change can come from the top, but it can also come from below. The Lua and their allies will have to keep pushing, and more sympathetic people, such as the DPNP's new director, will need to take charge. Then, perhaps, the parties involved will become more aware of institutional barriers and the need to understand and address them. In a best-case scenario, people of goodwill will come to see one another's ways of knowing not as oppressive or backward but as merely different and mutually informing.

Reflections on the Adivasis (Jeff Snodgrass)

A precipitous drop in forest cover has led the Indian state to shift its policy away from commodity extraction and toward the sustainable use of forests by local communities. This has led to many new initiatives meant to actively involve locals in new forms of state-local 'co-' or 'joint' management. Despite this shift in policy, the RFD (the implementing agent of the state in this arena) continues to experience difficulty in its conservation and afforestation efforts. Winning the trust and the cooperation of local peoples in a true and abiding 'joint' natural resource management strategy is particularly difficult for the RFD.

India's Indigenous Adivasis are especially important here, because they often live in and near protected forests and parks; they are economically dependent on these lands (for timber, fuel, food, fodder, medicine, and slash-and-burn agriculture) and are impoverished and growing in numbers, which increases pressure on these natural areas. Further, tribal communities often display a sophisticated knowledge of the forest and even their own 'ethnoforestry' and thus can help to identify priorities and actual management techniques in these collaborative conservation efforts.

As a way to build tribal commitment to state efforts and establish trust between tribals and the Indian state, an increasing number of studies point to a strong interconnection of religion and ecology in the Indian subcontinent, a focus of my own research and thoughts in this book. Rajasthan in particular is well known for its sacred groves, and Rajasthan's tribals, although often describing themselves as Hindus, are animists and so worship their environment in the form of trees, rivers, grasses, stones, hills, and the forest itself. As a consequence, religion can be a useful way to mobilize and to stimulate tribal conservation sentiments.

A flurry of first-rate research has begun to assess the prospects of a range of contemporary forest management efforts in India, as well as of community natural resource management more generally in other parts of the world. However, these studies have not closely examined the feasibility of implementing such programs in a sacred idiom. Based on ethnographic and survey research into the connection between Indigenous religion and forest conservation, and the current examination into the practical use of religion to promote forest conservation, this research has begun to fill the gap in the literature.

My findings suggest that religion can play an important role in conservation and sustainable forest management efforts in the area, especially in concert with the building of meaningful social bonds between state and local governing bodies. Although social bonds between the governing bodies are common in new governmental initiatives, I think that communicating these initiatives, for example, to Adivasis in culturally resonant idioms can be central to the success of such initiatives. Among other things, communicating in this way – recognizing Adivasi idioms – signals respect for tribal history and traditions and can thereby win trust and cooperation. Religious specialists such as shamans generally command tremendous respect within local Indigenous communities. Winning the cooperation of religious leaders in state-sponsored conservation might be of great tactical importance as a way to encourage others to utilize forest resources sustainably. Shamans' central position in the rite of distributing saffron is an example of this in the current context, since *they* organize this ritual, which in turn organizes villagers for collective management decisions.

Using religion as a way to encourage conservation could be useful in other cultural settings as well, and so having a broader view of what 'religion' might mean in Indigenous or other development contexts is helpful. (I use the term *religion* here in Durkheim's sense of going beyond mere symbols and rites to include the social, material, and political realities infused by these symbols and rites.) For example, Bhil *religion* brings together sacred personal and institutionalized values, as well as the social and material contexts to which those values connect. I therefore do not think it wise to limit an understanding of religion to just the symbolic *value* dimensions of experience but to include the way those values are embodied in material and political relations to the environment.

Thus I agree that one must avoid the romantic trap of thinking that religion operates separately from material and political contexts and similarly avoid the idea that summoning gods, spirits, and invisible symbolic realities might be enough to ensure successful land management. I similarly eschew any related fantasy that Indigenous persons are so tightly tied to divine and sacred powers as not to be practical-minded economic and political actors. Livelihoods and politics should not be banished from either our definitions of religion or from the Indigenous conservation equation in these village contexts.

Nevertheless, I don't favor the common modern view that that livelihoods and politics work most effectively when disconnected from deep values and sentiments couched in a religious idiom. The key to successful conservation and land management, as we have suggested throughout this book, is the continued economic and political strength of individuals and collectivities that sanction and legitimate natural resource management decisions. But, at least in the Indigenous contexts discussed in this book, such bodies are at once economic, political, and also *sacred*.

Thus a strategy that incorporates religion can further conservation and management goals.

Reflections on the Lakota (Kathy Pickering Sherman and Richard Sherman)

Natural resources reside in the heart of Lakota culture. The desire to repair the severed tie between the people and the land pervades discussions of not only co-management but also of economic development, housing, health and well-being, education, and cultural and language preservation. A special reverence is shown to Lakota knowledge holders, who are helping the younger generations to re-establish that connection to the land. Bureaucratic obstacles to Lakota families having beneficial use and control of their lands, such as federal trust status and government policies favoring commodity agricultural interests, are being actively questioned, challenged, and circumvented by reservation residents. Along with these visions of a recovered relationship with the land comes a restored pride in the cultural values and philosophies that defined Lakota conceptions of people's place within the natural world.

Nevertheless, the impact of a century of imposed Western use values and Western management approaches has left deep wounds on the land and on the people. The barriers of lack of recognition, narrow definitions, and codification and ownership of knowledge have continued into co-management relationships. The institutional divide between tribal governance, on the one hand, and state and federal power, on the other, often generates worse-case scenarios of each side plunging forward unmodified and unmonitored by the other, instead of benefiting from the best of each.

The major difficulty we see in co-managing the natural protected areas of the Pine Ridge Reservation is the lack of continuity for stewardship. On the tribal side, politicians commandeer the natural areas program without knowledge of the Indigenous or the Western system, but simply with knowledge of how to manipulate colonial political structures. Politicians yield to pressure from sports hunters and cattle interests rather than keeping traditional subsistence practices at the fore. Two-year tribal terms of office, a product of imposed structures of Western-style governance, make continuity virtually impossible. Changing political winds result in changing tribal management policies and practices, some of which are detrimental to the resource.

On the Western side, National Park Superintendents come and go every few years. Some are extremely sympathetic to the need for tribal self-determination and are supportive of genuine co-management approaches. Others are skeptical of the contribution to be gained from including tribal perspectives and wary of creating a precedence of inclusion. Because of the tremendous power of the National Park Service, and the discomforts and difficulties of reaching out to tribal communities, the easiest path becomes one of all or nothing: either the tribe conducts the program without support or assistance from the National Park Service, or the National Park conducts the program without interference from the tribe. These are not collaborative arrangements, and so they suffer from the deficiencies of privileging one management system over the other. The last Superintendent was Native American and worked aggressively to integrate tribal participation and tribal voice into every aspect of the park's activities, including an explicit public process to determine the best management approach between the park and the tribe. During his three years as Superintendent, he received heavy criticism from outside the reservation for his efforts to highlight Indigenous ways of thinking about and managing natural resources. Even then the actual Indigenous involvement was relatively minor compared to the vision of the Indigenous Stewardship Model. The new Superintendent will probably not provide the same level of support to the tribal initiatives and co-management of the park.

We see the need for Indigenous approaches and Western science in both protecting and preserving the natural resources on the reservation. Unfortunately, some tribal managers want to exclude scientists, often because of past negative experiences with condescending Western management agencies who similarly want to exclude Indigenous participation. Scientists have no knowledge of the Lakota approach, and Lakota managers have little knowledge of science. However, tribal resource managers can no longer work completely within the Indigenous approach, because in the modern world we have to deal with Western scientists all the time.

Our greatest concern is that the South Unit of the Badlands National Park, the only semi-wilderness area left on the reservation, will be destroyed forever if it is not managed properly. The protected area within the South Unit is only 208 square miles out of the entire 6,000 square miles of reservation lands. This is the context in which the Indigenous Stewardship Model has the best chance to be effective. It remains to be seen whether politics and lack of continuity will ultimately undermine the shared interests of the National Park Service and the Oglala Sioux Tribe in preserving this unique and critical wildlife area.

As Lakota people, we claim to see the interconnections among everything. Therefore, it is up to us to see the changes and re-establish the balance between modern economic interests, such as cattle and sports hunting, and the traditional and subsistence uses of wild plants and animals on the reservation. The Indigenous Stewardship Model looks at the interconnectedness of humans in the natural world, showing the connections between hunting, microenterprise, and economic development and providing ways to improve the conditions for everyone on the reservation. The approach is inclusive of everyone, not just beholden to politicians or wealthy economic interests.

Western managers often assert that too many of the cultural practices of Indigenous communities have been lost and that therefore the knowledge is no longer of any use in creating a management approach. What are not lost, however, are the values and philosophies of the people. If those Indigenous values and philosophies are used as the guiding principles for management, that is more than sufficient to ensure a sound approach. By following this approach, any management system can be changed so that it is workable in an Indigenous sense.

Figure 7.1 Carpet snake stone arrangement, Gummingurru, Queensland (photograph by A. Ross).

Reflections on Co-Management in Australia (Annie Ross)

Various forms of collaborative management between Indigenous land owners and the state are now common in protected-areas management in many parts of Australia. Despite the government rhetoric that co-management provides Indigenous Australians with the opportunity to once again manage their own resources, the opportunities for genuine decision making by Indigenous traditional owners are limited, even in Indigenous Protected Areas.

The Gummingurru Aboriginal stone arrangement site (Figure 7.1), although not formally a protected area, is one small piece of land where Aboriginal Australians at first glance appear to have full control over their heritage. This site, near the town of Toowoomba on the Darling Downs west of Brisbane (see Figure 4.2), was originally a secret, sacred men's initiation site, but following European settlement in 1871, use of the site for this purpose gradually ceased. Today the site is used by traditional custodians for reconciliation activities and public education about Aboriginal culture (Ross 2008).

In 2003 the 5-hectare paddock on which this site occurs was purchased by the Indigenous Land Corporation (ILC), a national organization funded by the Australian Commonwealth to buy land for Aboriginal peoples whose connection to traditional lands has been extinguished by freehold land acquisition. In the years following acquisition by the ILC, the Gummingurru Aboriginal Corporation (GAC), comprising members of the Aboriginal community with traditional connections to the site, worked with ILC staff to demonstrate that the GAC could manage this place without government intervention. Following almost six years of planning, budgeting, and development, the GAC was able to demonstrate that Gummingurru could be a financially viable site, and in March 2008 the land was formally handed back to the traditional custodians.

The GAC manages the site with input and assistance from a range of agencies: the local shire council; the local Natural Resources Management body (the Condamine Alliance – a federally funded agency with a charter to assist a range of local land managers, both Aboriginal and non-Aboriginal); nearby universities (The University of Queensland and the University of Southern Queensland); and a local Aboriginal arts business. This partnership between Aboriginal custodians and local white and black organizations has been very successful, with the GAC now running regular school and community tours of the site and continuing ongoing maintenance of the site with the help of volunteers.

On the surface, Gummingurru appears to be an example of a small but successful amalgam of Indigenous and Western management. But scratch this surface a little and it is clear that the GAC is able to be

Figure 7.2 Traditional GAC custodian, Brian Tobane, resurrects the Gummingurru site by searching for buried rocks that make up now-hidden stone arrangements (photograph by A. Ross).

successful only if its members continue to meet white expectations. Complex legislation provides obstacles to every effort by the traditional custodians to use Gummingurru for the purposes the community has identified. The GAC has the 'resurrection' of Gummingurru as its primary aim. Resurrection entails the ongoing maintenance of the site, but this involves not just keeping the grass mown and the fences repaired, as required by the ILC. Members of the GAC are also keen to find new stone arrangements buried in the shallow soils of the site (Figure 7.2) and to mend arrangements that have become misshapen through decades of neglect. However, by doing this, the GAC is 'interfering' with a registered Aboriginal cultural heritage site, protected under the Queensland Aboriginal Cultural Heritage Act of 2003 (ACHA). Section 25 of the ACHA makes it clear that the excavation and relocation of cultural heritage objects are offenses against the Act. Although the GAC owns the *land* on which the site occurs, under s.20 of the ACHA, the *site* is owned by the state.

The ACHA defines Aboriginal heritage areas or objects as 'evidence, of *archaeological* or historic significance, of Aboriginal occupation of an area of Queensland' (emphasis added). The archaeological and historic significance of Gummingurru lies in the value of the intact, original stone arrangements and the integrity of the site complex in its traditional configuration. Furthermore, the ACHA requires that registered sites such as Gummingurru are accompanied by 'a plan of the area and *a detailed description of its boundaries*' (Section 48 – emphasis added). But the boundaries of Gummingurru, and the plan of the site, are constantly changing as the GAC finds or creates new stone arrangements. Although there is, at present, no suggestion that the traditional custodians will be indicted for interference with a registered site, the existing legislation does allow for such legal action to be taken.

Although Gummingurru, an original Aboriginal ceremonial site, is now formally owned by the GAC, management of the site must meet ILC imposed business plans, ACHA definitions, and Western academic data. The example of Gummingurru, along with the previous case studies from Australia, leads me to be pessimistic about Australia's readiness for the kind of management based on genuine collaborative partnerships and shared knowledge outlined in the Indigenous Stewardship Model. Nevertheless, at least governments in Australia are keen to develop co-management, and, conceivably with leads from other parts of the world, Australia will eventually recognize that there is a place for Indigenous knowledge in natural and cultural resource management.

Perhaps this book will act as a catalyst to overcome the inertia of the Australian system. In this book we have demonstrated that Indigenous knowledge can and should have a place in co-management arrangements. Indigenous voices, along with support from those with an understanding of Indigenous ways of knowing and managing, *can* be a strong lobby for natural resource management. Governments need not only to listen but to act.

REFERENCES

ABC News. 2009a. Uluru debate: To climb or not to climb? Australian Broadcasting Corporation July 8, 2009, www.abc.net.au/news/stories/2009/07/08/2620405. htm. Accessed November 2009.

———. 2009b. Rudd urged to veto Uluru climbing ban. Australian Broadcasting Corporation July 9, 2009, www.abc.net.au/news/stories/2009/07/09/2620775. htm. Accessed November 2009.

———. 2009c. Uluru climb ban in doubt. Australian Broadcasting Corporation October 20, 2009, www.abc.net.au/news/stories/2009/10/20/2719023.htm?site=brisbane. Accessed November 2009.

Agrawal, A. 1995. Dismantling the divide between Indigenous and scientific knowledge. *Development and Change* 26: 413–439.

Allen, J., and S. Holdaway. 1995. The contamination of Pleistocene radiocarbon determinations in Australia. *Antiquity* 69(262): 101–112.

Alvard, M. 1998. Indigenous hunting in the neotropics: Conservation or optimal foraging? In T. Caro (Ed.), *Behavioral ecology and conservations biology*, pp. 474–500. Oxford University Press, New York.

———. 2003. Comment on 'Huna Tlingit traditional environmental knowledge, conservation, and the management of a "wilderness" park' by E. S. Hunn, D. R. Johnson, P. N. Russell, and T. F. Thornton. *Current Anthropology* 44(Supplement): S93–S94.

Ambler, M. 1990. *Breaking the iron bonds: Indian control of energy development.* University of Kansas Press, Lawrence.

Anderson, E. N. 2000. Maya knowledge and 'science wars'. *Journal of Ethnobiology* 20(2): 129–158.

Antweiler, C. 2004. Local knowledge theory and methods: An urban model from Indonesia. In A. Bicker, P. Sillitoe, and J. Pottier (Eds.), *Development and local knowledge: New approaches to issues in natural resources management, conservation and agriculture*, pp. 1–34. Routledge, New York.

Appadurai, A. 1986. Introduction: Commodities and the politics of value. In A. Appadurai (Ed.), *The social life of things: Commodities in cultural perspective*, pp. 3–63. Cambridge University Press, Cambridge.

Arnold, D., and R. Guha (Eds.). 1995. *Nature, culture and imperialism: Essays on the environmental history of South Asia.* Oxford University Press, New Delhi.

Ash, J. 1988. The location and stability of rainforest boundaries in northeastern Queensland, Australia. *Journal of Biogeography* 15: 619–630.

Atran, S. 1990. *Cognitive foundations of natural history: Toward an anthropology of science.* Cambridge University Press, Cambridge.

———. 1998. Folk biology and the anthropology of science: Cognitive universals and cultural particulars. *Behavioral and Brain Sciences* 21: 547–609.

Baker, L., S. Woenne-Green, and the Mutitjulu community. 1992. The role of Aboriginal ecological knowledge in ecosystem management. In J. Birckhead, T. de Lacy, and L. Smith (Eds.), *Aboriginal involvement in parks and protected areas,* pp. 65–74. Aboriginal Studies Press, Canberra.

Baker, N. 2005. Fraser Island's Dingoes learn new tricks. *Australasian Science* (36)1: 20–22.

Balme, J., and W. Beck. 1996. Earth mounds in southeastern Australia. *Australian Archaeology* 42: 39–51.

Barker, T., and A. Ross. 2003. Exploring cultural constructs: The case of sea mullet management in Moreton Bay, South East Queensland, Australia. In N. Haggan, C. Brignall, and L. Wood (Eds.), *Putting fishers' knowledge to work: Conference proceedings,* pp. 290–305, Fishers Centre Research Report, volume 11(1) University of British Columbia, Vancouver.

Basso, K. 1996. *Wisdom sits in places: Landscape and language among the Western Apache.* University of New Mexico Press, Albuquerque.

Baviskar, A. 1995. *In the belly of the river: Tribal conflicts over development in the Narmada Valley.* Oxford University Press, New Delhi.

Bellwood, P. 1985. *Prehistory of the Indo-Malaysian Archipelago* (revised edition). University of Hawai'i Press, Honolulu.

Berkes, F. 2003. Comment on 'Huna Tlingit traditional environmental knowledge, conservation, and the management of a "wilderness" park' by E. S. Hunn, D. R. Johnson, P. N. Russell, and T. F. Thornton. *Current Anthropology* 44(Supplement): S94–S95.

———. 2008. *Sacred ecology* (2nd edition). Routledge, New York.

———. 2009. Evolution of co-management: Role of knowledge generation, bridging organizations and social learning. *Journal of Environmental Management* 90: 1692–1702.

Berkes, F., J. Colding, and C. Folke (Eds.). 2003. *Navigating social-ecological systems: Building resilience for complexity and change.* Cambridge University Press, Cambridge.

Berkes, F., and C. Folke (Eds.). 1998. *Linking social and ecological systems: Management practices and social mechanisms for building resilience.* Cambridge University Press, Cambridge.

Berkes, F., and M. Kislalioglu Berkes. 2009. Ecological complexity, fuzzy logic, and holism in Indigenous knowledge. *Futures* 41: 6–12.

Berlin, B. 1991. *Basic color terms: Their universality and evolution.* University of California Press, Berkeley and Los Angeles.

———. 1992. *Ethnobiological classification: Principles of categorization of plants and animals in traditional societies.* Princeton University Press, Princeton, NJ.

Beteille, A. 1998. The idea of Indigenous people. *Current Anthropology* 39: 187–191.

Bicker, A., P. Sillitoe, and J. Pottier (Eds.). 2004. *Development and local knowledge: New approaches to issues in natural resources management, conservation and agriculture.* Routledge, New York.

Bigge, C. 2008. Are Torres Strait Islanders over-harvesting dugongs? An evaluation of anthropological and Western scientific perspectives of dugongs in the Torres

Straits. Unpublished B.A. Honours thesis, School of Social Science, The University of Queensland, Brisbane.

Bird-David, N. 1991. Animism revisited: Personhood, environment, and relational epistemology. *Current Anthropology* (40): 67–91.

Bodley, J. 2008. *Victims of progress* (5th edition). AltaMira Press, Lanham, MD.

Boldt, G. 1974. *United States vs. State of Washington*, 384 F. Supp. 312.

Bolt, A. 2004. Yorta Yorta: Money for myths. *Herald Sun Newspaper*, May 5.

Bomford, M., and J. Caughley (Eds.). 1996. *Sustainable use of wildlife by Aboriginal peoples and Torres Strait Islanders*. Australian Government Publishing Service, Canberra.

Booth, A., and H. Jacobs. 1990. Ties that bind: Native American beliefs as a foundation for environmental consciousness. *Environmental Ethics* 12: 27–43.

Bourdieu, P. 1960. *Algeria* (1979 translation). Cambridge University Press, Cambridge.

———. 1972. *Outline of a theory of practice* (1977 translation). Cambridge University Press, Cambridge.

Boster, J. 1996. Human cognition as a product and agent of evolution. In R. F. Ellen and K. Fukui (Eds.), *Redefining nature: Culture, ecology, and domestication*, pp. 269–289. Berg Publishers, Oxford.

Bowdler, S. 1977. The coastal colonization of Australia. In J. Allen, J. Golson, and R. Jones (Eds.), *Sunda and Sahulk: Prehistoric studies in Southeast Asia, Melanesia and Australia*, pp. 205–246. Academic Press, New York.

Bowman, D. M. J. S. 1998. The impact of Aboriginal landscape burning on the Australian biota. *New Phytologist* 140: 385–410.

———. 2000. *Australian Rainforests: Islands of green in a land of fire*. Cambridge University Press, Cambridge.

Bowman, D. M. J. S., and W. J. Panton. 1993. Decline of *Callitris intretropica*: R. T. Baker and H. G. Smith in the Northern Territory: Implications for pre- and post-European colonization fire regimes. *Journal of Biogeography* 20: 373–381.

Bradley, J. 1995. Fire: Emotion and politics – A Yanuywa case study. In D. B. Rose (Ed.), *Country in flames: Proceedings of the 1994 symposium on biodiversity and fire in North Australia*, pp. 25–31. Department of Environment, Sport and Territories and North Australia Research Unit, Australian National University, Darwin.

———. 1997. Li-anthawirriyarra, people of the sea: Yanyuwa relations with their maritime environment. Unpublished PhD thesis, Northern Territory University, Darwin.

———. 1998a. 'How can a whitefella know it all?' Indigenous science – Western science and marine turtles. In R. Kennett, A. Webb, G. Duff, M. Guinea, and G. Hill (Eds.), *Marine turtle conservation and management in northern Australia*, proceedings of a workshop held at the Northern Territory University Darwin 3–4 June 1997, pp. 25–32. Centre for Indigenous Natural and Cultural Resource Management and Centre for Tropical Wetlands Management, Northern Territory University, Darwin.

———. 1998b. 'We always look north': Yanyuwa identity and the maritime environment. In N. Peterson and B. Rigsby (Eds.), *Customary marine tenure in Australia*, pp.125–124. Oceania Monograph 48. Oceania Publications, University of Sydney.

Bradley, J. 2001. Landscapes of the mind, landscapes of the spirit: Negotiating a sentient landscape. In R. Baker, J. Davies, and E. Young (Eds.), *Working on country: Contemporary Indigenous management of Australia's lands and coastal regions*, pp. 295–307. Oxford University Press, Melbourne.

———. 2008. When a stone tool is a dingo: Country and relatedness in Australian Aboriginal notions of landscape. In B. David and J. Thomas (Eds.), *Handbook of landscape archaeology*, pp. 633–637. Left Coast Press, Walnut Creek, CA.

Bradley, J., M. Holmes, D. N. Marrngawi, A. I. Karrakayn, J. Miller, W. Ninganga, and I. Ninganga. 2006. *Yumbulyumbulmantha ki-Awarawu = All kinds of things from Country:* Yanyuwa Ethnobiological Classification Report Series, volume 6. Aboriginal and Torres Strait Islander Studies Unit, The University of Queensland, Brisbane.

Breeden, S. 1997. *Uluṟu: Looking after Uluru-Kata Tjuta the Anangu way.* J. B. Books, Marleston, SA.

Breman, J. 1985. *Of peasants, migrants and paupers: Rural labour circulation and capitalist production in West India.* Oxford University Press, New Delhi.

Brosius, J. P. 2000. Endangered forest, endangered people: Environmentalist representations of Indigenous knowledge. In R. Ellen, P. Parkes, and A. Bicker (Eds.), *Indigenous environmental knowledge and its transformations: Critical anthropological perspectives*, pp. 293–318. Overseas Publishers Association, Harwood Academic Publishers, Amsterdam.

Brower, B. 1991. *Sherpa of Khumbu: People, livestock, and landscape.* Oxford University Press, New Delhi.

Broughton, J. M. 2003. Comment on 'Huna Tlingit traditional environmental knowledge, conservation, and the management of a "wilderness" park' by E. S. Hunn, D. R. Johnson, P. N. Russell, and T. F. Thornton. *Current Anthropology* 44(Supplement): S95.

Bruner, J. 1996. Frames for thinking: Ways of making meaning. In D. R. Olson and N. Torrance (Eds.), *Modes of thought: Explorations in culture and cognition*, pp. 189–215. Cambridge University Press, Cambridge.

Butlin, N. 1983. *Our original aggression.* George, Allen, and Unwin, Sydney.

Byrne, D. 1991. Western hegemony in archaeological heritage management. *History and Anthropology* 5: 269–276.

———. 2005. Messages to Manilla. In I. Macfarlane with M-J. Mountain and R. Paton (Eds.), *Many exchanges: Archaeology, history, community and the work of Isabel McBryde*, pp. 53–62. Aboriginal History Monograph 11.

———. 2008. Counter-mapping in the archaeological landscape. In B. David and J. Thomas (Eds.), *Handbook of landscape archaeology*, pp. 609–616. Left Coast Press, Walnut Creek, CA.

Byrne, D., and M. Nugent. 2004. *Mapping attachment: A spatial approach to aboriginal post-contact heritage.* Department of Environment and Conservation, Sydney.

Campbell, B. 2004. Indigenous views on the terms of participation in the development of biodiversity conservation in Nepal. In A. Bicker, P. Sillitoe, and J. Pottier (Eds.), *Investigating local knowledge: New directions, new approaches*, pp. 149–168. Aldershot, Ashgate.

Capriccioso, R. 2009. Obama ushers in a new era for Indian Country. *Indian Country Today*, November 5, www.indiancountrytoday.com/home/content/69340852.html. Accessed November 2009.

Carlson, L. 1981. *Indians, bureaucrats, and land: The Dawes Act and the decline of Indian farming.* Greenwood Press, Westport, CT.

Carlsson, L., and F. Berkes. 2005. Co-management: Concepts and methodological implications. *Journal of Environmental Management* 75(1): 65–76.

Carpenter, K. A., S. K. Katyal, and A. R. Riley. 2009. In defense of property. *The Yale Law Journal* 118: 1022–1125.

Casey, E. 1996. How to get from space to place in a fairly short time. In S. Feld and K. Basso (Eds.), *Senses of place,* pp.13–42. School of American Research Press, Santa Fe, NM.

Castile, G. P. 1998. *To show heart: Native American self-determination and Federal Indian policy, 1960–1975.* University of Arizona Press, Tucson.

Cheater, A. (Ed.). 1999. *The anthropology of power: Empowerment and disempowerment in changing structures.* Routledge, New York.

Clark, J. L. 1985. *Thus Spoke Chief Seattle: The story of an undocumented speech – Prologue* 18(1), National Archives and Records Administration, online reference: www.archives.gov/publications/prologue/spring_1985_chief_seattle.html. Accessed October 2004.

Clark, R. 1981. The prehistory of bushfires. In P. Stanbury (Ed.), *Bushfires: Their effect on Australian life and landscape,* pp. 61–74. The Macleay Museum, University of Sydney, Sydney.

———. 1983. Pollen and charcoal evidence for the effects of Aboriginal burning on the vegetation of Australia. *Archaeology in Oceania* 18: 32–37.

Clarke, A. 2002. The ideal and the real: Cultural and personal transformations of archaeological research in Groote Eylandt, northern Australia. In Y. Marshall (Ed.), *Community Archaeology,* pp. 249–264. *World Archaeology* 34(2).

Clarke, D. 1973. Archaeology: The loss of innocence. *Antiquity* 47: 6–18.

Cleveland, D. A., and D. Soleri (Eds.). 2002. *Farmers, scientists and plant breeding: Integrating knowledge and practice.* CABI Publishing, Wallingford.

Clifford, J. 2007. Varieties of Indigenous experience: Diasporas, homelands, sovereignties. In M. de la Cadena and O. Starn (Eds.), *Indigenous experience today,* pp.197–223. Berg Publishers, Oxford.

Cohen, F. 1986. *Treaties on trial: The continuing controversy over northwest Indian fishing rights.* University of Washington Press, Seattle.

Cole, J. R. 1993. Cult archaeology and unscientific method and theory. *Advances in Archaeological Method* 3: 1–33.

Cole, N., G. Musgrave, L. George, T. George, and D. Banjo. 2002. Community archaeology at Laura, Cape York Peninsula. In S. Ulm, C. Westcott, J. Reid, A. Ross, I. Lilley, J. Prangnell, and L. Kirkwood (Eds.), *Barriers, borders, boundaries: Proceedings of the 2001 Australian Archaeological Association Annual Conference,* pp.137–150. Tempus 7. Anthropology Museum, The University of Queensland, Brisbane.

Coombs, H. C., M. M. Brandl, and W. E. Snowdon. 1983. *A certain heritage: Programme for and by Aboriginal families in Australia.* CRES Monograph 9, Australian National University, Canberra.

Cordell, J. 1991. *Managing Sea Country: Tenure and sustainability of Aboriginal and Torres Strait Islander marine resources.* Consultancy Report for the Ecologically Sustainable Fisheries Working Group, Canberra.

Cottrell, M. 1985. Tomato Springs: The identification of a jasper trade and production center in southern California. *American Antiquity* 50: 833–849.

Craig, D. 1992. Environmental law and Aboriginal rights: Legal framework for Aboriginal joint management of Australian national parks. In J. Birckhead, T. de Lacy, and L. Smith (Eds.), *Aboriginal involvement in parks and protected areas*, pp. 137–148. Aboriginal Studies Press, Canberra.

Cronon, W. 1995. The trouble with wilderness, or getting back to the wrong nature. In W. Cronon (Ed.), *Uncommon ground: Toward reinventing nature*, pp. 69–90. W. W. Norton and Company, New York.

———. 2003. *Changes in the land: Indians, colonists, and the ecology of New England* (20th anniversary edition). Hill & Wang, New York.

Cullen, M. 2007. Competing Knowledge in Natural Resource Management: Dugong Management in the Great Barrier Reef World Heritage Area. Unpublished Bachelor of Environmental Management thesis, The University of Queensland, Brisbane.

D'Andrade, R. G. 1980. Cultural cognition. In M. I. Posner (Ed.), *Foundations of cognitive science*, pp. 795–830. MIT Press, Cambridge, MA.

———. 1995. *The development of cognitive anthropology*. Cambridge University Press, Cambridge.

———. 2008. *A study of personal and cultural values: American, Japanese, and Vietnamese*. Palgrave, New York.

Darlington, S. M. 1998. The ordination of a tree: The Buddhist ecology movement in Thailand. *Ethnology* 37(1): 1–15.

———. 2000. Rethinking Buddhism and development: The emergence of environmentalist monks in Thailand. *Journal of Buddhist Ethics*, www.buddhistethics.org/7/darlington001.html. Accessed January 2003.

David, B. 2006. Indigenous rights and the mutability of cultures: Tradition, change and the politics of recognition. In L. Russell (Ed.), *Boundary writing: An exploration of race, culture and gender binaries in contemporary Australia*, pp. 122–148. University of Hawai'i Press, Honolulu.

Delcore, H. 2000. Localizing development: Environment, agriculture, and memory in northern Thailand. Unpublished PhD thesis, University of Wisconsin-Madison.

———. 2003. Non-governmental organizations and the work of memory in northern Thailand. *American Ethnologist* 30(1): 61–84.

———. 2004. Symbolic politics or generification? The ambivalent implications of tree ordinations in the Thai environmental movement. *Journal of Political Ecology* 11(1): 1–30.

———. 2007. The racial distribution of privilege in a Thai national park. *Journal of Southeast Asian Studies* 38(1): 83–105.

Deloria, E. C. 1944. *Speaking of Indians*. Friendship Press, New York.

DeMallie, R. J., and D. R. Parks. 1987. *Sioux Indian religion: Tradition and innovation*. University of Oklahoma Press, Norman.

Department of Environment, Water, Heritage and the Arts. 2009. *Nganana Tatintja Wiya – 'We never climb'*, www.environment.gov.au/parks/uluru/visitor-activities/do-not-climb.html. Accessed November 2009.

Department of Natural Resources and Water. 2008. *Cape York Peninsula Heritage Act—What does it mean for the Indigenous community?* Fact Sheet, www.nrw.qld.gov.au/factsheets/pdf/land/l157.pdf. Accessed January 2009.

Diamond, J. 1986. The environmentalist myth. *Nature* 324(6092): 19–20.

———. 1988. The Golden Age that never was. *Discover* 9(December): 70–79.

Diamond, J. 2005. *Collapse: How societies choose to fail or succeed.* Penguin Books, London.

Dodson, J., R. Fullagar, and L. Head. 1992. Dynamics of environment and people in the forested crescents of temperate Australia. In J. R. Dodson (Ed.), *The naïve lands: Prehistory and environmental change in Australia and the Southwest Pacific*, pp.115–159. Longman Cheshire, Melbourne.

Doherty, K. 1996. Even if you go you'll never never know: A critical review of pre-visit literature in cultural tourism. Unpublished Bachelor of Applied Science (Natural Systems and Wildlife Management) Special Project thesis, The University of Queensland, Gatton.

Dortch, J. 2004. Archaeology at Lancefield Swamp: Report of the February 2004 excavations. Unpublished Report to the University of Sydney, www.earthsci.unimelb. edu.au/~mlcupper/Lancefield%20Swamp.pdf. Accessed November 2009.

Dunbar, K. 1995. How scientists really reason: Scientific reasoning in real-world laboratories. In R. J. Steinberg and J. Davidson (Eds.), *Mechanisms of insight*, pp. 365–395. MIT Press, Cambridge, MA.

Dundes, A. 1962. Earth-diver: Creation of the mythopoeic male. *American Anthropologist* 64(5): 1032–1051.

Eamon, W. 1990. From the secrets of nature to public knowledge. In D. C. Lindberg and R. S. Westman (Eds.), *Reappraisals of the scientific revolution*, pp. 333–365. Cambridge University Press, Cambridge.

Ede, A., and L. B. Cormack. 2004. *A History of science in society: From philosophy to utility.* Broadview Press, Peterborough, Ontario.

Eichstaedt, P. 1994. *If you poison us: Uranium and Native Americans.* Red Crane Books, Santa Fe, NM.

Ellen, R. 2003. Variation and uniformity in the construction of biological knowledge across cultures. In H. Selin (Ed.), *Nature across cultures: Views of nature and the environment in non-Western cultures*, pp. 47–74. Kluwer, Amsterdam.

———. 2004. From ethno-science to science, or 'What the indigenous knowledge debate tells us about how scientists define their project.' *Journal of Cognition and Culture* 4(3-4): 409–450.

Ellen, R., and H. Harris. 2000. Introduction. In R. Ellen, P. Parkes, and A. Bicker (Eds.), *Indigenous environmental knowledge and its transformations: Critical anthropological perspectives,* pp. 1–33. Overseas Publishers Association, Harwood Academic Publishers, Amsterdam.

Ellis, B. 1994. Rethinking the paradigm: Cultural heritage management in Queensland. *Ngulaig* Monograph # 10. Aboriginal and Torres Strait Islander Studies Unit, The University of Queensland, Brisbane.

Engelhardt, R. A. 1989. Forest-gatherers and strand-loopers: Econiche specialization in Thailand. In *Culture and environment in Thailand: A symposium of the Siam society*, pp. 125–141. Siam Society, Bangkok.

EPA (Environmental Protection Agency). 1999. *Conservation and management of the dugong in Queensland 1999–2004.* EPA and Queensland Parks and Wildlife Service Conservation Plan Series, Queensland State Government, Brisbane, www. derm.qld.gov.au/register/p00523aa.pdf. Accessed November 2009.

———. 2007. *Conservation and management of dugongs in Queensland.* EPA and Queensland Parks and Wildlife Service Conservation Plan Series, Queensland State Government, Brisbane, www.derm.qld.gov.au/register/p02268aa.pdf. Accessed November 2009.

Evans-Pritchard, E. E. 1969. *The Nuer: A description of the modes of livelihood and political institutions of a Nilotic people*. Oxford University Press, New York.

Fabian, J. 1983. *Time and the other: How anthropology makes its object*. Columbia University Press, New York.

Fanon, F. 1967. *Black skin, white masks*. Grove Weidenfeld, New York.

Feit, H. A. 1987. Waswanipi Cree management of land and wildlife: Cree ethnoecology revisited. In B. A. Cox (Ed.), *Native people, native lands: Canadian Indians, Inuit and Metis*, pp. 75–91. Carleton Library Series No. 142, Carleton University Press, Ottowa, Canada.

———. 1994. The enduring pursuit: Land, time, and social relationships in anthropological models of hunter-gatherers and in hunters' images. In E. S. Burch and L. J. Ellanna (Eds.), *Key issues in hunter-gatherer research*, pp. 421–439. Berg Publishers, Oxford.

———. 1998. Reflections on local knowledge and institutionalized resource management: Differences, dominance, decentralization. In L. J. Dorais, M. Nagy, and L. Muller-Wille (Eds.), *Aboriginal environmental knowledge in the North*, pp.123–148. Université Laval, Gétic, Québec.

Fernández-Gimenez, M. 2000. The role of Mongolian nomadic pastoralists' ecological knowledge in rangeland management. *Ecological Applications* 10: 1318–1326.

Fforde, C., J. Hubert, and P. Turnbull (Eds.). 2002. *The dead and their possessions: Repatriation in principle, policy and practice*. Routledge, New York.

Field, J., J. Barker, R. Barker, E. Coffey, L. Coffey, E. Crawford, L. Darcy, T. Fields, G. Lord, B. Steadman, and S. Colley. 2000. 'Coming back': Aborigines and archaeologists at Cuddie Springs. *Public Archaeology* 1(1): 35–38.

Field, J., M. Fillios, and S. Wroe. 2008. Chronological overlap between humans and megafauna in Sahul (Pleistocene Australia–New Guinea): A review of the evidence. *Earth-Science Reviews* 89: 97–115.

Field, J., and R. Fullagar. 2001. Archaeology and Australian megafauna. *Science* 294: 7a.

Fixico, D. L. 1998. *The Invasion of Indian Country in the Twentieth Century: American Capitalism and Tribal Natural Resources*. University Press of Colorado, Niwot, CO.

Flannery, T. 1994. *The future eaters: An ecological history of the Australasian lands and people*. Reed New Holland, Sydney.

Foucault, M. 1977. *Discipline and punish: The birth of the prison*. Penguin Books, New York.

Fox, J. 2002. Siam mapped and mapping in Cambodia: Boundaries, sovereignty, and Indigenous conceptions of space. *Society and Natural Resources* 15: 65–78.

Freeman, M. M. R., L. Bogoslovskaya, R. A. Caulfield, I. Egede, I. I. Krupnik, and M. G. Stevenson. 1998. *Inuit, whaling, and sustainability*. AltaMira Press, Walnut Creek, CA.

Gadgil, M., F. Berkes, and C. Folke. 1993. Indigenous knowledge for biodiversity conservation. *Ambio* XXII(2-3): 151–156.

Gadgil, M., and R. Guha. 1992. *This fissured land: An ecological history of India*. University of California Press, Berkeley and Los Angeles.

———. 1995. *Ecology and equity: The use and abuse of nature in contemporary India*. Routledge, London.

Gegeo, D. W., and K. A. Watson-Gegeo. 2001. 'How we know': Kwara'ae rural villagers doing Indigenous epistemology. *The Contemporary Pacific* 13(1): 55–88.

———. 2002. Whose knowledge? Epistemological collisions in Solomon Islands community development. *The Contemporary Pacific* 14(2): 377–409.

George, M., J. Innes, and H. Ross. 2004. *Managing sea country together: Key issues for developing co-operative management for the Great Barrier Reef World Heritage Area*, CRC Reef Research Centre Technical Report, CRC Reef Research Centre Ltd., Townsville.

Gelman, R. 1990. First principles organize attention to and learning about relevant data: Number and the animate-inanimate distinction as examples. *Cognitive Science* 14: 79–106.

Getches, D., C. Wilkinson, and R. Williams. 1998. *Cases and materials on Federal Indian Law*. West Group, St. Paul, MN.

Gillespie, R., D. R. Horton, P. Ladd, P. G. Macumber, T. H. Rich, R. Thorne, and R. V. S. Wright. 1978. Lancefield Swamp and the extinction of the Australian megafauna. *Science* 200: 1044–1048.

Gilligan, B. 2006. *The National Reserve System Programme 2006 Evaluation*. Department of the Environment and Heritage, Canberra, www.environment.gov. au/indigenous/publications/pubs/ipap-evaluation.pdf. Accessed November 2009.

Godwin, L. 1988. Around the traps: A reappraisal of stone fishing weirs in northern New South Wales. *Archaeology in Oceania* 23: 49–59.

———. 2005. 'Everyday archaeology': Archaeological heritage management and its relationship to native title in development-related processes. *Australian Aboriginal Studies* 2005(1): 74–83.

Godwin, L., and Weiner, J. 2006. Footprints of the ancestors: The convergence of anthropological and archaeological perspectives in contemporary Aboriginal heritage studies. In B. David, B. Barker, and I. J. McNiven (Eds.), *The social archaeology of Australian Indigenous societies*, pp. 124–138. Aboriginal Studies Press, Canberra.

Gold, A. G., and B. G. Gujar. 2002. *In the time of trees and sorrows: Nature, power, and memory in Rajasthan*. Duke University Press, Durham, NC.

Golschewski, K. 2004. Expanding concepts of heritage: An investigation into the concept of cultural landscape and its inclusion into heritage management practice and legislation. Unpublished B.A. Honours thesis, The University of Queensland, Brisbane.

Goody, J. 1977. *The domestication of the savage mind*. Cambridge University Press, Cambridge.

———. 1986. *The logic of writing and the organisation of society*. Cambridge University Press, Cambridge.

———. 1987. *The interface between the written and the oral*. Cambridge University Press, Cambridge.

Gorring, D. A. 2002. 'Country and western landscapes': Is there a 'place' for the Yanyuwa Tiger Shark song cycle within cultural heritage legislation and management practices in Australia? Unpublished B.A. Honours thesis, School of Social Science, The University of Queensland, Brisbane.

———. In prep. 'Talking the talk, walking the walk': A journey from ancient stories to modern narratives. Unpublished PhD thesis, School of Social Science, The University of Queensland, Brisbane.

Gorring, D., and A. Ross. 2004. Contestation between the State and Aboriginal traditions: Is tradition 'the magic that is ever present'? Unpublished paper delivered to the Department of Anthropology, Colorado State University, Fort Collins.

Gott, B. 1983. Murnong – *Microseris scapigera*: A study of a staple food of Victorian Aborigines. *Australian Aboriginal Studies* 1983(1): 2–17.

Gould, R. A., and S. Saggers. 1985. Lithic procurement in central Australia: A closer look at Binford's ideas of embeddedness in archaeology. *American Antiquity* 50: 117–136.

Greer, S., R. Harrison, and S. McIntyre-Tamwoy. 2002. Community-based archaeology in Australia. In Y. Marshall (Ed.), *Community Archaeology*, pp. 265–287. *World Archaeology* 34(2).

Guha, R. 2000 [1989]. *The unquiet woods: Ecological change and peasant resistance in the Himalaya*. University of California Press, Berkeley and Los Angeles.

Guha, R., and J. Martinez-Alier. 1997. *Varieties of environmentalism: Essays north and south*. Earthscan Publications, London.

Guha, S. 1999. *Environment and ethnicity in India 1200–1991*. Cambridge University Press, Cambridge.

Hall, H. J. 1984. Fishing with dolphins? Affirming a traditional Aboriginal fishing story in Moreton Bay, southeast Queensland. In R. J. Coleman, J. Covacevich, and P. Davie (Eds.), *Focus on Stradbroke: New information on North Stradbroke Island and surrounding areas, 1974–1984*, pp. 16–22. Boolarong Press, Brisbane.

Hall, T. D. 1986. Incorporation in the world-system: Toward a critique. *American Sociological Review* 51: 390–402.

———. 1987. Native Americans and incorporation: Patterns and problems. *American Indian Culture and Research Journal* 11: 1–30.

Hall, T. D., and J. V. Fenelon. 2009. *Indigenous peoples and globalization: Resistance and revitalization*. Paradigm Publishers, Boulder, CO.

Hanson, P. 1999. Press release regarding High Court decision in *Yanner vs. Eaton*, October 8, 1999, www.onenation.com.au. Accessed November 1999.

Hardiman, D. 1987. *The coming of the Devi: Adivasi assertion in western India*. Oxford University Press, New Delhi.

Hardin, G. 1968. The tragedy of the commons. *Science* 162: 1243–1248.

———. 1991. The tragedy of the unmanaged commons: Population and the disguises of providence. In R. V. Anderson (Ed.), *Commons without tragedy: Protecting the environment from overpopulation – A new approach*, pp. 162–185. Shepheard-Walwyn, London.

———. 1993. *Living within limits: Ecology, economics, and population taboos*. Oxford University Press, New York.

Harrison, P. 2007. *The fall of man and the foundations of science*. Cambridge University Press, Cambridge.

Harrison, R. 2002. Shared histories and the archaeology of the pastoral industry in Australia. In R. Harrison and C. Williamson (Eds.), *After Captain Cook: The archaeology of the recent Indigenous past in Australia*, pp. 37–58. Sydney University Archaeological Methods Series 8. Archaeological Computing Laboratory, University of Sydney, Sydney.

Harvey, J. 1999. History or science, history and science, and natural sciences: Undergraduate teaching of the history of science at Harvard, 1938–1970. In M. W. Rossiter (Ed.), *Catching up with the vision: Essays on the occasion of the 75th anniversary of the founding of the History of Science Society*, Isis volume 90 Supplement. University of Chicago Press, Chicago.

Hassrick, R. B. 1964. *The Sioux*. University of Oklahoma Press, Norman.

Havermann, P., D. Thiriet, H. Marsh, and C. Jones. 2005. Traditional use of marine resources agreements and dugong hunting in the Great Barrier Reef World Heritage Area. *Environmental and Planning Law Journal* 22: 258–280.

Head, L. 1990. Conservation and Aboriginal land rights: When green is not black. *Australian Natural History* 23: 448–454.

———. 2000. *Second nature: The history and implications of Australia as Aboriginal landscape.* Syracuse University Press, New York.

Heinsohn, R., R. Lacy, D. Lindenmayer, H. Marsh, D. Kwan, and I. Lawler. 2004. Unsustainable harvest of dugongs in Torres Strait and Cape York (Australia) waters: Two cases using population viability analysis. *Animal Conservation* 7: 417–425.

Hobsbawm, E. 1983. Introduction: Inventing traditions. In E. Hobsbawm and T. Ranger (Eds.), *The invention of tradition*, pp. 1–14. Cambridge University Press, Cambridge.

Hiscock, P. 1996. The New Age of alternative archaeology of Australia. *Archaeology in Oceania* 31(3): 152–164.

———. 2008. *Archaeology of ancient Australia.* Routledge, New York.

Horton, D. R. 1982. The burning question: Aborigines, fire and Australian ecosystems. *Mankind* 13(3): 237–251.

———. 2000. *The pure state of nature: Sacred cows, destructive myths and the environment.* Allen and Unwin, St Leonards, Sydney.

Hughes, J. D. 1983. *American Indian ecology* (1st edition). Texas Western Press, University of Texas at El Paso.

———. 1996. *North American Indian ecology* (2nd edition). Texas Western Press, University of Texas at El Paso.

Hunn, E. S. 1993. What is traditional ecological knowledge? In N. M. Williams and G. Baines (Eds.), *Traditional ecological knowledge: Wisdom for sustainable development*, pp. 13–15. Centre for Resource and Environmental Studies, Australian National University, Canberra.

———. 2002. In defense of 'the ecological Indian'. Paper presented at the 9th International Conference on Hunting and Gathering Societies, Edinburgh, Scotland, 9 September 2002, www.abdn.ac.uk/chags9/1hunn.htm. Accessed October 2004.

———. 2003. Epiphenomenal conservation reconsidered. Paper delivered to American Anthropological Society Annual Meeting, Chicago, November 20, 2003.

Hunn, E. S., D. R. Johnson, P. N. Russell, and T. F. Thornton. 2003. Huna Tlingit traditional environmental knowledge, conservation, and the management of a 'wilderness' park. *Current Anthropology* 44(Supplement): S79, S103.

Huntington, H. 2000. Using traditional ecological knowledge in science: Methods and applications. *Ecological Applications* 10(5): 1270–1274.

Hurt, R. D. 1987. *Indian agriculture in America: Prehistory to the present.* University of Kansas Press, Lawrence.

Hytten, K., and G. L. Burns. 2007. Deconstructing dingo management on Fraser Island: The significance of social constructionism for effective wildlife management. *Australian Journal of Environmental Management* 14: 48–57.

Igoe, J. 2004. *Conservation and globalization: A study of national parks and Indigenous communities from East Africa to South Dakota.* Wadsworth, Belmont, CA.

Ingold, T. 1996. *The perception of the environment: Essays in livelihood, dwelling and skill.* Routledge, London.

Isager, L., and S. Ivarsson. 2002. Contesting landscapes in Thailand: Tree ordination as counter-territorialization. *Critical Asian Studies* 34(3): 395–417.

Jacobs, J. M., and F. Gale. 1994. *Tourism and the protection of Aboriginal cultural sites.* Australian Government Publishing Service, Canberra.

Janca, A., and C. Bullen. 2003. The Aboriginal concept of time and its mental health implications. *Australasian Psychiatry,* 11(1): S40–S44.

Johannes, R. E. 1987. Primitive myth. *Nature* 325(5): 478.

Jones, R. 1969. Fire-stick farming. *Australian Natural History* 16: 224–228.

———. 1973. Emerging picture of Pleistocene Australians. *Nature* 246: 278–281.

———. 1975. The neolithic palaeolithic and the hunting gardeners: Man and land in the antipodes. In R. P. Suggate and M. M. Cresswell (Eds.), *Quaternary Studies,* pp. 21–34. Bulletin 13 Royal Society of New Zealand, Wellington.

———. 1995. Mindjongork: Legacy of the firestick. In D. B. Rose (Ed.), *Country in flames: Proceedings of the 1994 symposium on biodiversity and fire in North Australia,* pp. 11–17. Department of Environment, Sport and Territories and North Australia Research Unit, Australian National University, Darwin.

Jones, R. M., and N. White. 1988. Point blank: Stone tool manufacture at the Ngilipitji Quarry, Arnhem Land, 1981. In B. Meehan and R. M. Jones (Eds.), *Archaeology with ethnography: An Australian perspective,* pp. 51–87. Department of Prehistory, Australian National University, Canberra.

Jonsson, H. 2005. *Mien relations: Mountain people and state control in Thailand.* Cornell University Press, Ithaca, NY.

Kalland, A. 2000. Indigenous knowledge: Prospects and limitations. In R. Ellen, P. Parkes, and A. Bicker (Eds.), *Indigenous environmental knowledge and its transformations: Critical anthropological perspectives,* pp. 319–335. Overseas Publishers Association, Harwood Academic Publishers, Amsterdam.

Kearney, A. 2008. Gender in landscape archaeology. In B. David and J. Thomas (Eds.), *Handbook of landscape archaeology,* pp. 247–255. Left Coast Press, Walnut Creek, CA.

Keil, F. C. 1994. The birth and nurturance of concepts by domain: The origins of concepts of living things. In L. Hirschfeld and S. Gelman (Eds.), *Mapping the mind: Domain specificity in cognition and culture,* pp. 234–254. Cambridge University Press, New York.

Kennett, R., C. J. Robinson, I. Kiessling, D. Yunupingu, N. Munungurritj, and D. Yunupingu. 2004. Indigenous initiatives for co-management of Miyapunu/Sea Turtle. *Ecological Management and Restoration* 5(3): 159–166.

Kershaw, A. P. 1976. A late Pleistocene and Holocene pollen diagram from Kynch's Crater, northeast Queensland, Australia. *New Phytologist* 77: 469–498.

———. 1985. An extended late Quaternary vegetation record from northeastern Queensland and its implications for the seasonal tropics of Australia. *Proceedings of the Ecological Society of Australia* 13: 179–189.

———. 1986. Climatic change and Aboriginal burning in northeast Australia during the last two glacial/interglacial cycles. *Nature* 322: 47–49.

Keyes, C. F. 1987. *Thailand: Buddhist kingdom as modern nation-state.* Westview Press, Boulder, CO.

Kimmerer, R. W. 2002. Weaving traditional ecological knowledge into biological education: A call to action. *Bioscience* 52(5): 432–438.

King, M. 1997. Too old to lose, too rich to ignore: Aboriginal plant use knowledge in protected area planning. Unpublished Special Project thesis, Department of Natural and Rural Systems Management, The University of Queensland, Gatton.

Kleinman, D. L., and S. P. Vallas. 2001. Science, capitalism and the rise of the 'knowledge worker': The changing production of knowledge in the United States. *Theory and Society* 30: 451–492.

Kloppenberg, J. 1988. *First the seed: The political economy of plant biotechnology, 1492–2000.* Cambridge University Press, Cambridge.

Kolff, D. 1990. *Naukar, Rajput, and Sepoy: The ethnohistory of the military labour market in Hindustan, 1450–1850.* Cambridge University Press, Cambridge.

Kothari, A. 2006. Community conserved areas: Towards ecological and livelihood security. *Community Conserved Areas* 16(1): 3–13, http://cmsdata.iucn.org/downloads/parks_16_1_forweb.pdf#page = 5. Accessed November 2009.

Krech, S. 1999. *The ecological Indian: Myth and history.* W. W. Norton and Company, New York.

Kuhn, T. 1962. *The structure of scientific revolutions.* University of Chicago Press, Chicago.

Kunstadter, P., and E. C. Chapman. 1978. Problems of shifting cultivation and economic development in northern Thailand. In P. Kunstadter, E. C. Chapman, and S. Sabhasri (Eds.), *Farmers in the forest: Economic development and marginal agriculture in northern Thailand*, pp. 3–23. East-West Center, Honolulu.

Kuper, A. 2003. The return of the native. *Current Anthropology* 44(3): 389–412.

Langton, M. 1978. Self-determination as oppression. Preface to H. C. Coombs, *Australia's policy towards Aborigines, 1967–1977*, p. 5. Minority Rights Group Report No. 35. Minority Rights Group, London.

———. 1996. Wilderness and terra nullius. In *Perspectives on indigenous people's management of environment resources: Ecopolitics IX Conference papers and resolutions*, pp. 11–24. Ecopolitics Conference, Northern Land Council, Casuarina N.T.

Lanyon, J. 2003. Distribution and abundance of dugongs in Moreton Bay, Queensland, Australia. *Wildlife Research* 30: 397–409.

Latour, B. 1988. *The pasteurization of France.* Harvard University Press, Cambridge, MA.

Lewis, H. 1982. Fire technology and resource management in Aboriginal North America and Australia. In N. M. Williams and E. S. Hunn (Eds.), *Resource managers: North American and Australian hunter-gatherers*, pp. 45–68. Selected Symposium #67. Westview Press, Boulder, CO.

———. 1991. A parable of fire: Hunter-gatherers in Canada and Australia. In R. E. Johannes (Ed.), *Traditional ecological knowledge: A collection of essays*, pp. 11–19. IUCN Gland, Switzerland.

Lewis, H. 1993. Traditional ecological knowledge: Some definitions. In N. Williams and G. Baines (Eds.), *Traditional ecological knowledge: Wisdom for sustainable development*, pp. 8–12. Centre for Resource and Environmental Management, Australian National University, Canberra.

Lindberg, D. C. 1990. Conceptions of the scientific revolution from Bacon to Butterfield: A preliminary sketch. In D. C. Lindberg and R. S. Westman (Eds.), *Reappraisals of the scientific revolution*, pp. 1–26. Cambridge University Press, Cambridge.

Lohmann, L. 1999. Forest cleansing: Racial oppression in scientific nature conservation. *Cornerhouse briefing* 13, www2.mtnforum.org/oldocs/1564.pdf.

Lourandos, H. 1980. Change or stability? Hydraulics, hunter-gatherers, and population in temperate Australia. *World Archaeology* 11: 245–264.

Lourandos, H. 1997. *Continent of hunter-gatherers: New perspectives in Australian prehistory*. Cambridge University Press, Oakleigh, Victoria.

Loy T. H., and A. R. Wood. 1989. Blood residue analysis at Çayönü Tepesi, Turkey. *Journal of Field Archaeology* 16: 451–460.

Marsh, H., I. Lawler, D. Kwan, S. Delean, K. Pollock, and M. Alldredge. 2004. Aerial surveys and the potential biological removal technique indicate that the Torres Strait dugong fishery is unsustainable. *Animal Conservation* 7: 435–443.

Marsh, H., and D. F. Sinclair. 1989. Correcting for visability bias in strip transect aerial surveys of aquatic fauna. *Journal of Wildlife Management* 53: 1017–1024.

Marshall, Y. 2002. What is community archaeology? In Y. Marshall (Ed.), *Community Archaeology*, pp. 211–219. *World Archaeology* 34(2).

Martin, B. 1984. *Uprooting war*. Freedom Press, London.

Martin, B., S. Callaghan, and C. Fox, with R. Wells and M. Cawte. 1997. Challenging bureaucratic elites, www.uow.edu.au/~bmartin/dissent/documents/Schweik_cbe/97cbe.pdf. Accessed November 2009.

Marx, K. 1867. *Das Kapital: Kritik der politischen Ökonomie*, volumes 1 and 2, Friedrich Engels (Ed.), English translation. Progress Publishers, 1954–1959, Moscow.

Maybury-Lewis, D. 2002. *Indigenous peoples, ethnic groups, and the State* (2nd edition). Allyn & Bacon, Boston.

McAnany, P. A., and N. Yoffee (Eds.). 2009. *Questioning collapse: Human resilience, ecological vulnerability, and the aftermath of empire*. Cambridge University Press, Cambridge.

McBryde, I. 1984. Exchange in southeastern Australia: An ethnohistorical perspective. *Aboriginal History* 8(2): 132–153.

McCaskill, D., and K. Kempe (Eds.). 1997. *Development or domestication? Indigenous peoples of Southeast Asia*. Silkworm Books, Chiang Mai, Thailand.

McChesney, F. 1992. Government as definer of property rights: Indian lands, ethnic externalities, and bureaucratic budgets. In T. L. Anderson (Ed.), *Property rights and Indian economies*, pp. 109–146. Rowman and Littlefield Publishers, Inc., Lanham, MD.

McKinnon, J., and W. Bhruksasri. 1983. *Highlanders of Thailand*. Oxford University Press, New York.

McMullin, E. 1990. Conceptions of science in the scientific revolution. In D. C. Lindberg and R. S. Westman (Eds.), *Reappraisals of the scientific revolution*, pp. 27–92, Cambridge University Press, Cambridge.

McNickle, D. 1973. *Native American tribalism: Indian survivals and renewals*. Oxford University Press, Oxford.

McNiven, I. J. 2008. Sentient sea: Seascapes as spiritscapes. In B. David and J. Thomas (Eds.), *Handbook of landscape archaeology*, pp.149–157. Left Coast Press, Walnut Creek, CA.

McNiven, I., and A. Bedingfield. 2008. Past and present marine mammal hunting rates and abundances: Dugong (*Dugong dugon*) evidence from Dabangai Bone Mound, Torres Strait. *Journal of Archaeological Science* 35: 505–515.

McNiven, I. J., and L. Russell. 2005. *Appropriated pasts: Indigenous peoples and the colonial culture of archaeology*. AltaMira Press, Lanham, MD.

Mearns, L. 1994. To continue the Dreaming: Aboriginal women's traditional responsibilities in a transformed world. In E. S. Burch and L. J. Ellanna (Eds.), *Key issues in hunter-gatherer research*, pp. 263–288. Berg Publishers, London.

Meehan, B. 1982. *Shell bed to shell midden*. Australian Institute of Aboriginal Studies, Canberra.

———. 1988. The 'dinnertime camp'. In B. Meehan and R. Jones (Eds.), *Archaeology with ethnography: An Australian perspective*, pp.171–181. Department of Prehistory, Research School of Pacific Studies, the Australian National University, Canberra.

Memmott, P., and D. Trigger. 1998. Marine tenure in the Wellesley Islands region, Gulf of Carpentaria. In N. Peterson and B. Rigsby (Eds.), *Customary marine tenure in Australia*, pp. 109–124. Oceania Monograph 48. Oceania Publications, University of Sydney.

Merchant, C. 1995. Reinventing Eden: Western culture as a recovery narrative. In W. Cronon (Ed.), *Uncommon ground: Toward reinventing nature*, pp. 132–159. W. W. Norton and Company, New York.

Merculieff, I. L. 1994. Western society's linear systems and aboriginal cultures: The need for two-way exchanges for the sake of survival. In E. S. Burch and L. J. Ellanna (Eds.), *Issues in hunter-gatherer research*, pp. 405–415. Berg Publishers, Oxford.

Merlan, F. 1998. *Caging the rainbow: Places, politics, and Aborigines in a North Australian town*. University of Hawai'i Press, Honolulu.

———. 2009. Indigeneity: Global and local. *Current Anthropology* 50(3): 303–333.

Mgbeoji, I. 2007. Lost in translation? The rhetoric of protecting Indigenous peoples' knowledge in international law and the omnipresent reality of biopiracy. In P. W. B. Phillips and C. B. Onwuekwe (Eds.), *Accessing and sharing the benefits of the genomics revolution*, pp. 111–142. Springer, New York.

Milton, K. 1996. *Environmentalism and cultural theory: Exploring the role of anthropology in environmental discourse*. Routledge, New York.

Mithen, S. 1996. *The prehistory of the mind: A search for the origins of art, religion, and science*. Thames and Hudson, London.

Montree, C., K. S. Bunthida, K. Orawan, L. Pinkaew, M. Petchmala, P. Darunee, T. Kitti, and R. Noel. 1992. People and forests of Thailand. In L. Pinkaew and R. Noel (Eds.), *The future of people and forests in Thailand after the logging ban*, pp. 151–196. Project for Ecological Recovery, Bangkok.

Moore, D. S., A. Pandian, and J. Kosek. 2003. The cultural politics of race and nature: Terrains of power and practice. In D. S. Moore, J. Kosek, and A. Pandian (Eds.), *Race, nature, and the politics of difference*, pp. 1–70. Duke University Press, Durham, NC.

Morgan, M. 1991. *Mutant message down under*. MM Co., Lees Summit, MO.

Murray Li, T. 2000. Locating indigenous environmental knowledge in Indonesia. In R. Ellen, P. Parkes, and A. Bicker (Eds.), *Indigenous environmental knowledge and its transformations: Critical anthropological perspectives*, pp. 121–149. Overseas Publishers Association, Harwood Academic Publishers, Amsterdam.

Mutitjulu Community. 1990. An *insight into Uluru: The Mala Walk and the Mutitjulu Walk*. Parks Australia and Mutitjulu Community Incorporated, Aboriginal Cultural Centre, Uluru Kata Tjuta National Park.

Nabokov, P. 2002. *A forest of time: American Indian ways of history*. Cambridge University Press, Cambridge.

Nadasdy, P. 1999. The politics of TEK: Power and the 'integration' of knowledge. *Arctic Anthropology* 36: 1–18.

Nader, L. 1996a. Anthropological inquiry into boundaries, power and knowledge: Introduction. In L. Nader (Ed.), *Naked science: Anthropological inquiry into boundaries, power and knowledge*, pp. 1–25. Routledge, New York.

Nader, L. 1996b. Preface in L. Nader (Ed.), *Naked science: Anthropological inquiry into boundaries, power and knowledge*, pp. xi–xv. Routledge, New York.

Needham, J. 1954 [2000]. Foreward. In D. Raven, W. Krohn, and R. S. Cohen (Eds.), *The social origins of modern science*, pp. xi–xiv. Kluwer Academic Publishers, Boston.

Needham, R. 1975. Polythetic classification: Convergence and consequences. *Man* 10(3): 349–369.

Niezen, R. 2003. *The origins of indigenism: Human rights and the politics of identity.* University of California Press, Berkeley and Los Angeles.

Nursey-Bray, M. J. 2005. 'Having a yarn': Engaging Indigenous communities in natural resource management. CRC Reef Research, Townsville, Queensland, www.engagingcommunities2005.org/abstracts/S69-nursey-bray-mj.html. Accessed November 2009.

O'Connell, J. F., and F. J. Allen. 1998. When did humans first arrive in greater Australia and why is it important to know? *Evolutionary Anthropology* 6: 132–146.

Odora Hoppers, C. A. 2002a. Indigenous knowledge and the integration of knowledge systems. In C. A. Odora Hoppers (Ed.), *Indigenous knowledge and the integration of knowledge systems: Towards a philosophy of articulation*, pp. 2–22. New Africa Books, Claremont, South Africa.

———. 2002b. Introduction. In C. A. Odora Hoppers (Ed.), *Indigenous knowledge and the integration of knowledge systems: Towards a philosophy of articulation*, pp. vii–xiv. New Africa Books, Claremont, South Africa.

Olney, J. 1998. *Members of the Yorta Yorta Aboriginal Community vs. The State of Victoria & Ors (1998) Federal Court of Australia* 1606 FCA (18 December 1998), www.austlii.edu.au/au/journals/ILB/1999/9.html. Accessed November 2009.

Omura, K. 2003. Comment on *The Return of the Native* by Adam Kuper. *Current Anthropology* 44(3): 395–396.

O'Reilly, K. 2005. *Ethnographic methods.* Routledge, Oxford.

Ortner, S. B. 2006. *Anthropology and social theory: Culture, power and the acting subject.* Duke University Press, Durham, NC.

Palmer, K. 1998. Customary marine tenure at Groote Eylandt. In N. Peterson and B. Rigsby (Eds.), *Customary marine tenure in Australia*, pp. 142–153. Oceania Monograph 48, Oceania Publications, University of Sydney.

Pardoe, C. 1988. The cemetery as symbol: The distribution of prehistoric Aboriginal burial grounds in southeastern Australia. *Archaeology in Oceania* 23: 1–16.

Peacock, S., and N. Turner. 2000. 'Just like a garden': Traditional resource management and biodiversity conservation in the interior plateau of British Columbia. In P. Minnis and W. Elisens (Eds.), *Biodiversity and Native America*, pp. 133–179. University of Oklahoma Press, Tulsa.

Peloquin, C., and F. Berkes. 2009. Local knowledge, subsistence harvests, and social-ecological complexity in James Bay. *Human Ecology* 37(5): 533–545.

Peluso, N. L., and P. Vandergeest. 2001. Genealogies of the political forest and customary rights in Indonesia, Malaysia, and Thailand. *Journal of Asian Studies* 60(3): 761–812.

Perkins, M. 2001. *The reform of time.* Pluto Press, London.

Perry, R. 1996. *From time immemorial: Indigenous peoples and state systems.* University of Texas Press, Austin.

Peterson, N., and B. Rigsby (Eds.). 1998. *Customary marine tenure in Australia.* Oceania Monograph #48, Oceania Publications, University of Sydney, Sydney.

Phoenix-O'Brien, L. 2002. Dingo tales: An examination of the barriers to the integration of Indigenous and Western knowledge in natural resource management. Unpublished BA Honours thesis, School of Social Science, The University of Queensland, Brisbane.

Pickering, K. 2000. *Lakota culture, world economy.* University of Nebraska Press, Lincoln.

———. 2001. Legislating development through welfare reform: Indiscernible jobs, insurmountable barriers, and invisible agendas on the Pine Ridge and Rosebud Indian Reservations. *Political and Legal Anthropology Review* 24(1): 38–52.

———. 2004. Decolonizing time regimes: Lakota concepts of work, economy and society. *American Anthropologist* 106(1): 85–97.

Pickering, K. A., and B. Jewell. 2008. Nature is relative: Religious affiliation, environmental attitudes, and political constraints on the Pine Ridge Indian Reservation. *Journal for the Study of Religion, Nature and Culture* 2(1): 135–158.

Pickering Sherman, K., J. Van Lanen, and R. T. Sherman. 2010. Practical Environmentalism on the Pine Ridge Reservation: Confronting structural constraints to Indigenous stewardship. *Human Ecology* 38(4): 507–520.

Pinkaew, L. 2002. *Redefining nature: Karen ecological knowledge and the challenge to the modern conservation paradigm.* Earthworm Books, Chennai.

Pinkerton, E. W. 1992. Translating legal rights into management practice: Overcoming barriers to the exercise of co-management. *Human Organization* 51(4): 330–341.

Poole, D. C. 1881 [1988]. *Among the Sioux of Dakota: Eighteen months' experience as an Indian agent, 1869–1870.* Raymond DeMaillie (Ed.), Minnesota Historical Society Press, St. Paul.

Posey, D. A. 1992. Interpreting and applying the 'reality' of Indigenous concepts: What is necessary to learn from the natives? In K. H. Redford and C. Padoch (Eds.), *Conservation of neotropical forests: Working from traditional resource use*, pp. 21–34. Columbia University Press, New York.

———. 1998. Comment on 'The Development of Indigenous Knowledge' by Paul Sillitoe. *Current Anthropology* 39(2): 241–242.

———. 2000. Ethnobiology and ethnoecology in the context of national laws and international agreements affecting Indigenous and local knowledge, traditional resources and intellectual property rights. In R. Ellen, P. Parkes, and A. Bicker (Eds.), *Indigenous environmental knowledge and its transformations: Critical anthropological perspectives*, pp. 35–54. Overseas Publishers Association, Harwood Academic Publishers, Amsterdam.

Povinelli, E. 1993. 'Might be something': The language of indeterminacy in Australian Aboriginal land use. *Man* (New series) 28: 679–704.

Prangnell, J., A. Ross, and B. Coghill. 2010. Power relations and community involvement in landscape-based cultural heritage management practice: An Australian case study. *International Journal of Heritage Studies* 16(1-2): 141–155.

Press, T. 1995. Fire, people, landscapes and wilderness: Some thoughts of North Australia. In D. B. Rose (Ed.), *Country in flames: Proceedings of the 1994 symposium on biodiversity and fire in North Australia*, pp.19–23. Department of

Environment, Sport and Territories and North Australia Research Unit, Australian National University, Darwin.

Pretty, J., B. Adams, F. Berkes, S. Ferreira de Athayde, N. Dudley, E. Hunn, L. Maffi, K. Milton, D. Rapport, P. Robbins, E. Sterling, S. Stolton, A. Tsing, E. Vintinner, and S. Pilgram. 2009. The intersections of biological diversity and cultural diversity: Towards integration. *Conservation and Society* 7(2): 100–112.

Prucha, F. P. 1992. *The Great Father: The United States Government and the American Indians.* University of Nebraska Press, Lincoln.

Queensland Fisheries Management Authority (QFMA). 1997. *Moreton Bay Fishery, Discussion Paper Number 6.* Queensland Fisheries Management Authorities, Brisbane.

Rabinow, P. 1996. *Making PCR: A story of biotechnology.* University of Chicago Press, Chicago.

Rangarajan, M. 1996. *Fencing the forest: Conservation and ecological change in India's Central Provinces 1860–1914.* Oxford University Press, New Delhi.

Redford, K. 1990. The ecologically noble savage. *Orion Nature Quarterly* 9: 24–29.

Redford, K., and A. M. Stearman. 2003. Forest-dwelling native Amazonians and the conservation of biodiversity: Interests in common or in collision? *Conservation Biology* 7(2): 248–255.

Reynolds, C. J. (Ed.). 1993. *National identity and its defenders: Thailand, 1939–1989.* Centre of Southeast Asian Studies, Monash University Clayton,Victoria.

Reynolds, H. 1987a. *Frontier: Aborigines, settlers and land.* Allen and Unwin, Sydney.

———. 1987b. *The law of the land.* Penguin Books, Ringwood, Victoria.

———. 2001. *An indelible stain? The question of genocide in Australia's history.* Viking, Penguin Books, Ringwood, Victoria.

Richards, P. 1985. *Indigenous agricultural revolution: Ecology and food-crop farming in West Africa.* Hutchison, London.

Richardson, J., and L. Mason Hanks. 2001. *Tribes of the north Thailand frontier.* Yale University Press, New Haven, CT.

Rigsby, B. 1998. A survey of property theory and tenure types. In N. Peterson and B. Rigsby (Eds.), *Customary marine tenure in Australia*, pp. 22–46. Oceania Monograph 48, Oceania Publications, University of Sydney.

Riley, A. R. 2005. 'Straight stealing': Towards an Indigenous system of cultural property protection. *Washington Law Review* 80: 69–164.

Robbins, P. 2000. The rotten institution: Corruption in natural resource management. *Political Geography* 19: 423–443.

Robinson, C. J., and N. Munumgguritj. 2001. A Yolngu framework for cross-cultural collaborative management. In R. Baker, J. Davies, and E. Young (Eds.), *Working on country: Contemporary Indigenous management of Australia's lands and coastal regions*, pp. 92–107. Oxford University Press, Melbourne.

Robinson, C. J., H. Ross, and M. Hockings. 2006. *Development of co-operative management arrangements in the Great Barrier Reef: An adaptive management approach.* CRC Reef Research Centre Technical Report No. 55. CRC Reef Research, Townsville, Queensland.

Roopnaraine, T. 1998. Indigenous knowledge, biodiversity and rights. *Anthropology Today* 14(3): 16.

Rose, D. B. 1986. Passive violence. *Australian Aboriginal Studies* 1986(1): 24–30.

Rose, D. B. 1992. *Dingo makes us human: Life and land in an Australian Aboriginal culture.* Cambridge University Press, Cambridge.

———. 1995. Introduction. In D. B. Rose (Ed.), *Country in Flames: Proceedings of the 1994 symposium on biodiversity and fire in North Australia,* pp. 1–5. Department of Environment, Sport and Territories and North Australia Research Unit, Australian National University, Darwin.

———. 1996a. Land rights and deep colonizing: The erasure of women. *Aboriginal Law Bulletin* 3(85): 6–13.

———. 1996b. *Nourishing terrains: Australian Aboriginal views of landscape and wilderness.* Australian Heritage Commission, Canberra.

Ross, A. 1994. Traditional hunting in national parks and the cultural heritage paradigm. *Ngulaig* Monograph, volume 11. Aboriginal and Torres Strait Islander Studies Unit, The University of Queensland, Brisbane.

———. (Ed.). 1998. *Fire management today.* Video, produced by Video-Vision, The University of Queensland, Brisbane. ISBN 1864990295, 67 minutes.

———. 2008. Managing meaning at an ancient site in the 21st century: The Gummingurru Aboriginal stone arrangement on the Darling Downs, southern Queensland. *Oceania* 78: 91–108.

Ross, A., B. Anderson, and C. Campbell. 2003. Gunumbah: Archaeological and Aboriginal meanings at a quarry site on Moreton Island, southeast Queensland. *Australian Archaeology* 57: 75–81.

Ross, A., and C. Bigge. 2009. Australia. In C. Wessendorf (Ed.), *The Indigenous world 2009,* pp. 232–241. International Working Group on Indigenous Affairs, Copenhagen.

Ross, A., and S. Coghill. 2000. Conducting a community-based archaeological project: An archaeologist's and a Koenpul man's perspective. *Australian Aboriginal Studies* 2000(1&2): 76–83.

Ross, A., and D. Moreton. In press. Gorenpul knowledge of Moreton Bay. In P. Davie (Ed.), *Wild guide to Moreton Bay* (2nd edition). Queensland Museum, Brisbane.

Ross, A., T. Donnelly, and R. Wasson. 1992. The peopling of the arid zone: Human-environment interactions. In J. R. Dodson (Ed.), *The naive lands: Prehistory and environmental change in Australia and the Southwest Pacific,* pp. 76–114. Longman Cheshire, Melbourne, Victoria.

Ross, A., and K. Pickering. 2002. The politics of reintegrating Australian Aboriginal and American Indian Indigenous knowledge into resource management: The dynamics of resource appropriation and cultural revival. *Human Ecology* 30(2): 187–214.

Ross, A., J. Prangnell, and B. Coghill. 2010. Archaeology, cultural landscapes and Indigenous knowledge in Australian cultural heritage management legislation and practice. *Heritage Management* 16(1–2).

Ross, A., and Quandamooka. 1996a. Aboriginal approaches to cultural heritage management: A Quandamooka case study. In S. Ulm, I. Lille, and A. Ross (Eds.), *Australian Archaeology '95: Proceedings of 1995 Australian Archaeological Association Conference.* Tempus Publications, volume 6, pp. 107–112. The University of Queensland, Brisbane.

———. 1996b. Quandamooka perspectives on cultural heritage *Place* 2: 1, 5–6.

Ross, A., and H. Tomkins. In press. Fishing for data: The value of fine mesh screening for fish bone recovery: A case study from Peel Island, Moreton Bay. In J. Specht and R. Torrence (Eds.), Val Attenbrow Festschrift, Records of the Australian Museum, Technical Report Series.

Rowlands, M. 1994. The politics of identity in archaeology. In G. Bond and A. Gilliam (Eds.), *Social construction of the past: Representation as power*, pp. 131–135. Unwin Hyman, London.

———. 2004. Return of the 'noble savage': Misrepresenting the past, present and future. *Australian Aboriginal Studies* 2004(2): 2–14.

Rowse, T. 2000. *Obliged to be difficult: Nugget Coombs' legacy in Indigenous affairs*. Cambridge University Press, Melbourne.

Russell, H. 1980. *Indian New England before the Mayflower*. University Press of New England, Hanover, NH.

Sahlins, M. 1972. *Stone Age economics*. Aldine de Gruyter, New York.

Salmon, E. 2000. Kincentric ecology: Indigenous perceptions of the human-nature relationship. *Ecological Applications* 10(5): 1327–1332.

Santasombat, Y. 2003. *Biodiversity, local knowledge, and sustainable development*. Regional Center for Social Science and Sustainable Development, Chiang Mai University, Chiang Mai, Thailand.

Schafersman, S. 1997. An introduction to science, scientific thinking and the scientific method, http://pbisotopes.ess.sunysb.edu/esp/files/scientific-method.html. Accessed October 2004.

Scott, C. 1996. Science for the West, myth for the rest? The case of James Bay Cree knowledge construction. In L. Nader (Ed.), *Naked science: Anthropological inquiries into boundaries, power and knowledge*, pp. 69–86. Routledge, London.

Scott, J. C. 2009. *The art of not being governed: An anarchist history of upland Southeast Asia*. Yale University Press, New Haven, CT.

Sharp, N. 1998. Reimagining sea space: From Grotius to Mabo. In N. Peterson and B. Rigsby (Eds.), *Customary marine tenure in Australia*, pp. 47–65. Oceania Monograph 48, Oceania Publications, University of Sydney.

Sherman, R. T. 1988. A study of traditional and informal sector micro-enterprise activity and its impact on the Pine Ridge Indian Reservation economy. Aspen Institute for Humanistic Studies. Washington, D.C. Manuscript. Available from rtsherman@q.com.

———. 2005. Honor the Earth Northern Plains Buffalo caretaker survey results. Unpublished manuscript. Available from rtsherman@q.com.

———. 2007. Indigenous Stewardship Model: A traditional strategy to restore ecosystem balance and cultural well being utilizing values, philosophies and knowledge systems of Indigenous peoples. Available from rtsherman@q.com.

Shiva, V. 1997. The enclosure of the commons. In V. Shiva, A. H. Jafri, G. Bedi, and R. Holla-Bahr (Eds.), *The enclosure and recovery of the commons*. The Research Foundation for Science, Technology and Ecology, India.

———. 1998. Intellectual property rights, www.psrast.org/vashipr.htm. Accessed April 2005.

Shore, B. 1996. *Culture in mind: Cognition, culture, and the problem of meaning*. Oxford University Press, Oxford.

Silberbauer, G. 1994. A sense of place. In E. S. Burch and L. J. Ellanna (Eds.), *Key issues in hunter-gatherer research*, pp. 119–146. Berg Publishers, Oxford.

Sillitoe, P. 1998. The development of Indigenous knowledge: A new applied anthropology. *Current Anthropology* 39(2): 223–235.

Sillitoe, P. 2002. 'Maggots in their ears': Hunting incantations and Indigenous knowledge in development. *Journal of Ritual Studies* 16(2): 64–77.

Sillitoe, P., A. Bicker, and J. Pottier (Eds.). 2002. *Participating in development: Approaches to Indigenous knowledge*. Routledge, New York.

Singh, G., A. P. Kershaw, and R. Clark. 1981. Quaternary vegetation and fire history in Australia. In A. M. Gill, R. H. Groves, and I. R. Noble (Eds.), *Fire and the Australian Biota*, pp. 23–54. Australian Academy of Science, Canberra.

Sivaramakrishnan, K. 1999. *Modern forests: Statemaking and environmental change in colonial eastern India*. Stanford University Press, Stanford, CA.

Skaria, A. 1999. *Hybrid histories: Forests, frontiers and wildness in western India*. Oxford University Press, New Delhi.

———. 1987. *Usage of marine resources by Aboriginal communities on the east coast of Cape York Peninsula*. Great Barrier Reef Marine Park Authority Publications Series, Townsville.

Smith, B. R. 2005. 'We got our own management': Local knowledge, government and development in Cape York Peninsula. *Australian Aboriginal studies* 2005(2): 4–15.

Smith, C., and H. Burke. 2003. In the spirit of the code. In L. Zimmerman, K. Vitelli, and J. Howell-Zimmer (Eds.), *Ethical issues in archaeology*, pp. 177–197. AltaMira Press, Walnut Creek, CA.

———. 2004. Joining the dots: Managing the land and seascapes of Indigenous Australia. In I. Krupnik and R. Mason (Eds.), *Northern ethnographic landscapes: Perspectives from the circumpolar nations*, pp. 379–400. Smithsonian Institution Press, Washington, D.C.

Smith, D. E. 2005. *Researching Australian Indigenous governance: A methodological and conceptual framework*. CAEPR Working Paper 29. Centre for Aboriginal Economic Policy Research, The Australian National University, Canberra.

Smith, E. A., and B. Winterhalder. 1992. *Evolutionary ecology and human behavior*. Aldine de Gruyter, New York.

Smith, E, A., and M. Wishnie. 2000. Conservation and subsistence in small-scale societies. *Annual Review of Anthropology* 29: 493–524.

Smith, M. A., J. R. Prescott. and M. J. Head. 1997. Comparison of ^{14}C and luminescence chronologies at Puritjarra Rock Shelter, central Australia. *Quaternary Science Reviews (Quaternary Geochronology)* 16: 299–320.

Smith, N. 2001. Are Indigenous people conservationists? Preliminary results from the Machiguenga of the Peruvian Amazon. *Rationality and Society* 13(4): 429–461.

Smyth, D. 2001. Joint management of national parks. In R. Baker, J. Davies, and E. Young (Eds). *Working on country: Contemporary indigenous management of Australia's lands and coastal regions*, pp. 75–91. Oxford University Press, Melbourne.

———. 2006. Indigenous protected areas in Australia. *Community Conserved Areas* 16(1), http://cmsdata.iucn.org/downloads/parks_16_1_forweb.pdf#page = 5. Accessed November 2009.

Snodgrass, J. G. 2006. *Casting kings: Bards and Indian modernity*. Oxford University Press, New York.

Snodgrass, J. G., and K. Tiedje. 2008. Introduction to JSRNC theme issue. Indigenous nature reverence and conservation: Seven ways of transcending an unnecessary dichotomy. *Journal for the Study of Religion, Nature, and Culture* 2(1): 6–29.

Snodgrass, J. G., M. G. Lacy, S. K. Sharma, Y. Singh Jhala, M. Advani, N. K. Bhargava, and C. Upadhyay. 2008. Witch hunts, herbal healing, and discourses of indigenous 'eco-development' in North India: Theory and method in the anthropology of environmentality. *American Anthropologist* 110(3): 299–312.

Snodgrass, J. G., S. K. Sharma, Y. Singh Jhala, M. G. Lacy, M. Advani, N. K. Bhargava, and C. Upadhyay. 2007. Beyond self-interest and altruism: Herbalist and Leopard Brothers in an Indian wildlife sanctuary. *Human Dimensions of Wildlife* 12(5): 375–387.

———. 2008. Lovely leopards, frightful forests: The environmental ethics of indigenous Rajasthani shamans. *Journal for the Study of Religion, Nature, and Culture* 2(1): 30–54.

Sobel, D. 1995. *Longitude: The true story of a lone genius who solved the greatest scientific problem of his time*. Penguin Books, New York.

Spence, M. D. 1999. *Dispossessing the wilderness: Indian removal and the making of the national parks*. Oxford University Press, New York.

Sponsel, L. 1998. The historical ecology of Thailand: Increasing thresholds of human environmental impact from prehistory to the present. In W. Balee (Ed.), *Advances in historical ecology*, pp. 376–404. Columbia University Press, New York.

Stevenson, M. G. 2006. The possibility of difference: Rethinking co-management. *Human Organization* 65(2): 167–180.

Strauss, C., and N. Quinn. 1997. *A cognitive theory of cultural meaning*, Cambridge University Press, Cambridge.

Sullivan, P. 1998. Salt water, fresh water and Yawuru social organization. In N. Peterson and B. Rigsby (Eds.), *Customary Marine Tenure in Australia*, pp.96–108. Oceania Monograph 48. Oceania Publications, University of Sydney.

Sullivan, S. 1993. Cultural values and cultural imperialism. *Historic Environment* 10: 54–62.

———. 1996. Reflexions of 27 years. In S. Ulm, I. Lilley, and A. Ross (Eds.), *Australian archaeology '95: Proceedings of 1995 Australian Archaeological Association Conferences, Gatton College*. Tempus volume 6, pp. 1–11. The University of Queensland, Brisbane.

Sundar, N. 1997. *Subalterns and sovereigns: An anthropological history of Bastar, 1854–1996*. Oxford University Press, Oxford.

Surin, P. 1985. Ethnoarchaeology with the Phi Tong Luang (Mlabrai): Forest hunters of northern Thailand. *World Archaeology* 17(2): 206–221.

Suzuki, D. 1992. A personal forward: The value of native ecologies. In D. Suzuki and P. Knudtson, *Wisdom of the elders: Sacred native stories of nature*, pp. xxvii–xliv. Bantam Books, New York.

Suzuki, D., and P. Knudtson. 1992. *Wisdom of the elders: Sacred native stories of nature*. Bantam Books, New York.

Swidler, N., K. E. Dongoske, R. Anyon, and A. S. Downer (Eds.). 1997. *Native Americans and Archaeologists: Stepping stones to common ground*. AltaMira Press, Walnut Creek, CA.

Tannenbaum, N. 2000. Protest, tree ordination, and the changing context of political ritual. *Ethnology* 39(2): 109–127.

Tapp, N. 1989. *Sovereignty and rebellion: The white Hmong of northern Thailand*. Oxford University Press, Singapore.

Tapp, N., J. Michaud, C. Culas, and G. Yia Lee. 2004. *Hmong/Miao in Asia*. Silkworm Books, Chiang Mai, Thailand.

Taylor, G. 1980. *The New Deal and American Indian tribalism: The administration of the Indian Reorganization Act, 1934–1945.* University of Nebraska Press, Lincoln.

Taylor, K. 2001. Trees, farms, ecosystems and 'places': A constructivists approach to an ecological problem. Unpublished Honours Project, School of Natural and Rural Systems, The University of Queensland, Gatton Campus.

Taylor, P. J. 1996. *The way the modern world works: World hegemony to world impasse.* John Wiley and Sons, New York.

Taylor, S. G. 1990. Naturalness: The concept and its application to Australian ecosystems. *Proceedings of the Ecological Society of Australia* 16: 411–418.

The Australian. 2009. PM wants Uluru climb to stay open, www.theaustralian.com. au/news/pm-wants-uluru-climb-to-stay-open/story-0-1225748234270, July 10. Accessed November 2009.

Tiedje, K., and J. G. Snodgrass (Eds.). 2008. Indigenous nature reverence and environmental degradation: Exploring critical intersections of animism and conservation. Special theme issue of the *Journal for the Study of Religion, Nature, and Culture* 2(1): 5–159.

Thornton, R. 1987. *American Indian holocaust and survival: A population history since 1492.* University of Oklahoma Press, Norman.

Torrence, R. 1986. *Production and exchange of stone tools: Prehistoric obsidian in the Aegean.* Cambridge University Press, Cambridge.

Traweek, S. 1988. *Beamtimes and lifetimes: The world of high energy physicists.* Harvard University Press, Cambridge, MA.

Trigger, B. 1969. *The Huron farmers of the north.* Holt, Rinehart and Winston, New York.

Trigger, D. S., and C. Dalley. 2010. Negotiating indigeneity: Culture, identity and politics. *Reviews in Anthropology* 39(1): 46–65.

Tucker, B. 2003. Comment on 'Huna Tlingit traditional environmental knowledge, conservation, and the management of a "wilderness" park' by E. S. Hunn, D. R. Johnson, P. N. Russell, and T. F. Thornton. *Current Anthropology* 44(Supplement): S98.

Ulm, S. 1995. Fishers, gatherers and hunters of the Moreton fringe: Reconsidering the prehistoric Aboriginal marine fishery in south eastern Queensland, Australia. Unpublished BA Honours thesis, Department of Anthropology and Sociology, The University of Queensland, Brisbane.

Ulm, S., F. Petchey, and A. Ross. 2009. Towards an understanding of marine reservoir variability in Moreton Bay, southeast Queensland. *Archaeology in Oceania* 44: 160–166.

United Nations. 2004. The concept of indigenous peoples. Background paper prepared by the secretariat of the permanent forum on indigenous issues. Department of Economic and Social Affairs, www.un.org/esa/socdev/unpfii/documents/workshop_data_background.doc. Accessed May 2010.

Unnithan-Kumar, M. 1997. *Identity, gender and poverty: New perspectives on caste and tribe in Rajasthan.* Berghahn Books, Oxford.

Upshal, D. 2000. *Dances with myths.* Video. Channel Four Television Corp. London.

Vandergeest, P. 1996. Mapping nature: Territorialization of forest rights in Thailand. *Society and Natural Resources* 9: 159–175.

———. 2003. Racialization and citizenship in Thai forest politics. *Society and Natural Resources* 16: 22.

Vandergeest, P., and N. L. Peluso. 1995. Territorialization and state power in Thailand. *Theory and Society* 24: 385–426.

Vella, W. F. 1978. *Chaiyo! King Vajiravudh and the development of Thai nationalism.* University of Hawai'i Press, Honolulu.

Wallerstein, I. 1992. The West, capitalism, and the modern world-system. *Review* 15: 561–619.

———. 2001. *The end of the world as we know it: Social science for the twenty-first century.* University of Minnesota Press, Minneapolis.

———. 2003. Anthropology, sociology, and other dubious disciplines. *Current Anthropology* 44(4): 453–465.

Walsh, F. 1990. An ecological study of traditional Aboriginal use of 'country': Martu in the Great and Little Sandy Deserts, Western Australia. In D. A. Saunders, A. J. M. Hopkins, and R. A. How (Eds.), Australian ecosystems: 200 years of utilization, degradation, and reconstruction. *Proceedings of the Ecological Society of Australia.* 16: 23–37.

———. 1992. The relevance of some aspects of Aboriginal subsistence activities to the management of national parks: With reference to Martu people of the Western desert. In J. Birckhead, T. de Lacy, and L. Smith (Eds.), *Aboriginal involvement in parks and protected areas*, pp. 75–97. Aboriginal Studies Press, Canberra.

Walsh, F., and P. Mitchell. 2002. *Planning for country: Cross cultural approaches to decision making on Aboriginal lands.* IAD Press, Alice Springs.

Waswo, R. 1997. *The founding legend of Western civilization: From Virgil to Vietnam.* Wesleyan University Press, Middleton, CT.

Weatherford, J. 1988. *Indian givers: How the Indians of the Americas transformed the world.* Random House Publishing Group, New York.

Weber, R., T. Butler, and P. Larson. 2000. Conservation and Indigenous peoples. In R. Weber, T. Butler, and P. Larson (Eds.). *Indigenous people and conservation organizations: Experiences in collaboration*, pp. 3–6. World Wildlife Fund, Washington, D.C.

Weiner, J. 2002. Diaspora, materialism, tradition: Anthropological issues in the recent High Court appeal of the Yorta Yorta. *Land, rights, Laws: Issues of Native Title* 2(18): 1–12.

Wellings, P. 1995. Management considerations. In T. Press, D. Lea, A. Webb, and A. Graham (Eds.), *Kakadu: Natural and cultural heritage management*, pp. 238–270. Australian Nature Conservation Agency and North Australia Research Unit, The Australian National University, Darwin.

Whaley, R., and W. Bressette. 1992. *Walleye warriors: An effective alliance against racism and for the Earth.* New Society Publishers, Philadelphia.

Wilkinson, T. 2004. Little Big War. www.backpacker.com, pp. 66–73; 115–119.

Williams, E. 1987. Complex hunter-gatherers: A view from Australia. *Antiquity* 61: 310–321.

Williams, N. M., and G. Baines (Eds.). 1993. *Traditional ecological knowledge: Wisdom for sustainable development.* Centre for Resource and Environmental Management, Australian National University, Canberra.

Williams, N. M., and D. Mununggurr. 1989. Understanding Yolngu signs of the past. In R. Layton (Ed.), *Who needs the past? Indigenous values and archaeology*, pp. 70–83. Unwin Hyman, London.

Willis, J. 1992. Two laws, one lease: Accounting for traditional Aboriginal Law in the lease for Uluru National Park. In J. Birckhead, T. de Lacy, and L. Smith (Eds.),

Aboriginal involvement in parks and protected areas, pp. 159–166. Aboriginal Studies Press, Canberra.

Windschuttle, K., and T. Gillin. 2002. The extinction of the Australian pygmies. *Quadrant* June 2002, www.sydneyline.com/Pygmies%20Extinction.htm. Accessed November 2009.

Winichakul T. 1994. *Siam mapped: A history of the geo-body of a nation.* University of Hawai'i Press, Honolulu.

———. 2000a. Travel and ethno-spatial differentiation of Siamese subjects, 1885–1910. In A. Turton (Ed.), *Civility and savagery: Social identity in Tai states,* pp. 38–62. Curzon, London.

———. 2000b. The quest for '*siwilai*': A geographical discourse of civilizational thinking in late nineteenth and early twentieth-century Siam. *Journal of Asian Studies* 59(3): 528–549.

Wise, T. 1985. *The self-made anthropologist: A life of A. P. Elkin.* George, Allen and Unwin, Sydney.

Wolfley, J. 1998. Ecological risk assessment and management: Their failure to value Indigenous traditional ecological knowledge and protect tribal homelands. *American Indian Culture and Research Journal* 22: 151–169.

Wyatt, D. K. 1984. *Thailand: A short history.* Yale University Press, New Haven, CT.

Xaxa, V. 2003. Tribes in India. In V. Das (Ed.), *The Oxford India companion to sociology and social anthropology,* pp. 373–408. Oxford University Press, Oxford.

Yanner vs. Eaton. 1999. High Court of Australia Finding in *Yanner v Eaton* [1999] HCA 53 (21 December 1999), www.austlii.edu.au/au/cases/cth/high_ct/1999/69.html. Accessed November 2009.

Yanyuwa Families, J. Bradley, and N. Cameron. 2003. *'Forget about Flinders': A Yanyuwa atlas of the southwest Gulf of Carpentaria.* J. M. McGregor, Ltd, Queensland.

Yorta Yorta Aboriginal Community vs. Victoria. 2002. High court of Australia Finding in *Yorta Yorta Aboriginal Community vs. Victoria & Ors* [2002] HCA 58 (12 December 2002), www.austlii.edu.au/au/cases/cth/HCA/2002/58.html. Accessed November 2009.

Yos, S. 2003. *Biodiversity, local knowledge, and sustainable development.* Regional Center for Social Science and Sustainable Development, Chiang Mai University, Chiang Mai.

Young Bear, S., and R. D. Theisz. 1994. *Standing in the light: A Lakota way of seeing.* University of Nebraska Press, Lincoln.

Zilsel, E. 1939 [2000]. *The social origins of modern science.* Collection of papers edited by D. Raven, W. Krohn, and R. S. Cohen. Kluwer Academic Publishers, Boston.

Subject Index

Moreton Bay (*see* Quandamooka)

Nan Province, 12, 19–21, 170–184, 225–230
narrow definitions (*see* barrier B)
National Park Service (USA), 236–237, 245, 255–257, 279–280
native title (Native Title Act 1993), 13, 23, 73, 135–136, 189, 205–206
natural resources management, 9–10, 17, 28, 37–38, 42–43, 60–61, 95–113, 150–151 (*see also* stewardship)
natural resources, use of, 16–17, 18, 21, 43–46, 60, 75–78, 88–92, 109–112, 119–120, 123–125, 129–132, 144–152, 161–184, 203, 205–207, 209–211, 217–230, 238–239, 241, 243–248, 250–253, 261, 276–278
NGOs (Non-Governmental Organizations), 19–20, 29, 46, 77–78, 111, 156, 170, 173–175, 182–183, 228–230
nonvalidation of Indigenous knowledge (*see* barrier C)

outsider knowledge (*see* barrier I)
overcoming barriers, 156–158, 173–177, 182–183, 203, 205–207, 209–211, 217–232, 235–260, 263–275, 276
overcoming environmental degradation, 235–260
ownership of knowledge (*see* barrier G)

Pine Ridge Indian Reservation, 14–17, 137–160, 235–260, 262, 278–280
politics and NRM, 22, 24, 35–36, 56–58, 61–62, 72–78, 110–113, 134–135, 138–139, 154–157, 174–175, 183–184, 193–233, 237–238, 243, 259, 279–280
power (*see* barrier M)

prairie dogs, 146–147, 150, 151–152
property rights, 57, 71, 83, 96, 101–103, 141–142, 189
population growth, 43–46, 71–72, 88–89, 161, 166, 277–278
Phulwari ki Nal, 16–19, 160–170

Quandamooka, 11–13, 60, 80–81, 125–127, 129–133, 281–284
Queensland, 11–14, 66–67, 116–137, 215–216, 281–284
Queensland Parks and Wildlife Service (QPWS), 11, 67, 122–126, 134–135

racial/cultural inferiority (*see* barrier L)
Rajasthan, 12, 16–19, 40, 160–170, 217–225, 276–278
Rajasthan Forest Department (RFD), 19, 160–170, 217–225, 276–278
reconciliation, 241, 282–284
religion and ritual, 34, 53, 62–67, 72, 103–106, 144–145, 167, 174, 179, 183, 217–230, 238–239, 260, 277–278
resource management (*see* natural resources management)
Royal Forestry Department (Thailand), 77, 170–184, 225–230

science (*see* scientific knowledge)
scientific knowledge, 31–35, 48, 53, 66–67, 261; and experts/specialists, 36–37, 100, 107, 126–129; vs. Indigenous knowledge, 34–38, 49–50, 53, 66–67, 69, 70–75, 85–86, 98, 106, 157, 231, 255–257; and integration (*see* Indigenous Knowledge integration); and privilege over IK, 72, 92–93, 101, 117–129, 210–216, 231 (*see also* control); and proof, 33, 35, 40, 56, 62–66, 85, 96, 101, 111, 117–120; and thinking like Indigenous people, 40–43, 50

Name Index

About the Authors

Anne (Annie) Ross is a senior lecturer in anthropology and archaeology at The University of Queensland, Australia. Her main research interests relate to Aboriginal knowledge of natural resources and cultural heritage, and the contestation between Indigenous and Western ways of constructing and managing heritage places. She has undertaken research in coastal southeastern Queensland, the Darling Downs in inland Queensland, and the Solomon Islands. She has published extensively in archaeology, ecology, and Indigenous studies.

Kathleen (Kathy) Pickering Sherman is professor and chair of the Department of Anthropology at Colorado State University, where she has been on the faculty since 1997. Before starting graduate school, she worked as a legal services attorney on the Pine Ridge Indian Reservation in South Dakota, and she continues to conduct research there on household subsistence and community-based economic development. Her research interests include economic anthropology, traditional ecological knowledge, tribal economic development, collaborative ecosystem conservation and natural resource management, and the effects of globalization on Indigenous communities. Her seven-year longitudinal study of household economic dynamics on the Pine Ridge Reservation, funded by the National Science Foundation, is providing baseline data for a wide variety of reservation development programs, including workforce development, small business expansion, Lakota-based education models, and natural resource management. She is author of *Lakota Culture, World Economy* (University of Nebraska Press), and co-author of *Welfare Reform in Persistent Rural Poverty* (Pennsylvania State University Press). She completed her graduate studies at University of Wisconsin-Madison and has a law degree from New York University School of Law.

Jeffrey (Jeff) Snodgrass is associate professor of anthropology at Colorado State University. His research specialization is in cognitive and psychological anthropology. He has published widely on caste, ritual performance, spirit possession, and religious healing in India. His early research with the formerly untouchable *Bhat* community of bardic performers culminated in the publication of *Casting Kings: Bards and Indian Modernity* (Oxford University Press 2006). Currently Snodgrass is working to understand how loss of access to forest spaces and resources – for example, through deforestation and people's displacement from a wildlife preserve in central India – affect Indigenous peoples' health and systems of healing.

Henry (Hank) Delcore is a professor of anthropology at California State University, Fresno, where he directs the Institute of Public Anthropology. His research concerns the cultural politics of agricultural and environmental change in Thailand. His published work covers cultural constructions of the past, Buddhist environmentalism, and the relations between people and national parks.

Richard Sherman was born and raised on the Pine Ridge Indian Reservation in South Dakota and is a member of the Oglala Sioux Tribe. He has worked most of his life on all aspects of fisheries, wildlife, and buffalo management, ethnobotany, and Indigenous stewardship methods. He drafted the first comprehensive fish and wildlife code for the Oglala Sioux Tribe and created methods of inventory for wildlife conservation Reservation-wide. As Wildlife Biologist, Executive Director, and Board Member of Oglala Sioux Parks and Recreation, he actively managed the tribal buffalo herd for more than 30 years, using the values and philosophies of the Lakota people to maintain them in a wild state. He conducted several studies on the Pine Ridge Reservation focused on subsistence practices and wildlife management, including a study of the importance of home-based micro-enterprise activity for the Reservation economy and a study of small-scale native bison operators on Pine Ridge, Rosebud, and Yankton. He studied wildlife management at Utah State University and has a Master's Degree in regional planning from University of Massachusetts, Amherst.

Made in the USA
Las Vegas, NV
02 June 2023

72856054R00177